THE AMERICAN JUDICIAL TRADITION

PROFILES OF LEADING AMERICAN JUDGES

G. Edward White

New York

OXFORD UNIVERSITY PRESS

1976

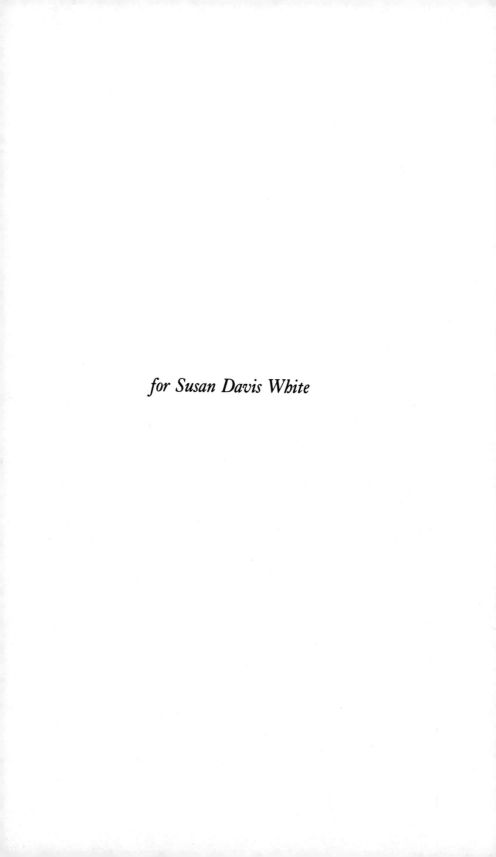

for Susan Davis White

The American Judicial Tradition

Preface

This book did not actually take shape during the years I participated in an informal legal history group at Harvard Law School, but its genesis was there. As with several other people currently teaching in law schools and history departments across the country, my interest in legal history can be traced to that experience. Jerome Cohen was the founder and moving spirit of that group; he has been a catalyst to the emergence of modern scholarship in American legal history.

I never met the late Richard Hofstadter, whose *American Political Tradition* served as a point of reference for this study. I am not certain that Hofstadter and I would necessarily have agreed on historiographical issues. I find Hofstadter's scholarship to be provocative in the best sense of the word, and I appreciate his willingness to synthesize or theorize and his concern with stylistic elegance. This present book, however, is about a judicial, as distinguished from a political, tradition and about judges as distinguished from politicians. I take those distinctions to be real, profound, and worth writing about.

A somewhat revised version of Chapter 6 appeared in the January 1975 issue of the *American Journal of Legal History*, and I am grateful to the editors for permission to reprint it.

Daniel Flanigan, William H. Harbaugh, Stanley N. Katz,

Daniel J. Meador, William E. Nelson, and Calvin Woodard have
read the entire manuscript in various drafts and improved it with
their suggestions. Morton Horwitz, A. E. Dick Howard, John C.
McCoid, Harvey S. Perlman, and J. Harvie Wilkinson III have read
portions of it and given me the benefit of their critical comments.
Roger J. Traynor has been kind enough to react to an early draft of
the chapter on his career, although that essay is in no sense authorized. Merrill D. Peterson was supportive of the work and helpful to
me in early stages. Linda Carroll Moore has been an outstanding
research assistant, and the book has benefited considerably from her
editorial suggestions. The secretarial staff of Virginia Law School,
notably Sandy Durham, has been a great help throughout its composition. Grants from the American Council of Learned Societies
and the Virginia Law School Foundation facilitated its progress.
The last stages of publication have profited by the incisiveness of
Susan Rabiner and the conscientiousness of Mary Ellen Evans of
Oxford University Press.

Alexandra Valre White and especially Susan Davis White have
immeasurably enriched my life while I have been working on the
book. They would have done so had the book not existed.

Charlottesville
December 1975

Contents

The American Judicial Tradition

Introduction

The relation between the title and the subtitle of this book requires a preliminary comment. The title is intended to suggest a generalized argument that there has been and is a tradition of American appellate judging; that it contains, at a minimum, certain identifiable elements; and that it has persisted, in a complex and variegated fashion, through time. The subtitle suggests, however, that this tradition is here being examined through a series of individual and group portraits of leading judges. The portraits are not intended to be complete or definitive. They stress themes and traits I found central to an understanding of the subjects and their times; they seek to capture essences. The book, then, is intended to communicate on varying levels of abstraction and concreteness, some levels involving broad generalizations about the judicial role in American history and others involving anecdotal or analytical comments on the life and work of a particular judge.

Given the length of the book, a summary of its central generalized argument may be useful. I begin by maintaining that the American judicial tradition, as I define it, did not exist at the formation of the nation, but was created during the tenure of John Marshall, and largely through his efforts. The tradition Marshall passed on at his retirement contained three identifiable elements, which I describe and analyze at various points in the narrative. The elements can be summarized here as a tension between independence and accountability, a delicate and unique relation to politics, and a recurrent trade-off between acknowledged powers and freedoms in the individual judge, and acknowledged constraints on the institution of the judiciary.

The first eight chapters describe, through profiles of leading judges, the course of the tradition in the nineteenth century. Central to that description is an argument that judging was not regarded in the nineteenth century as an exercise in making law. Rather, law was conceived of as a mystical body of permanent truths, and the judge was seen as one who declared what those truths were and made them intelligible—as an oracle who "found" and interpreted the law. The core elements of the tradition were derived from the oracular theory of judging and its interaction with politics in America. The oracular theory, I argue, persisted throughout the great part of the nineteenth century, despite important shifts in American jurisprudential attitudes.

The final seven chapters follow the path of the American judicial tradition in the twentieth century. Here the argument shifts. The characterization of the judge as an oracle came to be discredited in the early years of this century, I maintain; judges were acknowledged to be lawmakers, not law-finders. But the central elements of the tradition remained intact. This continuity was made possible by a series of successive jurisprudential theories that supplied various checks on judicial performance. Judicial reasoning was transformed from an exercise in law declaration to an exercise in justifying autocratic power in a democratic society. A nineteenth-century contrast between the "will of the judge" and the "will of the law" was replaced by a twentieth-century contrast between the results a judge reached and the reasons he gave for them. I conclude by suggesting that despite the dramatic changes in the posture of the appellate judiciary during Earl Warren's Chief Justiceship, and despite current jurisprudential ferment, the experience of contemporary American judges has some continuity with that of their predecessors in the tradition.

A work that presents a broad sweep of history through profiles of individuals necessarily presents problems of inclusion and exclusion. The judges selected for treatment have not been chosen arbitrarily, although some readers may quarrel with their presence. One criterion used in the selection process has been termination of service: no judges active at the time of the writing of the book were included. Although this criterion has resulted in the omission of some interesting and influential careers, such as that of recently retired Justice William O. Douglas of the United States Supreme Court, or those of Chief Justice Walter V. Schaefer of the Supreme Court of Illinois and Judge Henry Friendly of the Court of Appeals for the Second Circuit, it rests on the premise that a judge's impact is not entirely perceptible until his retirement.

A second criterion has been historical interest. Here more than one individual might have served to embody a theme or represent an attitude, and a further refinement has been necessary; or a less well-known individual has been thought deserving of attention for his historical significance. Utilization of this criterion has eliminated Chief Justice John Bannister Gibson, who served on the Supreme Court of Pennsylvania in the early nineteenth century, and Thomas Ruffin, Chief Justice of the Supreme Court of North Carolina at the same time. Other judges, such as James Kent, Joseph Story, and Roger Taney, were thought to personify points of view roughly similar to those of Gibson or Ruffin. In the same fashion Thomas McIntyre Cooley of the Supreme Court of Michigan has been chosen over John Forrest Dillon of the Supreme Court of Iowa, whose jurisprudential attitudes greatly resembled Cooley's.

Where two men could be said to personify a similar point of view and to have made a roughly comparable impact on history, a third criterion has been employed, that of availability of information on a prospective subject's personal life. One function of a biographical-essay format is to sketch the character and personality of a subject; and since judges do not always reveal themselves in their decisions, additional information is generally necessary to flesh out the portrait. In the case of Ruffin and Dillon the relative paucity of such information contributed to their exclusion. Only in the treatment of Roger Traynor, the one living judge studied, has personal information been underemphasized.

Finally, perceptions of the current state of knowledge on various subjects has affected the breadth of their coverage. Justices Holmes and Brandeis, for example, are contained in a single chapter, though Justices Jackson and Traynor receive separate treatment. These judgments on coverage were based not on an implicit ranking of the stature or importance of the subjects but on a desire to provide fresh perspectives on the mind-set of individual judges,

thereby avoiding as often as possible the repetition of familiar information or conventional analysis. In some instances I sought a new
perspective in a group portrait; in others, through a more detailed
focus on an individual character.

A far more systematic set of criteria than the above would still
not insure an infallible selection process. Indeed, the use of the
biographical-essay format as a means of writing history presents obvious difficulties. The format sacrifices exhaustiveness of detail for
distillations and syntheses; it seeks, as used herein, to capture
habits of mind, impulses of thought and feeling, style and influence. History as biography also overemphasizes individual contributions: no "great man" theory is advanced here, and care has
been taken to point out the cultural imperatives of time and place
that confine human influence within prescribed channels.

Identifying and describing a "tradition" of American appellate
judging assumes a certain cohesiveness and continuity in the process of appellate adjudication over time. This study does not go so
far as to suggest, as Roscoe Pound once did, that social and economic conditions are merely pieces of evidence fitted in to the
workings of a "taught legal tradition." * It suggests, rather, that judging is bound to reflect the governing social and intellectual assumptions of various periods in American history, and that its relation
to its social context is one of total integration. But in examining
appellate judging in America one cannot ignore its distinctive
institutional characteristics, which have remained relatively constant
over the years and which have affected judicial behavior.

This study's emphasis on continuity and tradition is not intended
to identify it with a "consensus" view of American history or with
any alternative view. Conflict and consensus are not terms that lend
themselves readily to judicial history. Adjudication has as its essential function the resolution of social conflict, but it performs that
function in part through appeals to consensual attitudes as they
have manifested themselves in past legal decisions, whether by
judges or legislatures. It is not the purpose of this study to assess
the validity of treating American history from one theoretical perspective or another; its purpose is rather to try to convey, in a
broad sense, an understanding of what it has meant to be an American appellate judge.

* R. Pound, *The Formative Era of American Law* 82 (1938).

Throughout this work, judging and a judicial tradition are identified with courts of appeal rather than with trial courts. In this sense its focus is narrower than its title might perhaps imply. It emphasizes a more abstract component of judging, one with an emphasis on the content and meaning of legal doctrine, than that which is often emphasized at the trial-court level. Nothing is said here about the functions of examining witnesses, charging juries, making rulings on points of evidence, or creating a trial record, all of which form in part the business of trial judging. This is not to minimize the importance of those functions: they simply do not lend themselves as well to jurisprudential or historical analysis as does the work of appellate courts, nor, from one perspective, are they as significant.

Not all the subjects portrayed here have been treated with admiration. No effort has been made to perpetuate a mystique of judges as being innately wise and dignified human beings. Still, a tinge of respect has suffused the portraits, respect not only for many of the individuals involved but also for the institution of the appellate judiciary. As a professional ideal it demands balanced judgment and honesty from those who personify it; it attempts to make complex adjustments in human relations and yet requires intelligence and rationality in the undertaking. It can serve, in its finest performances, as a solidifying force in our culture.

1

John Marshall and the Genesis of the Tradition

In pre-Revolutionary America the specific responsibilities of the appellate judge varied from colony to colony, but judges generally served in two capacities: as intermediaries between colonial executives and local communities and as leadership figures in the localities. The judges of the Superior Court of Massachusetts, for example, passed on the validity of tax assessments and entertained damage suits against sheriffs, jailers, customs officials, and moderators of town meetings. As such, they were agents of the provincial government, functioning as executive bureaucrats. Being men of high status, they were usually pillars of their local communities. They were also asked to use their power and prestige to preserve local order and tranquility.[1]

The specific responsibilities of colonial judges assured them of a wide range of petty powers but of little independence. They were accountable to those who appointed them and to those affected by their decisions. They could not entirely ignore their administrative responsibilities, and neither could they enforce distasteful judgments. In addition, colonies such as Massachusetts sought to limit judicial power further by giving great weight to jury verdicts while restricting the power of judges to influence juries—through trial court instructions—or to modify jury findings on appeal.[2] Finally, the independence of the appellate judiciary in the colonies was limited by the predominant jurisprudential assumption that judges merely "found" the law, mechanically applying existing rules to new situations. This assumption fostered an image of judges as oracles who could discover the law's technical mysteries but who could not influence the content of law itself.

The advent of the Revolution and the introduction of the Constitution changed the structure of the appellate court system in America but did not dramatically change the status of judges. The history of the Supreme Court from 1789 to 1801, the year of John Marshall's appointment as Chief Justice, was marked by three phenomena: the minimal extent of Court business; the disorganization and disunity of the Court itself—most notably with regard to the question of its authority to pass on the constitutionality of Congressional legislation—and the increasing involvement of the Court in partisan politics.[3]

Between February 1790, when the Court began its first term, and February 1793, it heard only five cases. From 1790 to 1801 it decided only fifty-five. The Court had two Chief Justices during this period. The first, John Jay, felt so little burdened by his office that he remained active in Federalist party politics while on the bench, and finally resigned in 1795 to run for Governor of New York. His successor, Oliver Ellsworth, was ill much of the time and spent most of the rest of his tenure in the diplomatic corps.[4] The Court membership numbered six until 1801, and five between 1801 and the 1803 term.[5] Justices often gave separate opinions for their decisions, and they revealed themselves divided on, among other things, their own power to construe, and possibly invalidate, acts of Congress in light of the Constitution. The most notable case decided in this first decade of the Court, *Chisholm v. Georgia*,[6] which allowed a citizen of one state to sue another state in a federal court, was overruled by the 11th Amendment in 1798.

Worst of all, the passage of the Alien and Sedition Acts of 1798 embroiled the justices in partisan politics.[7] The Court failed to declare that controversial legislation unconstitutional; in response, the Virginia and Kentucky Resolutions, which argued that state legislatures, not the Court, were the ultimate interpreters of the Constitution, were drafted. After Jefferson's election in 1800, the outgoing Federalists "packed" the federal judiciary with party supporters; their opponents, the Republicans, responded by bringing impeachment charges against several judges, including Justice Samuel Chase of the Supreme Court. John Jay, who was again offered appointment to the Court, this time in 1800 by President John Adams, characterized the state of judicial affairs in his respectful but firm rejection of the position. The Court, he told Adams, labored "under a system so defective" that it could not possibly "obtain the energy, weight, and dignity which were essential to its affording due support to the National Government, nor acquire the public confidence and respect which, as the last resort of the justice of the nation, it should possess." [8] This was the branch of government John Marshall was named to head in 1801.

The genesis of the American judicial tradition was the transformation of the office of appellate judge under John Marshall. This tradition has, since its origins, contained certain core elements: a measure of true independence and autonomy for the appellate judiciary from the other two branches of government; the extension, within limits, of judicial authority to questions of politics in addition to technical questions of law; and the presence of a set of internalized constraints upon the office of judge that circumscribe judicial freedom of choice and give the office an identity discrete from the personalities of the individuals who occupy it at any specific time. Since Marshall the appellate judiciary in America has been consciously aloof from direct participation in politics and an active and weighty political force; at once the least regulated and the most constrained branch of American government. Marshall was the primary creator of this unique institutional role.

Each of the tradition's central elements can be seen as having been derived by Marshall in response to the particular difficulties the judiciary faced at the opening of the nineteenth century. In response to the problems of excessive accountability and uncertain status, Marshall declared the independence of judges in *Marbury v. Madison*, [9] making the appellate judiciary the final interpreter of the supreme law of the land. In response to the limiting effects of an oracular theory of judging, which sought to divorce "law" from community values, Marshall developed a technique of decision-making that retained an oracular style but grounded decisions on appeals to the first principles of American civilization. And while entangling the Court in the resolution of questions of social, economic, and philosophical importance—questions that were political in the grander sense of the term—Marshall took steps, in response to the problem of partisanship, to disassociate the Justices of the

Supreme Court from orthodox political affairs and to secure unanimity among them. Out of Marshall's efforts came the distinctive
blend of independence, sensitivity to political currents, and appearance of impartiality that has since constituted the challenge of ex-
cellence in appellate judging in America.

I

Any attempt to understand Marshall must take into account his extraordinary personality, a central trait of which was inoffensiveness. After three and a half volumes, Marshall's first major biographer, Albert Beveridge, lamented that his subject remained "so
surpassingly great and good" that Beveridge virtually despaired of
finding "some human frailty [to identify] his hero with mankind."
The discovery of personal weakness in Marshall would have been
"most welcome" for Beveridge, but he confessed to have uncovered
only "some small and gracious defects." [10] On Marshall's death the
attorneys and officers who had served before him testified to his
"equanimity," "benignity of temper," and "amenity of manners,"
which were said to be so pronounced that "none of the judges who
sat with him on the bench, . . . no member of the bar, no officer
of the court, no juror, no witness, no suitor, in a single instance,
ever found or imagined, in any thing said or done, or omitted by
him, the slightest cause of offence." [11]

Part of Marshall's inoffensiveness may be traced to his informality and lack of pretension: Americans have long admired modesty
and humility in their public servants. Although his age prided itself
on style and dress and made them badges of status, Marshall did
not conform to such conventions. Numerous contemporary observers commented on his unkempt hair, his dangling knee buckles,
the mud on his boots; his appearance was more than once described
as awkward or slovenly. He spoke freely to strangers on the street
and regularly performed menial domestic tasks, such as marketing
or carrying firewood, which seemed inconsistent with his station.
"In his whole appearance, and demeanour, dress, attitudes, ges-
ture, sitting, standing, or walking," wrote a contemporary, "he is as
far removed from the idolized graces of Lord Chesterfield, as any
other gentleman on earth." [12]

If Marshall was a "simple, unaffected man," unconcerned with his personal appearance, contemptuous of "studied manners," [13] and given to humor at his own expense, he was also aware of his mental capabilities and was self-confident in his exercise of them. Justice Joseph Story, who sat on the Supreme Court with Marshall for twenty-four years, said that "no one ever possessed a more entire sense of his own extraordinary talents." [14] In an oral argument as a lawyer, Marshall would begin tentatively and awkwardly, then appear to pick up confidence from his own argument, to become almost magisterial at the end. He preferred to make closing arguments so that he could draw information and ammunition from his opponents' presentations. [15] At the Supreme Court it was said that he encouraged lengthy oral arguments, using them to educate himself on the particulars of a case. During his Chief Justiceship there was no limit on the length of arguments, and lawyers sometimes spoke continuously for four or five days. Yet Marshall had the gift, contemporaries wrote, "of developing a subject by a single glance of his mind, and detecting at once the very point on which every controversy depends." [16] His mind "possessed the rare faculty of condensation; he distilled an argument down to its essence." [17]

The ability to "master the most complicated subjects with facilty" was joined in Marshall with a certain disinclination toward academic learning and "some little propensity for indolence." [18] His legal education consisted of a six-week lecture course given by George Wythe at William & Mary College in 1780, during which, if Marshall's notebook may be trusted, he devoted at least as much thought to the pursuit of his future wife, Polly Ambler (whose name was scrawled at prominent places throughout his law notes), as to the offerings of Mr. Wythe. [19] As a lawyer in Virginia, and later as a judge, he was not prone to the use of legal authorities, and on several occasions his arguments in Virginia rested on no precedents at all. [20] On the Supreme Court his "original bias," according to his colleague Story, "was to general principles and comprehensive views, rather than to technical or recondite learning." [21] His greatest strength both as a lawyer and as a judge was not technical expertise, but the ability, as a contemporary remarked, to lay "his premises so remotely from the point directly in debate, or else in terms so general and so spacious, that the hearer . . . was just as willing to admit them as not." [22] Once Marshall's premises were conceded, his opponents were at a distinct disadvantage, for his skill in reasoning syllogistically downward from premises to results was so pronounced that Thomas Jefferson reportedly said, "When conversing with Marshall, I never admit anything. So sure as you admit any position to be good, no matter how remote from the conclusion he seeks to establish, you are gone." [23]

Marshall was generally regarded as being far fonder of leisure than of work. A French visitor to Virginia in 1796 reported that Marshall was perceived as "being a little lazy . . . but that does not prevent him from being a most superior person when he sits down to his work." [24] He unquestionably did not like legal research, preferring to prepare himself by refuting or accepting the insights of others while incorporating them. It was not his custom to work long hours either as a lawyer or as Chief Justice. In Richmond he often walked the streets in search of conversation, gave luncheons or dinners, or played quoits at his club. After he was appointed Chief Justice in 1801 he divided his time among Richmond, Raleigh, Washington, and his estate in Fauquier County, Virginia. In February the Supreme Court opened its term in Washington, with the entire term lasting no more than six weeks from 1801 until 1827, and no more than ten weeks until Marshall's death in 1835. After the Court adjourned, Marshall left for Richmond, where he held Circuit Court there for approximately three weeks, beginning in the third week of May. In the middle or at the end of June he left Richmond for Raleigh, where he held court for no more than a week. He then retired to Fauquier County, where he often remained through October. The third week in November he reopened court in Richmond for another three-week period; after New Year's he returned to Raleigh for another brief stay. At the end of January he returned to Washington. [25]

Even allowing for time in transit, which was not inconsiderable, this represents a working year of no more than twenty weeks, and in most years closer to fifteen. But Marshall wrote some opinions over the summer, and, at any rate, the working day of a Supreme Court Justice cannot be measured by the amount of time he sits in court. Between 1801 and 1807 Marshall wrote only twenty-seven opinions for the Supreme Court, but he wrote an additional fifty-six while sitting on circuit, and in addition produced a five-volume biography of George Washington. During the thirty-four years of Marshall's tenure as Chief Justice, the Supreme Court decided 1,215 cases, 1,006 by written individual opinion. In 519 of these 1,006 cases Marshall spoke for the Court. [26] Marshall thus wrote an average of fifteen opinions a year during his tenure. This figure can be contrasted with the approximately ninety-eight opinions a year issued by the Court from 1950 to 1970—an average of eleven opinions per Justice.[27] Although there is abundant evidence that Marshall sought out and enjoyed leisure (he was continually regretting his inability to work on the Washington biography because of the necessity to remain on his summer estate),[28] the impression he creates is that of a man with a peculiarly quick, penetrating, and facile mind, able to take a variety of intellectual short cuts.

As a businessman Marshall was less than totally successful in his ventures. He seemed to be incapable of giving business transactions his full attention. Between 1790 and 1800 he engaged in land speculation ventures that resulted in extended litigation and that, in one instance—the ill-fated purchase of the Fairfax Estate in Northern Virginia—left him with a due note of £14,000 and nearly ruined him financially. These difficulties first led him to accept an appointment as an envoy to France and later to undertake the biography of Washington, from which he expected to earn $50,000 eventually.[29] He initially set aside one year to complete the biography, which he planned as a four- or five-volume work, each volume to be 400-to-500 pages. He was two years into the project before he wrote a word.[30]

The intellectual acuteness, the disorderliness, the amiability, and the unpretentiousness of Marshall blended admirably in the performance of his office. He assumed the office of Chief Justice at a time when the Court was beleaguered by partisan strife and internal doubts about its role in the emerging American government. Marshall was confident enough of his philosophical premises and skillful enough in the use of his intellectual powers to assert and justify an active, expansive role for the federal judiciary. But he was also sufficiently acute in his understanding of human nature and sufficiently likable and admirable as a human being to make palatable, in his own person, the judicial power he asserted. Consequently under Marshall's guidance the Court became not only an increasingly important force in national politics but also a source of pride and inspiration to the men appointed to its bench. Its blossoming was tied not only to Marshall's personal impact but also to the manner in which he infused into the jurisprudence of his time his own philosophical premises.

II

Marshall's social thought, like that of many of his contemporaries, rested on the assumption that man held inalienable natural rights in the abstract, and these he brought with him into society. In a hypothetical state of nature, human beings possessed, merely by virtue of their humanity, such rights as life, liberty, property, and the pursuit of their own happiness. Social organizations reflected the common opinion of mankind that some measure of ordered cooperation was necessary for the full enjoyment of these rights, but they did not reflect any judgment that the exercise of the rights could arbitrarily be limited by society. In an abstract sense, society existed not to circumscribe natural rights but to preserve and promote them.

At the more concrete level of specific social interactions between persons, however, certain circumscriptions were inevitable. A right to liberty did not mean freedom to kill one's neighbor with impunity, nor did a right to life mean that one could never forfeit that right. A right to hold and enjoy property was likewise not absolute, but could, on specific occasions, be interfered with, the test of the legitimacy of the interference being whether it promoted natural rights in the aggregate. Those such as Marshall who began their observations of society by making such assumptions tended to have many of their intellectual disputes over the status of natural rights in practice: which individual rights could be infringed upon by society in order for society to survive, and how extensively could society infringe upon these rights in order to promote the general good? [31] Marshall found himself often more inclined to support particular infringements on rights than did some of his contemporaries, such as Jefferson.

Thus, although as a Congressional candidate he could criticize the Alien and Sedition Acts, which suppressed certain forms of speech critical of the national government, as a Supreme Court Justice Marshall held that these same Acts were constitutional. And since he conceived of the Constitution as being grounded in natural rights theory, the Alien and Sedition Acts were, moreover, philosophically justifiable. But the particular occasions on which he tolerated the confinement of natural rights were matched with occasions in which he believed that the extent of such confinement should be severely limited. In the trial of Aaron Burr, for example,

Marshall gave a very narrow reading of the extent of governmental power to punish for treason. He believed that criminal statutes should be construed strictly; that the writ of habeas corpus, which allowed an individual to challenge his incarceration, was a necessary mechanism for an enlightened society; and that governmental interference with the holding or use of private property was presumptively suspect.[32]

On balance, Marshall had a strong and consistent commitment to the general inalienability of natural rights. To that commitment was joined, however, an acute perception of the need to have in society a set of governing institutions exercising real and extensive supervisory power, even though those institutions were ultimately controlled by their constituents. Men might have natural rights, but they did not always perceive or execute them sensibly. Although one could build a society on the reasonable assumption that man was self-interested and would seek to promote his own interests, this was not to assume that the behavior of the individual subject could be left unregulated, for man was also passionate and given to excesses.

Implicit in this formulation was a presupposition, held by Marshall throughout his life, that there was a distinction between an enlightened elite and the masses at large; between men of "character" and the common man. This paternalistic belief served to justify for Marshall the existence of government itself and the need for governmental power. Discounting the moderation and wisdom of the common man as a social being, Marshall supported Virginia's system of county courts, whose membership was entirely appointive and self-perpetuating; opposed vigorously the election of Andrew Jackson, whom Marshall felt to embody in his person the incarnation of unchecked common passions; and distinguished sharply between a republican form of government, which he identified with "order," and a democratic form, which he associated with "chaos." [33]

If Marshall was an elitist and a paternalist, he was by no means an aristocrat. The central organizing principles of society for him were not social status, not breeding, intelligence, or culture, but self-interest and acquisitiveness. He began with a suspicion of communal organizations that required men to subordinate their self-interest to the general welfare—at least where that subordination involved self-deprivation of one's tangible physical possessions.

Society was better off, he felt, when individuals were encouraged to pursue their own interests; ultimately such pursuits would benefit all. Trade, commerce, and industry were inevitably profitable undertakings in a nation with abundant resources and a growing population, and were to be encouraged.[34] Property rights were to be protected if they symbolized the freedom to make use of one's acquisitive skills, but not if they represented simply the fruits of inheritance. Thus, primogeniture could be summarily abolished by the state, but the right to make use of the fruits of one's labor could not be so cavalierly curtailed.[35] The relatively free acquisition of wealth and status through enterprise was a prime ingredient of Marshall's social thought; class lines could give way to the acquisitive impulse. Yet a certain hierarchical structure remained. The masses were encouraged to be industrious, but remained in another sense the masses.

For Marshall the other side of the coin of acquisitiveness was tolerance and humanitarianism. As one encouraged individual men to pursue self-interest, so one respected their idiosyncrasies and responded in some measure to their unique demands upon society. But humanitarian policies were implemented in the light of their social utility. One might recognize the original right of Indians to the possession of lands in the New World, but one also conceded the right of American settlers to self-preservation and took into account the powers that flowed from conquest. At some point, then, the property claimed by Indians, although indisputably theirs in the natural-rights sense, became part of the indistinguishable mass of property held by the citizens of the American nation, and its appropriation by settlers became justifiable.[36] Similarly, slavery was, in the abstract, a clear violation of the natural right of man to the fruits of his own labor; yet an economic system resting on the classification of slaves as property could be sanctioned (at least on a short-run basis) because it allowed *slaveowners* the free and secure use of their own property. Marshall tended to regard slavery as a pernicious institution, but primarily, although not exclusively, because it threatened security.[37]

The intricate and sometimes strained devices to which Marshall resorted to reconcile natural rights with the legitimate demands of an ordered society were characteristic of the arguments and rationales of other social planners of his time. The public men of the Revolutionary generation derived a good share of their creativity from the fusion of two contradictory social insights. Man was fit to govern himself, but he could not be trusted to exercise self-government in a moderate and disinterested fashion. The question was how to design a society incorporating organizations in which these contradictions could be reconciled or, alternatively, contained. At some point, as Marshall and others saw, orderly government led to tyranny, oppression, and a frozen status system; at another point, alternatively, popular sovereignty led to violence, chaos, and mob rule. The ultimate search of statecraft was therefore a search for balance and moderation. Where the points of equilibrium lay was a matter of individual temperament, depending upon the extent to which one feared or trusted the common masses, the degree to which one was willing to circumscribe the rights of his fellow man in order to obtain some security and tranquility, and how deeply one was convinced of the wisdom and beneficence of a class of educated gentlemen. On these issues Marshall's viewpoint, in the context of the late eighteenth century, was middle-of-the-road. He stood with Washington against the tyranny of monarchy and the comparable tyranny of mob rule.

III

Law and legal institutions, as conceived by the Revolutionary generation, were aids in the process of balancing the virtues and excesses of the sovereign people against the virtues and excesses of their government. A first premise of the Founding Fathers, including Marshall, was that the sovereign people were not above the laws, although they had the power to change them. Considerable time and thought were devoted by Marshall and his contemporaries to operationalizing this principle in the form of a national government. Their solution was the creation of a series of balanced but often ambiguous power relations between the branches of the government and between those branches and their sovereign constituency. The term federalism has been characteristically used to describe this solution, but the term has difficulties.

When applied to the late eighteenth and early nineteenth centuries, federalism has two distinct connotations. It may refer either to a constitutional frame of government, with its emphasis on a union as distinguished from a confederation, or to the ideas of a po-

litical party that came to be known as Federalists. Marshall's jurisprudence complemented federalism in the first sense but not always
in the second. If he was a nominal Federalist before becoming
Chief Justice, he ceased being one while on the Court; on the other
hand, he remained a thoroughgoing advocate of the federal union
form of government. In the latter posture, however, he was in the
mainstream of his generation: as Jefferson said, the framers of the
new nation were all federalists and all republicans. Marshall staked
out a distinguishable position and quarreled with others among the
Founding Fathers primarily over the role of the judiciary in a federal union. He believed that federalism required the presence of an
independent federal judiciary; others, such as Jefferson, could concede the desirability of a federal system without seeing any necessity for judicial independence of the kind Marshall advocated. An
independent judiciary was logically the ultimate necessity in Marshall's jurisprudence, the culmination of his beliefs about law and
government. He sought to show that judicial independence was not
merely a side effect of federalism but a first principle of American
civilization.

The principle of judicial independence was derived from a series
of jurisprudential inquiries made by Marshall that began with a
cataloguing of the appropriate sources of law. One source, he believed, was the principles of natural rights. In coming to America,
Englishmen had brought their natural rights with them; in codify-
ing certain rights for themselves in the Constitution, however,
American citizens had not given up those other rights conferred
upon man in his original state. Hence, certain "vested"
property rights were protected from state interference not only
by the Constitution's obligation of contracts clause but also by
their permissibility in a state of nature. Marshall held thereby that
he was free to ground his decisions alternatively in "general principles which are common to our free institutions," or in "the particular provisions of the Constitution of the United States"; [38] on occasion he resorted to both when each alone seemed insufficient.

Precedents laid down by past courts, an important source of the
law in England and in colonial America, were diminished in value
by Marshall's jurisprudence, especially in cases of constitutional interpretation. Several conditions combined to insure the degraded
status of precedent: first, the sparsity of reports of English decisions
in America; second, the divergence of the new American nation

from England in its governmental structure and, apparently, in its philosophical assumptions; third, Marshall's own penchant for reasoning on the level of broad generalities; fourth, the relative absence, especially in the early years of Marshall's Chief Justiceship, of judicial interpretations of the Constitution. When, in the course of his career, Marshall had the opportunity to reason from his own precedents, he tended to treat a precedent not only as an authority in itself but also as an illustration of a fundamental principle of American government, which he then reaffirmed anew. Thus, his decisions in *Gibbons v. Ogden* [39] and *McCulloch v. Maryland* [40] had announced, respectively, the federal government's power to regulate commerce and its immunity from state taxation; his subsequent decision in *Brown v. Maryland* [41] explicitly made both those principles the basis for holding that foreign goods imported into a state could not be taxed by the state while they were held by the importer in the "original package."

In sum, Marshall's sources of law were arranged in a hierarchy, with the first principles of American civilization, in abstract and generalized form, given a higher ranking than specific manifestations of those principles. Wherever possible, Marshall sought to justify a particular decision in the broadest terms possible, so that it could be regarded as an unassailable manifestation of fundamental American beliefs.

Among the first principles Marshall articulated were four concerning the functions of American governmental institutions and the relations of these institutions with one another. The first principle concerned the discretionary powers of a government. The fact that government existed to protect individual rights did not mean that its officials were precluded from making the judgment that infringement of some rights was necessary for the protection of others. On this principle Marshall based his justifications for government suppression of such acts as seditious speech and domestic violence. The people's possession of natural rights in the abstract did not preclude the restriction of these rights in specific instances once the people had consented to be governed.

The second and third principles were derived from Marshall's understanding of the particular meaning of sovereignty to federalism. In establishing the Constitution, Marshall believed, the people of the states had consented not only to be governed but to be united as well. A dual delegation of power had been made by indi-

vidual citizens of the Republic: a grant of sovereignty to their respective states, then a further grant to the federal government of a
more inclusive but limited set of sovereign powers. The sovereign
power of the federal government transcended state boundaries and
was thus superior to the sovereign power of the states, but only
with respect to the federal powers enumerated in the Constitution.
Where the scope of federal sovereignty was unclear, a court, in
resolving the controversy, could resort to constitutional interpretation in the broadest sense of the term. It could, for example, ask itself whether the area in dispute was "national" or "local" in its nature, and in making that inquiry consider the extent to which local
interests had surrendered their parochial concerns or had chosen to
remain autonomous when they ratified the national government.
Using this approach, Marshall found that the states had surrendered to the national government the power to regulate coastal navigation for commercial purposes, [42] but had retained for themselves
the power to dam up navigable creeks that eventually spilled into
coastal waterways.[43]

The third principle likewise dealt with the consequences of the
people's tacit surrender of sovereignty to their national government.
Although the people were the ultimate sovereign, in consenting to
be governed they had chosen a particular form of governmental
control, the republican form. That form, in Marshall's view, constrained the people as much as it allowed them self-government.
Against the potential chaos attendant on mass participatory democracy, republicanism erected the institutional buffers of legislative
representatives and an independent judiciary. The excesses of the
people were moderated by representation, a process by which their
passionate demands were reformulated by an enlightened and reasonable class of public servants. The need of the populace for an articulation of their individual rights under law was met by the presence of a body of judges not beholden to the masses in any
immediate, partisan sense. One purpose of such buffers was to
preclude mass lawmaking.

These first three principles envisaged delicate interactions between the various branches of the national government, between
that government and the states, and between governments at large
and their popular constituencies. The effective functioning of government in America appeared to rest on a precise knowledge of the
limits of federal power, of the points at which state sovereignty was

to be supplanted by federal sovereignty, of the degree to which discretionary authority could be used by governmental institutions, and of the limitations on popular rule. Marshall's fourth principle underscored the balancing processes at the core of American government and entrusted these processes primarily to the judiciary.

According to this principle the Constitution granted the branches of the national government discretionary powers, but also created in them reciprocal obligations. Intertwined with the untrammeled authority possessed by Congress or by the Executive within the limits of their respective jurisdictions was a duty not to transgress these limits. The laws of the nation were the source of the power of government officials; and such officials had to obey those laws. They had been given powers in connection with the assignment of particular tasks oriented toward the achievement of great national objectives; governmental powers were hence inseparable from governmental obligations. Whether particular branches of government had met their obligations or ignored them, whether they had appropriately exercised their powers or gone beyond them, whether they had utilized discretion strictly within the limits of their jurisdiction or usurped the province of another branch—those were questions involving interpretations of the laws and, as such, were proper questions for consideration and resolution by the judicial branch of government. Judicial consideration of such questions was proper even though the judiciary did not make laws but merely construed them as they applied to individuals.

The role of the judiciary, in this view, was founded on a paradox. Courts were second-line institutions; they merely carried through the general commands of the legislature in particular instances, and could not alter the form of those commands. Yet in the process of construing generalized law in its particulars, the courts could decide whether the branch of government issuing the general command—the legislature or its delegate, the executive—had been constitutionally authorized to issue it. The courts, then, were bound by the Constitution, but they determined what it meant in specific instances. They were obliged to defer to the lawmaking authority of other branches but were empowered to decide the constitutional limits of that authority. Marshall's view of the special role of the national judiciary in America, and (by implication) of the office of judge at large, attempted to make this paradox intelligible.

Despite his broad mandate for judicial interpretation, Marshall

did not think of judges as exercising discretion in the modern sense
of the term. He did not believe that "interpreting" the law could be
seen as synonymous with "making" it, or that determinations by
judges of the limits of judicial power could be seen as representing
an unwarranted exercise of that power. He saw legal principles as
omnipresent and immutable. Over time the enumerated powers in
the Constitution were to remain fixed; the social ends (the great objects) to which those powers were related were also fixed. The
meaning of the Constitution was hence *not* intended to change with
time. Once a particular passage had been interpreted, that interpretation was to remain until the people chose to amend the document
itself. The notion that different generations of Americans might attach different meanings to constitutional language was alien to Marshall.

The apparent inconsistency between this static, constrained, passive view of the function of the judiciary and the increasingly active
and dominant role played by the Supreme Court in national politics
during Marshall's tenure becomes readily apparent. Yet Marshall
did not find the two inconsistent. For although courts were bound
only to "interpret" laws and to decide only "legal" questions, yet in
their search for fundamental principles on which to rest their decisions courts were empowered to go beyond the letter of the law to
the general set of philosophical beliefs on which the law was founded. Where, for example, a question arose as to the limits of the
powers of the general government or one of its branches, that question, although in one sense a question of "politics," was in another
sense a question compelling recourse to the fundamental principles
inherent in the creation of the American nation. If those principles
constituted the foundations of the law governing the nation, and
the jurisdiction of courts to interpret the law was as broad as the
law itself, then consideration of questions involving those principles
was a proper task of the judiciary.

Marshall's celebrated argument on behalf of judicial review of the
constitutionality of Congressional legislation in *Marbury v. Madison*
was a variant on this theme. As has frequently been pointed out,[44]
Marshall's opinion in *Marbury v. Madison* tended to assume away
the very issue in dispute: whether an independent judicial consideration of the constitutionality of acts passed by Congress was
permissible. *Marbury v. Madison* raised the question whether the
Secretary of State could choose not to deliver a Justice of the Peace

commission once the designate of that commission had been confirmed by the Senate, and his commission signed and sealed. The designate in question, William Marbury, applied to the Supreme Court for a writ of mandamus to compel the President to show cause why his commission had not been delivered, basing his appeal on a 1789 Act of Congress that gave the judiciary authority to issue writs of mandamus to "persons holding office under the authority of the United States." Marshall's opinion decided that the Court had jurisdiction to consider Marbury's case since, although the President had unlimited discretion to appoint federal officials, he could not arbitrarily remove them once appointed; that the Executive should therefore show cause why the commission had not been delivered; but that the Supreme Court lacked power to issue the writ of mandamus because the 1789 Act violated the section of Article III in the Constitution conferring original jurisdiction on the Court. Thus, in the process of construing a U.S. law, Marshall decided at least three arguably "political" questions: first, that the President had discretion to appoint federal officers at his will; second, that once appointed, he could not arbitrarily remove them; and third, and most celebrated, that the Court had the authority to decide that an act of Congress violated the Constitution.

In *Marbury v. Madison* the portion of Marshall's opinion authorizing judicial review of Congressional legislation made use of the following syllogism:

major premise, the laws of a nation were to be interpreted by its courts;
minor premise, the Constitution was a law of the United States;
conclusion, the Constitution was to be interpreted by the federal courts, the Supreme Court being the ultimate interpreter.

This syllogism, of course, turned on a definition of "law" that blinked the distinction between "political" and "legal" questions, thereby suggesting that the Constitution was an exclusively legal rather than a political document. Under this formulation a power in the judiciary to interpret "laws" necessarily involved a further power to decide whether a dispute arising out of the construction of a law raised "legal" or "political" questions.

Even if Marshall's opinion in *Marbury v. Madison* tended to assume away the central point in dispute, the case should not necessarily be viewed as an exercise in judicial subterfuge. The power of judicial review, though not explicitly sanctioned until *Marbury*, had been widely championed at the time of the framing of the Constitution and was a respectable intellectual position in the climate of late eighteenth-century jurisprudence.[45] If the theoretical framework of the Constitution was one of natural rights, and if the Constitution was not the exclusive source of those rights but merely an important one, then the lines between "law," philosophy, and politics were not always clear. There is evidence that certain of the Founding Fathers, notably Hamilton, envisaged judicial review as an exercise in politics through which an independent judicial elite could temper the democratic excesses of legislatures by affirming the republican political balances inherent in the Constitution.[46] In this view the role of the judiciary was explicitly political, and law and politics were virtually inseparable. Marshall's opinion in *Marbury v. Madison* rejected this position for one that conferred "political" powers on the judiciary only insofar as principles of fundamental law could be said to subsume basic political judgments.

The national judiciary, then, could play a role in the political process, but a role of a specially conceived kind. The judicial branch of government could fashion, through its power to search for fundamental principles of law, the locus and scope of institutional authority, and could intervene to protect certain "fundamental" private rights against governmental interference. In its interpretations of the Constitution, for example, it could define the scope of Congress's power to regulate commerce as against competing power claims by the states; it could, more generally, determine the points where state sovereignty gave way to national sovereignty; and it could carve out the areas in which vested private rights were to be protected against infringements by government.

The court's constituency, in this view, was twofold: the educated professional elites who served as buffers between government and the people, and the people themselves. If the judgments of courts, in Marshall's jurisprudence, were, in terms of their language and reasoning, directed at an elite rather than at a common audience, the judiciary was nonetheless ultimately the servant of the people, being at the mercy of political change as manifested in the current whims of the multitude. This was true not only because the people, through their elected representatives, staffed the courts, but also because the changing social views of the public affected the kinds of controversy brought to the courts. Thus, when Andrew Jackson's election seemed imminent in 1828, Marshall, who had anticipated retirement, decided to stay on as Chief Justice in order to deprive Jackson of the ability to name his successor, whom Marshall felt would undoubtedly be a man far less distressed than he about the increasing demands of democratic mobs for political change. Hence the dependence of an "independent" judiciary upon the political branches of government was inescapable. Although this sense of dependence frustrated Marshall in his last years on the bench, it was conceptually consistent with his jurisprudence.

IV

Marshall's intellectual abilities, social and philosophical assumptions, and jurisprudential premises were all manifested in the rhetoric of his opinions. The rhetorical outlines of his opinions roughly resembled the following pattern:

first, broad formulation of an abstract and seemingly innocuous general principle of law and government, with little effort to tie this principle in a precise way to the case before him;

second, investigation of the particular legal language, whether constitutional or statutory, whose interpretation was in question, and consequent refinement of that language;

third, the statement of a secondary principle based on Marshall's refinement of the language;

fourth, the setting forth of a series of implications that necessarily followed from the secondary principle;

fifth, decision of the case on the basis of those implications, but in terms incorporating the initial general principle, so that the decision had immense potential significance for future cases.

This pattern was not exclusively followed, nor its order always adhered to, but its presence was common enough to be distinctive. Three examples will suffice.

The case of *Fletcher v. Peck*, which Marshall decided in 1810, was a dispute feigned to elicit a judicial resolution of a controversy involving the sale of land claims in Georgia. The background of the case was heavy with corruption, fraud, and politics. At one point Marshall confided to the Court reporter that he had been reluctant to decide it because of the patently spurious character of the lawsuit.[47] The central question was whether a state could rescind title to land previously granted to private persons if the state itself had been the original grantor.

Marshall began his opinion with a characteristically artful tactic. He underscored the absence of power in the national judiciary to scrutinize the actions of a state legislature.[48] In examining the constitutional validity of legislative activity, he found that the courts could not inquire into the motives of a legislature. Even the motive of corruption, present in *Fletcher v. Peck*, did not permit judicial involvement. Having made this bow to legislative authority, Marshall then announced that "certain great principles of justice" ought "not to be entirely disregarded" in the case. Those included the "rules of property," which were "common to all the citizens of the United States," and the "principles of equity," which were "acknowledged in all our courts."[49] Under these principles innocent purchasers of land titles were entitled to protection of their rights, and a legislature could ignore them only by nakedly asserting its sovereign power. "The nature of society and of government" as well suggested "some limits to the legislative power." Where were those limits, Marshall asked, "if the property of an individual, fairly and honestly acquired, may be seized without compensation"?[50]

This general principle of inviolate "natural" private rights against the state was not, however, explicitly made applicable to the case, for Georgia, Marshall argued, was not "a single, unconnected sovereign power" but a member of the American Union, and hence restrictions on the states imposed by that Union's Constitution were relevant. Among those was the clause declaring that no state could pass a law impairing the obligation of contracts, and Marshall turned to an interpretation of the language of that clause in the circumstances of *Fletcher v. Peck*. In the course of his interpretation he made the refinement that a grant was a "contract" within the meaning of the Constitution, since every grant contained within it an implied contract by the grantor not to reassert his rights to the property granted. If a grant was a contract, Marshall then reasoned, the next question was whether the Constitution distinguished between types of contracts, either "executory or executed" or private or public, in its obligation of contracts clause. He found that it did not: "the words are general, and are applicable to contracts of every description." [51] Hence the Constitution included a general prohibition against impairing the obligation of contracts.

By means of implications following from his reading of "contract," Marshall had by this point in the opinion reached the desired result that Georgia could not rescind title to a deed previously granted. He then proceeded to ground that result on the broadest possible principle: Georgia was restrained "either by general principles which are common to our free institutions" or by "the particular provisions of the constitution of the United States." [52] The decision in *Fletcher v. Peck*, then, appeared to affirm the absolute inviolability of "vested" private rights against interference by state governments. Yet this broad principle was not essential to the decision of the case, for the result actually turned on the secondary principle that the impairment of contracts clause in the Constitution was to be read to cover "grants" as well as "contracts" and public grants as well as private grants. Jefferson, in an 1823 letter to Justice William Johnson, called this technique a "practice . . . of travelling out of [the] case to proscribe what the law would be in a moot case not before the court." [53]

Nine years after *Fletcher v. Peck* came the most controversial of Marshall's decisions, *McCulloch v. Maryland*. It considered the constitutionality of a state law enacting a tax on notes issued by a branch of the Bank of the United States in Baltimore, and, preliminarily, the constitutionality of the Bank's charter itself. The constitutional position of the Bank had been discussed at length, Hamilton and Jefferson having issued contrasting opinions on the validity of a national bank at the time of the Bank's original charter in 1791. There has been speculation [54] that Marshall had written portions of his opinion in *McCulloch v. Maryland* prior to the arguments in the case; the suit, another arranged controversy, had been pending for a year before being argued before the Court, and Marshall was known to be thoroughly versed in the issue of national versus state sovereignty that it raised.

Marshall's opinion considered first the constitutionality of the Bank's charter. He began by asking, rhetorically, whether the Constitution was a creation of the sovereign states or of the people who made up those states. This was a question to which he and republicans of his time knew the answer. The ultimate sovereignty rested in the people, and the fact that they had delegated powers to state governments did not preclude their delegating powers to the federal government. Indeed, a primary purpose of the Constitution was to delegate particular powers to a central government. Once delegated, those enumerated powers prevailed over competing state powers. If the federal government was "emphatically, and truly, a government of the people," whose "powers [were] granted by them, and [were] to be exercised directly on them, and for their benefit," then (Marshall maintained) that government was "the government of all" and "act[ed] for all." And thus "the nation, on those subjects on which it can act, must necessarily bind its component parts." That is to say, the federal government was "supreme within its sphere of action": this "would seem to result necessarily from its nature." [55]

At this point Marshall was merely restating a familiar tenet of his, that of the locus of sovereignty in a republican government and its implications for a federal system. But he subsequently made effective use of this general principle. First he formulated a derivative principle, and then put it to work in an interpretation of constitutional language. A constitution, being an instrument for the delegation of certain powers toward the achievement of certain "great objects," was not meant to resemble a code: it designated only "its great outlines" and "its important objects," leaving "the minor ingredients which compare these objects [to] be deduced from the nature of the objects themselves." Otherwise "it would probably never be understood by the public." [56] If this view of the Constitution's "nature" were accepted, then its necessary and proper clause was to be read as meaning not that Congress could only enact legislation "absolutely" necessary to the exercise of its enumerated powers, but that Congress had wide discretion to choose the means by which "great objects" were to be achieved. The necessary and proper clause, then, authorized Congress to enact legislation incidental to the purposes for which it had been granted specific powers. If it had the power to lay and collect taxes, borrow money, and regulate commerce, it could charter a bank to help effectuate those goals. "The power being given," argued Marshall, "it is the interest of the nation to facilitate its execution. It can never be their interest, and cannot be presumed to have been their intention, to clog and embarrass its execution by withholding the most appropriate means." [57]

By means of his secondary principle concerning the "nature" of the Constitution and his reading of the necessary and proper clause, then, Marshall had reached the result of upholding the constitutionality of the Bank's charter. He then tied this result back to his original sovereignty dictum with the celebrated phrase,

Let the end be legitimate, let it be within the scope of the Constitution, and all means which are appropriate, which are plainly adapted to that end, which are not prohibited, but consistent with the letter and spirit of the Constitution, are constitutional.[58]

In other words, the theory of sovereignty implicit in the Constitution's framing gave to the federal government unlimited discretionary power within the scope of its enumerated powers. If one accepts this reading, the significance of *McCulloch v. Maryland* becomes extraordinarily vast.

That Marshall intended the opinion to be read broadly can be seen from his treatment of the second issue in the case: whether, assuming that the Bank was constitutional, Maryland could tax it. He began by conceding that the delegation of a power of taxation to the federal government did not preclude concurrent taxing power in the states. But he then asserted that if a state's use of its taxing power was incompatible with the objects for which the federal government's powers were created, the taxing power of the state could be abridged, even though state taxation of the particular subject in question was not expressly prohibited by the Constitution.

Marshall next established this assertion in the context of the *McCulloch* case. The assertion rested, he maintained, on the "great principle . . . that the constitution and the laws made in pursuance thereof are supreme; that they control the constitution and laws of the respective states, and cannot be controlled by them." [59] From that principle were "deduced" certain "corollaries" relevant to the taxation issue in *McCulloch*. Thus, a power to create implied a power to preserve; a power to destroy, "if wielded by a different hand," was incompatible with the powers to create and preserve; and where this "repugnancy" existed, "that authority which is supreme must control." It was "too obvious to be denied" that Maryland could "destroy" the Bank if allowed to tax it. The state's power to destroy might thereby defeat the power in Congress to create a bank; consequently conflict existed, and the principle of national supremacy came into play. Therefore not only could the State of Maryland not tax a national bank (result in *McCulloch*); the

states, moreover, had "no power, by taxation or otherwise, to retard, impede, burden, or in any manner control the operations of
the constitutional laws enacted by Congress to carry into execution
the powers vested in the general government." [60] With this statement Marshall returned to his original principle of unlimited discretionary power in the federal government within the scope of its
enumerated powers.

In *McCulloch v. Maryland* Marshall seemed to be saying not only
that the states could not tax any operations of the federal government, but also that it was unclear whether they could retard those
operations by any means at all, provided the operations could be
tied to the "great objects" envisaged by the Constitution. This was,
of course, an extraordinary claim, and contemporary critics were
not unaware of its being so or of the devices used by Marshall to arrive at such conclusion. Judge Spencer Roane of the Virginia Court
of Appeals, writing under a pseudonym, declared that the *Mc-
Culloch* decision tended "to strip [the states] of some of the most important attributes of their sovereignty." If Congress, Judge Roane
observed, "should think proper to legislate to the full extent upon
the principles now adjudicated by the Supreme Court, it is difficult
to say how small [will be] the remnant of powers left in the hands
of the State authorities." James Madison's criticism took a different
tack. "The occasion [of *McCulloch v. Maryland*]," he wrote to Judge
Roane, "did not call for the general and abstract doctrine interwoven with the decision of the particular case. I have always
supposed that the meaning of a law, and for a like reason, of a Constitution, so far as it depends on judicial interpretation, was to
result from a course of particular decisions, and not . . . from a
previous and abstract comment on the subject. The example in this
instance tends to reverse the rule." [61]

If Marshall's opinion in *McCulloch* was his most controversial—
ultimately resulting in his responding anonymously to the criticism
it incurred [62]—his opinion in *Gibbons v. Ogden* was probably his
most widely read. [63] *Gibbons* was of particular interest and magnitude in that it combined the political question of state sovereignty
with the economic question of monopolistic control of navigation.
At issue was the constitutionality of a grant from New York State
to Robert Livingston, Robert Fulton, and their successors and li-
censees (of whom Ogden was one), of the exclusive right to operate
steamboats on New York waters. The grant had been challenged

by one Gibbons, who had chosen to operate coastal steamers on the Hudson River between New York and New Jersey in defiance of the Livingston-Fulton monopoly. The existence of the monopoly had long been an object of controversy: in 1812 the New York courts had sustained its constitutionality,[64] and in 1818 and 1822 New Jersey, Connecticut, and Ohio had passed retaliatory statutes forbidding the Livingston steamboats from using their waters.

Marshall opened his opinion in *Gibbons v. Ogden* with one of the most useful of all his starting general principles: the notion that the enumerated powers delegated to the federal government in the Constitution could be liberally construed. A liberal construction of the Constitution was possible, Marshall maintained, because the framers, and, ultimately, the people, intended to use words "in their natural sense"; and if, over time, that sense had become imperfect, then it was to be clarified by resort to the purposes of the document itself. Under this formulation language in the Constitution was to be read as in ordinary usage; the meaning of language was its common and "natural" one.[65]

From this starting point Marshall quickly deduced the working principle of his opinion—that the word "commerce" in the Constitution comprehended navigation. Commerce, in its natural sense, was more than "traffic," it was "intercourse"; [a]ll America" understood it to comprehend navigation; a power "to regulate navigation [had been] expressly granted [to Congress] as if that term had been added to the word 'commerce.' " [66] And if navigation was included in the term "commerce," then the power granted to Congress to regulate commerce "among" the several states meant that Congress had power over navigation within the limits of each state as far as that navigation could be connected with interstate or foreign trade.[67]

But the question remained whether there was not a concurrent power in the states to regulate commerce, analogous to the taxing power that Marshall had conceded to the states in *McCulloch*. Here again Marshall's refinements of language proved helpful. If Congress had been granted a power to regulate interstate navigation, and had exercised that power, its power was exclusive, so that if states attempted simultaneously to regulate trade that made use of interstate navigable waterways, they could not do so under any concurrent "commerce" power. They did, of course, have certain powers to affect interstate commerce, such as the power to establish health standards on vessels using their waters or the power to charge tolls for ferries. These, however, were "internal police" powers; in the field of regulatory interstate commerce Congress remained supreme, and might "control State laws [based on internal police powers] so far as it [might] be necessary to control them, for the regulation of commerce." [68]

There was a conflict, then, between the coastal license granted Gibbons by Congress and the New York grant to Livingston, first, because the New York grant ultimately regulated interstate navigation; second, because the coastal license, in Marshall's reading, conferred not only the right to engage in "foreign" coastal commerce but also the right to navigate the waters of the United States. And in this conflict the federal statute inevitably prevailed. Its supremacy did not rest on the character of the monopoly in question, for whether sailboats or steamboats were involved was unimportant since "the act of a State inhibiting the use of [its waters] to any vessel having a license under the act of Congress" came in "direct collision with that act." [69] The implications of the decision were thus clear: the powers expressly granted to the federal government could not "be contracted, by construction, into the narrowest possible compass," nor could "the original powers of the States [be] retained, if any possible construction will retain them." [70] In Marshall's judgment the decision in *Gibbons v. Ogden* rested ultimately on "the safe and fundamental principles" of dual sovereignty in a federal republic.

As in *McCulloch v. Maryland*, contemporary commentators understood the aim of Marshall's rhetoric in *Gibbons*. John Randolph wrote to a friend, in reference to the decision, that "[a] judicial opinion should decide nothing and embrace nothing that is not before the Court." Marshall could have rested the decision, Randolph pointed out, on the narrow ground of conflict between a coastal license and a state navigation monopoly in those areas where conflict patently existed. Instead he had used the occasion to carve out an exclusive power in Congress to regulate navigation that seemed massively broad in its scope. "No one admires more than I do," Randolph confessed, "the extraordinary powers of Marshall's mind; no one respects more his amiable deportment in private life. He is the most unpretending and unassuming of men." But Marshall's long experience as an advocate, Randolph thought, had perhaps "injured . . . the tone of his perception . . . of truth or false-hood." [71]

Randolph was perceptive in his appraisal of Marshall's rhetoric if not necessarily fair in his judgment about the effects on Marshall of his career as a practitioner. It was Marshall's supreme mastery of the existing rhetorical techniques of his time that gave his admittedly partisan results their unassailable quality. He understood the axioms of republican political theory and the steps of syllogistic reasoning, but, above all, he knew how to use them in dazzling combination, so that techniques of language construction were interwoven with appeals to "fundamental" political principles to produce the impression that the results reached were inevitable. Grant Marshall his starting principles, however vague and bland, and swiftly those principles, in refined form, led him to his desired outcome. Grant him that outcome, and it was made illustrative of a general principle of government that, if followed, decided countless other cases. "[W]rong, all wrong," Randolph allegedly said on reading one Marshall opinion, "but no man in the United States can tell why or wherein." [72]

In Marshall's hands the judiciary, while remaining aloof from politics, allegedly deciding legal, not political questions, and only interpreting and declaring the law, became a political force comparable in stature to the other branches of government. Marshall's tenure saw the genesis of a judicial tradition in America, and that tradition consequently has borne the marks of his personal interpretations of eighteenth-century social philosophy, jurisprudence, and politics. Under Marshall's guidance, judging in America became a technique of exercising power through the use of institutional constraints, themselves derived from broader jurisprudential assumptions. Since judges were obligated to discover and follow the laws made by other branches of government, they could and should be politically independent. Since the law was discoverable and, as manifested in the Constitution, "sacred," the idiosyncrasies of individual judges were necessarily subordinated to higher principles. Politics in the narrow partisan sense was thus incompatible with judging, and consequently a tyrannical judiciary was not to be feared, for judges could only follow the laws, and the people could change their content.

The legitimacy of the judiciary, from Marshall on, rested on its

ability to persuade the people that its members had indeed been
subject to these constraints in reaching their decisions. The source
of judicial authority, then, was the process of judicial reasoning.
Reasoning illustrated the extent to which judges merely "followed"
the law; reasoning illuminated the fundamental principles of American government at stake in a case. Rhetoric, in a judicial opinion,
had thus a dual function: that of interpreting the law and that of
justifying the exercise of the judicial function in a politically independent manner. But rhetoric necessitated an audience, and that
audience could fail to be persuaded by it. Implicit in Marshall's
blueprint for the American judiciary was the possibility of violent
public reaction against the implications of a decision.

2

Kent, Story, and Shaw: The Judicial Function and Property Rights

The legacy handed down by Marshall to his judicial successors had been a considerable one. Appointed to a court that could easily have become and nearly did become a resting place for minor political officials, Marshall gave to succeeding judges a national judiciary able to stand as an equal alongside the other two branches of the federal government. While maintaining that judges were aloof from politics, he had made the judiciary a national political force. While asserting that "judicial power is never exercised for the purpose of giving effect to the will of the judge, always for the purpose of giving effect . . . to the will of the law," [1] he had made judging an exercise in statecraft, a high form of applied political theory. He had more closely associated the art of judging with the positive qualities of impartiality and disinterestedness, and yet he had made his office a vehicle for the expression of his views about the proper foundations of American government. And through the artistry of his reasoning and the acuteness of his political judgments, he had linked the public image of the judiciary to his own formidable self. The strides made by the judiciary during Marshall's Chief Justiceship were considerable. By his death in 1835 the federal judiciary had become a dynamic force in American government.

Although Marshall's legacy was broad in one sense, it was still narrow in another. Marshall's primary concern as Chief Justice had been to demonstrate the relevance of an independent, powerful judiciary to an eighteenth-century model of balanced government, and in this he had succeeded almost beyond all expectations. He had concentrated on the high political issues of his day, and his decisions survive as impressively broad statements of the principles on which the American Republic was founded. His opinions became and remain important guidelines for future relations among the institutions of American government. But as the delicate equilibrium envisaged by the eighteenth-century model of government was upset by new pressures of nineteenth-century America—a surging economy and the increased prominence, especially in the states, of political movements in mass democracy—the Marshall legacy showed some limitations. It rested on fixed assumptions about the nature of man and the manner in which society was ordered; as these assumptions came to be challenged, social and legal problems surfaced that Marshall had not and perhaps could not have considered.

In particular, two situations evolved that called for judicial attention of a different character. The first was the need within the states for a set of coherent, accessible legal authorities as guidelines for ordinary private activity: a corpus of jurisprudence. The second, closely tied to the first though more specific in nature, was the need for a body of law defining and regulating the new forms of private and semiprivate enterprise, such as internal improvement franchises, utilities, and corporations, that had emerged with the expanded economy of nineteenth-century America. Marshall had helped sketch the broad outlines of state sovereignty in the new republic, and had underscored the importance of private enterprise and property rights to the framers of the Constitution. That importance was to be re-evaluated several times during the nineteenth century as those two concepts took on new dimensions.

Three early-nineteenth-century judges distinguished themselves in their efforts to modify the Marshallian legacy in the light of the circumstances of their time. James Kent, Chief Judge of the New York Supreme Court and later Chancellor of New York, Joseph Story, Associate Justice of the Supreme Court from Massachusetts, and Lemuel Shaw, Chief Justice of the Supreme Court of Massachusetts, were members of the post-Revolutionary generation of American judges. Although their careers, especially Kent's, overlapped that of Marshall, they were not his contemporaries. They had been too young to serve in the Revolutionary War; they had not been party to the framing of the Constitution; their concern was not so much with establishing the fundamental bases of American law as with elaborating legal doctrine and adapting it to a rapidly changing environment. Their attention centered on the development and consequent use of a body of judicially interpreted law (the "common" law) to meet a variety of new social problems. One major set of problems was spawned by the interaction of state governments and private entrepreneurs in an atmosphere of rapid and turbulent economic growth.

I

The careers of Kent, Story, and Shaw possessed a rough similarity that illustrates the close connection of the nineteenth-century judicial profession to state politics. Before being appointed to the bench all three men served in their respective state legislatures—Kent as a Federalist in the New York General Assembly from 1790 to 1793, Story as a Republican in the Massachusetts General Court from 1805 to 1808, and Shaw as a Federalist in that same body from 1811 to 1815, from 1820 to 1822, and from 1829 to 1830. In each man's case, experience as a state legislator formed a prelude to service on the bench. Kent's closeness to Governor John Jay, for whom he had worked as a legislator, secured him a nomination to the State Supreme Court in 1798; Story's service in the Massachusetts legislature helped put him in a position to secure a nomination to Congress in 1808, where he met James Madison, who appointed him to the Supreme Court in 1811; through Shaw's involvement in Federalist party politics he met Daniel Webster, who was influential in persuading him to accept the Chief Justiceship of Massachusetts in 1830.

As state politicians and rising lawyers all three demonstrated a concern for the interests of established men of means and a degree of resistance to political or economic change. Kent, according to his biographer, was "true to all the traditions—and prejudices— . . . of the complacent class to which by fortune he belonged"; [2] Story, though nominally a Republican, was by 1807 being characterized by Federalist Harrison Gray Otis as "a young man . . . who commenced Democrat a few years since and was much fondled by his

party," but who "acted on several occasions with a very salutary
spirit of independence." "[A] little attention from the right sort of
people," Otis added, "will be very useful to him and to us." [3]
Shaw, in 1815, on celebrating the end of the War of 1812, hoped
"that the day of idle theory, of frivolous experiment, and of dangerous trifling with our great national interests, which commenced
with the Administration of Mr. Jefferson, has passed away." [4]

But if there were parallels in their backgrounds and early social
views, the three men also had marked dissimilarities of temperament and developed contrasting interpretations of their judicial office. Kent was diffident, shy, and austere. As a young man, his lack
of gregariousness and his apparent disdain for the common man
kept him from attracting much business for his law practice and
from becoming a successful legislator. He did not particularly enjoy
advocacy, being an indifferent speaker and disinclined to engage in
heated debate. [5] His ambition (which was marked) was channeled
primarily into intellectual pursuits; he early identified professional
success with a thorough grounding in the historical antecedents of
English common law and in the classics generally. [6] His eventual
high reputation as a practitioner was acquired on the basis of his
skill at marshaling and presenting ancient authorities. [7]

Kent's ultimate goal, a judicial career, was eventually attained
in his thirty-fifth year, when Governor Jay appointed him to the
New York Supreme Court. He remained on that Court, first as
Puisne Justice and then as Chief Justice, until 1814, when he was
named Chancellor of the system of equity courts (which in New
York remained separate from law courts). The office of judge was
compatible with Kent's temperament. Its field of inquiry was as
much that of scholarly research as of contemporary affairs, and
Kent was essentially the judge as scholar. Yet the office of judge
still retained a certain political aspect, not so much in the active
partisan sense as in the realm where social philosophy and politics
came together, and Kent had from his youth possessed strong political views, and in adulthood continued to exhibit a certain rigidity
and zeal in his efforts to promote them. But it also cloaked its
adherents in a mantle of austerity that appealed to Kent's pride and
diffidence: the story is told [8] that one time Kent's son found his father, then in his eighties, sitting astride a cherry tree branch on his
farm in New Jersey. On being advised to take care in coming down

from the tree, Kent replied: "My son, I am used to elevated sta-
tions, and know how and when to descend with dignity."

At his maturity Kent was a leading jurist of his day. He had
come to dominate the Supreme Court of New York to such an extent that Marshall felt compelled, on overruling him in *Gibbons v.
Ogden*, to praise his reputation. He had single-handedly revolu-
tionalized equity practice in New York, transforming it from a haphazard, unorganized collection of random decisions to a system
with its own rather rigid and technical rules and procedures; and
with the publication between 1826 and 1830 of his *Commentaries* he
had emerged as the first of the great treatise writers of the early
nineteenth century.

He was also identified—especially in the latter portion of his
judicial career—as a judge whose doctrines tended to erect barriers
to the broadening of economic or political power. For this reason he
had become anathema to radical Democrats in the New York legislature, who were delighted to invoke a mandatory retirement statute for state judges when Kent reached the age of 60.[9] Kent, for his
part, responded in kind: his political convictions were fierce, and he
did not temper his passions with a sense of humor. He vociferously
damned advocates of universal suffrage and opponents of established property rights, and attempted to show, in his *Commentaries on American Law*, the fallacy of these doctrines. His political
friendships, such as those with Jay and Alexander Hamilton, were
of long standing, as were his animosities. Aaron Burr, who had run
unsuccessfully for Governor of New York in 1804, fell into the second category. Kent, in fact, was named by Burr in the complaint
that served as a starting point for his 1804 duel with Hamilton. Ten
years after that incident, Kent encountered Burr on Nassau Street
in Lower Manhattan, and, shaking his cane in Burr's face, blurted
out: "You are a scoundrel, sir!—a scoundrel!" Burr allegedly replied that the opinions of the learned Chancellor of New York were
always entitled to the highest consideration.[10]

Joseph Story came to be one of Kent's first friends. The two
held remarkably similar political views, mirrored each other in
many respects in their professional careers, and found companionship in their later years through a correspondence in which
they railed against the outrages of President Jackson and his judicial
appointees. But where Kent was rigid in his approach to ideas and

people, Story was mercurial; where Kent was distant and remote, Story was approachable and convivial.

Story's outstanding characteristic was his remarkable nervous
energy. A bombastic, pugnacious child, a restlessly ambitious
youth, an adult dogged by misfortunes, among them the loss of his
first wife six months after their wedding, and the death of most of
his children before their adolescence, Story found constant activity
a respite from his anxieties. "[M]y cheerfulness," he confessed, "is
the effect of labor and exertion to fly from melancholy recollections, and to catch at momentary joy." [11] His exuberance not only
endowed him with a reputation as one of the great monologuists in
an age when travel induced lengthy conversation, it resulted in a
staggering number of professional accomplishments as well. Between 1811, when he was appointed to the Supreme Court, and
1845, the year of his death, Story performed the duties of a Justice
(which included circuit riding in New England as well as sitting in
Washington), wrote nine multi-volumed commentaries on legal
subjects, served for sixteen years as a full-time professor of law at
Harvard and for over twenty years as president of a Massachusetts
branch of the National Bank, produced a volume's worth of
speeches and addresses and a larger number of letters, and engaged
in a great deal of behind-the-scenes political activity, at both state
and national levels.

This last interest stemmed from Story's life-long concern with
politics. From an early age he had sought out and engaged in political controversy, needling his acquaintances, and occasionally, in his
youth, becoming involved in fist fights. [12] He subsequently learned,
however, to suppress overt hostilities and to moderate his political
stances. As a law professor he advised his students "[a]lways [to]
have in readiness," in legal or political debate, "some of those un-
meaning but respectful formularies [such as] 'the learned gentleman.' " [13] His approach to politics rested on the belief that "[h]e
who lives a long life and never changes his opinions may value himself upon his consistency; but rarely can be complimented for his
wisdom." [14]

Political activity for Story was not at all inconsistent with the office of judge. He viewed his office as a forum from which he could
give unofficial advice on any number of political subjects. The
specter of judicial conflicts of interest did not loom large to nineteenth-century Americans, and Story seems to have given such

issues only indifferent attention. Although he once went on record as declining "to avail myself of my judicial station . . . to affect the opinion of others," [15] he repeatedly attempted to use his influence with Treasury Department officials to secure large bank deposits in the branch bank of which he was president; [16] he sat in judgment of cases involving the Bank of the United States while retaining his bank presidency, and helped Daniel Webster draft a reply to President Jackson's message vetoing the National Bank's charter in 1832; and he also participated in the decision in the famous *Charles River Bridge* case of 1837, notwithstanding the fact that Harvard University, of which he was both a member of the faculty and a Fellow of the Corporation, received annual income from one of the litigants.

Story's energetic participation in contemporary affairs and his combative temperament provoked animosities in spite of his acknowledged wit and charm. With Justice William Johnson he carried on a protracted feud that occasionally erupted in open sniping by both parties in the United States Reports. [17] After Johnson's death Story clashed repeatedly with Justice Henry Baldwin. [18] He eventually became estranged from his friend Henry Wheaton, Court Reporter during much of Story's tenure, who in 1837 called Story a prevaricator and a hypocrite. [19] When Thomas Jefferson, no admirer of Story during his lifetime, was alleged posthumously to have referred to Story as a "pseudo-republican," Story responded by stating that that term was employed for "every one . . . who dared to venture upon a doubt of [Jefferson's] infallibility." [20]

Kent and Story had both been precocious in their professional development. Both were admitted to practice at twenty-two; both were serving in their state legislatures by twenty-seven; at twenty-nine Story was a Congressman, at thirty Kent was Professor of Law at Columbia; at thirty-two Story was on the U.S. Supreme Court, and at thirty-five Kent was on the New York Supreme Court. In contrast, Shaw was a late bloomer. At twenty-four, after his first year in practice, he earned approximately $200. He did not argue a case before the Supreme Court of Massachusetts until he was twenty-nine. At thirty he was a Justice of the Peace for Suffolk County. But after 1811, when he was elected to the Massachusetts legislature, Shaw began to prosper. In the interval between that year and 1830, when he was appointed Chief Justice of the Massachusetts Supreme Court, he married an affluent merchant's daughter, served as a member of the Massachusetts Constitutional

Convention of 1820, became chief counsel to and a director of a bank, developed a thriving law practice, declined nomination to a judgeship on the Court of Common Pleas, and was elected president of the elite Suffolk Bar Association. By 1830 he was earning over $15,000 a year and had to be strongly persuaded before accepting the Chief Justiceship.[21]

In considering whether to undertake a judicial career, Shaw indicated that he was "conscious that I cannot . . . discharge the duties [with distinction]." Others, he noted, had assured him that he could, but the prospect gave him "apprehension and alarm."[22] There was a rational basis for Shaw's fears. He was not a legal technician; as a practitioner he had been impatient with legal research, relying on others to search for authorities.[23] His skill lay in counseling clients, where his honesty, straightforwardness, and common sense served him well. He associated judging with "patient research and persevering investigation"; his disinclination for those tasks nearly resolved him against accepting the position of Chief Justice, giving way at the eleventh hour to his sense that he had harbored similar doubts of his abilities with regard to "other arduous undertakings," and yet had "upon trial . . . found my strength equal to the occasion."[24]

Shaw, as a judge, appeared to contemporaries as a formidable, even awesome, figure. His physical appearance, short and massive, with a huge head and lined face, suggested strength in homeliness; his demeanor in the courtroom was ponderous, deliberate, bluff, and grave; he suffered no levity or disturbance and was capable of abusing counsel or peremptorily dismissing him;[25] he scrupulously avoided participation in political activity, considering his judicial office to be "quite aloof from political controversy";[26] he so dominated his Court that he wrote only one dissent in thirty years and had the unanimous approval of his fellow judges in forty-seven of his fifty opinions in constitutional law. His austerity and his accomplishments as Chief Justice were coupled with a striking lack of vanity, and this, as one contemporary noted, "gave a grandeur to his mind." Another stated that members of the Massachusetts bar were wont to speculate whether Shaw was "a divine institution or a human contrivance."[27]

In writing opinions, Shaw de-emphasized precedents, as Marshall had, preferring arguments based on what he called "the plain dictates of natural justice."[28] His greatest ability was in modifying existing legal doctrine in the context of the demands of contemporary society. He could see the policy implications in legal rules, he was receptive to change, and he had few partisan convictions that prevented his taking a detached view of a legal problem. In consequence, the tone of his opinions differed markedly from that of Kent or of Story. To some extent the difference was a function of time, for Shaw began his judicial career after Kent had completed his, and Shaw continued in service until 1860.

In the period in which Shaw wrote, the empty spaces of American jurisprudence had begun to be filled in, thanks largely to the work of Kent and Story themselves. The judicial task of undertaking a painstaking review of the historical antecedents of a problem had been greatly simplified by the publication of Kent's and Story's treatises. Moreover, judges in America had come, in the early years of the nineteenth century, to give increasing attention to the policy implications of legal doctrines.[29] But even in this context Shaw's work was distinctive. Where Kent or Story might rest a decision on a technical distinction, Shaw grounded it on rough common sense. Where Kent and Story might string together sets of authorities, Shaw completely ignored them. And where Kent and Story might pursue a legal principle to its consistent, logical conclusion, Shaw emphasized its ambivalences and suggested that it could lead to contradictory results in diverse instances.

III

The judicial world that Kent, Story, and, later, Shaw confronted was still shaped by the semiprimitive conditions of life on the American continent. Judges literally brought the law to the people—a task filled with physical and intellectual obstacles. Circuit riding to county courthouses in back-country settlements was a lonely and arduous practice: time in transit—if the circuit was extensive—often matched time in court. The judge carried his law books with him, since there were no public law libraries. There were few law books at best: until 1775 only forty-eight had been published in America,[30] and until 1790 there were few published reports of judicial decisions. During the first decade of the nineteenth century only the Supreme Court and a handful of state courts had printed records of their earlier cases. Under such circumstances judges were accustomed to deciding cases on an impressionistic basis and to seeing their decisions rapidly vanish into obscurity. The informality of the process was augmented in post-Revolutionary America by a popular prejudice against English common law and lawyers themselves, an attitude manifesting itself in the toleration of rough, *ad hoc* justice meted out without resort to technicalities. "It is our duty to do justice between parties," an early-nineteenth-century judge from New Hampshire announced, "not by any quirk out of Coke and Blackstone—books that I never read and never will." [31]

To Kent and Story, men with an inclination toward scholarship, an exalted image of their profession, and a certain class consciousness, such conditions were intolerable. "The progress of jurisprudence," Kent noted, "was nothing in New York prior to 1793." [32] What was most particularly absent, for Kent and Story, was a body of established authorities from which judges could derive rules for the resolution of cases coming before them. Marshall, faced with this void, had created his own body of working principles, but Marshall's task had been the initial formulation of the jurisprudence of the American Revolution, not its preservation and maintenance. Moreover, for the most part Marshall had not been called on to decide ordinary cases, but cases that raised issues of high politics. Kent, in his role as a state judge, and Story, who spent much of his time deciding lower-level federal cases for the New England circuit, needed more practical guidance.

Confronted with an absence of established American law, Kent and Story sought to create it themselves. A first step in that process was to secure publication and dissemination of court decisions, and, as a secondary goal, to ensure that the reporter charged with overseeing the publication would be sympathetic toward one's jurisprudential views. In William Johnson and Henry Wheaton, Kent and Story found two such men.

Johnson, who was appointed reporter of the New York Supreme Court in 1804, was a life-long personal and political friend of Kent. In 1814, when Kent was named Chancellor, he brought Johnson with him as reporter of equity decisions; by 1821 a speaker at the New York constitutional convention asserted that Johnson's reports were quoted "from Maine to New Orleans." [33] Johnson's *Chancery Reports* were dedicated to Kent and helped to make Kent's reputation. Chief Justice Isaac Parker of the Massachusetts Supreme

Court commented, also in 1821, that the bench of New York, "ever since we have been enabled to judge of its character by the masterly reports of Mr. Johnson, has been distinguished by great learning and uncommon legal acumen."[34] No English chancery decisions, noted the *London Law Magazine* in 1834, were "more frequently or more respectfully cited in the courts of South Carolina than the seven volumes of Mr. Johnson's reports of Kent's decisions."[35]

Story had ingratiated himself with Wheaton, shortly after Wheaton was named the Supreme Court's reporter, by helping draft a statute—the Reporter's Act of 1817—providing an annual salary for the office. From that point on, at least, Story found Wheaton receptive to the use of Court reports as a vehicle for Story's essays and also inclined to promote the distribution of Story's Court opinions. Story assisted Wheaton in his summaries of the Court's decisions,[36] contributed anonymous notes to Wheaton's early volumes,[37] planned to collaborate in a digest of Court decisions to be published under Wheaton's name,[38] and lobbied through Wheaton for publication in the several states of his own opinions.[39] Wheaton, for his part, was a willing participant in all these ventures, including the last. Thus, after Story had urged him to disseminate an opinion from which Justice William Johnson, Story's ardent foe, had dissented, Wheaton wrote, "Mr. Justice Johnson places the decision of the Court on a quicksand—yours on a rock. And I am therefore the more anxious to see it before the public."[40]

Reportage was but one means employed by Kent and Story to further their goal of developing American jurisprudence; another was the use of historical scholarship. For Kent and Story the canvassing of historical authorities served three functions simultaneously. It was, first of all, an exercise congenial to their temperaments. They were not only interested in scholarship for its own sake, they strongly pursued an ideal of cultivated gentility that had as one of its components intellectual exposure to history and the classics. They spoke, read, and wrote Latin, corresponding with each other in it; they immersed themselves in the civil law treatises of Europe; through Blackstone they were lead to Mansfield, Coke, Bacon, Glanvil, Bracton, and finally to Roman law. From these readings came the formidable succession of authorities that documented their judicial decisions. Behind an announced principle of law, in their analyses, lay the collective wisdom of the ages.

The personal and social fulfillment Kent and Story found in canvassing authorities was matched by professional pride. They saw the law as the vocation of gentlemen, requiring not only that its practitioners be learned, but that they be, in early nineteenth-century terms, "liberal"—that is to say, wide-ranging and imaginative in their intellectual pursuits. A dash of the classics or a smidgin of the ancient common law forms uplifted the quality of professional discourse. In this belief Kent and Story were not unique; one of the striking characteristics of nineteenth-century advocacy in America was a tendency on the part of appellate lawyers to project the gist of their arguments in Latin maxims.

There was another, less esoteric justification for historical research: the need to present American lawyers with a corpus of source material from which they could derive arguments. The more thorough the foray into the ancient authorities, the wider the range of possible precedents for an advocate; the more extensive that foray, the less the need for subsequent excursions. Scholarly exegesis, if full enough, thus came to serve as a form of lawmaking itself, as practitioners relied on Kent's or Story's canvasses rather than making their own. Since the purpose of Kent's and Story's digests was not merely to declare legal principles but implicitly, to argue for their existence, their synopses in a sense became modest exercises in making law.

This was the central function of the celebrated treatises of Kent and Story, first appearing in 1826 with the publication of the first volume of Kent's *Commentaries,* and continuing until Story's death in 1845. The treatises constituted an American version of small codes. They were not, technically, regarded as "authorities" in the same sense as were decisions of courts or statutes, but at a time when other published resources were scarce, they became for countless practitioners the starting points for research. The "law" of bailments, as Story would have been the first to admit, was not synonymous with *Story on Bailments,* which was published in 1832; yet the treatise's synopsis of legal principles was, practically speaking, a sufficient surrogate for the law itself. As such, the writings of Kent and Story, ostensibly collections of and glosses on "the authorities," became authoritative in themselves.

In addition to the personal and professional functions served by the historical scholarship of Kent and Story, there was a third function, one that might fairly be called political, in a broad sense of the term. Kent and Story used historical authorities not simply to bring additional information to bear on a legal problem, but also to prove the universality of certain propositions by demonstrating the ubiquity of their presence. Hence the appearance, in their decisions or commentaries, of a procession of ancients endorsing a particular legal proposition served as a means of indicating its truth. A practice of Roman law, commented on by Bracton, was seen to be duplicated in a common law rule, as explicated by Coke; and when an analogous civil law practice could be shown by reading the civilian commentators, the phenomenon took on the dimensions of a universal law of nature.

But the technique could work backward in time as well as forward. A theory of contemporary politics, assumed *arguendo* to be sound, could be shown to have such wide and deep historical antecedents as to constitute a social truth. One example of this was the universality of property rights: history showed for Kent "the gradual enlargement and cultivation of [the] sense [of property] from feeble force in the savage state to its full vigour and maturity among polished nations." [41] The demonstration of such a truth had a certain inevitability once one assumed, as did Kent and Story, that "a question of the highest moment" for statesmen was "how the property-holding part of the community may be sustained against the inroads of poverty and vice." [42]

IV

The role of the judiciary in demonstrating the inviolability of property rights and in preserving their sanctity had been an important concern of Marshall; maintaining this aspect of the judicial function was a central, self-designated task of Kent and Story. Associated with the protection of property rights, in Marshall's jurisprudence, had been an oracular theory of judging. Since the judiciary only "found" rather than "made" law, it could not be accused of protecting property rights for partisan or idiosyncratic reasons; alternatively, since an intention to secure autonomy for property could be found in sources of law such as the Constitution, the natural truth of that proposition was self-evident. But whereas Marshall harmonized protection of property rights with an allegedly nonpartisan role for the judiciary, maintenance of that harmony was to become a source of difficulty for Kent and Story. Ultimately, issues involving the place of property rights in the American legal system were to result in a modification not only of Marshall's view of property but of his theory of the judicial function as well. By the time Shaw became Chief Justice of the Massachusetts Supreme Court in 1830, the groundwork for that modification had already been laid.

Protection for property had been linked, in Marshall's jurisprudence, with the notion that security of property had been one of the original rights conferred upon man in a state of nature and brought with him into society. But this conception did not respond to the problem of determining which kinds of property should be protected when two property rights were in conflict. In one instance of conflict Marshall made a clear choice. He argued that property rights acquired by primogeniture or entail, being incompatible with a republican form of government, could be usurped by states at their pleasure; but by contrast, property that represented one's right to the fruits of his labor, such as lands acquired by contract, either with a state or with a private person, could not likewise be usurped.

This distinction between types of property rights was congenial to the dissolution of certain fixed badges of status that had prevailed in England and were considered anathema by Marshall's generation. Abolishing primogeniture and entail was comparable to abolishing titles or supplanting the monarchy with the Presidency: it participated in the self-definition of the new American nation. For Kent's and Story's generation, however, the task of ascertaining which property rights deserved protection became more complicated. A phalanx of vested property rights in the Revolutionary sense of the term had sprung up. During and after the Revolution, states had granted lands to entrepreneurs for various purposes, and in many instances those grants had resulted in the monopolization of large tracts of land or of certain public facilities, such as bridges, ferries, or turnpikes. As the American population grew and the national economy expanded, these property rights came to be regarded, in occasional instances, as barriers to further social or economic development. But a body of law, which Marshall had helped to create, apparently held that these rights could not be interfered with. Hence two competing conceptions of property emerged, one that emphasized its dynamic aspects, associating it with economic growth, and another that emphasized its static character, associat-

ing it with security from too rapid change. The inevitable clash between these two conceptions was not resolved with Marshall's decision in *Fletcher v. Peck*, but recurred again and again throughout the
nineteenth century.

Kent was prepared to concede the inapplicability in America of
English methods of restricting the transfer of property. "Entail-
ments are recommended in monarchical governments," he wrote,
"as a protection to the power and influence of the landed aristocracy; but such a policy has no application to republican establish-
ments . . . under which every individual of every family has his
equal rights, and is equally invited, by the genius of the institutions, to depend upon his own merit and exertions." [43] But to
doubt the appropriateness of a form of preventing transfers of land
was not to deny the principle that family influence and property,
once acquired, could be preserved and perpetuated. [44] For Kent, the
"sense of property" was bestowed on mankind for the "purpose of
rousing us from sloth, and stimulating us to action." It pervaded
"the foundations of social improvement"; it lead to the creation of
governments and the establishment of justice. Legislatures had no
right to limit the extent to which property could be acquired; a
state of equality as to property, in fact, was "impossible to be maintained," as being "against the laws of our nature." [45]

For Kent this conception of property rights translated itself into
four legal propositions: first, the powerlessness of legislatures to
disturb previously vested contract rights; second, the requirement
that if a legislature took private property for public purposes it
must compensate fully all those whose property was either appropriated or damaged in consequence of the appropriation; third, a
power in legislatures to regulate the use of property in accordance
with the safety or health of the community, subject to judicial approval; fourth, a power in courts to define what constituted "public
purposes," to determine the amounts required by full compensation, and to ascertain in which kinds of cases the regulation of property use was permissible. [46]

These propositions were not altogether bound to a static theory
of property. The second and third, in fact, were early statements of
the eminent domain and police powers of state governments, powers that emerged as important grounds for the promotion of new
economic enterprises by states throughout the century. But Kent's
formulation as a whole envisaged the judiciary, through its protec-

tion of vested rights and its ability to determine the conditions permitting legislative abrogations of property holdings, as a buffer between established property holders and the people. In Kent's view, judges could fairly find that a state grant of a monopoly in steamboat traffic to one entrepreneur prevented it from later granting a steamboat license to another; [47] that a state franchise to a bridge company could be used to prohibit subsequent bridge companies from competing with it; [48] and, in general, that the legislative grant of a franchise to a private corporation implicitly gave the corporation a privilege to enjoin its prospective competitors. [49]

Kent thus envisaged a peculiar relation between the legislature, the judiciary, and private entrepreneurs. To promote economic development, states had conceived the practice of granting lands or franchises to private entrepreneurs to pursue certain goals, such as making internal improvements. Under Kent's doctrines nothing prevented a state legislature from making these original grants or indeed from simply appropriating the property of its citizens for public purposes. Moreover, the state could insist that property be used one way rather than another if the public health or safety required it. But once the state granted away its lands, it could not regain them unless it had expressly reserved the right to do so. Nor could it permit subsequent potential grantees to pursue the very same economic objectives for which it had subsidized its original grantee. At some point, then, in Kent's view, property rights, having vested and created necessary attendant privileges in their owners, became static, and were guarantees of security against encroachment except under unusual circumstances. The chief institutional protector of security and ultimate apologist for a static view of property was the judiciary. Ultimately, judges were to side with those who held property against those who sought to obtain it—and this was perfectly acceptable to Kent. "Society," he announced in 1821, "is an association for the protection of property as well as of life, and the individual who contributes only one cent to the common stock ought not to have the same power and influence in directing the property concerns of the partnership as he who contributes his thousands." [50]

Kent's concern that economic expansion be stimulated yet not allowed to undermine the security of property led him to look favorably on forms of business enterprise that appeared to foster both those goals. One such form was the corporation, which simultaneously provided for the free, advantageous exertion of "industry, skill and enterprise," [51] and afforded "security to the persons of the members, and to their property." [52] Kent, however, regarded indiscriminate expansion of the corporate form as unwise, believing that it was best suited to high-risk public-service enterprises that required large capitalizations. Used indiscriminately it might tend to lessen competition.[53]

If Kent was cautious in his endorsement of the corporation, Story was not. Like Kent, Story was interested in maintenance of support for static property rights amidst a climate of economic expansion. He believed that "the sacred rights of property" were "to be granted at every point"; [54] that whenever legislation rendered "the possession or enjoyment of property precarious," it was "in its essence tyranny"; [55] that there could be "no freedom" where there was "no safety to property"; [56] and that government could "scarcely be deemed to be free [when] the rights of property [were] left solely dependent upon the will of a legislative body, without any restraint." [57] Accordingly, he sustained vested rights against legislative interference, either through use of the contracts clause of the Constitution,[58] a state constitution's prohibition against "retrospective laws," [59] or, when pressed, the principles of natural law themselves.[60] But Story did not see a static theory of property rights as necessarily incompatible with economic expansion. In his concurring opinion in the *Dartmouth College* case, for example, he simultaneously upheld the sanctity of vested rights against legislative infringement, and suggested a means by which legislatures could in subsequent charters to private enterprises reserve the right to repeal grants they had made.[61]

Story's concurrence in *Dartmouth College* was more important, however, for its effect upon the status of corporations. Corporate entities had existed in America since colonial times, but not primarily as business enterprises. Most colonial corporations were churches or municipalities; after 1800 the corporate form became associated with transportation companies chartered by legislatures to undertake special projects. Originally such charters conferred only limited discretionary powers, required special acts of the legislature for their implementation, and were not thought of as assuring limited liability for the corporation's stockholders. Perpetual charters, incorporation certificates, and limited liability were features evolving in the later nineteenth century, when the corporation began to assume its modern identification with business enterprise.

Dartmouth College approximated the colonial model of a corporation more than the later model. It was an organization that had been chartered not to pursue an economic venture but to provide education for the public. In the eighteenth and early nineteenth centuries, however, the close relations between state governments and private enterprise had spawned a legal doctrine that threatened to conflict with the notion of vested private rights: the theory that property rights "in the public domain" or "affected by a public interest" could be infringed by the state. This doctrine was made a basis for state involvement in cases such as those involving claims to riparian rights on the grounds that certain types of property, even if private in their ownership, were public in their use.[62]

A college corporation also seemed subject to public-interest restrictive legislation. Colleges functioned to educate the public; the state had an arguable interest in the nature and quality of the education a college provided. Hence the *Dartmouth College* case appeared to raise squarely the issue of whether a previous grant of a charter to a "public" corporation could be subsequently amended by the state in the light of the construction of the obligation of contracts clause advanced in *Fletcher v. Peck*. The issue seemed in doubt, despite the *Fletcher* decision, because of the public domain doctrine and because even the most tenacious defenders of the sanctity of property had conceded that some state restraints on its use were permissible. Marshall's opinion, however, seemed to draw a bright line between "private" and "public" corporations—a stance unresponsive to the subtleties of the case. In a literal sense Dartmouth College was a private institution, not an administrative wing of the state.[63] But in another sense it was surely "public"; Marshall's opinion simply chose to de-emphasize that aspect of its character.

Story's concurrence, however, spoke both to the relation of the *Dartmouth College* case to the public domain doctrine and to the political ramifications of the decision, which were quickly perceived by contemporaries.[64] The decision created for any arguably "private" corporation an umbrella of protection against state interference with the terms of its charter, despite the ability of states to interfere with property that was in the public domain or affected with a public interest. There were, Story maintained, two meanings of the term "public": a "popular" meaning and a "strictly legal" one. Any corporation serving the populace was public in the former sense, but its legal responsibilities flowed from the latter. If the "foundation" of a corporation was private, it was immune from state interference regardless of the uses to which it was put. Only corporations that remained actual governmental entities, such as municipalities, were "public" in the legal sense. Banks, insurance companies, transportation franchises, and educational institutions were private corporations, even though their "objects and operations" might "partake of a public nature." The phase "affected with a public interest" was to be strictly construed.[65]

But the freedom from state interference ascribed to private corporations, Story maintained, rested not on universal natural rights principles but on the more limited basis of the contracts clause in the Constitution. State or even royal charters to corporations were clearly "contracts," but nothing prevented states from reserving by the terms of its contracts a power to amend charters and thereby affect the rights of a corporation's members. Thus, while Story's concurrence in *Dartmouth College* served to limit the applicability of the public domain doctrine on a theoretical level, it also suggested a practical means by which states could control the expansion of private enterprises.

State legislatures were highly receptive to the practical proposal Story had advanced, and reservation of an amendment power became a common ingredient of incorporation charters in the nineteenth century.[66] But Story's suggestion that theory be tempered with practice was not so readily received. The public domain doctrine was not easily curbed; it revived itself in a variety of ways in the courts, and in 1837, in the *Charles River Bridge* case,[67] it captured a majority of the Supreme Court, to Story's "humiliation" and Kent's utter disgust.[68]

The revival of the doctrine was symptomatic of the emerging conceptions of property use associated with the century's second wave of economic expansion. From the Revolution through the first thirty-odd years of the nineteenth century, the internal development of the nation's economy was largely tied to ventures in transportation, and the form of the ventures was often that of partnerships between states and private groups organized around a single project. The turnpikes, ferries, bridges, and canals that made possible mercantile exchange between the seacoast and the interior were built primarily by state-chartered private monopolies. The original theory of state franchises for effecting internal improvements assumed that what the state could give it could take away, since the duration of monopolistic franchises was at state sufferance.

The contracts clause cases, such as *Fletcher* and *Dartmouth College*, served to modify the original partnership theory. State charters once created could not, absent an expressly reserved amendment power in the grantor, be abolished; temporary, risky internal improvement ventures were made into permanent, monopolistic enterprises. The owners of bridges or turnpikes could impose tolls to take advantage of the traffic in commerce their facilities had stimulated. In a few years, if they were well situated geographically, they could count on securing a return on their original investment and making monopoly profits besides.

With the continued growth of population in the nation's interior and the consequent rise in trade between the seacoast and the back-country, the demand for additional transportation routes became irresistible, and the enormous entrepreneurial potential of internal improvement franchises became widely perceived. At this point (occurring at different times in different localities), pressures toward a second wave of economic expansion mounted—a wave that treated ventures in transportation less as public service operations than as profitable business undertakings, and responded not so much to incentives created by a state to foster development of its resources as to demands of private persons for easy freight and passenger service between the interior and the seacoast. Consequently internal improvement schemes became focal points for the demands of a variety of interests: shippers who wanted an abundance of fast, cheap transportation; existent franchise holders who wanted a profitable return for their risk-takings; potential competing groups who wanted to enter the transportation services market; passengers who wanted safe, reliable, inexpensive transportation to previously inaccessible regions.

The theory of property rights advanced by Marshall and generally supported by Kent and Story was responsive to only one of these interest groups—established franchise holders. It suggested that a second wave of expansion in the transportation area could not take place if the first wave, that marked by state-private partnerships, had resulted in unreserved grants to private monopolies. The rights originally granted had now "vested." Competitive franchises could be enjoined, monopoly prices could be set, and subsequent expansion of transportation facilities was to be at the pleasure of the original franchise holders. In the view of Kent and Story the new expansionists, as Chief Justice Taney said in the *Charles River Bridge* case, were "obliged to stand still, until the claims of the old turnpike corporations shall be satisfied." [69]

That too many interests favored further expansion in the transportation sector to tolerate the continued primacy of the vested-rights doctrine was apparent by the 1830s. The Court majority in *Charles River Bridge* only codified the inevitable when it refused to enjoin a new bridge over the Charles River despite its obvious infringement on the vested rights of the existing bridge's stockholders. Less apparent were the legal theories to be utilized in developing protection for the emerging expansionist interests and their effects on the role of the judiciary, which had been conceived by Kent and Story as a buffer between those who held property and those who sought to acquire it.

Shaw began his judicial career at the crest of the expansionist wave. His thirty years on the bench witnessed a transformation of the status of vested property rights from an absolute bar to legislative activity to one of several ingredients that were balanced in a legislature's determination of the "public interest." This transformation served to resolve the tension between static and dynamic theories of property—and largely in favor of the dynamic theory. In helping to effectuate this change, Shaw utilized a breed of judicial activism whose audacity and originality were reminiscent of that of Marshall. Paradoxically, the result of his activism was to prescribe a far more passive role for the judiciary than that prescribed by Kent or Story.

In his reconsideration of the place of property rights in the society of his time, Shaw developed new usages for four existing legal doctrines: that of delegation of legislative powers, that of a public use, that of eminent domain, and that of state police powers. The doctrines were not original with Shaw, but in his hands they became the foundation for a new set of relations among private entrepreneurs, the legislature, and the judiciary.

The partnership form characterizing early-nineteenth-century economic ventures had been based on a particular interpretation of the powers of a state government. Governments, the theory assumed, had a power to control the use of private property if the common welfare so required. Although that power could be delegated to private persons, the state implicitly reserved the right to attach conditions to its delegation. An early application of this theory was the Massachusetts mill acts. Gristmills ran on water power, and thus required access to water and also tended to discharge water on adjacent farmland. At common law the owner of lands flooded by a nearby mill could enjoin the operation of the mill as a nuisance or sue the mill owner for damages. These sanctions acted as a deterrent to the development of mills; so in the mill acts Massachusetts delegated to mill owners its theoretical power to affect the use of private property, thereby allowing them to flood adjacent lands with impunity, but retained the right to oversee the rates they charged and the services they provided. The original justification for this legislative alteration of the common law was that the owners whose land was flooded, being farmers, received economic benefits from the presence of the mills, which helped to make their products marketable.

In the course of Shaw's tenure, several cases arose involving extension of the mill acts beyond gristmills to other kinds of enterprises. Iron mills or cotton mills, after 1830, were arguably not so similar to their earlier counterparts as to merit the same protection. They were merely one type of manufacturing enterprise in a diversifying state economy, and not necessarily indispensable requirements for economic health. Shaw, however, was prepared to sustain legislative delegations of an appropriation power to manufacturers. The "public interest," he maintained, was furthered by "the establishment of a great mill-power for manufacturing purposes . . . especially since manufacturing has come to be one of the great public industrial pursuits of the commonwealth." [70] And the same argument could be made in behalf of manufacturing enterprises that did not rely on water, such as factories and railroads. Shaw's test was whether, in a broad sense, the activity receiving special privileges constituted a benefit to the public.

This interpretation of the relation between state power and private enterprise was not, however, essentially designed to promote the interests of new forms of private enterprise at the expense of those injured by their operations. It also functioned to maintain the state's ability to continue regulation of private enterprise on the grounds of its "public" character. For if the justification for delegating privileges to certain enterprises was that they furthered the public interest, that same justification might be used for subsequent legislative control of their operations. Under this view the concept of vested rights became only one of a number of variables affecting the propriety of legislative regulation of private enterprise. If the public interest, on balance, was promoted by statutory infringements on vested rights, courts would not generally invalidate those infringements.

Shaw's approach to cases involving property rights entailed a delicate interweaving of the doctrines of eminent domain, public use, and police power. The doctrine of eminent domain, which had been recognized by Kent,[71] conceded to legislatures a power to appropriate land within their domain and tolerated delegation of that power to private enterprises to achieve certain "public" objects. The mill acts were early examples of delegations of this power. Its most extensive use, however, was in connection with the development of railroads.

The railroad industry required for its development the right to cut swaths of land for roadbeds out of existent property, and this need raised a series of questions involving the eminent domain doctrine. The first was whether the state could delegate its power of eminent domain to railroads. Shaw answered this affirmatively in *Boston Water Power Co. v. Boston & Worcester R.R.* and *Fuller v. Dame.*[72] The justification for an eminent domain power in railroads was that they were, like turnpikes, bridges, and mills, "public works," inasmuch as they were established by public authority for public use even though their construction was financed by private individuals. The second question was, assuming an eminent domain power in railroads, What was the effect of that power on vested contract rights? In a second case involving the Boston and Worcester Railroad and the Boston Water Power Company,[73] Shaw held that appropriation of land under the eminent domain power did not violate contract rights stemming from the original grant of that land. He distinguished between ordinary and extraordinary legislative powers, locating eminent domain in the latter category, since it rested on the demands of "public necessity." Original legislative grants to private individuals were assumed to benefit the public, since those "contracts," while creating rights in the grantees, implicitly reserved power in the grantors to recalculate the benefits of the arrangement. If on balance the public benefited from subsequent legislative infringement on existing rights based on the eminent domain power, the infringement was permissible.

Determining the proper relations between vested rights and eminent domain in any particular case was a matter, then, of ascertaining where the public interest lay. In certain instances, the public was aided by the maintenance of prerogatives for vested private interests, and existing contract rights could be protected. Hence the legislature could create a monopoly of railroad traffic along a certain route, and subsequent challenges to that monopoly by potential competitors could be overriden by the courts.[74] This was because the public was better served by a regulated monopoly than by competition in that particular situation, since competition between railroads over short routes fostered a waste of resources. Moreover, the possibility of subsequent competitors provided a disincentive for investors in the original railroad enterprise, and the public relied on private capital to subsidize the railroad industry.[75]

This resolution of the third question raised by the eminent domain doctrine—whether that doctrine created a presumption that vested rights were vulnerable to subsequent encroachment—left existing property holders a degree of autonomy. Competitors of railroads, or railroads themselves, could not infringe vested rights of others merely by showing proof of their incorporation by the legislature, for, if they had not expressly been granted specific eminent domain powers, they could not claim them by implication. Hence, railroads could not appropriate the existing roadbeds of turnpikes unless specifically authorized,[76] nor could they claim that a power to appropriate land exempted them from compensating owners of land not appropriated but damaged.[77]

There were, then, a series of judicially enforced limitations on delegation of the eminent domain power. Thus appropriation of land by eminent domain required compensation; the power extended only to those circumstances for which it had been expressly and unambiguously granted. The test in every instance was whether the object for which use of the power was employed constituted a benefit to the public or was merely a vehicle for private gain. In the first case, vested rights gave way to eminent domain; in the second, there was no need to disturb them, since their presence was assumed to benefit the public and their infringement only enhanced the economic position of certain private interests.

In short, private exercise of the eminent domain power was justified if the "use" to which it was being put was "public." And the presence of a public use justified the continued protection of the public interest in the relevant private enterprise. That protection could be effectuated through regulation: the legislature could set rates for railroads and mills and control their profits.[78] It could also be effectuated by outright prohibition of certain economic activity on the grounds that it was injurious to the public health. During Shaw's tenure the Massachusetts legislature moved from selective regulation of the liquor industry to more extensive regulation to outright prohibition. Shaw sustained each successive infringement,[79] limiting the legislature only by requiring that its regulations provide procedural safeguards for those persons whose property was being appropriated.

The eminent domain doctrine thus implied a "public use" of private enterprises that in turn implied the vulnerability of those enterprises to state regulation under the police powers. The concept of police power entered American jurisprudence during the years coincident with Shaw's tenure. It was a product of the partnership theory of state-private relations, the Tenth Amendment of the Constitution, and the eighteenth-century principle that all property, being "derived directly or indirectly from the government," was held "subject to those general regulations which are necessary to the common good and general welfare."[80] It implanted in the states the ability to restrict the use of property on the ground that a particular use jeopardized the general welfare; as Shaw put it, "the nature of well ordered civil society" required that "every holder of property, however absolute and unqualified may be his title, holds it under the implied liability that his use of it may be so regulated, that it shall not be injurious . . . to the rights of the community."[81]

Restriction of property through the police power was not a "taking," and hence did not require compensation.[82] The test of the constitutionality of a police power regulation was its "reasonableness," and regulations justified on the basis of state police powers were presumed to be valid; when found unconstitutional, they were voided only insofar as they affected the particular parties challenging them.[83] Under its police powers Massachusetts could suppress the liquor traffic,[84] regulate banks,[85] control the building of wharves,[86] and condemn buildings used as houses of prostitution.[87]

In sum, private property under Shaw was considered primarily with respect to its social usefulness. The public, through the legislature, was given considerable freedom to decide to what extent the impairment of particular property rights benefited the public at large. In tolerating this legislative calculus, Shaw was not only modifying the place of property rights in American jurisprudence, he was altering the Kent-Story conception of the function of the judiciary as well. Kent and Story had envisaged the judicial branch as an aristocratic barrier against the excesses of democratic legislatures, with the protection of existent property rights one of its major tasks. Under Shaw the judiciary became a partner with the legislature in shaping public policy. Individual cases were conceived of as manifestations of principles of civilized living and, as such, each new case could test the continued applicability of the principles it symbolized. "It is one of the great merits and advantages of the common law," Shaw wrote, "that instead of a series of detailed practical rules . . . [it] consists of a few broad and comprehensive principles founded on reason, natural justice, and enlightened public policy modified and adapted to the circumstances of all the particular cases which fall within it." [88] When new cases arose, they were to "be governed by the general principle . . . , modified and adapted to new circumstances by considerations of fitness and property, of reason and justice." [89]

Under this theory of the judicial function, great weight was given to the policy implications of a legal dispute. There were two primary sources of wisdom on matters of public policy: the decisions of prior courts (which were manifestations of "general principles" of reason and justice) and the enactments of legislatures (the principal expositors of public sentiment). Hence judges had a good deal of freedom to modify precedents in the light of changed circumstances, extracting their principles and reasoning by analogy, but little freedom to modify the decisions of legislators. Constitutional limitations on legislative activity were few, and judicial review of the actions of legislatures was narrow in its scope. The constitutionality of statutes was presumed; where alternative readings of a statute were possible, the one preserving its constitutionality was to be preferred; the invalidity of part of a statute did not void the whole; and the parties challenging the constitutionality of a statute had to prove its adverse effect on them.[90] Although the contracts clause of the federal Constitution was acknowledged by Shaw to be a limitation on state legislative activity, it was used to strike down statutes only three times in his thirty-year tenure.[91] Established property rights were considered as deserving of judicial protection only when their presence furthered the public interest [92] or they were being infringed in a shockingly arbitrary fashion.[93]

V

In one of the nation's most influential states, then, property rights had by 1860 lost their specially protected status and were subject to usurpation in the public interest. Shaw had supported and furthered this transformation of status; Kent and Story had opposed it. The transformation could be seen as a triumph for aspiring entrepreneurs and property holders as against established landowners. Insofar as the expanding character of the American economy required judicial tolerance of new uses of property, such transformation was progressive as opposed to reactionary. But identifying Shaw's approach to property rights issues as "liberal" and that of Kent and Story as "conservative" is not particularly useful. For one thing, it offends against the parlance of the time, under which Kent and Story regarded their views as representative of a liberal frame of mind.[94] Further, it de-emphasizes Shaw's use of the eminent-domain doctrine to promote corporate interests and maintain the security of stockholders of transportation ventures. And it leads to a distortion of the legal history of the post-Civil War period, where the theories of Kent and Story were revived not to protect "vested" interests but to preclude further governmental regulation of corporate entities, such as railroads, which had greatly expanded their operations under state control and now wanted further room to expand.

A more appropriate contrast between Kent and Story and Shaw involves their interpretation of the Marshallian view of the judicial function in the light of the exigencies of nineteenth-century America. Marshall's legacy, in this respect, had four features: an active judiciary, distrust of the popular will and its manifestation in acts of legislatures, sympathy toward entrepreneurial as opposed to static uses of property, and a method of deciding cases by appeal to principles of high politics. In the nineteenth century, continuing economic expansion—supervised and encouraged by state legislatures—created a tension between certain aspects of this legacy, most particularly between its preference for dynamic uses of property and its distrust of the popular will. Since this tension ultimately involved basic assumptions about the nature of man and his place in society, it affected the Marshallian method of decision-making, which rested on the assertion of shared principles of social organization in America. Consequently judges who followed Marshall were faced with a troublesome choice. They could develop either a method of decision-making that identified the judiciary with economic expansion and made it a tacit partner of the legislature, or a method that retained the judicial branch as a check on legislative activity and a protector of static uses of property. Shaw chose the former method, and with it Marshall's belief that judicial interpretation was a matter of returning to first principles; Kent and Story chose the latter, making it an exercise in partisan historical scholarship.

In a transitory fashion history supported Shaw's choice, so that a passive, although free-wheeling, conception of the judicial function supplanted the more active and rigid view of Kent and Story for a time. It would be inaccurate, however, to state that consequently Shaw made a greater contribution to the development of the American judicial tradition than Kent or Story. The latter two men provided their profession, through their scholarship, with a synthetic body of "law" with which to work, and with it a perspective in which emerging legal problems could be viewed. Masterfully broad in some respects, that perspective was narrowly partisan in others, and it was in those areas, such as property rights, that it first came to be abandoned. Shaw's form of abandonment, which created a new way of thinking about property rights, was particularly responsive to new features of the nineteenth-century American economy, and thereby enormously influential. But Shaw built on Kent and Story as much as he moved beyond them. On Shaw's retirement in 1860 a group of lawyers who had practiced before his court remarked that "[i]t was the task of those who went before you, to show that the principles of the common and the commercial law were available to the wants of communities which were far more recent than the origin of those systems. It was for you to adapt those systems to still newer and greater exigencies." [95] Both efforts were part of the function of the judge in nineteenth-century

America, so that in praising Shaw the Massachusetts Bar was praising Kent and Story as well.

A conception of law as a body of shared principles was decisive
in determining the judicial approach of Kent and Story and also the
contrasting approach of Shaw. Kent and Story saw what they had
once perceived as common American values revealed as class values; and having come upon that insight, they retreated into history
to find the sources of legal doctrine. In so doing they rendered their
pronouncements vulnerable to changed circumstances. A historical
definition of property rights, however once universalized, could
become anti-utilitarian and obsolete. Principles of law, in the sense
used by Kent and Story, could be modified with time. Shaw, who
had the benefit of Kent's and Story's scholarship, also saw its im-
permanence: to him principles of law meant something closer to
contemporary communal values. In defining principles in that fashion and in appealing to them in his opinions Shaw was reminiscent
of Marshall, but with an important difference. Marshall had appealed to principles he thought immutable as well as incontrover-
tible. Shaw's appeal was to the public utilitarian calculus of the
moment. In his hands judges were not so much oracles as public
servants. What, then, if a judge misread public sentiment; what if
the first principles on which he grounded his opinions were politically unacceptable? That difficulty, avoided by Shaw, was to haunt
his contemporary Roger Taney.

3

Roger Taney and the
Limits of Judicial Power

In a surviving portrait of Roger Taney his disheveled hair and pained, meditative expression create an ascetic appearance more appropriate to a saint than to the man who has come to be called the judicial defender of racism and human bondage. His reputation has been resurrected several times by scholars, who have pointed out that he was a judge of considerable talent and stature and that his association with the infamous *Dred Scott* decision [1] needs to be viewed in the context of his other accomplishments.[2] Yet he remains a symbol of the moral nadir of the American judicial tradition, when the Supreme Court of the United States publicly declared the "degraded status" of blacks in America and the inherent inferiority of their race, and gave legal sanction to the enslavement of blacks by whites. With *Dred Scott* to remind us of the ignorance and viciousness long embedded in American culture, Taney's reputation may never be completely vindicated. He forces us to see the extent to which our institutions of government and our system of laws can become, even while administered by the educated and well-intentioned, affronts against humanity.

Taney was representative of educated professional Americans of his generation. Confronted with a rapidly expanding economy, changing political alignments, and the growth of cultural schizophrenia of which the system of black slavery was a root cause, he sought to adjust the nation's institutions so that they might survive in the new conditions created by these phenomena. Like many other statesmen of his day, Taney tried and failed to solve the slavery problem, but his response to the problem, no more unsuccessful than any other response, has become particularly offensive with time. The tension between the humanitarian and egalitarian ideals associated with the founding of the American nation and the presence of black slavery was simply too debilitating and pervasive to admit of peaceful consensual solution; moreover, it occurred at a time when consensual values were noticeably lacking throughout American civilization. The internal conflicts, of which the slavery issue was the most dramatic example, were never truly resolved, but engendered a forced reconciliation of the nation, with one set of attitudes summarily superimposed on another. Taney can hardly be faulted for failing to provide a set of fundamental constitutional principles by which the question of slavery could be amicably settled. Indeed, given the ideological context of his time, none existed. But he can, from another perspective, be faulted for the political and moral choices he made in attempting to settle the question.

Between 1836, the year when Taney replaced Marshall as Chief Justice, and 1857, the year of the *Dred Scott* decision, an affirmative justification for racially based enslavement was developed and refined in America. On the Court, Taney provided legal support for that justification. His intention was benign; he was concerned not with preserving slavery as such but with maintaining peaceful coexistence between competing ideologies in the nation. One cannot, however, ignore the fact that, despite his motives, Taney attempted to use the power of the judicial branch of government to further the existence of a subculture in which persons of one race were considered the property of persons of another. In this use of his office Taney demonstrated the moral and political limits of judicial power in America.

I

Taney served on the Court in a period of striking change, diffusion, and ambiguity in American civilization. Competing models of social organization existed in numerous areas of life in early-nineteenth-century America: static versus dynamic theories of property-holding; a stratified, restrictive system of political participation as opposed to successive movements appealing to the rhetoric of mass democracy; humanitarian reform in contrast to slavery. Taney reflected these contradictory impulses himself. The son of an established propertyholder, he was first elected to the Maryland legislature in 1799 largely because of the prominence of his father, and in his first term resisted a series of efforts to restrict the influence of the landed gentry. Yet in the 1820s and 1830s he aligned himself with the Democratic Party, which advocated mass suffrage, and became a strong supporter of Andrew Jackson and a prominent figure in the Jacksonian campaign against the Second Bank of the United States, regarded by both supporters and opponents as an assault on social and economic privilege. Despite his close identification with the landed gentry of his region, he became a principal spokesman on the Court for doctrines curtailing the power of landowners in an expansionist economy. While a member of the Maryland legislature he had actively promoted the rights of black freedmen and slaves, calling slavery "a blot on our national character," [3] and freeing his own slaves; [4] yet as attorney general under Jackson he gave his official opinion that "the African race in the United States" were "every where a degraded class," not endowed with inalienable rights and not entitled to political privileges. [5]

Throughout his life Taney was involved in politics, thus tempting one to attribute the contradictions in his thought to considerations of expediency. If such motivation existed, it was not generally noted by his contemporaries. Daniel Webster called Taney "cunning," but Webster was rarely dispassionate in his appraisal of his political opponents; a more representative comment described Taney as having "an air of so much sincerity in all he said that it was next to impossible to believe he was wrong." [6] The general impression Taney made was that of a gentle, moderate, and likable man, with a capacity to defuse through his person the passions his actions engendered. Story, who had deplored Taney's appointment, described him as one who in his judicial duties "conducted himself with great urbanity and propriety"; [7] Justice Samuel Miller, who sat with Taney during the latter's final two years in office, was less grudging in his praise. "When I came to Washington," Miller recalled, "I had never looked upon the face of Judge Taney, but I knew of him. I remembered that he had attempted to throttle the Bank of the United States, and I hated him for it. . . ."

He had been the chief Spokesman of the Court in the Dred Scott case, and I hated him for that. But from my first acquaintance with him, I realized that these feelings toward him were but the suggestions of the worst elements of our nature; for before the first term of my service in the Court had passed, I more than liked him; I loved him." [8]

A striking feature of Taney's career was the relatively few personal attacks made on him by his enemies, especially in the light of his continued participation in controversial matters. Hostile contemporary commentators on his actions as a Maryland politician resorted only to standard mild caricature, and he escaped much of the calumny heaped on the Jackson administration, despite being the central figure in attacks on the Bank of the United States. Only after *Dred Scott* did he undergo savage public criticism.

Part of Taney's ability to avoid personal antagonisms can be traced to his ethereality. He was frail and withdrawn, preoccupied with his health and that of his family. He was not ambitious, although he never declined advancement to a higher office; and despite the sensitivity of his disposition, he was not upset by criticism and was scrupulously moderate when provoked. He retreated from work whenever his physical energies were taxed to their limit (which was frequently), and was often absent from the Court, but he persevered for twenty-eight years as Chief Justice and died in harness, as he had said he would. He was morbidly fearful of crowds, suffering from stage fright as an advocate, and his voice was variously described as feeble and hollow; yet he was markedly effective in argument. It was said that his presentations were so clear and created such an impression of conviction that his audience never focused on his unprepossessing appearance. [9]

In personal relations Taney's strong suits were subtlety and tact. He was neither a gregarious nor a dominating personality and was never able to mold the Court to his views as Marshall had been able to do. Under Taney's tenure two of the solidifying features of the Marshall Court—the absence of dissenting opinions and the practice of having the Justices live together during the Term—disappeared. Characteristic of Taney's approach to his office was his assignment of two [10] of the first three important cases of his first term to associates, keeping only the *Charles River Bridge* [11] opinion for himself. All three cases involved major issues and represented significant departures from the Marshall Court—types of cases Mar-

shall had appropriated for the Chief Justiceship. Taney preferred to
influence others through the power of suggestion rather than of persuasion, as a letter to President Jackson in 1833 indicates. Taney's
object was to induce Jackson to remove deposits from the National
Bank and to appoint him Secretary of the Treasury. To that end he
summarized the difficulties involved in the deposit policy, stating
that although no man but Jackson was "strong enough to meet and
destroy [the Bank]," [12] the risks were perhaps too great, and he
(Taney) would understand if the effort were not made; and he indicated that he thought himself not well qualified to be Secretary of
the Treasury, but was willing to defer to Jackson's wishes. The effect of the letter was to feed Jackson's competitive spirit, rouse him
to action against the Bank, and secure Taney the Treasury nomination.

Taney's reticence and equanimity masked a capacity for passionate opinions, stubbornness, and irascibility, which as an adult he
completely suppressed in public. Having once made his mind up
on an issue, he was not apt to change it; and when he regarded the
issue as a matter of principle, he was willing to go the limit in its
defense. His early misgivings about slavery had been superseded
by a conviction that the states had complete independence in dealing with the slave trade and that any interference with their sovereignty in this respect was intolerable. This judgment led him not
only to declare the unconstitutionality of the Missouri Compromise,[13] but also, in a hypothetical opinion, that of Lincoln's Emancipation Proclamation.[14]

The tradition of judicial performance that Taney had inherited
from Marshall assumed considerable participation by the judiciary
in high affairs of state and a large measure of judicial freedom to interpret the Constitution in accordance with the changing "crisis of
human affairs." Though Taney was to differ with Marshall on specific issues and on the extent of permissible judicial involvement in
"political" questions, he essentially accepted Marshall's activist
theory of the judicial function and attempted to adapt it to what he
regarded as the peculiarly pressing social needs of his time. He
sought, in this task, a technique of analyzing questions of commerce in order to resolve conflicts raised by economic expansion; a
theory of sovereignty in a federal system in order to reflect the diffusion of political power in nineteenth-century America; and a judicial reconciliation of the divisive slavery issue. He pursued each

goal in the activist tradition he had inherited from Marshall, but he was ultimately unable to make use of the principal justification for Marshallian activism: appeal to the common philosophical principles on which American civilization was founded. In Taney's tenure Americans were divided on first principles; denied that appeal, Taney turned cautious, then stubborn, leaving himself and his office unguarded.

II

The Marshall Court, in the course of its existence, had proved alternatively receptive and hostile to economic development. Its constructions of the contracts and commerce clauses of the Constitution had created major incentives, then barriers, to the unrestricted private use of property. The contracts clause, as interpreted in the vested rights doctrine, gave original property holders a right to "the fruits of their labor," and also allowed them to block further use of lands they had been granted. The doctrine of federal pre-emption of commerce had fostered traffic on the nation's waterways, but by the 1830s it apparently precluded state regulation of commercial enterprises, often an incentive for state subsidization of private entrepreneurial activity. Pressure on Marshall Court doctrines from the second wave of economic expansion in the early nineteenth century could be seen in the almost unprecedented dissension fostered in that Court by the *Charles River Bridge* case, first argued in 1830 and undecided for six years.[15]

Taney's opinion in *Charles River Bridge* represented an intermediate position between the primacy given vested rights by the Marshall Court and the eventual subordination by courts, such as the Supreme Judicial Court of Massachusetts under Shaw, of property rights to the public welfare. Taney rested his arguments on the assumption that a state had the power to "promote the happiness and property of the community" and could restrict private property rights in the process. Surrender of that power through grants of absolute monopolies was possible but should not be presumed unless the legislature had explicitly indicated such a purpose, for "the whole community" had an interest in reserving the power in the state. Unless a particular grant openly surrendered the power, then it should be construed as "preserving it undiminished." In

Charles River Bridge the original grant was not explicit, and hence it was to be read in favor of the public. The rights of private property were to be "sacredly guarded," but only when intentionally immunized from legislative scrutiny, for "the community also [had] rights, and . . . the happiness and well being of every citizen depend[ed] on their faithful preservation." [16]

The interpretation of the contracts clause advanced in *Charles River Bridge* set the tone for subsequent treatments of vested rights by the Taney Court. Infringements by states of the rights of previous grantees were generally tolerated on the basis that certain powers, such as taxing [17] or eminent domain,[18] were implicit in state sovereignty and would be considered reserved by the states unless explicitly surrendered. This approach did not prevent the occasional protection of vested rights when they were affected by changes in state mortgage laws [19] or in laws taxing banks.[20] But in general the contracts clause barrier to state regulation of private economy activity was removed during Taney's tenure. This development did not, as Story feared, deter entrepreneurs from entering into risky new ventures; in fact it created incentives for state support of those ventures, since the states could rely on retaining control over the enterprises they subsidized. The massive growth of the railroad industry between 1850 and 1860 was a product of such thinking. Railroad proprietors were permitted to infringe the rights of competing transportation franchises but remained under potential state control regarding the location of their routes and the pricing of their services.

A second potential constitutional barrier to economic expansion was the commerce clause, as interpreted by the Marshall Court. In *Gibbons v. Ogden*,[21] that Court had held that where a federal statute affecting commerce conflicted with a state statute, the federal regulation prevailed. The Court did not directly resolve the question whether the commerce clause prevented all state regulation of interstate commerce or merely those regulations that conflicted with existent federal statutes. At least one Justice, Johnson, had taken the position that the federal government had pre-empted the field so that no state regulation of interstate commerce was permissible even in the absence of federal activity. This view, if followed by the Taney Court, would have had profound effects on the commercial development of the nation, for it would have meant that any business engaged in interstate commerce would have been immune from state regulation. It also had implications for the growth of slavery, since by the 1830s several states had passed laws regulating the slave traffic and providing procedures for the capture and return of fugitive slaves. Pre-emption of that power by Congress would have immeasurably affected the investment of Southern states in the slave trade.

Taney quickly moved to dispel the notion of federal pre-emption, but had difficulty articulating an overriding rationale to which his whole Court could subscribe. *New York v. Miln* [22] tested the validity of a New York statute requiring the masters of ships entering the Port of New York to supply the state with information about the health and financial condition of immigrant passengers. The purpose of the statute was to enable New York to prevent impoverished immigrants from entering the state. The Court sustained the statute against a claim that it regulated interstate commerce, holding that persons were not articles of commerce and the act was a legitimate exercise of the state's police powers. In the *License Cases*,[23] however, that distinction was not possible, since the contested statutes regulated the sale of liquors. Taney, in a concurring opinion, attempted to set forth a new theory of federal-state relations under the commerce clause. His theory assumed a concurrent power in states to regulate commerce within its borders, even if that commerce subsequently passed beyond the state, so long as the regulation of internal traffic did not conflict with an existing federal statute. In the case of liquor, Congress had sanctioned its importation; hence no state could prevent that. But the liquor traffic, having entered a state, had an internal commerce within it that the state could regulate in the absence of Congressional regulation. Taney's theory thus required a twofold inquiry under the commerce clause: whether the traffic regulated was "internal," and whether Congress had occupied the field. If the first question was answered in the affirmative and the second in the negative, state regulation was permissible.

Under this formula Taney had no difficulty distinguishing subjects that states could regulate from those they could not. States could tax immigrants entering their ports, but not American citizens; [24] they could authorize construction of bridges in the absence of Congressional action, even though the bridges obstructed navigation; [25] but they could not tax shipments for export, since Congress had pre-empted that field.[26] Further, a state could enact bankruptcy laws, even though Congress possessed that power—but such state laws had no force outside the state.[27] Similarly, a state could tax out-of-state legatees of property even if Congress attempted, through a treaty, to create a tax exemption for certain foreigners.[28] In short, the commerce clause did not preclude all state regulation of commerce; state sovereignty set limits on the exclusivity of federal regulatory power.

Taney's formulation nonetheless allowed a considerable range of federal autonomy. One decision of his greatly expanded the admiralty jurisdiction of the federal courts and thereby the federal control of navigation on the inland waterways;[29] another allowed the development of a uniform federal commercial law by holding that federal courts were not bound to follow the decisions of state courts in commercial cases involving citizens of more than one state;[30] still another broadened federal court jurisdiction over corporations.[31] This last case promoted the interests of corporations by making it easier for them to escape hostile state courts but, in general, Taney was not inclined to protect banks or corporations from state regulation unless the privileges they claimed, such as immunity from taxation[32] or the right freely to engage in business in a state other than that of its domicile,[33] had been explicitly granted.

By and large, Taney's views on constitutional issues affecting economic development reflected his own attitudes toward various forms of entrepreneurial activity. He remained sympathetic toward landholding, including mortgage-holding,[34] hostile toward banks, suspicious of corporations, tolerant of federal power in a few limited areas such as navigation, and zealously protective of state powers in most instances, especially where implicit or dormant federal powers were the basis of pre-empting state activity. His decisions reflected those views, but rested on narrow and subtle distinctions that did not bring to his side a majority of his Court and rarely secured unanimity. The distinctions indicated more than lawyers' artfulness and political caution. They reflected the contradictory impulses of economic life in early-nineteenth-century America, where the antinomies of security and progress, stability and expansionism, and order and efficiency maintained an uneasy coexistence.

III

Taney's re-evaluations of the commerce and contracts clauses rested on a novel theory of sovereignty designed to respond to the diffusion of political power in America, to the greater diversity of attitudes and interests manifested in its growing population, and, above all, to the need of the South to maintain and expand its unique system of labor. Taney's purpose was to recast the conceptions of sovereignty held by the Founding Fathers and assumed by Marshall in the light of the growing sectional character of nineteenth-century American civilization.

Taney's theory underscored the states' role in a federal system. His theory counterpointed Marshall's: it began with the same assumptions—that after the Revolution sovereignty rested in the people, who then delegated it in part to various governments—but then emphasized the powers reserved for the states rather than those surrendered to the general government. Taney conceded that the states had surrendered particular powers to the federal government, but maintained that they were otherwise "absolutely and unconditionally sovereign within their respective territories." [35] These two starting points spawned a series of "angry and irritating controversies between sovereignties," [36] since the extent to which the federal government could disturb asserted state supremacy, by actions "necessary" to implement its own conceded powers, had not been determined. The limits of state and federal power were to be determined ultimately by the Supreme Court, which functioned not only to maintain the supremacy of the national government but also to protect the states from federal usurpation of their reserved powers.

The Court was an appropriate institution to resolve controversies between sovereignties because it was not like a state court, yet, unlike other federal courts, it was not solely the creation of Congress. It had been "erected," according to Taney, "and . . . powers . . . conferred upon it, not by the Federal government, but by the people of the States, who formed and adopted that Government." [37] It owed its allegiances neither to federal nor to state governments as such but to the people, in their capacity as citizens of both the nation and their respective states.

Since controversies between states and the federal government had recurred increasingly with the diffusion of political power in the early nineteenth century, Taney's view assumed, in some areas, the presence of an activist judiciary, upholding federal supremacy where necessary but emphasizing primarily the importance of the states in a federal system. In its reinterpretations of the commerce clause, the vested rights doctrine, admiralty jurisdiction, and the

relations between state and federal law, the Taney Court proved itself as bold and free-wheeling as its predecessor. But in other respects his Court set limitations on its exercise of power. In cases between 1838 and 1854 Taney employed the "political questions"
doctrine to preclude judicial determination of the legitimate composition of Rhode Island's state legislature [38] and of the right of a
foreign government to recognition by the United States,[39] and
maintained that the Court could not resolve state boundary disputes involving jurisdiction rather than physical property.[40] He
also read narrowly the Constitution's requirement that courts decide only "cases and controversies," holding that the Court could
not review the findings of a territorial court with regard to land
claims of Spanish citizens against the United States,[41] and could
not review judgments of the Court of Claims if those judgments
were to be executed in the future.[42] In commercial law, by contrast, the Court, in the famous case of *Swift v. Tyson*,[43] claimed
power to disregard the findings of state courts. By 1851 a commentator claimed that in commercial law both the state courts and the
Supreme Court were "courts of final and coordinate jurisdiction." [44]

Despite these qualifications on the Court's power, Taney's conception of the judicial function assumed that the appellate judiciary
would continue to be a source of political statesmanship. His
theory of sovereignty was meaningless, in the face of Marshall
Court precedents, without active participation by his Court to
redress the balance between federal and state sovereignties. The
theory rested in fact on the assumption that in matters of peculiarly
sectional concern the states were the appropriate regulatory forum,
and their judgments were presumptively entitled to respect.
Taney's preference for state supremacy proved explosive in the area
of slavery.

IV

The slavery controversy incorporated within itself the major
themes of Taney's term of office. At one level it was an issue involving economic expansion in that it questioned whether a particular system of labor could be prohibited in new areas of the nation
where conditions appeared favorable for its use. At another level it

tested the extent to which political diffusion and sectional diversity would be tolerated in America by asking whether a region committed to the practice of slavery could remain an influential political force in the American nation, or even a part of that nation at all. Finally, it asked to what extent American society was grounded on ideological principles and to what extent those principles could be abandoned in practice. Were all men, or only white men, created equal? Were all men endowed with the rights of life and liberty, or could blacks be summarily deprived of those rights?

The extent to which the slavery issue raised these fundamental questions was not immediately perceived by nineteenth-century Americans. In the early years of the century there seems to have been a general belief, expressed by Taney as a Maryland state legislator, that slavery was an objectionable practice, that it was not flourishing and would gradually be abandoned, but that it should not forcibly be eradicated. The opening up of the trans-Mississippi West, however, destroyed whatever consensus existed on slavery. Certain portions of the unsettled West appeared, in a geographical sense, capable of supporting an agricultural economy similar to that of the lower South, in which the economic importance of slave labor was inestimable. Moreover, even if cotton or rice or indigo were unsuited to the trans-Mississippi West, slavery might be useful in other areas, such as produce farming or even mining; and further expansion of the American nation might include areas of the Caribbean to which slavery was clearly adaptable.

Most important, the projected expansion of slavery highlighted the moral implications of the existing slave system. It was one thing to tell a Southerner how to manage his household, another to object in principle to a system that treated human beings as property and to deplore its emergence in new territories. But attacks on slavery at large invariably became attacks on the practices tolerated by particular Southern states, so that the South felt compelled to protest the most abstract form of criticism and to oppose the eradication of slavery even in territories, such as Oregon, in which it was apparently neither feasible nor desired by the residents. Increasingly in the 1840s and 1850s the slavery issue became a vehicle for pitting one region against another. The successive Congressional "compromises" on slavery, including the Missouri Compromise and the Compromise of 1850, rigorously preserved an absolute balance of power between North and South, as though a deviation from this equilibrium would result in the imposition of one region's ideology on the other.

By the time Taney replaced Marshall as Chief Justice it was clear that no easy or wholly satisfactory solution to the slavery issue was forthcoming, and the Court was reluctant to involve itself in the dispute. Issues of social controversy are often translated into appellate litigation, however, and in 1841 the case of *Groves v. Slaughter* [45] came before the Court. The case involved the constitutionality of a clause in the Mississippi Constitution prohibiting the introduction of slaves into Mississippi after 1833. A contract had been signed to bring slaves into the state after that year, and the question was whether the contract was voided by the state Constitution, and, if so, whether the state Constitution conflicted with the federal Constitution's commerce clause. Potentially at stake were the answers to the critical questions as to whether slaves were persons or articles of commerce, and whether, if they were persons, they were citizens of the United States.

The Taney Court, on that occasion, managed to avoid deciding both those questions by finding that the clause in the Mississippi Constitution required enabling legislation to be effective, and since no such legislation had been passed, the contract was valid. Justice McLean, however, wrote a concurring opinion in which he faced the commerce question and found that state sovereignty prevailed over the commerce clause with regard to the slave trade. McLean's intent was to show that antislavery states could prohibit the introduction of slavery, but his opinion was also read as conceding to the slave states a power to prohibit free blacks from entering their borders. [46]

Groves v. Slaughter hinted at divisions within the Taney Court on the slavery issue; they came to the surface in *Prigg v. Pennsylvania*, [47] decided in 1842. *Prigg* involved a Pennsylvania statute modifying the Fugitive Slave Act of 1793. The question it raised was whether the power of Congress to prescribe regulations for the return of fugitive slaves was exclusive. The Court found that it was, and so held the Pennsylvania statute unconstitutional. In the course of his opinion, however, Story maintained that this exclusive federal power over fugitive slaves prohibited the states not only from enacting laws modifying the effect of the Fugitive Slave Act, but even from enacting laws implementing it. Between 1843 and 1848, six Northern states enacted legislation forbidding compliance with the Act; in 1850 Congress responded with a more comprehensive fugitive slave law. Taney dissented from the latter portion of Story's opinion, maintaining that state noncompliance with the Fugitive Slave Act was impermissible.

Reaction to the *Prigg* decision demonstrated how inextricably the Court had been drawn into the politics of the slave issue. Northern newspapers denounced the Court for upholding the Act; a Southern senator called *Prigg* "one of the most unfortunate decisions in its effect upon the South of any that has ever been made." [48] While a new fugitive slave law was being debated in Congress, efforts were made to expose the Court's pro-Southern composition and to suggest that it would invariably support the South on slavery questions. Senator Charles Sumner of Massachusetts went so far as to suggest that Congress could ignore the decisons of the Court. [49]

In 1851 Taney delivered the opinion of the Court in *Strader v. Graham*. [50] That case involved the question whether slaves who had gone from Kentucky (a slave state) to Ohio (a free state) and then returned to Kentucky had lost their slave status. The Kentucky Court of Appeals had held that they had not. The Supreme Court refused to divide the case, finding that the question was one of Kentucky law and that nothing in the Constitution was contrary to it. Thus, no federal question existed, and the Court was without jurisdiction to review the decision of the Kentucky Court of Appeals. Taney's opinion, grounded on the narrowest of holdings, had wider implications, however, since the individual determination of slave status in cases of this kind were left to slave-state courts. Characteristically, Taney's opinion was subtle and cautious, its broad ramifications made implicit rather than explicit.

If *Strader v. Graham* seemed to settle questions regarding the interchange of slaves between slave states and free states, it had not resolved the question of the effect of a slave's subsequent residence in one of the territories of the trans-Mississippi West. The status of slavery in those territories reappeared as a national issue after 1848, when the Mexican War vastly increased the western holdings of the United States. The Missouri Compromise has prohibited slavery in certain territories, but in 1854 it had been repealed by the Kansas-Nebraska Act, and the choice of slavery had been left to the settlers of the new territories. Meanwhile, the *Dred Scott* case had begun to work its way up to the Court. By 1852 the Missouri Supreme Court had held that Scott, originally a slave in Missouri, subsequently taken into Illinois and Upper Louisiana Territories and then returned to Missouri, had become a slave on return. Scott's lawyers, anxious to secure a disposition of the issue by the Supreme Court, then arranged to have him sold to Dr. J. F. A. Sanford, a resident of New York, in order to attain the diversity of citizenship requisite for bringing an appeal to the Circuit Court of Appeals. That effect was successful. The Court of Appeals in 1854 ruled against Scott, and the case was certified to the Supreme Court that same year.

The *Dred Scott* case was remarkably similar to *Strader v. Graham*, and seemed dispositive on similar grounds. There were, however, two complicating factors: for one thing, Scott had gone from a slave state to a territory where Congress had outlawed slavery, not to a free state; further, Scott was claiming United States citizenship by virtue of his suit in a federal court. Potentially, then, the case raised three issues: first, whether a slave permanently lost his slave status when taken into a free territory; second, whether Congress could outlaw slavery in the Territories; and third, whether a black alleging himself to be free was a citizen of the United States. The first question was virtually on all fours with that decided in *Strader v. Graham*, and the latter two were politically so explosive that it was doubtful that the Court would decide them—or so commentators at the time thought.[51]

The Taney Court divided first on whether it could entertain the case at all because of the jurisdictional question raised by Scott's citizenship, and in May 1856 the case was set down for reargument. While it was pending, the Presidential election of 1856 was held. James Buchanan was elected, and was to assume the office in March of 1857. A series of extraordinary events then took place. *Dred Scott* was reargued in December 1856, and the Justices first considered it in conference in February 1857. There a majority of the Court decided, with two dissenters, to resolve the case by following *Strader v. Graham*—that is, holding that Missouri law determined Scott's status in Missouri and that since Scott was considered a slave in Missouri he could not bring suit in a federal court. This decision avoided passing either on the citizenship question or on the constitutionality of the Missouri Compromise. Taney, himself a member of the majority, assigned Justice Samuel Nelson (New York) the task of writing the Court's opinion. The dissenters, Justices John McLean (Ohio) and Benjamin Curtis (Massachusetts), resolved, however, to address in their opinions the constitutionality of the Missouri Compromise and to sustain the power of Congress to prohibit slavery in the territories.

Learning of this, the members of the majority reconsidered, and some, notably Justice James Wayne (Georgia), determined to counter the dissenters by reaching the constitutionality of the Missouri Compromise and declaring it void. Wayne persuaded four of the majority Justices, Taney among them, to abandon Nelson's opinion and replace it with one by Taney that would decide all the issues in the case. Nelson and Justice Robert Grier (Pennsylvania) tentatively refused to commit themselves to this procedure, so that a bare 5–4 majority now appeared to exist in behalf of a comprehensive disposition of the case.

At this point Justice John Catron (Tennessee) wrote a letter to President-elect Buchanan suggesting that he write Justice Grier and impress him with the necessity for settling all the points at issue in the case. Catron did not tell Buchanan the proposed outcome of the case, but Grier's position was particularly significant in that, whereas the other five Justices who had formed the new majority— Taney, Wayne, Catron, John Campbell (Alabama), and Peter Daniel (Virginia)—were all Southerners, Buchanan, like Grier, was a Pennsylvanian. Buchanan wrote Grier, and Grier responded by telling Buchanan the outcome of *Dred Scott*, agreeing to concur with Taney's opinion and informing Buchanan that the opinion would not be handed down before March 4, Buchanan's Inauguration Day. Having received that letter, Buchanan said in his Inaugural that the question of the permissibility of slavery in the territories was a judicial question to be decided by the Court, and he would "cheerfully submit" to the Court's decision, which he expected would "finally settle" the issue.[52]

The decision by the new majority to resolve all the issues raised by the *Dred Scott* case was all the more remarkable because by deciding the citizenship issue against Scott they made irrelevant the issue of the constitutionality of the Missouri Compromise and left themselves open to the charge that passing on its constitutionality was a gratuitous invasion by the Court into the political arena. Equally remarkable was the strong language used by Taney in his historical argument that Africans had not been considered American citizens. Taney said, among other things, that at the time of the framing of the Constitution blacks were considered "a subordinate and inferior class of beings"; that they "had been subjugated by the dominant race, and whether emancipated or not, yet remained subject to their authority"; that they "had no rights or privileges but such as those who held the power and the Government might choose to grant them"; and that they had "no rights which the white man was bound to respect." [53] Such attitudes Taney described as "universal[ly]" held. Contemporary critics of the *Dred Scott* opinion immediately asserted that this language represented Taney's own views rather than the views of most Americans at the time the word "citizen" was introduced into the Constitution. [54]

Finally, Taney's argument with regard to the constitutionality of the Missouri Compromise stretched his talent for subtle legal distinctions to its limits. He made a very narrow reading of the constitutional clause empowering Congress to make rules and regulations respecting the territories of the United States. He distinguished "rules and regulations" from more general legislation, proposed that the federal government merely held territories in trust for "the benefit of the people of the several states," and concluded that acts of Congress prohibiting slavery in territories prevented American citizens from bringing their property into these territories, thereby depriving them of property without due process of law. [55]

Few decisions of the Court have stimulated as much heated commentary as the *Dred Scott*. The striking aspect of the commentary was its tendency to regard the decision as a venture by the Court into politics rather than an ordinary opinion. Both friends and critics of the decision called it a "stump speech" and an attempt by the Court to "thrust itself into the political contests," making it "a mere party machine." [56] Opponents of the decision called for a remodeling of the Court, [57] and for civil disobedience; [58] supporters suggested that resistance to the decision was tantamount to treason. [59] Taney was called "subtle, ingenious, sophistical and false," a "tricky lawyer" rather than an "upright judge," and one who "walked with inverted and hesitating steps," his forehead "contracted," his eyes "sunken," and his face with "a sinister expression." [60] A commentator at the time summarized the impact of such characterizations. "The country," he wrote, "will feel the consequences of the decision more deeply and more permanently, in the loss of confidence in the sound judicial integrity and strictly legal character of their tribunals." [61] Among other things, the decision stimulated irreparable conflicts among the Court's members, and Taney became so estranged from Curtis over the early publication of his dissent that Curtis resigned at the close of the 1857 term. To the end of his life Taney resisted criticism of the decision. As he wrote Franklin Pierce in 1857, he had "an abiding confidence that this act of [his] judicial life will stand the test of time and the sober judgment of the country," [62] and he persisted in believing that attempts by the federal government to interfere, even in wartime, with relations between slaves and their owners were unconstitutional. [63]

V

It is easy to criticize the Taney Court for deciding the *Dred Scott* case at all or for deciding it in the manner chosen, and the facts behind the decision suggest that it was one of the least detached exercises of judicial power in American history. To choose to resolve highly controversial questions in a format in which their resolution was hardly necessary for a decision was surely a tactical error, doubtless the effect of the passions the case generated among the Justices. It is too much to say, however, that the case precipitated the Civil War; it merely represented another unacceptable attempt to resolve the essentially unresolvable dilemma of the presence of slavery in America. It was not the Taney Court's failure to solve the problem of slavery that disgraced it, but the manner in which its attempt was made.

Taney's career, at its close, illustrated the inescapably political character of judging in America; yet it also demonstrated the limitations of the judiciary as a political force. Under Taney the Court had been sensitive to economic and political change and had reinterpreted existing constitutional doctrines to make them responsive to new features of nineteenth-century American society. Several of its decisions in the areas of economic development and federal-state relations had been "popular" in the sense of providing judicial interpretations that harmonized with prevailing social attitudes or responded to emergent economic and political interests. The very tentativeness of the Court's course in those areas can be seen as politically skillful. Although the pace of change was acute, its direction seemed uncertain, and Taney's subtle distinctions helped steer a middle course between inertia and frenzy. But in the *Dred Scott* decision, by contrast, Taney chose not to reflect the ambivalences in public sentiment but to attempt a permanent resolution of an issue that had become increasingly unresolvable. By the time it reached the Taney Court, the *Dred Scott* case had become a symbolic manifestation of a conflict in values. A sizable minority of the nation had a heavy social and economic investment in the "peculiar institution," slavery; another sizable minority found it morally offensive. When conflict in social values becomes that pervasive and profound, judicial reasoning cannot assuage it; sublety becomes artificiality, and statesmanship partisan politics.

The judiciary in America has not proved to be suited to the resolution of controversies in such instances. The legitimacy of judicial decisions rests on the public's willingness to accept the expertise and authority of the judicial office, which is itself based on the ability of judges to persuade by a process of reasoning in their opinions. Judicial reasons are in essence articulations of values; they persuade by appealing to shared beliefs whose existence may be only dimly perceived by the public at large. A judicial decision is "right" not by virtue of some transcendent quality of logic or reason, but because the values it affirms and appeals to are perceived as important and worthwhile by the general public. When no set of first principles emerges from the analysis of a case—when in fact the case dramatizes either the absence of such principles or a deep disagreement as to the appropriate values to be affirmed—judicial reasons lose their impartiality. At this point the judiciary can no longer effectively function, for its legitimacy rests on its separation from and transcendence of partisan discourse. If a court may be judged to have entered the political arena and is criticized on that arena's terms, as the Taney Court was after *Dred Scott*, it cannot help but lose stature.

In the end, the infamy that Taney brought upon himself by his opinion in *Dred Scott* stemmed from the fact that he made the alleged inferiority of blacks a principle of law. As the subsequent history of the nation has shown, a good many Americans have not been particularly disturbed by the *practice* of racial discrimination, even if that practice has been at odds with national ideals of fairness and equality. What was disturbing in *Dred Scott* was the *open justification* of discrimination by the legal system— the announcement that in a constitutional sense blacks were not equal, not deserving of fair treatment, and not entitled to the full panoply of inalienable natural rights. If this were so, the principle of the Declaration of Independence that all men were created equal either was a mockery without moral force or had a special set of racially based limitations. Some Americans were prepared to go to war over the question of whether one race could treat another as subhuman, and many would not abide a judicial declaration that such treatment was legitimate. In attempting that declaration, Taney overstepped the limits of judicial power. Under the pressure of events, he departed from his usual practice and sought a ringing affirmation of overriding principles, in the Marshall tradition. But the first principles had vanished; available in their place were only opposing sets of deeply held values. His choice between those sets of values exacerbated tensions in his own time and has left him vulnerable to the moral censure of later generations.

4

Miller, Bradley, Field, and the Reconstructed Constitution

The three constitutional amendments of the Reconstruction era reflected the ideological crisis represented by the Civil War. They addressed themselves to the nub of that crisis, the discrepancy between the natural-rights groundings of American citizenship and the legal status of blacks in America. The Thirteenth Amendment eradicated the slave status of blacks, the Fourteenth clarified their citizenship status, overruling *Dred Scott*, and the Fifteenth conferred upon them the right to vote. These were among the primary purposes of the amendments, but they served also the psychic function of assuaging the guilt created by the explicit assertion in *Dred Scott* that Americans of African descent were considered subhuman.

Other aspects of the amendments had potentially broader impact. In particular, the Fourteenth Amendment, after conferring American citizenship on "all persons born or naturalized in the United States," declared that no state could abridge the privileges and immunities of United States citizens, or deprive any person of life, liberty, or property without due process of law, or deny any person the equal protection of the laws. The generality of this language augured a possible revamping of the system of American federalism. If the privileges and immunities, due process, and equal protection clauses were interpreted broadly, the ambit of state regulatory power over private individuals might be considerably reduced. Although one fair interpretation of these clauses in the Fourteenth Amendment was that they were designed primarily to prevent Southern states from discriminating against freed blacks, there were other possible readings that could expand the meaning of the term "persons," widen the content of the privileges and immunities clause, and give impact to the equal protection and due process clauses outside the area of racial discrimination.

Among the uncertainties raised by the constitutional changes of the Reconstruction period, then, were questions regarding the content of the general clauses of the new Amendments, notably the Fourteenth; the prospective beneficiaries of the Amendments, which might include other minorities and possibly inanimate persons in addition to freed blacks; the effect of these Amendments on other clauses in the Constitution, especially the commerce clause; and, implicitly, the role to be assumed by the federal appellate judiciary in interpreting the reconstructed Constitution. From 1870 to the 1890s these questions were a source of continual interest and difficulty for the Supreme Court.

If the early years of the nineteenth century had been marked by the simultaneous presence of clashing and contradictory modes of thought, those after the Civil War were characterized by pressure to resolve those ambivalences by some ideological synthesis. A search for unifying principles marked numerous areas of American life. Intellectual disciplines attempted to create formalistic methodologies that would yield permanent academic truths; politicians rallied around the concepts of national unity and patriotism; businessmen sought a means to control and predict the course of economic growth.[1]

The very persistence of ambivalences and conflicts in American life after the Civil War seemed to make their reconciliation a matter of greater urgency. The presence of military governments in the South after the war underscored the fact that regional differences persisted, and sectional power blocs remained divisive forces in national politics.[2] A neoclassical model of economics, emphasizing communal harmony and state paternalism, survived in the face of increasing entrepreneurial activity by private corporations that no longer needed state subsidization to remain solvent.[3] Americans remained deeply uncertain about concrete applications of natural-rights benefits to blacks, despite the abstract commitment to that principle embodied by the aftermath of the Civil War. Gradually

the inclination of nineteenth-century Americans to implicitly tolerate internal contradictions in their civilization gave way, once those
contradictions resurfaced in the late nineteenth century, to strident
attempts to discover and affirm unifying national values.[4] In this
context renewed pressure developed for the promulgation of first
principles by the judiciary, suggesting a potential renaissance of
Marshallian judging. But the America in which this pressure surfaced was immeasurably altered from that of Marshall's time.

Against this backdrop, two trends developed between 1870 and
1890 in the Supreme Court's interpretations of the Reconstruction
Amendments. The first was an increasingly broad use of the Fourteenth Amendment as a barrier against state regulation of private
conduct. The second was a gradual shift in the content of that
amendment and consequently in the character of its beneficiaries.
Originally interpreted as a device by which the federal government
could protect the rights of freed blacks against state interference,
the Fourteenth Amendment gradually came to be used by the
Court to bar state regulation of industrial enterprises. Implicit in
this last development were two collateral themes: a disinclination
on the part of the Court to protect the civil rights of blacks as it became more inclined to safeguard the property rights of entrepreneurs, and an increasingly active role for the Court, and the federal
appellate judiciary, as the overseer of state legislation. By 1890 a
majority of the Court stood on the threshold of interpreting the
Fourteenth Amendment's due process clause as a mandate to evaluate the substantive worth of state statutes curtailing property
rights.

The primary representatives of this phase of the American judicial tradition were three Associate Justices of the Supreme Court,
Samuel Miller, Joseph Bradley, and Stephen Field. The dominance
of Associate Justices on the Court was itself significant, since for
the sixty-three years preceding Taney's death in 1864 the Court
had primarily reflected the views and personality of its Chief Justice. With the appointment of Salmon Chase to succeed Taney that
pattern was altered, and Chief Justices were overshadowed by their
associates for the next sixty-six years.[5] Miller, Bradley, and Field
together served under three Chief Justices, of whom none was an
original theorist or inspired stylist. In contrast, each of these three
associates had the ability to reshape a Court in his image, but each
was prevented from so doing by the resistance of the other two and

of Justice John Harlan, who together with Miller, Bradley, and Field made the Court in the 1870s and 1880s a singular collection of strong-minded and contentious men.[6]

I

Samuel Miller was generally admired by his contemporaries, from Chief Justice Taney, who praised his "courtesy, . . . zeal, and powers of mind," [7] to Justice Horace Gray, who believed that had Miller's training been less "unsystematic and deficient" he would have been second only to Marshall in stature.[8] He was not, in turn, invariably generous in his appraisals of others or reserved in communicating negative impressions. Of Chief Justice Chase, Miller said that "his first thought in meeting any man of force was . . . how can I utilize him for my presidential ambitions"; [9] of another, Morrison Waite, he noted that he was "sadly wanting" in both "firmness and courage." [10]

Miller's temperament seems to have consisted of gruffness superimposed on sensitivity. He would occasionally express open distaste for the argument of an advocate before the Court, and he chastised spectators who whispered during his reading of his opinions. Yet observers spoke of "the real kindliness and goodness of [his] heart"; [11] he was the most popular Justice of his day with the Court staff, and was said to be "as ready to talk to a hod-carrier as to a cardinal." [12] He had been driven to abandon the profession of medicine, which he had been preparing for before taking up law, because he was too much affected by the sufferings of the incurably ill; he was opposed to capital punishment and would construe criminal statutes as narrowly as possible.

Miller was not self-effacing. He lobbied hard for his Supreme Court nomination, campaigned through intermediaries for the Chief Justiceship in 1873, and took an active interest in attempting to get men to whom he was favorably disposed appointed to the Court. In 1869 he advised his brother-in-law, William Ballinger, that he was "making a strenuous effort" to have a new judicial circuit created that would include Texas, Arkansas, Louisiana, and Mississippi, for which he hoped to have his friend Judge Henry C. Caldwell appointed.[13] Five years later he wrote Ballinger that he "hope[d] yet to see you in our Court." [14] Then in 1877 a vacancy appeared when Justice David Davis resigned to serve in the Senate. In accordance with overtures to reconcile the South that took place in connection with the disputed Hayes-Tilden election of 1876, the nomination was purportedly assured to a Southerner. Miller immediately entered into a series of machinations to secure the nomination for Ballinger (a Virginian) by working through Grey Bryan, a brother-in-law of Ballinger who was close to President Hayes. From March to October of 1877, Miller wrote Ballinger encouraging letters, rounded up endorsements from politicians, met with Hayes, lobbied in Ballinger's behalf with his fellow Justices, and had a confidential meeting with Hayes's private secretary in which he argued against other potential nominees, including John Harlan, the eventual designate. When Harlan was appointed, Miller responded by attacking Hayes, suggesting that "[i]t is a sickening fact that all appointments to office thus far, which are worth considering can be traced to personal friendship or obligation of the President." [15]

Not a graceful or calm loser, Miller complained after Harlan's nomination that he was losing interest not only in the politics of judicial appointments but in his work at the Court. Such outbursts were characteristic of him in times of disappointment. Upon being thwarted in his efforts to secure the Chief Justiceship in 1873, he had written that President Grant would "not give it to any man except as a personal favor conferred on a friend and associate," since "Fitness for the office has at no time been an element of his choice." [16] He spoke periodically of retiring from the Court, saying in 1877 that no Justice ought to serve after age seventy; yet when he had reached that age he said that he did "not believe a healthy man of seventy years accustomed to any kind of work, mental or physical, ought to quit it suddenly," [17] and remained active until his death at seventy-four in 1890.

In general, Miller was a self-assured, opinionated, dominant man who liked to have his own way and occasionally regarded the Court as his own province. He clashed with other strong personalities and influenced those of his peers with malleable views. "I have had," he wrote in 1879, "strong passions, an excitable temperament, ardent desires and powerful antipathies, and . . . sometimes . . . have not been as forgiving and as lenient to the errors of others as a more perfect character would have been." [18] His lamentations when fatigued or thwarted revealed the extent to which he sought to impose his will on others. "I certainly strove very hard last term," he confessed on one occasion to Ballinger, "to have things go right and to get all the good out of our Chief and my brethren that could be had. But . . . I can't make a silk purse out of a sow's ear. I can't make a great Chief Justice out of a small man. I can't make [Nathan] Clifford and [Noah] Swayne, who are too old, resign. . . . I can't hinder Davis from governing every act of his life by his hope of the Presidency. . . . It is vain to contend with judges who have been at the bar the advocates for forty years of railroad companies, and all the forms of associated capital, when they are called upon to decide cases where such interests are in contest. . . . I will do my duty but will fight no more." [19] Miller was saved from utter despair and vindictiveness, however, by his sense of humor, which could be directed at himself as well as others. On one occasion, commenting on his difficulties with Bradley, he reportedly said that "the trouble with Bradley is that he does not recognize my intellectual preeminence." [20]

Miller's political and social views altered with the changing course of events and ideas in the late nineteenth century. He grew up in Kentucky and developed an abhorrence of slavery there; in 1849, when a Kentucky constitutional convention voted against emancipation of the slaves, Miller resolved to leave the state. In Iowa, where he settled, he joined the Republicans after the Whig party disintegrated in the 1850s, but never considered himself an abolitionist. As a small-town lawyer and a Westerner, he was antagonistic toward expansionist Eastern railroads and suspicious of finance capitalists. He decried the "gambling stockbroker[s] of Wall Street" in a case involving municipal bonds,[21] and wrote in 1878 that he had "met with but few things of a character affecting the public good of the whole country that has shaken my faith in human nature as much as the united, vigorous, and selfish effort of the capitalists—the class of men who . . . live solely by interest and dividends. . . . They engage in no commerce, no trade, no manufactures, no agriculture. They produce nothing." [22] His early Court decisions reflected sympathy for black rights and a certain hostility toward corporate interests; but later in his career he was somewhat more sympathetically inclined toward large-scale private enterprise [23] and less concerned with preserving the rights conferred on black freedmen by the framers of Reconstruction.[24] At the end of his career he expressed a fear of immigrants, and denounced socialists, anarchists, communists, foreign agitators, and all others who threatened the sanctity of private property.[25]

If Miller was for a large part of his career unfamiliar with and hostile toward large corporate interests, Joseph Bradley was eminently acquainted with them; if Miller was a boisterous, effervescent, informal man, Bradley was meticulous, self-contained, analytical, pedantic, and given to occasional eccentricities. His intellectual vantage point was self-education. The son of an upstate New York farmer, he reportedly declared to his father at age eighteen that he "*must* have an education." [26] Then, being unable to travel to New York, he engaged a local tutor in Latin and Greek and entered Rutgers College at twenty. After graduation he worked in a law office and read law for six years, and was admitted to the New Jersey bar in 1839. His educational experiences led him to place a high premium on varied and original research. Bradley particularly enjoyed synthesizing diverse texts and reducing them to manageable size. In this effort he continued to demonstrate the intellectual persistence that characterized his earlier efforts. At fifteen he had spent a year attempting an arithmetical solution to a problem that had puzzled his country-school teachers; when he found, through correspondence with a friend, that the problem was easily solved through algebra, he walked five miles to borrow an algebra textbook, "and hardly ate, drank or slept until [he] knew that book from beginning to end." [27]

Bradley's education gave him great confidence in his ability to extract meaning from original sources, and an attendant disinclination to rely on the spadework of his peers. He had, a contemporary observed, "little or no deference for the mere opinion of others." [28] Justice William Strong once remarked that if there was a rationale no one else had thought of on which a case could be decided, Bradley would be attracted to it.[29] He had a passion for pursuing inquiries, however tangential, to their roots. As a schoolboy he had made copious annotations of his texts; as a Justice he read voluminously and wrote critical essays on such thinkers as Hobbes and Carlyle; he developed a model for Noah's Ark and attempted to pinpoint the date of Jesus's crucifixion; he designed an all-purpose calendar and drafted legislation for a "natural solar year"; and he charted the development of English translations of the Bible.[30]

Bradley's meticulousness was combined with an impatience toward others who were less rigorous. He remarked that "[a] man is most happy when he is most perfect"; [31] he was once so agitated by a horsecar driver's failure to deposit him at the correct church that he could not bring himself to attend church for the next month; [32] he reportedly missed a train one time through his wife's insistence that he put on a new pair of trousers, and reacted by cutting the pants to ribbons with a penknife. [33] For Bradley, truth was attainable, man was perfectible, painstaking and careful labor bore its own rewards, and intellectual rigor and moral virtue were linked. "[O]nly when [the mind] acquires sufficient strength and courage to mount above the floating current of popular thought," he wrote at twenty-four, could it "pursue . . . that straight and luminous path to the pure and immutable sources of intellectual and moral perfection." [34] With so much at stake, sloppiness was unforgivable.

The last passage suggests that in Bradley's thought there was a division between intellectual pursuits and "popular thought" which might give rise to an aloofness from politics. Bradley did as a judge attempt such a course, [35] but was not altogether successful. His appointment to the Court was tainted by the political imbroglio over the *Legal Tender* cases, which twice tested the constitutionality of the Legal Tender Act of 1862, giving the status of legal tender to United States treasury notes. In 1870 the Court, then being temporarily reduced in size to seven members, held the Act unconstitutional, [36] but a year later it reversed itself, [37] with the two new Justices, Bradley and Strong, voting with the new majority. Between the 1870 decision and the reargument a year later, various political maneuvers were made by friends of the decision to prevent the case from being reargued. Justice Miller, who had dissented in the first case, claimed that Chief Justice Chase, who was with the original majority, had "resorted to all the strategems of the lowest political trickery to prevent [the reargument from] being heard." [38] Critics of the 1871 reversal charged that President Grant had packed the Court and that Justice Bradley had declared his views on the case before being appointed. Evidence indicates that Bradley's position was relatively easy to guess, but that no collusion took place prior to his nomination. [39]

Even more controversial was Bradley's role in the disputed Hayes-Tilden election of 1876. Bradley was the last appointment to the fifteen-member Electoral Commission created by Congress to allocate twenty disputed electoral votes between Hayes and Tilden. He replaced David Davis, the original choice by virtue of his lack of party affiliation, when Davis was named to the Senate in early 1877. As he was the odd member in a commission of seven Democrats (including Justice Field) and seven Republicans (among them Justice Miller), Bradley's vote would be decisive. In every major Commission vote, Bradley voted with the Republicans, his party. In the case of disputed electoral votes in Florida, he may have changed his vote under pressure. He was said [40] to have drafted an opinion finding for the Democrats, then supplanted it with one holding for the Republicans after receiving visits later in the same day from two old friends, Commission member Frederick Frelinghuysen and George Robeson. Bradley denied the charge, claiming that he had merely written out decisions on both sides to clarify his thinking; but that disclaimer has been doubted. [41]

In 1882 Bradley wrote that "[s]o far as I am capable of judging my own motives, I did not allow political, that is, party, considerations to have any weight whatever in forming my conclusion. I know that it is difficult for men of the world to believe this, but I know it, and that is enough for me." [42] "If I have the ill-fortune to be unjustly judged," Bradley continued, "I am not the first who has been in that predicament. We must take the world as it is, and having done what we conceived to be our duty, trust the rest to a higher power than that [which] rules the ordinary affairs of man in society." [43] On this blend of self-assurance, fatalism, and spirituality rested Bradley's actions. He was apt to agonize over his decisions, but once having arrived at them he was confident that his intellectual powers, his zeal to get to the root causes of things, his systematic and thorough habits, and his lofty disinterestedness resulted in decisions that would be sanctioned over time. Like Miller, Bradley was impressed with his own abilities, impatient with the foibles of others, and not apt to bend to the will of those about him. Despite these qualities and his humorlessness, he was appreciated by contemporaries. Justice Miller's brother-in-law called him "a thorough ready lawyer, and the most complete business man I have ever seen on the bench." [44]

Business, of course, was an honorable word in the later nineteenth century, and if Bradley was a business man in one respect, Stephen Field was one in another, being first a representative of and later an apologist for the swashbuckling entrepreneurs who emerged with expanding private enterprise. The son of a New England Congregationalist minister, Field shared the inclination of his brothers, Cyrus, an inventor, and David Dudley, a New York City law practitioner, to seek their fortunes outside the church. A graduate of Williams College, a member of the New York bar, and a sixth-year apprentice in his lawyer brother's office, Field set out for California in pursuit of gold at age thirty-three. He settled in Marysville, northeast of San Francisco, where he became a land speculator, a magistrate with expansive powers, and something of a lawyer. Here he made the first of his numerous enemies, William Turner, later a state judge, who once said in a letter to the Marysville newspaper that Field's life, "if analyzed," would be "found to be one series of little-mindedness meanlinesses, of braggadocio pusillanimity, and contemptible vanity." [45] Field later settled his score with Turner by securing election to the California State Legislature and drafting a bill rearranging the state's judicial districts so that Turner's district was relocated in a remote area in northwestern California.

Field's actions in the Turner affair were characteristic: he hated fiercely and long, and was tireless in his efforts to avenge himself on those who had crossed him. When Grover Cleveland, the first Democratic President after the Civil War, was elected in 1884, Field, who had himself been prominent in Democratic circles, asked Cleveland not to appoint certain California enemies of Field to federal offices. When Cleveland subsequently did appoint some of those men, Field vowed never to enter the White House while Cleveland was President. Cleveland returned the compliment by pointedly overlooking Field's candidacy for Chief Justice when Morrison Waite died in 1888.

Field's capacity for controversy and his immersion in the roughest sort of human affairs were encapsulated in the Terry affair, perhaps the most sensational piece of drama in which a Justice of the Supreme Court has ever participated. David Terry, who had served with Field in the California Supreme Court in the 1850s, had married one Sarah Hill. When a law suit involving a contested former marriage of Mrs. Terry came before Field, sitting on the Ninth Circuit, he delivered an opinion finding against Mrs. Terry, in the course of which he gave a detailed history of her less than solid past. Upon hearing this, Mrs. Terry jumped up from her seat in the courtroom and protested that Field had been paid to rule against her. Field ruled her out of order and asked that she be removed from the room. Terry responded by knocking down a mar-

shal and brandishing a knife. He and Mrs. Terry were subsequently sentenced to jail for contempt of court. Both made
threats against Field's life.

In the summer of 1889, just when the Terrys were due to be released from prison, Field was returning to California to sit on the
Ninth Circuit. He was advised not to make the trip and could have
avoided it, since circuit visits could be made at two-year intervals.
He resolved to go, however, with the comment, "I should be
ashamed to look any man in the face if I allowed a ruffian, by
threats against my person, to keep me from holding the regular
courts in my circuit." [46] Protection was arranged for Field in the
person of a bodyguard, David Neagle. In August, Field was returning by train from Los Angeles, where he had held court, to
San Francisco, with Neagle accompanying him. The Terry couple
happened to board the same train. While taking breakfast in the
dining car, Field and Neagle encountered them.

Field had seated himself at a table between the Terrys and the
door. Mrs. Terry, on seeing him, rapidly left the dining car.
Slightly later, Terry rose and headed toward the door, but as he
reached Field's table he suddenly struck Field twice on the side of
the face. Neagle leaped from his seat and cried "Stop, stop!" Believing that Terry was drawing a knife, he shot him twice, killing
him. Mrs. Terry then returned, carrying a satchel with a gun, to
find her husband dead. Neagle was taken into custody and removed
from the train at Stockton.

Mrs. Terry filed a complaint charging Neagle and Field with the
murder of her husband, and Field was actually arrested; but when
the U.S. Attorney General's office put pressure on the local authorities, he was released. Neagle was subsequently exonerated, but
not before his case had reached the Supreme Court on a question
about the issuance of a federal writ of habeas corpus. The Court,
with Field not sitting but rooting in the wings,[47] held that the issuance of the writ in Neagle's behalf was proper.[48] Field never
buried the incident, and when, a year later, a California journalist
who had written a moderately approving account of Terry's life
was nominated by President Harrison to the position of Register of
the U.S. Land Office in San Francisco, Field used his influence to
force withdrawal of the nomination. "When Field hates," a contemporary observed, "he hates for keeps." [49]

The Terry affair revealed much about Field: his stubbornness, his self-righteousness, his vindictiveness, his penchant for arousing hostility in others. These qualities combined with a creative and innovative mind to make Field a formidable and controversial judge. Even Terry had called Field "an intellectual phenomenon," who could "give the most plausible reasons for a wrong decision"; [50] Field's opinions had the self-assurance and righteous fervor of an Old Testament prophet, which numerous contemporaries thought him to resemble. It has been suggested [51] that the increasingly strident and self-righteous tone of Field's opinions in his later years masked deep anxieties. He allegedly came to see dark threats to the private enterprise system in the radical philosophies, such as Communism and Socialism, that were emerging in late-nineteenth-century Europe.

Whatever the reasons, the balance of values Field weighed in his decision-making shifted decisively after 1870 to the side of private property rights. In his earlier opinions, especially those on the California Supreme Court, he had shown an inclination to tolerate legislative interference with private property in order to protect the public health or welfare; later he was to regard such activity as subversive and to generate a theory of judicial review that allowed the judiciary to function as a guardian of established economic interests. Although Field thought of himself as a conservative, noting once to a friend that he "should be glad to go to the Pacific Coast this summer . . . to add my voice to strengthen, if I could, all conservative men," [52] his theory of judging was in some respects a radical departure from the views that had come to prevail in the Taney Court. Field's success in securing acceptance for his view of judging—the view that dominated the Supreme Court by the time of his resignation in 1897—was a tribute to his creativity, his arrogance, and the energy and zeal of his attempts to dispel his anxieties.

II

After 1870 new factors were clearly affecting interpretations of the Constitution. The majoritarian syntheses reached by the Taney Court with respect to the allocation of power between the national government and the states, and with respect to the powers and limitations of state governments as regulators of the economy, needed further revision in the light of developments after *Dred Scott*. For one thing, Taney's theory of concurrent sovereignty had been altered by the fact that the Southern states, at least technically, were under military rule; moreover, three amendments directly affecting the rights of American citizens as against state governments had been added to the Constitution; finally, private enterprise had evolved from its original dependence upon the states for economic support to a position in which it could survive without state subsidization. Circumstances suggested the possibility of a more expansive reading of the two principal clauses of the Constitution limiting state regulation of private enterprise—the contracts clause and the commerce clause. In addition, language in the Reconstruction Amendments, particularly in the Fourteenth, was itself sufficiently broad to suggest a potential set of new constitutional limitations. Attention turned, in legal treatises, to the role of constitutions, federal and state, as negative checks on state activity.[53] These developments, together with the increasing incidence of literature expressing confidence in private enterprise and propounding a theory of minimal governmental participation in economic affairs, foreshadowed a new chapter in American constitutional history and a new stance for the appellate judiciary. Changes, however, were to come slowly and seemingly without pattern or design. Antebellum theories of government persisted well after the Civil War, and few judges saw themselves as agents of change.

By the time of the Civil War, the contracts clause had diminished in importance from its previously exalted status in the Marshall Court. The principal reason for this diminution had been anticipated by Story in his concurrence in the *Dartmouth College* case. If, that is, state legislatures reserved an amendment power in their grants to corporations, the reserved power was considered part of the original contract, and subsequent legislative infringements of the rights of grantees did not violate the contracts clause. With this interpretation in mind, states continually reserved amendment powers in their charters, and obligation of contracts suits grew less frequent. There were still some occasions, however, when obligation of contracts cases came before the Court after the Civil War—notably, the *Legal Tender* cases.[54] Those cases tested the power of Congress to designate greenback notes as legal tender and thus, in certain instances, to reduce the value of pre-existing debts. Among the constitutional arguments against the Legal Tender Acts of 1862 was the belief that they impaired the obligation of contracts. In the second *Legal Tender* case, decided in 1871, Miller and Bradley joined the new majority, Bradley holding in a concurrence that the federal government's power to issue paper money and designate it legal tender followed not only from implications of its specific powers (such as to coin money), but also from its character as a national sovereign. Existing contractual rights were subservient to this power.[55] Field dissented sharply, arguing that payment of pre-existing debts in currency of lower value constituted a repudiation of those debts and hence an impairment of contractual obligations.[56] The Justices continued their split in subsequent cases, Miller and Bradley dissenting from a decision holding that payment in "specie" precluded payment in greenbacks,[57] and Field dissenting from all cases that followed the 1871 decision.[58] In the last of those cases Field, alone in dissent, reasserted the obligation of contracts argument and cited Madison's Federalist for its validity. Greenback legislation, he maintained, "directly operat[ed] upon and necessarily impair[ed] private contracts." [59]

Field, however, was not so wedded to an expansive reading of the contracts clause as to make great use of it as a barrier to legislative activity. He joined a dissent by Miller in a case in which a state that had expressly surrendered its power to tax private businesses was prevented from reviving it,[60] although he stopped short of endorsing Miller's view that the taxing power could never be contracted away. Field was subsequently to assert limitations on the taxing power of legislatures, but not by virtue of the contracts clause. He showed little interest in that clause as a constitutional limitation except in the specific context of legal tender cases. The clause was construed more and more infrequently during the late nineteenth century,[61] and by 1900 had ceased to be a factor in constitutional litigation.

The second potential constitutional protection for private enterprise against state regulation was the commerce clause, and here Taney's theory of concurrent sovereignty came under pressure after the Civil War. Two kinds of questions arose in the commerce clause cases of the late nineteenth century, one set involving the proper subject matter of state regulation, and the other the appropriate scope of state taxation of goods in interstate commerce. Both sets of questions followed from the Taney Court decision in *Cooley*

v. Board of Wardens,[62] where a concurrent power in the states to regulate interstate commerce was conceded, and the Court was empowered to inquire whether the subject matter being regulated was
of a kind that required uniformity of treatment or could admit of
local variations. In state taxation cases, that distinction broke down,
and the inquiry became a matter of whether the state would be permitted to use its sovereign powers to discriminate against nonresidents or to attach conditions to its favors. These issues spawned a
variety of views from Miller, Bradley, and Field.

Miller took a pragmatic approach to both sets of questions. In an
1867 opinion on circuit,[63] affirmed by the Supreme Court three
years later,[64] he held that railroad bridges over navigable waterways could be regulated by Congress; but eleven years later he
upheld the right of the states to construct dams over navigable
tributaries in their boundaries.[65] He sustained Illinois legislation
regulating grain elevator rates against a commerce clause attack,[66]
but nine years later invalidated a similar attempt on the part of Illinois to regulate interstate railroad rates, maintaining that uniformity of rates was essential to regulation of the railroad industry.[67]
In state taxation cases, Miller was concerned with the actual effects
of the tax in question rather than with the subject matter to be
taxed. He was not interested, for example, in distinctions between
taxes on freight and taxes on the receipts from freight; the question
for him was whether a state, by whatever means, was compelling
citizens of other states to pay taxes for the right to have their goods
transported through the state in the ordinary channels of commerce. If so, for Miller the tax was invalid.[68] Miller also reasoned
from the evils that constitutional language was originally designed
to prevent, arguing that a state could tax "imports" from other
states,[69] but not the sale of imports from abroad.[70]

Bradley's commerce clause opinions tended to be more doctrinaire. He attempted to reconcile two potentially opposing principles: the right of states to exercise a concurrent power of regulation
to its fullest extent when Congress had not occupied the field, vis-à-
vis the necessity of preserving uninterrupted traffic through the
states. Bradley was the principal architect of the "public interest"
doctrine announced by Chief Justice Waite in *Munn v. Illinois,* and
his research in English cases and treatises resurrected the theory of
public use (which had been an important common law principle in
states such as Massachusetts before the Civil War), expanding it to

justify state regulation of private enterprise "affected with a public interest." [71] Bradley reaffirmed his view in a dissent in *Wabash v. Illinois*, maintaining that state regulation of railroads was as permissible as regulation of grain elevators. He also resisted efforts to make the federal judiciary a supervisor of state regulatory legislation, arguing in *Chicago, Milwaukee and St. Paul Ry. Co. v. Minnesota* [72] that courts could not inquire into the reasonableness of rates set by a state railroad commission.

The scope of state regulation of interstate commerce was wide, Bradley believed, but regulation should not disturb the free flow of interstate traffic. Thus, if goods had reached their final destination in a state,[73] or if they were being prepared for exportation,[74] they could be taxed; but if they were merely part of the rolling stock of a railroad passing through a state, they were exempted.[75] Nonresidents importing goods into a state could not be taxed if residents conducting business in the state were not; [76] nonresident salesmen could not be taxed on their entrance into a state; [77] and the gross receipts of common carriers passing through states were not taxable.[78] Nor were Congressional franchises granted to railroads subject to local taxation,[79] although, anomalously, wharves used in interstate commerce were.[80] In general, Bradley favored regulation of commerce, but wanted it to be uniform, and preferred federal to state control where possible, but did not use the doctrine of federal plenary power to preclude any state regulation.

Field's opinions on the commerce clause illustrate the markedly ideological character of his judicial stance. He tended to see legal problems as symbolic of ideological conflicts and to analyze them primarily on that level. This tendency was illustrated by his slavish support of the fiction that a state could impose unconstitutional conditions on its grants of corporate charters, since it had the power to grant the charters in the first place. In Field's jurisprudence, contract rights were given great deference. He viewed franchise grants by states to private corporations as though they were arms-length bargaining agreements between private citizens: if a state tax was a condition imposed in return for the privilege of the franchise, it was valid even though it affected interstate commerce. Hence, state taxation cases for Field turned on whether or not the state legislature had exacted the taxing privilege as a price of the franchise grant. If not, he invariably voted to invalidate state taxes on goods in interstate commerce; [81] if so, he sustained them.[82]

Consequently, in this limited area Field tolerated a measure of state regulation of private enterprise, but for reasons that underscored his commitment to the autonomous exercise of private rights.

In the broader area of state regulatory powers Field tended to pay less attention to the commerce clause than did his peers. He deplored the "public interest" doctrine of *Munn v. Illinois* and sought to substitute for it the more limited concept of "public use," which he conceded gave rise to a power of regulation.[83] He believed that the proper inquiry in *Munn* and its companion cases was to what extent owners of franchises had surrendered pre-existing rights as a condition of securing the franchise;[84] that was the same inquiry he made in state taxation cases. In one case subsequently spawned by *Munn*,[85] he secured a concession from Chief Justice Waite that "under pretence of regulating fares and freights, the State cannot . . . do that which in law amounts to a taking of private property for public use without just compensation, or without due process of law."[86] Eventually he succeeded in shifting the area of focus, in cases involving state regulation of private enterprise, from the commerce clause to the due process clause of the Fourteenth Amendment. His approach had the virtue of clarity and ideological consistency in an area where confusion and temporizing appeared to reign.

III

Increasingly, the Fourteenth Amendment came to be the focus of judicial activity and controversy on the Court in the late nineteenth century. This amendment had been enacted in a period when race relations and civil rights were social issues of first priority in America, but by the 1890s those issues had been displaced in importance by issues involving economic theory. The flurry of Congressional activity in the years immediately following the Civil War testified to the dominant role of the legislative branch of government at that time; the Court, in contrast, had been disgraced by the *Dred Scott* decision and the partisanship of the *Legal Tender* cases. By the end of the century Congress was virtually inactive, no further constitutional amendment was to occur for another twenty years, and the Court was at one of its highest points of prominence. There were distinct winners and losers in this saga: corporations and advocates of limited government generally profited, and blacks and other minorities generally suffered from the Court's approach to the Fourteenth Amendment. When Field, having established what was then a longevity record, finally left the Court in 1897, he could look with pride at having been on the side of the winners most of the time, and also at having played a major part in developing a new conception of the function of the appellate judiciary in America. Miller and Bradley, for their part, had performed minor but significant roles in that process.

The Fourteenth Amendment raised a spate of potentially troublesome questions. One set involved its assertion of natural rights against the federal government and the states: thus, was it merely declaratory of existing individual rights, or did it create new ones, and if so, for whom? Another set involved the allocation of governmental power it envisaged. Concededly, one of its purposes was to enhance the authority of the national government as against the states, but how far did that authority extend? Of particular interest here was the amendment's declaration that persons born or naturalized in America were both citizens of the United States and citizens of their respective states, and that state governments could not abridge the privileges and immunities of citizens of the United States. Finally, the amendment raised a set of questions about its enforcement. Was it self-executing, or did its implementation require additional legislation? Did its coverage extend to the infringement by private citizens of the rights of other citizens? And who was the ultimate judge of its reach—Congress and state legislatures, through enforcement statutes, or the judiciary, through scrutiny of allegedly discriminatory legislative action?

The framers of the Reconstruction Amendments apparently intended, among other things, to secure full citizenship rights for freed blacks, thereby ensuring that attempts on the part of Southern states to deprive blacks of citizenship rights would be constitutionally prohibited.[87] Nonetheless, through the ingenious strategems of counsel, the first case asking the Court to determine the scope of the Fourteenth Amendment's protection involved not the civil rights of blacks but the economic rights of butchers in Louisiana.

The *Slaughter-House* cases, one of which came before Bradley on circuit in 1870, tested the right of Louisiana to establish a twenty-five-year monopoly on the abattoir business. Louisiana's action was in the established tradition of state-created economic monopolies. The question, as raised by former Justice Campbell in behalf of competing butchers, was whether that practice was now impermissible under the Fourteenth Amendment. Bradley held that it was, basing his decision not only on that amendment but also on a Civil Rights Act proposed in 1866. Among the privileges and immunities of national citizenship, he maintained, was the right "to adopt and follow [a] lawful industrial pursuit . . . without unreasonable regulation or molestation and without being restricted by . . . unjust, oppressive and odious monopolies." [88] This "sacred right of labor" was "one of the fundamental privileges of an American citizen." [89]

Bradley's decision (which was appealed to the Supreme Court) raised a delicate problem in political statesmanship. A measure of state regulation of private rights seemed essential to the efficient functioning of Reconstruction, since the South was being controlled—on the surface at any rate—by artificially-created legislatures. Yet the Fourteenth Amendment was clearly designed to underscore the inalienable rights of American citizens—or so its privileges and immunities, equal protection, and due process clauses suggested. The choice, then, was between construing those clauses narrowly or establishing the federal judiciary as an omnipresent check on state regulation. Miller, for a majority of the Court, chose the former option. The "one pervading purpose" of the Reconstruction Amendments, he argued, was protecting black freedmen; although others could share in this protection, Miller "doubt[ed] very much whether any action of a State not directed by way of discrimination against the [N]egroes as a class, or on account of their race [would] ever be held to come within the purview" of the equal protection clause. [90] As for the privileges and immunities clause, that pertained only to privileges and immunities *peculiar* to national citizenship, such as the right to travel to the seat of government, the right to move freely from one state to another, [91] and the right to claim diplomatic protection when out of the country. The Fourteenth Amendment, in Miller's view, did not change the relation between the national government and the states, it merely codified an existing relation. The privileges and immunities clause underscored the special rights attendant on national citizenship, rights that had been in evidence before Reconstruction; the equal protection clause was hypothesized as being exclusively designed to raise blacks to an equal footing with other citizens; the due process clause, which Taney had used in *Dred Scott*, pertained only to matters of procedure. "[W]e do not see in [the] amendments," Miller maintained, "any purpose to destroy the main features of the general [federalist] system." [92]

Bradley and Field dissented from this reading. Bradley believed that the purpose of the amendment was to protect rights of national citizenship, which he considered "primary," rather than those of state citizenship, which he described as "secondary and derivative." He also thought that by the Reconstruction Amendments the federal government had been made the basic protector of citizenship rights.[93] Field saw the Fourteenth as giving "practical effect" to "the sacred and inalienable rights of man," and repeated Bradley's argument on circuit that the privileges and immunities clauses conferred on private citizens the right to pursue a lawful calling unrestrained by monopolies.[94]

The *Slaughter-House* cases represented a turning point in the history of judicial construction of the Fourteenth Amendment. From that point the privileges and immunities clause ceased to be an object of judicial interest and the due process clause became the focus of controversy. Through continued glosses on that clause the scope of the amendment's protection was widened to include economic rights as well as civil rights. And in counterpoint the rights of blacks under the Reconstruction Amendments were narrowed, as though racial inequality was to be made the price of expanded protection for free enterprise. Miller, Bradley, and Field each participated in these developments.

Having rejected a substantive reading of the due process clause in the *Slaughter-House* cases, Miller then entertained such a reading in *Bartemeyer v. Iowa*,[95] decided a year later. *Bartemeyer* raised the question whether an Iowa prohibition law deprived a liquor dealer of his property without due process of law. Miller avoided facing the due process argument squarely, but indicated that it should be taken seriously. Field, strangely indifferent to the due process argument in the *Slaughter-House* cases, gave substantive meaning to the Fourteenth Amendment from that point on. He would have invalidated the legislation upheld in *Munn v. Illinois* on due process grounds, denying "the power of any legislature under our government to fix the price which one shall receive for his property of any kind." [96] He dissented in the *Sinking Fund* cases, which upheld a Congressional statute requiring certain railroads to set aside a portion of their profits as insurance against accumulated debts.[97] By 1888 he had succeeded in building a due process requirement of just compensation into state statutes setting rates for railroads.[98]

Field's most important contributions to the development of the Fourteenth Amendment came, however, in his circuit opinions in California. Abandoning his early practice of deferring to legislative supremacy even against due process challenges,[99] Field set out to make his Ninth Circuit the protector of private rights against state interference. From 1874 to 1882, in a series of cases [100] involving California statutes discriminating against Chinese immigrants, Field extended the amendment's equal protection clause to cover aliens, implicitly announcing a very broad judicial power under the amendment to scrutinize the reasonableness of state legislation. At the same time he gave tacit support to attempts to secure for corporations the protection of the due process and equal protection clauses on the ground that they were "persons."

That question had received contradictory answers in the lower courts after Reconstruction, a circuit opinion by Bradley implying that corporations were "citizens" of the United States,[101] an opinion by an Illinois state judge finding them persons within the due process clause to a limited extent,[102] and a circuit opinion by Justice William Woods holding them neither citizens nor persons within the Fourteenth Amendment.[103] Field's Ninth Circuit opinions in the Chinese immigrant cases created the anomaly of extended protection for aliens but no such protection for corporations; in response, arguments for including corporations within the Fourteenth Amendment were renewed. In *San Mateo v. Southern Pacific R.R. Co.*, an 1882 Ninth Circuit case, Field proved receptive to such arguments. If corporations were not persons within the meaning of the amendment, Field maintained, corporate property could be arbitrarily infringed by legislatures. "It would be a most singular result," he argued, "if a constitutional provision intended for the protection of every person . . . should cease to exert such protection the moment the person becomes a member of a corporation." [104] Four years later a unanimous Supreme Court, aided by disingenuous testimony by advocate Roscoe Conkling as to the original purposes of the framers of the Fourteenth Amendment,[105] summarily upheld Field's position,[106] and the due process clause of the amendment became a vehicle for the judicial assertion of economic theories.

As the economic content of the Fourteenth expanded, the original purpose of the Reconstruction Amendments became increasingly neglected. Although Miller was influential in enforcing the voting rights of blacks in some circumstances,[107] he allowed them to be curtailed in others.[108] Congressional statutes penalizing persons who deprived blacks of their constitutional rights were struck down or circumscribed in opinions by Bradley; [109] in his most celebrated opinion, the *Civil Rights* cases,[110] he held that the Fourteenth Amendment prohibited only discriminatory acts by states, not private persons, and that the Civil Rights Act of 1875, which had attempted to outlaw racial segregation in inns, was unconstitutional. The combination of this decision and the *Slaughter-House* cases meant that blacks could not expect the federal government to protect them from discriminatory acts by private individuals. What citizenship rights they had were rights primarily against official state action. Such decisions set the stage for the plethora of discriminatory legislation that emerged in the South after 1880.

Of the three Justices, Field was least sympathetic toward the rights of blacks. He supported Miller and Bradley in a construction of the Force Bill (1870), prescribing criminal penalties for conspiring to deny United States citizens their constitutional rights—a construction that exempted from its coverage the murder of a group of blacks participating in a political rally in Louisiana. He dissented from a case whose object was to insure black voters federal protection against those attempting to prevent them from exercising their rights,[111] and maintained, in dissent, that states could constitutionally exclude blacks from jury service.[112] The occasional sympathy he felt for the plight of racial minorities, as evidenced by some of his decisions in cases involving Chinese aliens, did not extend to blacks.

IV

By 1890, the year of Miller's retirement, the Court had prepared itself, through its interpretations of the Fourteenth Amendment, to re-emerge as a major political force in American life. Its preparation had been seemingly without design, for in its Fourteenth Amendment cases, as in its contracts and commerce clause decisions, it had shown neither uniformity of approach nor marked ideological trends. Tentative steps had been made in one direction and then another: *Munn* and then *Wabash;* the *Slaughter-House* cases and then the *Civil Rights* cases. Miller, Bradley, and even, on occasion, Field had moved in seemingly contradictory ways: alternately tolerant, then suspicious of attempts to regulate private property; at once champions of an expansive jurisdiction for the federal courts and of extensive delegations to the states of control over civil rights issues.

Despite these ambivalences, tendencies were evident. By the 1890s the Court had claimed the power to scrutinize the reasonableness of legislative activity to insure that property had not been seized in violation of due process. It had also transformed what Miller had declared to be the original meaning of the Fourteenth Amendment to a meaning more harmonious with the temper of the late nineteenth century, in which the concerns of private enterprise were taken far more seriously, by most Americans, than the concerns of blacks. It had apparently abandoned its efforts to secure some compromise between antebellum theories of economic regulation and the post-Civil War spirit of laissez faire; a majority of its Justices in the 1890s viewed as presumptively suspect legislative attempts to regulate industrial enterprise.

The Court was ripe for the acceptance of Field's theory of the judicial function, a theory that combined a hostile attitude toward governmental infringements of broadly conceived economic rights, with a conception of the appellate judiciary as an active check on legislative excesses. Judicial power, as Field observed on his retirement from the Court in 1897, was a "negative power, the power of resistance." [113] The Court had come full cycle, reasserting the inalienable rights of man as its governing principles and reviving the role posited by Marshall and Kent for the judiciary—a buffer between the people and their government. But it had returned to first principles only selectively. The distinction between natural-rights principles and constitutional principles, acknowledged by both Marshall and Story, had disappeared. The core values of American civilization, in Field's jurisprudence, were contained in the Constitution. The Reconstruction Amendments, together with the rest of the document, codified the natural rights of man. But the judiciary defined the meaning of those rights. Apparently the Supreme Court could choose to vindicate some "inalienable" rights and ignore others. Ironically, the original thrust of the reconstructed Constitution after the Civil War had been toward vindication of those rights that the late-nineteenth-century Court gradually and imperceptibly chose to ignore.

In his conceptualization of the judicial function, Field referred to the power of the judiciary as power to declare the law. That phrase hearkened back to the oracular theory of judicial decision-making, in which judges merely interpreted the commands of legislatures, the sole "lawmakers." Although that theory had never been repudiated in the course of the nineteenth century, it had been de-emphasized in the works of creative antebellum judges, such as Shaw and Taney, who had tacitly made the judiciary a repository of wisdom on matters of social policy. With Field and those who shared his perspectives, however, came an apparent de-emphasis on policy considerations and a professed return to immutable guiding axioms of the law, axioms that the judge applied merely to the facts before him to reach a sound result. This emphasis underscored the apparently limited nature of judicial decision-making, while de-emphasizing the fact that the governing axioms judges faithfully applied were often synonymous with congenial economic and social theories. Field, of course, did not believe that the right to use one's property free from governmental interference was merely a "theory"; he viewed it as a self-evident truth about mankind. Neither did he suspect that in determining the content of the Reconstruction Amendments the federal judiciary was "making law" in the boldest sense, substituting their views as to the proper beneficiaries of those amendments for the admittedly vague views of the framers.

Or if he did, he kept silent about it. For the theory of judicial performance articulated by Field for the Court in 1897 was a declaration of judicial power of a radical kind. It allowed an institution of government that was largely unaccountable to immediate popular criticism to decide for itself what was the proper relation of government to free enterprise in late-nineteenth-century America, and whether or not the citizenship guaranties conferred on blacks by the Reconstruction Amendments were to be enforced. It allowed the federal judiciary to interpret statesmanship as an exercise in undocumented kinds of social and economic theorizing. And it suggested that this form of statesmanship was important because of the need for safeguards against too-rapid political change. In order to uphold substantively conservative philosophical positions, then, Field was advocating a radical augmentation of judicial power.

The judiciary in America, however, becomes a hostile object of public attention when its power has been perceived as being overly concentrated or aggrandized. One of the elements of the American judicial tradition has been a dialectic of power between the judiciary and its constituencies. The judicial branch has used its apparently limited power to enhance its stature, and yet has been reminded of the fact that it is ultimately responsible for the political effects of its decisions, so that the more it ventures into the realm of political statesmanship, the more it risks having its goals frustrated. A combination of favorable social circumstances, incompetence in other branches of government, and the presence of able, strong-willed men on the Court enabled it to become by the 1890s the chief overseer of American economic development and to maintain that position for another twenty years. But its boldness was eventually to be the source of limits on its supremacy. In 1905 one of its own members announced that a Constitution was not made to embody any particular economic theory, whether paternalism or laissez faire, and that judges should not use their office to read their own social or economic prejudices into the law.

5

Political Ideologies, Professional Norms, and the State Judiciary in the Late Nineteenth Century: Cooley and Doe

I

The review functions of the federal appellate judiciary, as established by Marshall and refined by his successors, together with the potentially vast expansion in the jurisdiction of the federal courts augured by the Reconstruction Amendments, might have inclined one to predict, in the 1870s, that the resolution of significant legal issues by American appellate courts would henceforth take place primarily at the federal level. Such a prediction, however, would have ignored the intimate connection (already illustrated by the careers of Kent and Shaw) between state appellate judging and the regulation of the American economy.

Since state constitutions were patterned on the federal Constitution, with its tripartite division of powers, and since state legislatures were active in the area of economic regulation throughout the nineteenth century, delicate questions involving the allocation of power among governmental branches or the limits of legislative authority over private enterprise were regularly entrusted to the state judiciary before 1900. These cases represented ideological and political disputes of the first magnitude. Since Congress had tacitly allowed the states to take the lead in regulating entrepreneurial activity, the pattern of regulation tolerated by state courts came to serve as a pattern for the nation. The states became testing grounds for extensions of governmental power over the lives of individuals under the rubric of state "police powers"—powers derived from the perceived duty of the states to protect the health, welfare, safety, and morals of their citizens. The police powers doctrine had first been employed by state judges such as Shaw; its first major challenge was also to come in the state courts.

Closely tied to questions of legislative prerogative were separation-of-powers issues. Each time that a state court invalidated or tolerated legislative regulation of private activity it implicitly took a position on the scope of its own authority. If legislative control of a particular activity was impermissible, judicial control, through the evolutionary process of the common law, loomed as a possible alternative. A consequence of judicial invalidation of legislation, then, was the emergency of the judiciary as a protector of private economic or civil rights. Alternatively, judicial toleration of police power regulations suggested either a sympathy with the content of the regulation or a narrow view of the scope of judicial regulatory power. In each of these instances the decisions of state courts had political and ideological implications.

The state judiciary in nineteenth-century American was thus not isolated from matters of national political importance. Yet because of the nature of the decision-making process among state judges of that time and because of rapid and pervasive shifts in the political vocabulary of the nineteenth century, terms used traditionally to describe the ideological character of judicial decisions, such as "liberal" or "conservative," require special definition as applied to the late-nineteenth-century state judiciary. Twentieth-century perspectives on economic regulation, for example, confuse matters. If liberalism and conservatism are distinguished from one another in terms of a respective sympathy and antipathy toward rapid change and government regulation of private enterprise, then governmental policies from the New Deal through the 1960s can be considered liberal. On the other hand, belief in the autonomy of a system of "free enterprise" can be identified with conservatism. In the nineteenth century, however, American attitudes toward the issue of government regulation of private enterprise went through three phases, none of which can be categorized in twentieth-century terms.

In the first phase, which served as the ideological context for most of Kent's decisions, legislative promotion of entrepreneurial ventures, such as bridge and turnpike construction, was considered inimical to established landholding interests, since it prevented them from restricting the future use of their lands. Eminent domain, as conceived by Kent, was a device intended to insure compensation for established landholders, should portions of their property be confiscated by states to promote internal improvements. Under Shaw, however, eminent domain became a weapon for change. The state governments that granted franchises reserved the right to regulate them in the public interest; hence in this phase governmental regulation served to promote change and was resisted by existent elites.

As the effects of state promotion of privately financed internal improvements became clear, a reorientation of political attitudes took place. A turnpike or railroad charter, if interpreted to create an exclusive franchise in the grantee, was an immensely lucrative holding. Having secured a franchise, the builders of internal improvements naturally resisted competition, so that by the 1830s and 1840s economic liberty and equality became slogans of the Jacksonian Democrats. In the political alignments of that period, the Whigs, who favored government promotion and regulation of internal improvement ventures, could be said to have represented a conservative point of view.

The growth of the railroad industry and attendant industrialization after 1850 introduced yet another phase. In contrast to the older model of state-private partnership, railroad networks were built in the Midwest, South, and West with much less state participation. As extant railroad networks expanded, the federal government simply used its eminent domain power to grant swaths of state land for railroad beds. Interstate railroad traffic was within the regulatory ambit of the federal government, but Congress did not choose to exercise its regulatory powers. At the advent of the industrial revolution in America, then, the mode of transportation that helped engender that revolution was essentially free of government regulation.

In the absence of federal action, certain states attempted to reinstitute themselves as the regulators of transportation franchises. They were met by opposition from railroad interests and those industries whose shipping volume was sufficient to merit favorable treatment from the interstate railroads. Apologists for these groups articulated a philosophy of government that envisioned a free market without governmental interference. Although the groups they represented had become established elites with startling suddenness, they nonetheless were the "vested" interests of the post-Civil War years. In contrast, among the supporters of government regulation were farmers and small shippers, groups who were disadvantaged in a free-market situation.

The slogans of Jacksonian Democrats—free trade, economic liberty, equality of opportunity—were adopted by conservative political theorists of the late nineteenth century. The inviolability of private property came to be talked about in terms resembling those employed by Kent, but in a vastly different context. The ease with which Jacksonian concepts were employed to justify the dominant position of post-Civil War industrialists testified to the ambivalent character of the theories of economic equality and liberty advanced in the 1830s. On one hand, those theories constituted radical attacks on special privilege; on the other, they recalled notions of inviolate private property—notions that had originated in the eighteenth century. Updated, they made the principles of egalitarianism and libertarianism—when the reference was to economic issues—attractive to conservatives.

In a limited sense, then, judicial responses to state regulation of private enterprise in the nineteenth century may be seen as an index of political attitudes that were manifested in interpretations of the function of a judge. Kent viewed the judiciary as a buffer between established wealth and the excessively democratic legislature. Shaw tended to defer to legislative prerogatives—thereby circumscribing the role of the judiciary—but generally agreed with the regulatory policies expressed by the Massachusetts legislature during his tenure. Taney likewise applauded legislative attempts to curb corporate privilege and to maintain the prerogatives of slaveholders, and found support for them in the Constitution. Field, after sustaining paternalistic legislation while on the California Supreme Court, became one of the chief theorists of negative judicial activism, in which the judiciary was perceived as an omnipresent watchman against legislative usurpation of private property rights.

Justice Thomas Cooley of the Michigan Supreme Court and Chief Justice Charles Doe of the New Hampshire Supreme Court had as their collective period of service the years 1859–1896, in which nineteenth-century attitudes toward government regulation of private enterprise, notably railroads, were in their third phase. Each had discernible views about the value of government regulation and the proper role of the judiciary in that process. But the attitudes of Cooley and Doe toward the major political issues of their day do not altogether explain the impact of their careers or the source of their reputations. Cooley achieved prominence more as a treatise writer than as a judge, and some of his judicial decisions have been thought to deviate from the thrust of his scholarly writings.[1] Doe resists characterization in orthodox political terms: his reputation has been based primarily on his remarkably innovative approach to the process of judicial decision-making.

The careers of Cooley and Doe illustrate the presence of another set of variables affecting the work of appellate judges, especially at the state level. In addition to their political constituency of citizens who often directly elect them, state judges have a professional constituency: the lawyers who practice before them and the clients of those lawyers. In periods such as the late nineteenth century, when the function of state judges is essentially a common-law function of interpreting the meaning of existing judicial decisions in new factual circumstances, judicial innovation takes on an expanded meaning. It is more than "liberalism" or "conservatism"; it is, in most instances, a departure from established judicial practice. If prior judicial decisions may be thought of as guides of conduct to lawyers and their clients, the clearer and more unchanging the guideline the more certain can professional constituents be that actions they advise or undertake will not run counter to the law. Conversely, the less reliance a court places on its prior decisions, the less predictability it insures its professional constituents.

Opposed to the values of certainty and predictability in common law decision-making is that of flexibility. A prior decision is never an authoritative resolution of all future cases, unless those cases are identical to that previously decided. It is merely an analogy that may prove applicable in the next relatively similar case. It may not prove applicable, however, for any number of reasons, not the least being that considerations of public policy that lent support to the prior decision may not be operative in the next case or may have ceased to be thought important. If a court rigidly applies the prior decision to cover all succeeding similar cases, it may ultimately reach a result that in its particular context is thought unjust. Part of the value of common law decision-making, then, is that prior judicial decisions are regarded as persuasive but not conclusive; they can be distinguished or even overruled. In this manner a system of judge-made law responds to change.

At various times in American history, for reasons having to do with relations between ideology and changing social conditions, different theories of judicial decision-making have been in vogue.[2] Shaw, favoring flexibility, assumed in his adjudication calculus that previous decisions, being manifestations of larger principles, were always subject to modification. During the tenure of Cooley and of Doe the values of certainty and predictability came into fashion, primarily because of a perception of social chaos and widespread, rapid change that gripped late-nineteenth-century Americans, with a resultant need for intellectual theories that would lend stability and purpose to the universe. Law was not the only academic discipline affected by this need: rigid economic, sociological, and biological "laws" were created to afford stability at roughly the same time.[3] One class of persons particularly interested in achieving stability and predictability in their affairs was the large transportation and industrial interests. One way that state courts could respond to this concern was by slavishly following precedents.

An interest in achieving certainty or predictability through judicial decisions is not always the equivalent of conservatism, as a hypothetical example will illustrate. Assume that in the 1820s a state grants franchises to turnpike companies and supervises the rates charged by those companies. An 1830 decision of that state's highest court sustains the legislature's authority to ensure that the rates charged be "reasonable." Fifty years pass, and turnpikes are replaced by railroads as the major mode of transportation in the state. For a time the state legislature exercises no control over railroad rates, and the railroads make several types of price discriminations. In the 1880s protests against railroad rebates and other forms of price discrimination arise, and the state passes a law creating a commission empowered to fix railroad rates. The constitutionality of that law is challenged. In this situation the railroads could expect, in the face of the 1830 turnpike decision, that they would be treated like turnpikes and that the state's power to set rates would be sustained. This would be the predictable result. But the railroads would argue, in challenging the law, that railroads differed from turnpikes because of the economics of the industry, which necessitated price discriminations; or that new considerations of public

policy that had emerged in the fifty-year period necessitated a distinction between turnpikes and railroads; or that the earlier decision
had been an erroneous interpretation of legislative powers under
the state constitution.

In advancing these arguments the railroads would be emphasizing the value of flexibility in the common law to secure a result in
keeping with a conservative perspective. Since railroads had in the
fifty years after 1830 become an entrenched elite in the transportation field in the state, and since they had achieved this position in
the absence of state regulation, judicial support for the new regulatory statute would necessitate a radical change in their operations.
But if they secured a decision distinguishing them from turnpikes,
the railroads would be ensuring freedom for themselves to maintain
their business as they had maintained it for the past fifty years.

To be sure, common law issues can be seen as having a political
or ideological tinge: single plaintiffs sue large companies, landowners sue squatters, and some of those classes of litigants are more
eager to resist sweeping political change than are others. But in the
great range of state common law cases in the late nineteenth century the basic questions largely involved relations between the state
court and its professional constituency. Thus, was the court innovative, or inclined to follow the decisions of its predecessors? was
it interested in promulgating and maintaining a static system of
legal rules, or did it consider responsiveness to change one of the
chief responsibilities of interpreters of the common law? did it associate legal change with the judicial branch of government, or primarily confine innovation to the legislature? The response of leading state judges often turned not so much on their political
affiliations or their preference for one social class or group over
another as on their attitudes toward freedom and restraint in the
use of their office, their respect for the pronouncements of prior
courts, and their temperamental responsiveness to change.

II

Thomas Cooley shared with Joseph Story an appetite for scholarship, a clarity of expression, and an abundance of energy, but
lacked Story's charm, conviviality, attraction to controversy, and
flair. Both men were treatise writers of great influence, judges

whose tenure surpassed twenty years, public officials, successful private practitioners, and the dominant professors at a generative period of a major law school. But where Story made a strong impression, for better or for worse, on his contemporaries, Cooley made a mild one. Story's students at Harvard remembered him as the teller of delightful anecdotes, whereas Cooley's at Michigan recalled that he presented careful, clear lectures in a dry, measured monotone. Had Cooley not been a lawyer, a colleague speculated, he might have been a "great financier": [4] he was sound, meticulous, well-organized, moderate, and parsimonious. His tastes were simple, he never took a vacation, and he was a regular churchgoer. As a young practitioner, he was, like Kent, apparently too retiring in his manner to generate much business; as a trial advocate he was "not promine[n]t . . . and never could have [been]"; [5] he allegedly never sought advancement to any of the offices he held; and his best-known treatise, *Constitutional Limitations*, which first appeared in 1868, was the product of a series of lectures that Cooley wrote only after his colleagues on the University of Michigan Law School faculty had declined to do so.

Cooley was born in upstate New York and had only a minimal formal education, attending grammar school before first reading law at the age of eighteen in a law office in Palmyra. As with Bradley, there are familiar boyhood stories indicating that Cooley was eager for an education and was an intellectual self-starter.

Evidence of these traits appeared also in his later life, when he became an amateur historian and produced a history of Michigan published in 1885. After a year at Palmyra, Cooley traveled westward, apparently heading for Chicago, but settled in Adrian, Michigan, and there continued reading law until 1846, when he was admitted to the Michigan bar. For the next eleven years he was a relatively successful itinerant small town practitioner. In 1847 he formed a partnership with another lawyer in Tecumseh, Michigan; dissolved that and returned to a law office in Adrian in 1848; moved to Toledo, Ohio, to set up his own practice in 1854; and returned to Adrian in 1855. During the same period he dabbled in newspaper writing, farming, and real estate, and was a county circuit court commissioner and a village recorder.

In 1857 the Democrat-controlled Michigan legislature created a state supreme court, and in 1858 Cooley, a loyal Democrat, was named court reporter. At that time the office of reporter, as witnessed by the careers of Henry Wheaton and William Johnson, was one of special influence. Reporters commonly argued cases before the judges whose decisions they published. Cooley argued over forty cases before the Supreme Court of Michigan in the seven years he served as reporter. The reportership not only greatly enhanced Cooley's career as a practitioner; it also made him a logical candidate for the faculty of the state law school, which was established in 1859.

In 1864, "as if by a sort of natural selection," [6] Cooley was elected an Associate Justice of the Michigan Supreme Court on the Republican ticket. Like many other Democrats, he had changed parties during the Civil War (in several Northern states the Democratic party was impotent or discredited for several years after 1860). Cooley was closely acquainted with the Michigan Supreme Court justices (who were all Republicans until 1884), and particularly with James V. Campbell, who had been appointed with him as a charter member of the Michigan law faculty. Although Campbell may have been influential in securing Cooley's nomination in 1864, he was to clash continually with him on the bench until Cooley's resignation in 1885.

Cooley, after twenty years of service on the Supreme Court, was defeated for re-election by Allen B. Morse, a Democrat. Cooley's defeat has been attributed to his alienation of the growing labor movement in Michigan, his sympathy with the railroads and the general resurgence of the Democrats in the 1880s.[7] His retirement from the bench did not blunt his capacity for work, and he quickly found other outlets. Despite his intention to enter private practice, in 1886 he was appointed receiver of the bankrupt Wabash Railroad and in 1887 was named a commissioner of the newly created Interstate Commerce Commission, with which he remained until his retirement in 1891 for reasons of health.

Cooley rivaled Story in his ability to pursue several full-time jobs at once. In 1883, for example, in his sixtieth year, he wrote over 140 judicial opinions, heard 600 cases, gave 100 one-hour lectures in the law school and the political science department at the University of Michigan, published three scholarly articles and two new editions of treatises, was advisory counsel to the city of Ann Arbor (where he resided), managed his properties in Lansing and Bay City, served as President of the Michigan Law School Alumni Association, and planned and supervised an addition to his house.

When his health finally broke in 1891, he attributed it to compulsive labors of this sort.

Early in his career Cooley identified himself as a social theorist of Jacksonian democracy and its antecedents, among them, notably, the free-trade stance. He opposed special privilege and favored open access for all to economic benefits, opposed internal improvement schemes if they tended to favor particularistic interests, believed that local bodies were the most efficient units of government, and supported universal public education.[8] He was an active Democrat as a newspaper editor in Adrian in the 1840s and 1850s, and ran unsuccessfully for the office of Judge of the Toledo Court of Common Pleas. In some circles, however, his reputation has been that of an apologist for private enterprise who provided railroads and other giant "special interests" of the late nineteenth century with a legal rationale for their operations. One commentator has suggested that his treatise *Constitutional Limitations* supplied "laissez-faire capitalism . . . with a legal ideology." [9]

The apparent conflict between Cooley the democrat and Cooley the capitalist is partially illusory. The transition from Jacksonian attacks on economic privilege to post-Civil War support for unregulated capitalism was a relatively painless one, requiring only the superimposition of an older value system on a new set of economic conditions. The Jacksonian reformers favored the abrogation of special relations between privileged elites and governments. They wanted the purported restoration of a mythic society in which true equality of economic opportunity existed and no person could take advantage of inherited or otherwise privileged wealth. Extending this ideology to other areas, they favored universal suffrage and education as well; but the focus of their reform was on centers of economic power, such as the Bank of the United States.[10] By the close of the Civil War the concept of equality of economic opportunity had become useful to new elites that had risen to power through a combination of technological development and government support, but now desired widespread autonomy to pursue their operations and feared that too-close government supervision might prevent the consolidation schemes they envisaged as buffers against economic instability. Equality of economic opportunity, restated as "laissez faire," became a congenial ideology to those groups; they favored a "free market" approach to markets they controlled.

Cooley's treatise *Constitutional Limitations*, from an ideological point of view, was a reaffirmation of his Jacksonian tenets. What made the treatise a national bestseller was the context in which his pronouncements were made. For one thing, his focus was not on the federal government but on the states. The treatise collected and synthesized the numerous ways in which states could potentially be restricted from passing legislation by their own constitutions or by the federal Constitution. As such it focused attention on the major source of regulatory legislation in the nineteenth century and gave state constitutions a new uniformity and life. Again, Cooley chose as his chief source of limitations the due process clauses of state constitutions rather than the obligation of contracts clauses, which had been emasculated by states through the technique of reserving amendment rights in franchise grants. Particularistic legislation benefiting a certain class of persons, and excessively vague general legislation, Cooley argued, were both violations of due process. From this insight late-nineteenth-century judges such as Field were eventually to instill a substantive meaning to the phrase "due process of law."

The use of the due process clause as a bar to excessive restrictions on private property had been anticipated by Taney in *Dred Scott*, and the other "limitations" emphasized by Cooley stemmed from orthodox Jacksonian social assumptions. Particularistic legislation was suspect because it violated the principle of equality of economic opportunity; overly general legislation was "arbitrary and unusual" in its nature and infringed the right of "the whole community . . . to demand the protection of the ancient principles which shield private rights against arbitrary interference." [11] Cooley's contribution was to give these principles a new and potentially widespread applicability. A due process clause or an equivalent "law of the land" clause was included in virtually all state constitutions; its content was impressively vague, and its relevance to state attempts to invade the "liberty" of private enterprises or to legislate against particular economic organization was apparent.

Cooley stopped short, however, of fashioning the limitations of the due process clause into dogmas such as the doctrine of liberty of contract, through which judges, by maintaining the fiction of equal bargaining power in industrial workers and their employers, invalidated much of the welfare legislation passed by states in the late nineteenth and early twentieth centuries. For Cooley constitutional limitations were two-edged: they functioned not only to protect private enterprise from undue legislative supervision but also to prevent it from securing special benefits. This second function was emphasized by Cooley in his 1870 opinion in *People v. Salem*.[12]

The *Salem* case gave Cooley an opportunity to express his views on particularistic state taxation legislation, one of the most common means by which nineteenth-century legislatures had financed internal improvement ventures. A common means of state aid to railroads after the Civil War was the purchase by municipalities of bonds funded through local taxation.[13] A special act of the Michigan Legislature in 1864 authorized certain townships, including Salem, to execute and issue municipal bonds in behalf of the Detroit and Howell Railroad. The constitutionality of the act was challenged on the ground that it represented taxation without a "public purpose." In defiance of numerous other state courts and in disregard of the convention that courts should not substitute their views for those of legislatures on questions of the "public" nature of taxation unless the purpose of a tax statute was plainly and palpably not public,[14] Cooley held that a railroad was not a public entity for the purpose of taxation. In the course of the decision, he referred to an economic "equality of right," "a maxim of state government" that was violated by laws favoring particular classes or occupations.[15]

Cooley's decision in *Salem* made him something of a favorite among Republican Party reform elements, who revived in the 1870s earlier Democratic attacks on concentrated capital and special privilege. A coalition of Liberal Republicans (who had emerged as a splinter party) and Democrats sought to nominate Cooley either for Governor of Michigan or as a candidate for Congress. Neither effort was successful; their only tangible effects were to identify Cooley as a dissident and to prevent his being considered for the United States Supreme Court when vacancies developed during the Grant Administration.

In some respects Cooley's judicial decisions were closer to those of Taney than to those of Field. He construed the obligation of contracts clause strictly and was suspicious of its use to protect corporate privilege.[16] He asserted the supremacy of legislative power against private claims: a municipality, he maintained, could not delegate its powers to some private individuals to seek redress against others.[17] He articulated a narrow theory of judicial review of legislative,[18] executive,[19] or administrative activity;[20] and in a celebrated case involving the Michigan Tax Commission in 1882, he not only upheld the autonomy of the Commission's operations, he also inveighed against judges who "assaulted" statutes because they "did not like the legislation." [21] Finally, despite the harmony of Cooley's interpretation of the role of due process clauses in state constitutions with the delegation to the judiciary of wide powers to review legislation, he apparently never intended this result. [22]

In the face of his rather limited view of the scope of judicial power and his animosity toward corporate privilege, how did Cooley come to be pictured as one of the builders of the late-nineteenth-century judiciary-capitalist complex? The answer is that Cooley was simultaneously an opponent of concentrated wealth and one of the intellectual founders of legal justifications for unregulated capitalism. He and the economic elites of the post-Civil War years had two things in common: first, a faith that equality of economic opportunity could be achieved merely by the absence of governmental participation in the affairs of private enterprise; [23] and second, a belief that certainty and predictability in the law were attainable and desirable.

With respect to the second of these beliefs, Cooley functioned on a different level from that of advocates for large corporations who made ample use of his treatises. He believed that painstaking research and clear-headed analysis could uncover general principles of law, and that such principles were timeless. As a treatise writer his function was to extract such principles and set them forth as guides to conduct; as a judge his function was to apply them, whether they suited his fancy or not. In 1887, in an address to the Georgia Bar Association entitled "The Uncertainty of the Law," Cooley sought to show that certainty could be achieved. [24] His methods were simple. Law was a science, governed by axioms; one discovered the axioms, articulated and synthesized them, then applied them to resolve controversies. Solutions were evident, lines could be drawn, rules could be made. With this technique, over time, one could truly know what the law "was." At the bottom of Cooley's rules and principles, of course, were his own predilections, which had stimulated his search in the various state constitutions for clauses that limited legislative power to support privilege. But that search, for reasons Cooley would have disapproved had he entirely perceived them, made him an unwilling patron of the railroads and trusts whose existence he feared. His career came to illustrate the close connection, in the late nineteenth century, between academic methodologies seeking for immutable intellectual principles, and the political ideologies that supported the continued primacy of elites.

III

If Cooley's approach to judging was ultimately congenial with the ideological perspectives of an influential segment of late-nineteenth-century Americans—albeit not for conventional reasons—Charles Doe's approach cannot be associated with any dominant nineteenth-century political theory or ideology: it was uniquely and idiosyncratically his own. It cannot be characterized in traditional political terms; it invites, rather, an alternative analysis of judicial behavior. It served to isolate Doe from the jurisprudential climate of his day and to make him the most creative state judge of the late nineteenth century.

Doe's approach, in simplest terms, revived the role of judges as dispensers of justice rather than as builders of a system of law. He believed, as had one of his eighteenth-century New Hampshire predecessors, that it was his business "to do justice between the parties . . . by common sense and common honesty as between man and man." [25] Doe assumed this role, however, not in a society that had no jurisprudence at all, as Kent had put it, but in one with a legacy of reported decisions, a congeries of well-established interest groups who looked to the law as a potential repository of security in their affairs, entrenched systems of procedural rules, and a scientific ideal of lawmaking. Among the jurists of his day, with their increasing fondness for formal rules and immutable principles, Doe was an anarchist. He found judicial remedies wherever he found a violation of individual rights, expanded the jurisdiction of his office whenever necessary to do justice, ignored precedents that stood in his way or procedures that tied his hand, and single-handedly reformed the common law of New Hampshire.

Doe's unconventional approach to his office was in keeping with his temperament. He was born into a moderately affluent and influential family, attended Exeter, Andover, Harvard, Dartmouth, and Harvard Law School, married a member of the Portsmouth aristocracy, and became independently wealthy. But he was unpretentious, entirely oblivious of social niceties, eccentric in his habits, and contemptuous of ostentation. "A vulgar notion of display and an affectation of social rank," he once wrote to John Wigmore, "are besetting sins, so universal and so ruinous, that an old man fails in his duty when he neglects a fair opportunity to warn every young person who is worthy of a high place in the world." [26] Doe practiced his teachings so painstakingly as to give the appearance of utter poverty. He dressed his children in cloth smocks and denim overalls, he wore woolen mittens instead of dress gloves, he traveled in circuit wearing a horse blanket and a cloth cap, he never shined his shoes, and he wore the same Prince Albert coat for over twenty years. He shunned social contacts almost altogether, hated publicity and public praise, continually attributed his judicial innovations to others, and held that judges should not be celebrated until after their deaths.

In the courtroom Doe was notably informal and eccentric. While a trial judge, he occasionally sat alongside counsel rather than on the bench, held hearings in his hotel room, fraternized with indicted murderers, dispensed with as many procedural formalities as he could, and refused to wear a robe. He also attempted to prevent lawyers from haranguing witnesses,[27] ignored rules of evidence, selected the jurors himself, examined and cross-examined witnesses, and gave charges to the jury in common idiom.

Doe's informality was symptomatic of his general impatience with legal tradition and ritual unless it had some functional significance. He regarded precedents, for example, as simply evidence of the current state of the law, having no particular persuasive value. He believed that "the maxim which, taken literally, requires courts to follow decided cases" was merely "a figurative expression requiring only a reasonable respect" for prior decisions.[28] The variables that chiefly concerned him in a judicial decision involved the rough justice of the fact situation before the court: whether an injury had been done to the complaining party; whether he had a right to complain; how Doe felt, intuitively, about the equities of the situation. With this emphasis, precedents became merely tools to be used or abandoned at the discretion of the judge; the real "law" lay in the circumstances of the dispute itself.

The methodology employed by Doe in making decisions thus tended to reduce questions of substantive law to questions of factual analysis, based on common sense and perceptions of justice.

Legal doctrines in Doe's hands became generalized articulations of his perceptions; as such they could be revised or abandoned at will. Judging became an *ad hoc* process. No one case was ever precisely like another, no rule could be followed invariably, and the law abounded in artificialities and fictions that could be exposed and discarded at will. Continuity, certainty, predictability, and stability were desirable ends only if they conformed with reason and justice in the individual case; reform and innovation were inherent in the individualized process of judicial decision-making.

Despite Doe's disclaimers, he was the great common-law reformer of his generation. He broke down the custom of criminal lawyers of using their interrogations of witnesses as intimidation devices. He abolished the New Hampshire system of writ pleading—in which the success of a suit often turned on the particular phrasing of the complaint—by allowing complainants to amend their pleadings during a trial.[29] He allowed an error of law to be corrected at trial, rather than requiring a new trial;[30] he allowed suits in law to be converted to suits in equity in the course of a proceeding.[31] He converted the New Hampshire law of evidence from one based on artificial "presumptions" to one whose primary rule was that courts shall hear the "best evidence" available, the question of what evidence was "best" being one of fact.[32] He discarded the M'Naghten rules for criminal insanity, which presumed a defendant to be sane unless he could establish that he did not know the difference between right and wrong, and substituted a test whereby the jury considered all the available evidence with a view of determining, as a matter of fact, whether the crime had been an "offspring or product of mental disease."[33] He pioneered the development in torts of the "reasonableness" test for liability, in which the conduct of the defendant was evaluated against a hypothetical community standard of reason and prudence supplied by the jury, with liability resulting only if his conduct deviated from that standard.[34]

Doe did not confine his innovations to common law issues, although the bulk of his decisions were on common law subjects. He developed a theory of statutory and testamentary interpretation that tied the meaning of a document to the "intent" of its framers, the question of intent being one of fact to be determined by historical research.[35] Using such a test, he ignored the long-established "rule against perpetuities" in a case in which it functioned to defeat the intention of the maker of a will.[36] Complementing Doe's theory of interpretation was his belief that judges could fashion remedies out of necessity. He made available the writs of mandamus, quo warranto, and habeas corpus or injunctive relief—technical obstacles notwithstanding—if a plaintiff could show that he had been injured and was entitled to a remedy. Under his approach, judicial freedom to interpret laws enacted by legislatures was extensive, and judicial power to intervene in behalf of existing civil rights was wide-ranging.

Doe's inclination to regard legal doctrines as justifications for results based on common sense and natural justice, his unabashed interest in judicial "legislation," his disregard for formalities, his skepticism toward abstractions, and his conception of law as continually in flux link him with the legal realists of the twentieth century. Alongside other judges of his time, who solemnly maintained that the judicial branch merely "found" the laws and who seemingly accepted without question a conception of law as a science or a body of rules, Doe appears strikingly modern. Yet his theories of government were not of his own century, but of that which had preceded it. He regarded constitutions as social compacts and believed that individual rights were reserved by the people as conditions of their agreement to be governed.[37] He identified equality not with special treatment for oppressed minorities but with the right of all citizens to receive like economic or social [38] opportunities. He equated liberty with the protection of private property, and held that security in property was a foundation of all civil rights.[39]

Such views—which associate Doe with Marshall—led him to insist that state taxation not be imposed on one set of persons rather than another; [40] that local and state taxes be equally assessed within the appropriate governmental unit; [41] and that the practice of granting bondholders immunity from taxation be declared constitutionally invalid.[42] They also led him to oppose vigorously legislative attempts to control the assets of private corporations [43] or to regulate railroad rates.[44] In Doe's view, legislatures simply had no power to interfere with the use of private property.

Although the affairs of private enterprise were immune from legislative control, entrepreneurs were not absolved of any responsibility to the state. They were required to set "reasonable" rates, and the reasonableness of the rates was a question for the judiciary.

Here Doe revived the older conception of enterprise regulation that had prevailed in such states as Massachusetts in the eighteenth and early nineteenth centuries, where mill owners and turnpike franchises were held accountable to the public to maintain rates at a reasonable level. In making the supervision of railroad rates part of the province of the judiciary, however, Doe was again being innovative. Shaw, a pioneer in developing the regulatory police powers of the states, had suggested that only the legislative branch of government could impose regulations. Doe entrusted this function to the judiciary simply by assuming that private rights had been violated by railroad price discriminations, and that the courts could supply a remedy.

The combination of Doe's radical disrespect for tradition and formality, zealous adherence to eighteenth-century constitutional principles, and broad conception of the powers of his office assured his status as the most unconventional judge of his era. Two jurisprudential principles of Taney's generation—judicial deference to the will of the legislature, and an expanded conception of the powers of states to regulate the private affairs of their citizens—were decisively repudiated by Doe. This repudiation linked him to late-nineteenth-century innovators such as Field, but Doe never shared Field's solicitude for large corporate interests, nor his sanctimonious assertion of immutable legal principles. Nor did Doe espouse the economic egalitarianism of Cooley. For him private enterprise, though secure from legislative control, was ultimately required to behave in an economically reasonable manner.

On balance, all attempts to link Doe with any nineteenth-century political philosophy or ideology only render him *sui generis*. His importance lies more in his relation to the professional norms of his time. His career was a testament to his belief that certainty and predictability in the law were values of very little importance in the face of the dictates of reason and justice, and that judicial precedents—those indices of legal continuity on which nineteenth-century jurisprudes hoped to build a science of law—were nothing but manifestations of a past court's conception of justice, to be followed or abandoned at another court's discretion. In an age in which tradition, stability, and regularity were looked upon as barriers against chaos, and judges were increasingly expected to be mechanical and predictable, Doe maintained and expanded an older conception of homespun justice.

IV

The careers of Cooley and Doe underscore a dimension of the process of American appellate adjudication that has not always been made apparent in portraits of leading judges, particularly those on the Supreme Court. This dimension involves the dual constituencies, professional and political, of an appellate judge. At one level, an appellate decision is a resolution of a controversy between individual litigants with potential meaning for similarly situated persons in the future. Here it can function as a guideline for private conduct, since like cases, in Anglo-American jurisprudence, are presumably treated alike. An appellate decision is at another level, however, a resolution of competing social issues, extending (when constitutional controversies of great magnitude come before the Supreme Court) to an attempted reconciliation of pervasive value conflicts in the nation. At this level a decision has important political and ideological significance, and the positions adopted by individual judges can be considered in that context.

Although the professional and political constituencies of courts overlap, they are also distinguishable. Political conservatism in a judge is not always allied with institutional conservatism, nor is political liberalism necessarily allied with institutional activism. Though in the contexts of their times neither Cooley nor Doe was easily classifiable as a political liberal or political conservative, Cooley was decidedly an institutional conservative, attempting as he did to achieve continuity and predictability in judicial decisions, and Doe was decidedly an institutional activist, emphasizing change. Yet Doe's vision of an ideal America was grounded in a more distant past than Cooley's.

The tradition of appellate judging in America has thus involved more than a delicate and ambivalent relation between the judiciary and a changing political and ideological climate of opinion. It has involved also determinations by individual judges as to how much freedom and restraint they associate with the performance of their office. These determinations are not always capable of being characterized in conventional political terms. Neither Cooley nor Doe fits nicely into a "liberal" or a "conservative" package; their jurisprudence was based more on an institutional than an ideological perspective. That perspective, though perhaps most marked in the state appellate judiciary, has been a longstanding part of the cal-

culus of judging in America. A claimed power in appellate judges
to decide questions of great political import engendered, in the
nineteenth century, a search for fundamental principles of political
theory to which judicial decisions could appeal. Judicial power
begat a sense of its own limitations. Similarly, a strong judicial interest in perpetuating independence for the judiciary engendered a
sense of institutional constraints. Judges, like other visible officials,
were accountable to their constituents and to the other branches of
government. Their being oracles of the law's wisdom did not
change that fact.

6

John Marshall Harlan I:
The Precursor

After his death in 1911 he was virtually ignored by scholars for nearly forty years; in 1947 Justice Frankfurter called him an "eccentric exception" to the distinguished majority of judges, Frankfurter included, who had resisted making the Bill of Rights freedoms available to petitioning citizens against the states through the due process clause of the Fourteenth Amendment.[1] Two years later, however, a law review article predicted his "coming vindication";[2] in 1954 he was hailed by the *New York Times* as the progenitor of *Brown v. Board of Education;*[3] by the 1960s he was one of twelve Supreme Court Justices singled out as deserving of special biographical treatment;[4] and in a 1972 survey he was ranked as one of the twelve "great" Justices in the history of the Court.[5]

Thus has John Marshall Harlan I's reputation climbed from obscurity to prominence. Ironically, the same factors that alienated him from most of his peers and the scholarly public during his lifetime and long after his death have formed the basis of his reincarnation. More an ideologue than a jurist, he held views that were once distinctly out of phase; recently they have come into fashion. None of these slights or exaltations of history would have concerned Harlan, according to contemporaries. He allegedly went to sleep with one hand upon the Constitution and the other on the Bible, and thus secured the untroubled sleep of the just and the righteous.[6]

Harlan's career suggests that not all leading appellate judges can be classified by reference to theories of judicial performance. Two perspectives on federal appellate judging clashed during his tenure on the Supreme Court, one harmonious with antebellum economic and political theories and one responsive to the changes in late-nineteenth-century American life signified by Reconstruction and large-scale industrialization. The constitutional history of the Supreme Court in the latter part of the century exemplified the gradual replacement of the first perspective by the second. The first perspective, illustrated in the majority opinions in the *Slaughter-House* cases [7] and *Munn v. Illinois*,[8] tolerated state economic regulation, attempted to maintain concurrent sovereignty and an equilibrium between the federal and state systems, and read the Reconstruction Amendments as declaring that the existing civil rights of white American citizens now applied to blacks. The second perspective, illustrated by the majority opinions in the *Civil Rights* cases [9] and *Wabash v. Illinois*,[10] was suspicious of state economic regulation, read the Reconstruction Amendments as creating an increased role for the federal judiciary as protectors of private rights against the states, and distinguished between the kinds of rights protected, vindicating economic rights far more than civil rights. Many leading Justices of the late nineteenth century held one perspective or another: Waite, a prime advocate of the first; Field, the chief exponent of the second; Miller and Bradley, imperceptibly and irregularly sliding from the first to the second.

Harlan cannot be described in the same terms. He combined a passionate desire to vindicate the civil rights of blacks with a reverence for private property. He often opposed economic regulation by the states, but generally tolerated it when undertaken by the federal government. He had no affinity for the reform ideologies of the late nineteenth century—populism, syndicalism, and socialism. Yet he joined supporters of those movements in railing against and attempting to regulate the giant industrial enterprises of the period. Harlan's theory of judging was primarily designed to implement his individual convictions. It placed a premium on arriving at desirable results, not on internal consistency. It bound a judge only to his own intuitive sense of what was right. But Harlan's intuition that a paternalistic federal government could serve as a protector of the socially and economically disadvantaged struck fire with social reformers in the early and middle twentieth century. Once a maverick, Harlan has become a visionary prophet.

I

Harlan was deeply influenced throughout his judicial life by his early experiences as a Kentucky politician. His father was a Whig Congressman from Kentucky and a confidant of Henry Clay; and he himself adopted and maintained the Whig belief in a strong national government, never losing his sense of the Union's importance. He was also a Southern slaveowner, and the two affiliations proved increasingly difficult to reconcile. Before the Civil War he attempted to reconcile support for slavery with opposition to secession. During the war he chose nationalism over states' rights, repudiating his original position on slavery. In 1890 he declared that the Union could not exist "without a government of the whole" and that the "general government" was "supreme" with respect to its "objects," which he defined as those purposes for which "America has chosen to be . . . a nation." [11]

In the 1850s the Whig party in Kentucky found itself bankrupt as a result of the death of Clay and the ominous aspects of nationalism at a time when slaveholding seemed compatible only with states' rights. As the Kentucky Whigs disintegrated, Harlan sought other political bases from which he could simultaneously espouse slavery and support the Union: first the American party, whose chief positions were anti-Catholicism and opposition to immigration; then the Conservative Union party of the 1860s, which favored preservation of the Union but opposed emancipation and abolitionism. At various points from the 1850s to the 1870s Harlan spoke out against popular sovereignty, threatened secession if the war were made a mandate for emancipation, charged that the Emancipation Proclamation of 1862 was unconstitutional, opposed any grant of political privileges to blacks, called the proposed Reconstruction Amendments symbols of "a complete revolution in our Republican government," and maintained that blacks were socially inferior to whites and that segregation of the races was right and proper. [12]

Despite these efforts to defend the caste system of his youth,

Harlan increasingly found himself prepared to support the Union even at the price of eradication of slavery. In 1868 he joined the Republican Party and in 1871 ran for Governor of Kentucky on that ticket. In the course of that campaign he publicly repudiated his earlier views. He stated that he had "acquiesced in the irreversible results of the war," expressed regret at his earlier championing of slavery, and claimed that "there is no man on this continent . . . who rejoices more than I do at the extinction of slavery." [13] He supported Reconstruction legislation such as the Ku Klux Klan Act of 1870 and the Civil Rights Act of 1871, and renounced his earlier views on immigration. Defeated, he ran again in 1875, reaffirming his support for Reconstruction and civil rights, and once again lost.

Harlan's conversion on the issue of black rights and his persistent faith in the federal government as a uniform and efficient distributor of economic benefits were to form the intellectual cornerstones of his approach to judging. In his 1871 gubernatorial campaign both beliefs were in evidence. In addition to supporting the civil rights legislation of Reconstruction, Harlan proposed an extension of "the powers of industry and national wealth" through the abolition of interstate railroad monopolies, a graduated income tax to avoid imposing burdens on the poor, and an equalization of school taxes, based on the principle that "the rich owed it to the poor to contribute to the education of the latter." [14] Six years after that campaign, Harlan was a power in Republican Party politics. When he successfully maneuvered to swing the Kentucky delegation to Rutherford Hayes in 1876, he was rewarded with an appointment to the Supreme Court the next year.

Personality traits that strongly influenced Harlan's interpretation of his judicial office had also been exhibited in his political campaigns. He had entered politics early in life, making speeches for the American Party in 1856 when he was twenty-three and rapidly acquiring self-confidence and a sureness of his convictions. After his first public speech he became conscious, he later wrote, "of a capacity to say what I desired to say, and to make myself understood." [15] His ample proportions and striking appearance perhaps contributed to this self-esteem: Harlan's wife remembered that when she first saw him, when he was twenty-one, he walked "as if the whole world belonged to him." [16] A religious fundamentalism augmented his self-righteousness. He believed that nothing that the Bible commanded could "be safely or properly disregarded" and nothing that "it condemn[ed] [could] be justified." [17] The taunts of opponents who reminded him of his conversion on black rights only strengthened his beliefs. He would rather be "right," he said in 1871, "than consistent." [18]

Strength of conviction combined in Harlan with an approach to judicial decision-making that emphasized the achievement of results. His troublesome division between the Union and slavery, once resolved in favor of the Union, produced a messianic commitment to black rights. Harlan almost never failed to uphold the civil rights of black plaintiffs, never invalidated civil rights legislation when it pertained to freed blacks, and regularly dissented from cases that left black petitioners without a remedy against either discrimination by states or attacks by private citizens. To achieve those results Harlan was prepared to read the Thirteenth and Fourteenth Amendments exceptionally broadly [19] or, if required, to ignore procedural irregularities. [20]

In cases involving government regulation of economic affairs, Harlan was equally result-oriented. He believed in broad federal regulatory powers, and complained that Court decisions emasculating or invalidating federal statutes constituted "judicial legislation." [21] On the other hand, he opposed state attempts at rate regulation, was suspicious of the powers of federal executive officers, and believed that federal regulatory powers, though broad in scope, were limited in nature. In espousing these positions he described the judiciary as a guardian of private property, [22] trumpeted the rights of individuals against the government, [23] and made use of orthodox laissez-faire precepts such as the liberty-of-contract doctrine. [24] At the same time that he tolerated state regulation of working hours, maintaining that the judiciary had no right to "enter the domain of legislation and . . . annul statutes that had received the sanction of the people's representatives," [25] he invalidated a federal statute purporting to extend the commerce power to include private labor relations, claiming that it arbitrarily sanctioned an illegal invasion of personal liberty and property rights. [26]

Harlan's result-orientation testified to his sense that the law could be shaped to conform to a judge's personal convictions. He once stated to a group of students at George Washington University (where he taught constitutional law from 1889 until his death) that if Justices did not "like an act of Congress, we don't have much trouble to find grounds to declare it unconstitutional." [27] In his

own case a basis for animosity or preference was often deep-seated,
and he was rarely at a loss to justify it and rarely influenced by the
views of his fellow Justices. Chief Justice White, speaking gingerly
at a ceremony honoring Harlan, stated that Harlan's "methods of
thought . . . led him to the broadest lines of conviction, and as
those lines were by him discerned, . . . differences between himself and others became impossible of reconciliation." [28]

At least two disagreements between Harlan and his brethren
provoked open confrontations. During the reading of his dissent in
the case of *Pollock v. Farmers' Loan & Trust Co.*, which declared the
income tax unconstitutional, Harlan was reported to have
"pounded the desk, [shaken] his finger under the noses of Chief Justice [Fuller] and Mr. Justice Field," and to have "several times . . .
turned his chair" to glare at Field, Fuller, and Justice Gray.[29] Harlan claimed that Field had whispered and shuffled papers during
the reading of Harlan's dissent and had "acted like a mad man"
throughout the Court's consideration of the *Income Tax* cases.[30] At
the end of his career, Harlan became equally distressed at the *Standard Oil* [31] and *American Tobacco* decisions,[32] which gave power to
the judiciary to construe the Sherman Act in the light of a "reasonableness" standard. The decision represented a personal blow to
Harlan, since it modified his holding in the 1903 *Northern Securities*
case,[33] in which a judicial "rule of reason" had specifically been
repudiated. In his dissent in *Standard Oil* Harlan stated that "many
things are intimated and said in the Court's opinion which will not
be regarded otherwise than as sanctioning an invasion by the judiciary of the constitutional domain of Congress—an attempt by interpretation to soften or modify what some regard as a harsh public
policy." He described this tendency toward "judicial construction"
as "most harmful." [34] For Harlan, federal antitrust legislation was
intended to ensure that the weak were not mastered by the
strong—this being for him an essential part of rendering justice. In
such circumstances he was intolerant of "mere metaphysical conceptions or distinctions of casuistry," [35] and ill-disposed toward
those who would employ them to reach unjust results.

II

Harlan's orientation toward results and individualized views on
economic issues have made his opinions on government regulation

difficult to characterize. He has been alternatively called a "liberal nationalist" [36] and a "complete reactionary," [37] a "premature New Dealer" [38] and a "Whig-Progressive," [39] and "both an economic liberal and conservative." [40] Central to an understanding of Harlan's decisions involving government regulation of the economy is a sense of their timing. He came to the Court with well-developed ideas about the role of government in promoting and regulating industrial enterprise, but those ideas originally had no apparent applicability to contemporary circumstances, and later suggested solutions that were not entirely consistent with other aspects of Harlan's thought.

In summary, Harlan began his service on the Court holding economic views that were already outmoded, persisted in those views despite their obsolescence, then saw them take on different implications in the late 1880s and 1890s with the advent of collectivist ideologies. The interaction of Harlan's attitudes with the changing intellectual climate of his years of service made him appear first as an economic reactionary and then as something of a radical, but he disdained either characterization. If he and those favoring nationalization of the American economy were united in their hatred of giant corporate interests, this did not, Harlan felt, make him a socialist; [41] if he was anxious to secure for entrepreneurs an adequate return on their investments, this did not affiliate him with the captains of industry.

In 1877, when he joined the Court, Harlan had revealed himself as an orthodox Whig. He favored a "strong national economy," by which was meant support for the free flow of interstate commerce against particularistic local interests. He supported active government promotion of entrepreneurial ventures and held to a Marshallian interpretation of the commerce clause, which emphasized plenary federal control of commerce in the interest of economic expansion. To these tenets Harlan added a personal sympathy for economically disadvantaged persons, manifested in his 1871 and 1875 economics-reform proposals for Kentucky, which advocated the use of tax policies as a means of alleviating the burdens of the poor. In the 1870's there was virtually no intellectual home for these positions. The states, rather than the federal government, had emerged as the chief promoters and regulators of industrial enterprise. The focus of controversy in questions involving governmental regulation was not whether the states or the nation should do the regulating, but whether governmental institutions had any

right to regulate the use of private property. Pressure for federal
regulation as a means of combating excessive market power, as exemplified in the legislation creating the Interstate Commerce Commission in 1887, had not yet emerged. Poverty had not yet been
"discovered"; [42] the costs of industrialism were not yet so apparent
that policies intended to aid the victims of an industrial society had
very widespread appeal.

In this purview, Harlan's earliest decisions on government regulation—decisions involving the responsibility of defaulting states
and municipalities to their bondholders—indicated an appreciation
of the risks taken by investors, and revealed a rigorous application of
the impairment of contracts clause reminiscent of Marshall. [43] Recognition of the importance of capital investment in transportation
ventures and a belief in the sanctity of contracts were antebellum
Whig doctrines; Harlan persisted longer in use of the impairment
of contracts clause than any other post-Civil War Justice with the
possible exception of Field. [44]

A chief bugaboo of Harlan's, as manifested in the municipal
bond cases, was the restrictive effects of local legislatures on the development of enterprises financed by out-of-state investment. Harlan resorted to a number of devices to try to protect investors. In
addition to invoking the contracts and commerce clauses to invalidate state legislation adversely affecting their interests, he attempted to avoid the Eleventh Amendment's barrier to suits against
a state by citizens of another state, [45] supported efforts to expand
the diversity jurisdiction of the federal courts and to facilitate removal of cases from state courts, [46] and invoked the due process
clause to invalidate state regulation of foreign corporations. [47] These
were essentially negative decisions, linking him with an approach to
judging represented by Field. But they did not imply opposition to
all forms of government regulation; they were merely the obstruc-
tive half of a twofold policy designed to ensure uniform national
flow of capital and commerce. The other half of the policy was positive federal action.

Other factors complicating an assessment of Harlan's attitudes
toward governmental regulation include his distinction between
state efforts to interfere with capitalization and to regulate the use
of other goods and services, and his use of Marshall's distinction, in
commerce-clause cases, between "local" and "national" objects. He
was zealous to protect out-of-state insurance companies [48] and in-

vestors in railroads,[49] but he tolerated state regulation of liquor and oleomargarine.[50] He denied to states the authority to set railroad rates, but allowed them to prohibit railroad traffic on Sunday or control the points of stoppage on railroad lines.[51] He invalidated a federal statute attempting to regularize hours for union employees,[52] but sustained New York and Kansas statutes fixing hours for bakers and state employees against a similar challenge.[53] His result-orientation was doubtless partially responsible for the uneven pattern of these decisions. Religious and moral convictions informed his attitude toward Sunday closing laws, temperance legislation, and questionable business practices, while at the same time his strong desire to provide entrepreneurs a return on their investments made him suspicious of legislation that jeopardized the security of investors.

Harlan's philosophy of government regulation developed an added dimension after 1887, when federal regulatory statutes creating the Interstate Commerce Commission and prohibiting monopolies and conspiracies in restraint of trade provided an outlet for his dormant Whig attitudes. In the regulatory policies of a newly assertive federal government he saw the personification of the older American system, with its emphasis on the even-handed promotion of economic growth nation-wide. "Aggregations of capital," he felt, threatened to impose "another kind of slavery" on the American people.[54] A vigorous federal regulatory commission and rigidly enforced antitrust laws would prevent large enterprises from unfairly controlling the nation's business.

Thus, the antebellum Whig became the late-century paternalist who saw the federal government as an ally of those discriminated against by large-scale industrial enterprises. The powers delegated to the Interstate Commerce Commission to set railroad rates were to be strictly upheld by the courts; Supreme Court decisions emasculating the Commission constituted blatant judicial legislation.[55] The Sherman Anti-Trust law meant what it said: any industrial combination formed for the purpose of restraining trade was illegal. Whether the restraint was "reasonable" was not a question for the courts.[56] Sophistical judicial distinctions between "manufacture" and "commerce" intended to defeat the purpose of the antitrust laws were equally illegitimate.[57] A federal income tax that placed the costs of national economic growth on those who could most easily bear them was compatible with views long held by Harlan.

Invalidation of that tax by the Court seemed to him disastrous.[58]

Even while enthusiastically accepting paternalistic regulatory legislation, Harlan retained his older beliefs in the sanctity of individual rights. He decried "the effort of accumulated capital . . . to escape the burden of just taxation," [59] and maintained that "the greatest injury to the integrity of our social organization comes from the enormous power of corporations"; [60] yet he protested against arbitrary governmental interference with the property rights of citizens.[61] When these two beliefs came into conflict, such as when regulatory statutes infringed economic "liberties," Harlan resolved the tension by following his intuitions. He seemed to think that labor unions did not need special protection; [62] he accepted state regulation of wages and hours [63] more easily than state interference with creditor rights; [64] he did not usually maintain his general suspicion of state attempts to interfere with property rights in the area of taxation.[65] If this approach made Harlan unpredictable and inconsistent, it also prevented him from succumbing to the fear that gripped many American judges when collectivist doctrines began to be discussed in the late nineteenth century,[66] a fear often manifested by attempts to define the emerging problems of industrialization out of existence.

III

In civil rights cases the experience of Harlan's years in Kentucky immeasurably affected his stance. He had come to see the barbarity of a system in which whites treated blacks as chattels, and he could never look at cases involving the civil rights of blacks without invoking that vision. An incident from Harlan's domestic life is revealing of the symbolic meaning of the antebellum South for him. Shortly after his appointment to the Supreme Court, he had discovered in the Marshal's office at the Court an inkstand used by Taney in writing his decisions. On learning that Taney had used the inkstand to write *Dred Scott*, Harlan demonstrated such interest in it that he was given it as a present. After the inkstand had remained with Harlan for a time, he promised to give it to the wife of Senator George Pendleton of Ohio, who had expressed a desire to have it because Taney had been a relative of hers. Mrs. Harlan, believing that her husband would regret giving up the inkstand, secretly retrieved it from his study and hid it. Harlan told Mrs. Pendleton that the inkstand had inexplicably disappeared and subsequently forgot about it.

In 1883, when the *Civil Rights Cases* came before the Court, Harlan resolved to dissent, but was having difficulty writing a dissenting opinion. One Sunday morning, in the midst of his difficulties, Mrs. Harlan again intervened. Knowing that Harlan would not fail to attend services, she declined to accompany him, and while he was at church she retrieved Taney's inkstand, polished it and filled it with ink, placed it in a conspicuous spot in his study, and removed the other inkwells. When Harlan returned she called it to his attention and confessed her part in keeping it in the Harlan household. With the inkstand serving as a catalyst, Harlan began his dissent, the Reconstruction Amendments and the abolition of slavery linked in his mind. Out of those associations came sentences such as "I insist that the national legislature may, without transcending the limits of the Constitution, do for human liberty and the fundamental rights of American citizenship, what it did, with the sanction of this court, for the protection of slavery and the rights of the masters of fugitive slaves." [67]

Harlan's civil rights opinions were his representative performances. They brought together his emotional attachment to the plight of freed blacks, his broad reading of national power to protect citizenship rights under the Reconstruction Amendments, his willingness to shape legal doctrines to justify preferred results, the strength and stubbornness of his moral convictions, and his independence from the views of his colleagues. The cases, which were largely but not exclusively concerned with the rights of black plaintiffs, underscored for Harlan the federal government's responsibility to take affirmative action to protect the rights of disadvantaged minorities. In this area Harlan viewed the government's proper function as that of a benign despot continually intervening on the side of the underprivileged; and he would use whatever juristic tools were available to maintain the primacy of federal powers. The only extent to which he tolerated alleged racial discrimination was in matters of proof; if an affirmative case for discriminatory practices had not been made, Harlan would vote to deny a petitioner relief.[68] He was by all odds the leading judicial civil-libertarian of his time and the only nineteenth-century Justice whose approach to civil rights cases even faintly resembled that taken by the Warren Court.

Most of the civil rights cases considered by the Court in the early years of Harlan's tenure concerned federal legislation entitling blacks to trial by juries selected without racial discrimination, or preventing jurors from being excluded on account of race. Of all the black rights cases, the Court was most sympathetic to petitioners in this area. In 1880 Harlan joined three decisions sustaining federal legislation that gave blacks a right to be tried by juries selected without racial discrimination,[69] provided for indictments against state judges who excluded blacks from juries,[70] and permitted black petitioners to remove their cases to a federal court if a state did not allow nondiscriminatory jury selection.[71] In 1881 he wrote the opinion for the Court in a case in which the state of Delaware had systematically excluded blacks from juries, and a black petitioner had sued to have his conviction by an all-white jury reversed. Harlan read the 1880 jury cases as holding that the equal-protection clause of the Fourteenth Amendment itself prevented blacks from being tried by juries on which black jurors had been forbidden to serve on the basis of race. He maintained, however, that a prima-facie case of racial discrimination had to be made out; it could not merely be inferred from statistical evidence.[72]

For the remainder of his Court tenure, Harlan followed the approach to jury cases he had taken in the 1880s, with the continual support of a majority of the Justices. He invalidated state statutes excluding blacks from juries on the basis of race,[73] but only where real evidence of discrimination had been presented or where the states had not seriously entertained claims of proof.[74] In other instances, in which a prima-facie case of discrimination had not been made out, or where a state trial court had ruled the evidence insufficient,[75] Harlan denied relief. He also gave a relatively narrow scope to the right of removal from state courts in jury discrimination cases.[76] His jury decisions were unusual in that his position harmonized with that of most of his fellow Justices and in that they evidenced a relatively cautious attitude toward civil rights claims.

In Fifteenth Amendment cases Harlan's views gradually deviated from that of the Court. In 1884, in the case of *Ex parte Yarborough*,[77] the Court upheld federal legislation preventing private citizens from conspiring to deprive blacks of their right to vote in a federal election; Harlan joined the majority. Nineteen years later, however, at a high point in the Court's tolerance of racial discrimination, *Yarborough* was ignored by the majority in *James v. Bowman*.[78] That case involved the constitutionality of a federal statute preventing private citizens from interfering with Fifteenth Amendment rights through bribery or intimidation. Two citizens of Kentucky were convicted under the statute for harassing a black voter in Kentucky. The Court struck down as overbroad the statute's application to them, since the statute did not limit its reach to federal elections and since the Fifteenth Amendment did not prohibit private citizens, as opposed to states, from interfering with voting rights. Harlan, in dissent, rejected that reading of the Amendment.

In *Giles v. Harris*,[79] another 1903 case, the Court showed its then current tendency to avoid disturbing state schemes aimed at disenfranchising blacks. Alabama had established certain voting requirements that tended to prevent blacks from registering; a black petitioned for equitable relief in federal court, claiming that he and other blacks had been illegally prevented from registering. The Court denied relief, claiming that if Alabama's registration provisions were unconstitutional, the Court could not tolerate their presence by adding blacks to the registration rolls, and that since the Court could not enforce an equitable decree, it should not impose its views on state legislatures. Harlan, dissenting, maintained that the petitioner had made out a case for equitable relief and that the federal courts had the power to grant it.[80]

Harlan's reading of the Thirteenth Amendment also diverged from that of his peers. He believed, as he stated in the *Civil Rights Cases*, that the Amendment prevented not only "incidents" of slavery, such as compulsory labor or disqualification from holding property or making contracts, but also "badges" of slavery, such as exclusion of blacks from public accommodations. Harlan was willing to find evidence of "slavery" in acts of private creditors forcing black debtors to return to a state [81] or preventing blacks from working in a lumber mill,[82] in a state statute that made refusal to work prima-facie evidence of an intent to defraud an employer,[83] and in state statutes compelling seamen on private vessels to honor their contracts.[84] In this last case, Harlan maintained that "the condition of one who contracts to render personal services in connection with the private business of another becomes a condition of involuntary servitude *from the moment he is compelled against his will* to continue in

such service." [85] A prior practice in America of permitting the forcible return of seamen to their vessels was for Harlan unjustifiable
after the passage of the Thirteenth Amendment. In only one of
these cases was Harlan's position eventually upheld by the Court.[86]

It was in cases involving the Fourteenth Amendment, however,
that Harlan demonstrated his farthest isolation from the Court. He
had begun this estrangement in the *Civil Rights* cases, where he had
maintained that public accommodations and transportation franchises were instrumentalities of the states for purposes of the "state
action" clause of the amendment, and that the amendment's enforcement clause, taken together with its broad grant of citizenship
rights, meant that Congress could determine what legislation was
necessary to protect rights that were "fundamental in citizenship in
a free republican government." [87] This meant that, despite the apparent restriction of the Fourteenth's reach to discriminations by
states, the federal government still had broad potential powers to
prevent private discriminatory acts. From these positions stemmed
Harlan's dissents in subsequent Fourteenth Amendment cases.

In the area of transportation Harlan steadfastly maintained that
state-enforced segregation of blacks from whites was impermissible.
The first major transportation case in his tenure was *Louisville, New
Orleans, and Texas Ry. v. Mississippi*,[88] in which the Fuller Court
showed its inclination to uphold Southern states in their efforts to
prevent racial intermingling. In 1877 the Court, in a case in which
Harlan did not participate, had invalidated a Louisiana law forbidding racial discrimination on interstate steamboats passing through
the state, on the ground that such law constituted an undue usurpation of federal commerce powers.[89] The *Louisville* case presented an
analogous situation, since it tested the constitutionality of a Mississippi statute requiring racial segregation during the Mississippi portion of interstate railroad trips. The Court distinguished the earlier
case, claiming that compelling white passengers to share their
steamboat cabins with blacks was a far greater burden on interstate
commerce than compelling whites and blacks to have separate accommodations in Pullman cars. Harlan's dissent denounced the
spuriousness of this reasoning and held the statute an interference
with interstate commerce. Though technically he did not reach the
equal protection issue, he intimated that the statute violated the
Fourteenth Amendment as well.[90]

Louisville set the stage for *Plessy v. Ferguson*,[91] the notorious 1896 decision sustaining the constitutionality of a Louisiana statute requiring racially segregated railway cars against a Fourteenth Amendment challenge. For Americans of today the most striking aspect of Harlan's dissent in *Plessy v. Ferguson* has been the attitudes of racial toleration and the fears of racial antagonism that it expressed, as well as its conviction that "the destinies of the two races, in this country, are indissolubly linked." [92] But in a historical context those aspects of the opinion were overshadowed by Harlan's overriding assumption that the Fourteenth Amendment had radically equalized the status of all Americans. Inequality of citizenship rights, after the Reconstruction Amendments, was simply impermissible for Harlan. He admitted no distinctions between state and private action, between slavery and its vestiges, between reasonable and unreasonable governmental discrimination. He read the Reconstruction Amendments as creating a domain of protection for American citizens against inequitable treatment before the law and as making the federal government the supervisor of that domain. In his support for the civil rights conferred by the Amendments, his older beliefs in individual liberties against the government merged with his more recent sympathy for freed blacks, creating an phalanx of ideological and moral conviction.

Harlan went to extraordinary lengths to find support for his positions in the traditional authoritative sources of a judge. He read the Thirteenth Amendment as forbidding private actions that fostered incidents or badges of slavery despite strong evidence in the legislative history that its scope was confined to state activities. [93] He extended the scope of that amendment to reach areas, such as public accommodations, that it was very likely not intended to cover. [94] He interpreted the Fourteenth Amendment to apply to non-naturalized Indians who chose not to live on Indian reservations. [95] He believed that federal civil-rights legislation could be made to apply not only to protect citizens against attempted infringement of their rights by private persons, but to protect aliens as well. [96] Neither of these last two positions had the support of the Waite or Fuller Courts.

Most remarkable of all, in the context of his times, was Harlan's belief that the Fourteenth Amendment had assured that "not one of the fundamental rights of life, liberty or property, recognized by the Constitution of the United States, can be denied or abridged by a State in respect to any person within its jurisdiction." [97] Harlan meant by that statement that each of the first eight amendments to the Bill of Rights was incorporated in the Fourteenth Amendment's due process and equal protection clauses, and thus each applied against the states. He appears, in fact, to have meant even more than that, for he stated that fundamental U.S. citizenship rights were "principally" enumerated in the Bill of Rights, implying that others might be found and likewise applied as limitations on state conduct. In six cases between 1884 and 1908 involving the application of various Bill of Rights provisions to the states, Harlan affirmed this position.[98] No other member of the Court accepted it. Today, despite the long efforts of Justices Black and Douglas, "selective incorporation" of Bill of Rights provisions in the Fourteenth Amendment remains the majority doctrine. Yet for Harlan total incorporation was obvious: the Reconstruction Amendments had redefined the meaning of American citizenship and in the process had altered fundamentally the relation of the federal government to the states. United States citizens, after 1870, were wards of the nation.

IV

The dramatic turnabout in attitudes toward racial equality in the 1950s and 1960s seems to have been the chief catalyst in augmenting Harlan's reputation. The spectacle of a Southerner laying bare the prejudices and sophistries of his peers, appealing in his rhetoric to the same humanitarian feelings that lay at the base of the twentieth-century civil rights movement, demonstrating in his own person the zealousness that can be produced by a combination of insight and guilt, was an overwhelmingly attractive image to twentieth-century integrationists. Harlan's more general interest in the responsibilities of the federal government toward its citizens also contributed to his enhanced stature in a century in which national social-welfare legislation came into existence. But although he was the only late-nineteenth-century Justice to find paternalism at all congenial, he was a precursor of, rather than a spokesman for, judicial attitudes that later came into vogue. He had no integrated theory of judging, only his own convictions; he read the imperatives of his office only as a mandate to dispense his individualized kind of justice. Ultimately, his jurisprudence resists categorization, except as result-orientation, and his reputation becomes peculiarly vulnerable to changes in social attitudes. One generation's eccentric has become another's visionary, but his stature remains indeterminate. His currently high stature may be more transitory than it now appears.

Harlan's preoccupation with reaching results that satisfied his intuition and convictions raises a theme of great importance to the remaining judges in this study. In an age whose jurisprudence defined the judge as an oracle, result-orientation ostensibly never existed. Judging was an exercise in declaring the will of the law, not the will of the judge. But as Harlan's interpretative clashes with his colleagues revealed, the "law" was capable of being "declared" in a variety of ways for a variety of purposes.

The mystical, immutable principles of the law were the nineteenth-century judge's barrier against result-orientation. "The courts," Harlan's colleague David Brewer said in 1893, "hold neither purse nor sword; they cannot corrupt nor arbitrarily control. They make no laws. They establish no policy, they never enter into the domain of public action. They do not govern. Their functions . . . are limited to seeing that popular action does not trespass upon right and justice as it exists in written constitutions and natural law." [99] Not long after Brewer's statement the jurisprudential theory on which it rested was subjected to severe attack. The course of the American judicial tradition in the twentieth century was dramatically affected by that attack. A fear of unchecked result-orientation in the judiciary, covert for the most part throughout the nineteenth century, became starkly overt. The consequences of that development for twentieth-century judges require lengthy attention. First, however, a brief recapitulation of the tradition's course in the nineteenth century.

7

The Tradition at the Close of the Nineteenth Century

With the end of Harlan's tenure, American appellate judging entered the twentieth century. Harlan's performance exemplified this development in a symbolic as well as a literal sense. While memories that influenced his decision-making resurrected experiences of an older America, his special concerns foreshadowed major areas of twentieth-century judicial activity. He therefore affords a stopping place for some general observations on the path of American appellate judging from the opening to the closing of the nineteenth century.

The elements of judging central to Marshall's conception of his office—independence and accountability; detachment from, yet involvement with politics; a sense that judicial power was a constraining as well as a liberating force—survived intact throughout the nineteenth century. The times when the Supreme Court seriously lowered its own stature through imprudent or misguided decisions, as in *Dred Scott* or the conflicting *Legal Tender* cases, served to strengthen Marshall's legacy. *Dred Scott* and the *Legal Tender* cases were instances in which judges had been too openly responsive to political pressures or too ambitious in the use of their power. The lesson of those "self-inflicted wounds" [1] was that judicial independence could be achieved only through the appearance of genuine detachment and restraint. Those qualities were somehow associated with appeals in opinions to "first principles," the consensual norms and values of American civilization. To avoid such an appeal, as in the *Legal Tender* cases, or to make it imperfectly, as in *Dred Scott*, was to summon up the specter of judicial tyranny and to threaten the concept of an independent judiciary. None of the leading judges of the nineteenth century was as successful as Marshall in making this appeal, either because their sense of first principles differed from that of a majority of their contemporaries, because they were unable to perceive or articulate the consensual norms of their times, or because no clear consensus of values existed. But the challenge of Marshall's legacy remained intact throughout the century.

The legacy passed down by Marshall helped write additional themes emerging out of the experience of nineteenth-century appellate judging. One involved the complex relations between ideological beliefs and interpretations of the office of judge. A strong set of ideological convictions influenced the way that certain judges, notably Field and Harlan, interpreted their roles, but in other judges, such as Shaw, Cooley, or Doe, ideological positions were derivative of attitudes toward judicial performance. In still others, such as Marshall, Kent, and Story, political persuasions seemed to stimulate attitudes toward judging, and such attitudes, once independently developed, reinforced the judge's original political instincts. In addition, as the social context of judicial decisions altered during the course of the century, so did the implications of a particular theory of judging. Field resembled Story in his belief that judicial power could be used to safeguard property rights, but the character of the property rights he protected had changed and the climate of ideas in which he functioned had changed as well. Hence, to associate "activism" or "self-restraint" in nineteenth-century judges with "liberal" or "conservative" political views invites oversimplification unless the terms are used in context.

A second theme emerging in the nineteenth century involved the professional constituency of appellate judges and the related values of certainty, predictability, innovation, and flexibility. For certain judges, such as Shaw, Bradley, Cooley, and Doe, a trade-off between certainty and innovativeness seemed more central to their decision-making process than any other variable. For others, such as Harlan, this variable seemed inconsequential. In some instances, professionalist values can aid attempts to characterize the performance of a judge. A seemingly bizarre pattern of performance may clarify itself, as in the case of Doe, if professionalist values are substituted for political ones. But an understanding that judges often respond to the expectations of those most immediately affected by their decisions can be stretched out of proportion. Not all judges are instrumentalists, and the law is more than a series of responses to the demands of professional elites.[2] The theme appeared most dramatically in the nineteenth century at the state court level, where issues of vast political significance appeared with less frequency; it was perhaps less decisive in the calculus of most Supreme Court Justices. But it serves to highlight the variegated pressures on the office of judge in nineteenth-century America.

Another element of the tradition of American judging, the delicate relation between the judiciary and politics, engendered a third theme of the nineteenth-century experience. The tacit assumption that judges could remain aloof from the political arena at one level and yet participate in it at another created an ambiguity in American jurisprudence. From Marshall to Field, judges conceived of themselves as oracles whose function was simply that of rendering intelligible an already existing body of legal principles. Even the innovative judges of the mid-nineteenth century, such as Taney and Shaw, who modified legal doctrines to respond to altered economic and social conditions, believed that they were not making law but merely discovering its continual applicability to changing events. Yet critics of the American judiciary, from Marshall's tenure on, preceived the ability of judicial decisions to influence the course of politics. They learned early to read opinions at two levels: one, the immediate practical result reached and its professional and political consequences; another, the reasoning justifying that result, this reasoning serving as a rationale for the use of power by an undemocratic branch of government.

Since the reasoning process in its opinions constituted the undemocratic judiciary's essential means of justifying its power in a democratic society, that process needed to emphasize constraints on the behavior of judges, so as to deflect fears of judicial tyranny. A conception of judges as passive oracles making already existing truths intelligible aided in that deflection, but because of the political ramifications of judicial decisions, it did not at any time in the century forestall scrutiny of judicial reasoning. On scrutiny, judicial opinions periodically revealed themselves as something other than mere declarations of the state of the law. They expressed political and social points of view; they advanced theories of governmental and societal relations. At times they seemed so transparently opinionated as to threaten the oracular theory of judging itself. Hence a tension developed between the conception of judges as law-finders rather than lawmakers and the discernible impact of judicial decisions on political affairs. This tension ultimately resolved itself in a two-stage process in the early twentieth century: first, the articulation of a rigid version of the oracular theory, a version that denied any lawmaking function to judges at all; second, the exposure and eventual discrediting of the oracular theory itself. With the open concession that judges made law in some limited sense, the American judicial tradition began its twentieth-century phase.

8

Holmes, Brandeis, and the Origins of Judicial Liberalism

A sharp distinction between "nineteenth-century" and "twentieth-century" phases of the American judicial tradition has some artificial features. Older jurisprudential attitudes and theories of judging persisted after 1900; their persistence, in fact, is one of the features of American judicial history in the twentieth century. The striking twentieth-century changes in the intellectual climate in which judicial decisions were made, discussed in this chapter and subsequent ones, should not create an inference that the nineteenth century, by contrast, was static in its jurisprudence; the difference is one of degree. Finally, the prominence given in this and succeeding chapters to modern liberalism as a force helping to redefine judicial attitudes cannot, in the face of previous chapters, be read as suggesting that an ideological dimension to judging in America is peculiar to the twentieth century.

Nonetheless, a major reorientation of the American judicial tradition did occur sometime shortly after 1900. The oracular theory of judging ceased to be regarded as a universal principle, eventually became a minority viewpoint, and subsequently lost academic respectability altogether. Although none of the basic challenges of appellate judging in America disappeared, the intellectual context in which they were faced was altered. That process of alteration was part of a more general re-examination of attitudes and values in

America, out of which emerged the ideology of modern liberalism. The standard referents for political thought during most of the twentieth century have been the terms "conservatism" and "liberalism." So ubiquitous has been their usage that they have ceased to function as sharp characterizations and have become symbolic instruments of rhetoric. The incorporation of the term "liberalism" into our contemporary vocabulary in this fashion has some historical significance, since the term had, at its modern origins, a precise and revolutionary meaning. It had suggested then a radically new ideological perspective, based on a rejection of longstanding assumptions about the way in which society ought to be organized and on the creation of a novel relation between the individual citizen and his government. "Liberalism" has lost its original meaning largely because its premises have become so widely and loosely accepted. Before the 1920s the term, in its modern sense, was barely known; by the 1950s it was academically respectable to argue that liberalism had been the dominant ideology in the history of American civilization.[1]

The origins of modern liberalism in America coincided with the Supreme Court tenures of Justices Oliver Wendell Holmes and Louis Brandeis. The coincidence was accidental but of great import. The social thought of Holmes and Brandeis was not decisively affected by the emergence of twentieth-century liberalism, nor were their interpretations of their office markedly influenced by any desire to act as models of modern liberal judges. But the advent of liberalism provided critics of the judiciary with a new perspective from which to evaluate judicial performance. This perspective revealed innovative and contemporary elements in the jurisprudence of Holmes and of Brandeis and led to their apotheosis as heroic liberal judges.

I

Modern liberalism began in America with an insight, which dawned around the outbreak of World War I and revived in the 1920s, that the cultural unity of American civilization was disintegrating. There were numerous diverse manifestations of this perception, ranging from nervous reaffirmations of the purity of Anglo-Saxon America to attacks upon traditional symbols of virtue and respectability.[2] Linking these myriad forms of protest was a feeling that the core values of American culture had become meaningless slogans, capable of countless self-serving interpretations and hence no longer capable of functioning as a code of honorable behavior. As though for the first time, skeptics of the period saw that every unifying value engendered its own countervalue: morality begat hypocrisy; progress, exploitation; religiosity, bigotry; refinement, snobbishness; democracy, philistinism. As older consensual values became tarnished, former success models became figures of irony and pathos. The captain of industry, the self-made man, and the supersalesman were each regarded as having had a part in creating the stock market crash of 1929 and the ensuing depression.

Another perception followed from the original consciousness of value disintegration. Mature industrialism had created inequities and left a residue of victims. While rewarding a large segment of the nation's citizens, it had ignored or hurt other segments. It had not, for instance, eradicated poverty, or measurably improved the welfare of industrial laborers, or helped the increased percentage of elderly persons, or improved the quality of rural life. For these groups, progress had not necessarily been beneficial; for them industrialization had not brought success.

Over time, the sense of a wholesale loss of consensual American values merged with the perception of the costs of industrial progress to produce an affirmative ideology that supplanted the scattered "reform" movements of the late nineteenth and early twentieth centuries. The chief catalyst in the appearance of modern liberalism as a positive social philosophy in America was the crisis produced by the Depression of the 1930s. That crisis gave an immediacy to reform proposals that had been articulated in the 1920s by persons such as the advocates of a welfare state in Great Britain.[3] The principal innovation of modern liberalism was its utilization of the state as an agent to fill the void left by consensual value disintegration. The state, in this role, became a permanent force for social planning, order, and enlightened progress, substituting its administrative procedures for the discredited set of traditional values. It articulated common national goals by fiat and conceived and executed social policies consistent with those goals. The goals were not elaborately linked to consensual values; they were more often the tentative formulations of those who managed the state. The pursuit of social goals represented a form of coerced coherence necessitated by crisis and the dissolution of a previous value consensus.

Liberalism, at the time of its origin, represented a modification of some of the tenets of preceding reform movements in the light of a twentieth-century crisis in values. It retained a belief in an active, positive government; it also supported expansion of the class of government wards and beneficiaries. But it modified many of the substantive assumptions of advocates of one or another form of paternalism, embodying them, if at all, in standards of fair procedure. A comparison of liberalism with populism and the early-twentieth-century reform movement of progressivism illustrates the modifications. The populists and progressives both supported legislation intended to benefit industrial laborers; so did the liberals of the New Deal. The rhetorical emphasis of the first two groups was on removing the conditions—such as excessive size in industrial corporations and exploitation of workers by employers—that prevented workers from achieving freedom and independence in their jobs. The rhetorical emphasis of liberalism was on securing for industrial workers a forum, through unionization and collective bargaining, in which their interests could be fairly and equally represented. For populists or progressives, reform often had a moral content, evidenced in idealized roles for its beneficiaries, such as that of free and independent yeomen for industrial workers. Liberal reformers were not so much concerned with the life-style or moral character of those whose causes they supported as with insuring them a fair opportunity to air their grievances and promote their own self-interests.[4]

Although the idea of professionals in government was first articulated in the twentieth century by progressives, liberals gave it a new interpretation. The progressives, borrowing notions advanced by late-nineteenth-century elite reformers, argued that the presence in government of persons of high social and economic status would stimulate a revival of moral values because such persons would be above corruption and beyond the influence of special interests.[5] Liberals, though retaining a belief that government should be managed by elites, equated elite status more with technical and administrative expertise than with wealth or social position. This modification was in keeping with the assumption of modern liberals that professionalism's essential impact was to be felt in efficient and fair governmental procedures.

At its inception liberalism was an ideology based less on a commitment to shared values than on a response to their perceived disintegration. But as it evolved, its constant attention to the plight of casualties of progress became itself a value, often articulated as humanitarianism. As the victims of twentieth-century life came to include not only economic minorities but also ethnic, religious, or racial groups, a paradox developed. Humanitarianism compelled support for those whose minority status was made manifest by usurpations of their civil rights and liberties. Yet policies conceived and implemented by governmental officials inevitably produced such usurpations. What was the proper liberal response to government suppression of dissident speech in wartime, to wartime incarceration of naturalized American citizens who had retained or previously held citizenship in an enemy nation, to the invasion of welfare recipients' privacy by government agencies? Liberalism had as its major premise the validity of positive governmental intervention to further individual rights; what happened when the state acted to suppress them?

The paradoxes in modern liberalism were reflected in its ideals for judicial performance. On one hand, liberalism asked judges to reach results in keeping with the substantive values it cherished, such as those that sustained affirmative governmental action to alleviate economic and social inequalities or to help disadvantaged persons. On the other hand, liberalism asked judges to interpret their office in a professional manner—and by the 1920s judicial professionalism had taken on a new meaning. The model of judging embodied by Field had encountered strong criticism from legal scholars. The model permitted (so critics charged) an unwarranted imposition of the social and economic views of judges on the public at large. The apparent refusal of many members of the judiciary to respond to changed social conditions only exacerbated the situation.[6] Indeed some states, thwarted by the courts in their attempts to enact social welfare legislation, had responded by imposing elective checks, such as recall, on the performance of their judges. Two early-twentieth-century jurisprudential theories, Sociological Jurisprudence and a then nameless one that was eventually called Realism, had gained prominence on the strength of arguments that judging was a highly politicized and idiosyncratic process and that effective judicial performance could come only from constant attention to the social context of decisions, a full recognition by judges of the role that bias played in decision-making, and serious efforts on the part of the judiciary to confine the scope of its powers.[7]

The stunning effect of this criticism, in terms of the history of appellate judging, was its discrediting of the oracular theory of judicial decision-making. Deference by the judiciary to legislative activity was required (the critique maintained) for the reason that law could be shaped in the process of judicial interpretation to harmonize with the predilections of the judge. To claim that judicial theories of social organization or economics were outmoded was to imply that the law could be made synonymous with the social attitudes of judges. The vast majority of nineteenth-century jurists had not ignored the fact that judges had social attitudes, but they had insisted on a separation of those attitudes from the fabric of the law itself. Discovering the law remained a process independent of one's personal convictions, despite the social ramifications of discoveries. Sociological Jurisprudence and Realism found the separation between "law" and the interpretations of its officials to be artificial. Realism eventually took the step of equating law with the idiosyncratic judgments of judges and other lawmakers, but this step was not necessary to discredit the oracular theory of judging. All that was needed was the triumph of the belief that judges were, even in a limited sense, lawmakers rather than simply law finders.

All these factors combined to make what came to be called judicial self-restraint an important professional value. Competent professionalism, as defined by a set of academic critics in the early twentieth century, demanded that judges abandon the use of their office to bar "excessively democratic" legislation. Such a response was grounded simply on bias and was therefore intellectually unjustifiable. The appellate judiciary should not substitute its views on social issues for those of the legislature; the latter branch was far better suited to perceive and respond to social change. Judicial professionalism, if not humanitarianism, thus dictated deference on the part of judges to the affirmative governmental actions supported by liberals.

From the time of Holmes's appointment to the Court in 1902 through Brandeis's appointment in 1916 to Holmes's retirement in 1932, the general tenets of liberalism and its double-edged mandate for the judiciary gained increasing acceptance. At the same time a large number of appellate judges, including a shifting majority of the Justices on the Supreme Court, continued to scrutinize and in-

validate social welfare legislation, often using language that suggested a continued belief in the oracular theory of judging. In most
instances the scrutinized legislation constituted an intervention in
behalf of disadvantaged groups or individuals. From a liberal perspective, judicial self-restraint in such cases facilitated desirable
results. For reasons primarily related to their approach to judging,
Holmes and Brandeis both protested against judicial involvement in
the great majority of such cases and were subsequently hailed as
modern liberals.[8] In a smaller set of cases, the limits of government
power to suppress individual rights were tested. Here the Holmes-
Brandeis hegemony broke down, and differences between their jurisprudential views were revealed. In this latter group of cases their
images as liberals became somewhat clouded, and some of the inherent contradictions in judicial liberalism were first exposed.

II

The conspicious advantages of Holmes's youth—his family being
socially prominent, economically confortable, and at the center of
Boston's intellectual community—only served to fire his ambition
to divorce himself from his heritage and to distinguish himself in
his own right. His father was not merely a competent physician
and well-known poet but also a leading public figure of his time; he
loved publicity, social companionship, and good conversation, and
his public reputation was thereby so deeply entrenched that when
the younger Holmes was appointed to the Supreme Court in 1902,
at age sixty-one, he was chiefly described as Dr. Holmes's son.[9]
Holmes reacted early and sharply against the stature and impact of
his father. He was as solitary and self-preoccupied as his father was
garrulous; as serious and introspective as his father was effervescent
and glib. Dr. Holmes thought his son given to "looking at life as a
solemn show where he is only a spectator";[10] William James, less
charitable, found in him a "cold-blooded, conscious egotism and
conceit."[11] For his part, Holmes thought his father "largely distracted into easy talk and occasional verse": had Dr. Holmes been
"less popular," said his son, "he might have produced a great
work."[12]

     In Holmes's college years he seemed eager to arrive at some
organizing ideological or philosophical principle that would isolate

his way of thinking from that of his family circle. He rejected his father's religious views and at one point believed that "an all-comprehending science has embraced the universe . . . generalizing and systematizing . . . every vagary of the human mind." [13] In the 1850's, as the gap between North and South widened, Holmes became a rabid abolitionist and, when war came, enlisted in a regiment of Massachusetts volunteers in the Union army. Once at war, however, he found that life resisted a neat intellectual ordering and that the rightness or wrongness of beliefs was largely irrelevant. From these experiences came the celebrated paradoxes on which Holmes built his mature philosophic stance. Searching for general principles was the ultimate in intellectual satisfaction, but no generalization was worth a damn; fighting for ideals was heroic, but ideals were meaningless in themselves.

One can see the presence of these paradoxes in Holmes's scholarship, written largely in the nineteenth century; in his general attitude toward the relation of governmental institutions to social change; and in his interpretation of his judicial office. In his most extensive and impressive piece of scholarship, *The Common Law* (1880), he adopted an analytical technique that was to become characteristic: exposure of the fallacies of a prevailing system of thought, substitution of a counter-system, denial of the "truth" of that counter-system. In *The Common Law* the discarded system was nineteenth-century "logic," by which Holmes meant the formalistic, religion-based logic that reasoned downward syllogistically from assumed truths about the universe; the proposed counter-system was "experience," the changing "felt necessities" that reflected current social values and were altered by time and circumstances. Yet experience did not always produce wisdom, and change was not always for the better; so Holmes's system was not a model for lawmaking but merely a fatalistic acceptance that law was not so much the embodiment of reason as a manifestation of dominant beliefs at a given time.

Similar messages were conveyed in his two other major contributions to legal scholarship of the nineteenth century. In an essay, "The Path of the Law," he denied that the law was "a system of reason" or a series of "deduction[s] from principles of ethics"; [14] it was simply an embodiment of the ends and purposes of a society at a given point in its history. One could study current social purposes and, by referring legal rules to them, better understand the course of legal development. One could not, however, treat some purposes as invariably true or timeless and erect a logical jurisprudence on them. In another essay, "Law in Science and Science in Law," he argued, in fact, that one could even measure, through the techniques of statistics and economics, the intensity of the "competing social desires" that clashed in a lawsuit and, having made that measurement, arrive at a decision that kept law "in accord with the wishes and feelings of the community." But science, though a helpful tool, could not be thought of as an ultimate organizing principle. There would probably never be, Holmes felt, a "commonwealth in which science [was] everywhere supreme." It was only "an ideal—but "without ideals what is life worth?" [15]

Holmes apparently never read a newspaper (at least in his later life), and kept informed on contemporary events mainly through correspondence and conversation. Although he once said that academic life was half-life, his life-style while a judge, particularly during his tenure on the Supreme Court, was cloistered, focused on intellectual pursuits, and entirely isolated from national government and politics. Yet Holmes had no difficulty forming opinions on current political issues and resolving, as a judge, delicate questions of government. So integrated and flexible was his philosophic stance that it could absorb new issues, ideals, and events without disturbing its essential balance.

Life, Holmes assumed, was in constant flux, ideals gaining and losing primacy; one could not alter this process, however devoted one was to a particular viewpoint. The temporary triumph or defeat of ideas was determined by the unregulated intellectual marketplace. Hence there was no harm in tolerating the expression of ideas but no guarantee that any idea could survive for all time. Since America was a republic, majority opinion determined the acceptability of views, and a majority had the right to impose its beliefs on minorities. The principal vehicle for majoritarian expression was the lawmaking branch of the government; legislative power, grounded on majoritarian sentiment, was therefore limitless. But a majoritarian power to suppress minority viewpoints could be exercised only when the activities or viewpoints of a minority could reasonably be said to subvert social goals espoused by the prevailing majority. Up to that point, dissenting actions or opinions were protected, since they had a right to enter the intellectual marketplace to become "popular" or to be confined to oblivion.

Accordingly, the legislative branch of government could suppress speech, but only if the speech in question were clearly subversive of majoritarian social goals.[16] It could sterilize imbeciles if the ultimate eradication of mental defectives from the population were an end receiving majority support and if sterilization could reasonably be said to further that end.[17] It could prevent aliens from owning guns if the belief of a majority that aliens were inclined more than citizens to violence could be deemed reasonable.[18] A citizen might nonetheless campaign all his life against a war, in behalf of imbeciles, for equal treatment for aliens, or for the broader ideal of freedom to act and speak in a dissenting vein. American society had long recognized the latter ideal, and Holmes believed that he would be as willing as others had been to die for it.[19] But at some point civilized living in America required the recognition that unpopular views were ultimately impotent because the sentiments of the majoritarians determined the path of the law; and short of revolution, the laws of a majority were to be obeyed.

If Holmes's polity worked smoothly, dissenting actions and viewpoints continually beat against the wall of majoritarianism, the majority acted against them, and clashes in "social desires" resulted. The resolution of these clashes was the task of the courts, which held the "sovereign prerogative of choice." [20] But their freedom of choice was severely limited. To some extent, courts were bound by the choices of their predecessors; it was not generally the province of judges to "undertake to renovate the law." [21] Even on those occasions when precedents gave no guidelines, a series of institutional constraints derived from Holmes's notion of majoritarian sovereignty limited judicial freedom. The judiciary, not being elected representatives of the majority, was [not] to substitute its views for those of legislatures. The judiciary did not necessarily protect even constitutional rights against legislative infringement. All individual rights, for Holmes, were ultimately held at majority sufferance. Vindication of a right that the majority chose to circumscribe required a revolution and the forcible installation of a new majority.

Over and over, in his years on the Supreme Court, Holmes sounded these themes. Paternalistic social-welfare legislation was challenged before the Court; Holmes, who liked to play the cranky Social Darwinist, muttered about the frivolity or foolishness of the legislation but upheld the legislature's power to enact it. This interpretation of the judicial function came to be called tolerant or self-restrained or even statesmanlike by Holmes's admirers. Holmes, professing disdain for the last appellation, privately coveted it.[22]

In the end Holmes's intellectual vantage point was compatible with the opposing impulses that lurked, unarticulated, within him. He felt pride in the democratic and egalitarian consciousness of Americans, yet he was an intellectual and social snob, contemptuous of the "crowd." His personal relations were marked by barriers and distance. The archetypal Holmes friendship was a correspondence friendship, with the other participant being inaccessible to Holmes except for occasional visits. Even the most persistent of his correspondents, such as Harold Laski, rarely got beyond a certain level of intimacy. When Laski proposed, after many years of letters, that he call Holmes by his first name, he was summarily rebuffed.

Although much of Holmes's communication with others was at the level of intellectual abstraction, he also had an earthy, bawdy side, which punctuated his talk and occasionally his writings and revealed itself in his covert private life. Much of the distinctiveness of Holmes's style came from his juxtaposition of earthy or homely language with abstract ideas; although he held the two impulses apart in his activities, in his thoughts they easily intermeshed. "I wonder," he once said, "if cosmically an idea is any more important than the bowels." [23]

The internal tensions in Holmes ultimately led him to a fatalistic dependence on paradox and impotence, and this formed the basis of his jurisprudence. Consciously or unconsciously, he perceived the opposing impulses in himself, and gave up attempting to reconcile them. Whether man was inherently evil or perfectible, whether change ever constituted progress, even whether he himself existed—a question he took seriously—were unanswerable riddles. The easy solution was to acknowledge "ultimate facts"—power, force, and change—and let the "goodness or badness of laws" turn on "what the crowd wants," even though the crowd, "if it knew," would not want what it did.[24]

III

Late in his career Holmes came increasingly to parallel Brandeis, who had joined Holmes on the Court in 1916, in his voting record on certain constitutional issues. Chief Justice William Howard Taft, who was never enthusiastic about Brandeis as a colleague, said that in his later years Holmes was "so completely under the control" of Brandeis that it gave Brandeis two votes instead of one.[25] A 1927 press comment claimed that Holmes and Brandeis had "achieved a spiritual kinship that mark[ed] them off as a separate liberal chamber" of the Court.[26] The kinship of Holmes and Brandeis was one of the accidents of history. Neither their temperaments nor their philosophies were similar; the congruence of their views was largely a matter of time and circumstance.

As a young man Brandeis coveted the symbols of Holmes's inheritance: social prestige, affluence, and access to the Boston intelligentsia. The son of German immigrants who had settled in Kentucky, he entered Harvard Law School at eighteen in 1875 and rapidly became entranced by the intellectual atmosphere of Cambridge, determining for himself the "rising lights" among his professors [27] and "carefully not[ing] the names and addresses of eminent people." [28] He felt, as a Southerner, a Jew, and not a college graduate, that gaps existed between himself and his peers; he strove to narrow those gaps by adopting the life-styles of those about him. He was successful enough in this endeavor to lay the groundwork for a prospective law partnership in Boston with Samuel Warren, a wealthy socialite, and to secure for himself and his wife, a Jew from New York, a moderate degree of acceptance on the part of Boston society.[29]

Once economically and socially comfortable, however, Brandeis did not blend into Holmes's world. He was mindful, as he said to a close friend, that "whatever I have achieved, or may achieve is my own, pure and simple, unassisted by the fortuitous circumstances of family influence or social position," [30] and he retained a distance from the life in the trappings of which he surrounded himself. He joined clubs in order to "captivate" potential clients,[31] insisted that his wife adopt conventional upper-class dress standards, and dabbled in gentlemanly politics, such as civil service reform; yet in 1891 he attributed "the little successes I may have had" to "pressure from within" that stemmed from "a deep sense of obligation" rather than from "the allurement of a possible distinction." [32] Obligation for Brandeis meant adherence to a code of rigid personal standards, which included the tenets of self-denial, distaste for excess in any form, and moral righteousness. It was as though he were compelled by his conscience to follow these standards, with success following naturally upon them.

The Brandeis code justified, among other things, low heat in his law office to save expense, a short working day (to keep one's mind fresh), disdain for drinking, dancing, and like pursuits, the zealous molding of the lives of the underprivileged so that paupers might achieve "moral growth," [33] distaste for sloppy and inefficient business practices, and eventually, in his maturity, adoption of the public as his client in a series of lawsuits designed to dissolve the monopolistic positions held by gas utilities, life insurance companies, banks, and the New Haven Railroad. It was not important to Brandeis that in those suits he actually represented competitors of the various industries rather than their consumers. What was important was that his clients recognize the value of moderation, efficiency, and social responsibility in their business practices. The proper task of the legal profession was to aid them in that recognition. Lawyers at large should occupy the position Brandeis had carved out for himself: one of "independence between the wealthy and the people, prepared to curb the excesses of either." [34]

By the time of Brandeis's appointment to the Court, against the protests of an influential segment of the Boston legal and commercial community, who felt that the combination of an economic reformer and a Jew was too much to tolerate, the eligible beneficiaries of his wisdom were numerous. He had scrutinized business trusts and concluded that excessive size produced economic waste. The trust-busting aspects of Woodrow Wilson's New Freedom were largely his creation.[35] Scientific management, the efficiency-oriented program created by the engineer Frederick Taylor, had become one of his causes, even though it was opposed by labor unions whose members he wanted to liberate from their industrial slavery. The moral fervor of Zionism and its passion for social planning attracted him, and he began to deplore assimilation on the part of American Jews, calling it "national suicide." [36] He lobbied for reform of the banking industry and was one of the draftsmen of the Federal Reserve Act, which initiated national control over the distribution of currency and credit. Even institutions of government became objects of Brandeisian crusades. As counsel for *Collier's Weekly*, which had exposed mismanagement of Interior Department resources, Brandeis publicized the cause of a middle-level employee of Interior who had been muzzled for uncovering inefficiency and corruption in his superiors.

As with Holmes, a juxtaposition of competing impulses formed the core of Brandeis's philosophy. In his case the impulses were those of freedom and self-restraint. Excess size, inequities, or inefficiencies choked or stifled individual initiative, he believed, but success and accomplishment were ascribed to self-abnegation and a conservation of human resources. Brandeis found industrial laborers his "most congenial company," [37] and regarded the industrious among them as heroes (but was infuriated to see them smoking cigarettes). For him they were to be a counterpoint to the "intense materialism and luxuriousness" [38] of economic royalists. Freedom came, as it had in his case, from self-denial. In countless attempts to ingratiate himself with the eminent in Boston, in endless chilly days with overcoats substituted for radiators, in the husbanding of his early savings bonds, the moderation of pleasures, and the renunciation of luxuries were found the bits and pieces of Brandeis's eventual independence. When he joined the Court he was financially secure and beholden to no class or interest group. He was also convinced of his own righteousness, and zealous to impose his life-style on others.

The cosmic reach of Brandeis's philosophy suggested that he might come to the Court with developed views on the proper function of the judiciary. In actuality he had given little thought to the specific task of appellate judging, tending to include judges within his general observations on the legal profession. Two themes were central to his interpretation of law practice: the importance of empirical observation, and the lawyer's duty to be an intermediary between his clients and the public. Confronted with a legal problem, Brandeis sought to gather "the facts," and his great powers of organization and synthesis made fact analysis one of his special arts.

The facts having been collected and sifted, a course of action emerged. Each problem, he felt, formed the evidentiary basis of its own solution, since a sufficient supply of empirical data clarified the costs and benefits of various legal approaches. With the solution at hand, the next task was to persuade a client of its virtue. Here again, a grasp of "facts," including an understanding of the client's temperament, was a lawyer's best weapon. Empirical analysis, then, led to an inductive reasoning process in which costs were weighed against benefits; the process yielded a strategy with independent validity; a lawyer proceeded to persuade his client to adopt that strategy; in so doing, he not only gave good advice but influenced social policy and preserved his independence as well.

Judging, for Brandeis, was simply another exercise in this method. It was not a process of "reasoning from abstract conception," but one of "reasoning from life," taking "notice of facts."[39] In his first years on the Court, Brandeis seemed to make almost no distinction between his opinions and the briefs he had written as an advocate. He set forth the factual basis of his inquiry, undertook an extensive empirical investigation (complete with technical references), made a cost-benefit analysis of the effects of various policy choices made by a lower court or a legislature, chose the most efficient solution, and lobbied for it. In a case in his first year on the Court, *Adams v. Tanner*,[40] which considered the constitutionality of a Washington statute prohibiting employment agencies from charging fees, Brandeis asked himself what was "the evil which the people· of Washington sought to correct," why had they chosen "the particular remedy embodied in the statute," and what had been "the experience . . . of other states or countries in this connection."[41] Fifteen pages of labor statistics provided the answers. Private employment agencies had been corrupt and inefficient. It was reasonable for the people of Washington to want to eradicate corruption and inefficiency, and just for the Court to promote their cause.

For Holmes, this sort of partisan documentation was out of place in a judicial opinion[42]—and tedious as well. Holmes was not concerned with showing the positive value of paternalistic or regulatory legislation, but merely that its basis was reasonable. Therein lay a vital difference between him and Brandeis. Both men, as judges, believed that a legislative majority could infringe upon individual rights. "Above all rights," Brandeis said in one opinion, "rises duty to the community."[43] But whereas Holmes simply accepted the ultimate logic of that view, Brandeis needed to be personally convinced of the rightness of the majority's action. He was not receptive to, indeed was suspicious of, governmental power in the abstract, but when that power was being used for a moral purpose, he welcomed it. For example, Brandeis believed that economic independence and political democracy were interrelated. Excess size in enterprises was not only wasteful, he felt, but posed a threat to individual self-reliance, since the enterprise, as a unit, came to wield power over its own employees and other American citizens. Hence the use of governmental power to reduce the size of giant corporations amounted to a crusade for individual freedom. There was nothing inherently attractive in governmental power, however; "Big Government" was as much a potential threat to the individual as "Big Business."

Holmes, in contrast, recognized the "fact" of majority sovereignty and suggested to oppressed minorities that they consider revolution. In the historic struggles between the increasingly omnipotent governments of the twentieth century and various sets of individual rights, Holmes's reaction to government intervention—if he thought it anything but arbitrary—was generally passive; Brandeis's selectively enthusiastic or hostile. Consequently Holmes was almost uniformly indifferent to individual rights or liberties, whether economic or civil, whereas Brandeis, despite his view that all rights were ultimately subsumed in a broad obligation to society, occasionally approximated the stance of a civil libertarian.

IV

Of the thousands of opinions written by Holmes and Brandeis during their tenure on the Court, perhaps the most revealing, if not necessarily the most influential, were those in which they considered the effect of governmental regulation on two sets of liberties—first, the Fifth and Fourteenth Amendments' alleged guarantees of "liberty of contract"; second, the First and Fourteenth Amendments' guarantees of free speech.

The doctrine of liberty of contract, originally hinted at by Cooley in *Constitutional Limitations*, was developed in state courts in the 1880s,[44] was slowly and obliquely incorporated in Supreme Court decisions in the late 1880s and 1890s,[45] and was explicitly, though irregularly, accepted by a Court majority between 1905 and 1923.[46] Its advocates postulated an inalienable right in employers and employees to buy and sell their goods or services on terms they chose, deriving this right, originally, from the Fourteenth Amendment's protection against state interference with liberty and property. Later a similar gloss was made on the Fifth Amendment's protection of liberty and property rights from interference by the federal government, making liberty of contract a philosophical principle as well as a constitutional doctrine. In its most extreme form, liberty of contract declared that any governmental attempt to regulate private contractual relations was presumptively invalid. It was that presumption that jeopardized much of the welfare legislation of the early twentieth century.

Judicial use of the liberty-of-contract doctrine to invalidate paternalistic legislation became an object of controversy in the first decade of the twentieth century. Opponents of the doctrine, among them Roscoe Pound and Theodore Roosevelt, suggested that it was unsound for two reasons: it ignored "new conceptions of the relation of property to human welfare," [47] and it exemplified an artificial process of judicial reasoning in which predetermined beliefs were developed pseudologically "in the teeth of the actual facts." [48] If every man held his property subject to the general right of the community to regulate its use, property and contract rights were not inalienable. To exaggerate their importance in judicial formulas such as liberty of contract, which ignored the disadvantaged position of industrial workers in modern America, was to fail to adjust "[legal] principles and doctrines to human conditions." [49] This failure invited a characterization of judges as reactionaries or antiquarians.

Holmes identified himself with the opponents of liberty of contract in his first Supreme Court opinion, but his opposition stemmed from a different source. The case, Otis v. Parker, [50] tested the constitutionality of a California statute prohibiting sales of stock shares on margin. Holmes dismissed a claim that the statute limited unduly the freedom of adult persons to make contracts, by invoking his view on the proper allocation of institutional power in America. The fact that a statute could be said in a general way to violate the Constitution did not end the inquiry, he maintained, for "general propositions do not carry us far." The appropriate question for the Court in cases involving legislative infringement of "liberties" was not whether judges thought the statute "excessive, unsuited to its ostensible end, or based on [disagreeable] conceptions of morality," but whether it had a rational purpose and could be said to be a reasonable exercise of legislative power. [51]

At the outset of his career on the Court, then, Holmes indicated that his opposition to the liberty-of-contract doctrine could not be grounded on any enthusiasm for the paternalistic legislation that he sustained against its challenge. He thought that hours-and-wages laws merely "shift[ed] the burden to a different point of incidence"; [52] he professed indifference toward "legislation to make other people better"; [53] he did not believe that "wholesale regeneration" could be achieved "by tinkering with the institution of property." [54] He simply acquiesced in the apparent fact that "the liberty of a citizen to do as he likes" was "interfered with . . . by every state or municipal institution which takes his money for purposes thought desirable, whether he likes it or not." [55] When a legislative majority believed that an "important ground of public policy" called for restraint of individual liberties, Holmes felt that the Constitution permitted that restraint. "[T]he right to make contracts at will that has been derived from the word liberty in the [Fifth and Fourteenth] Amendments," he observed, had "been stretched to its extreme." [56]

From *Lochner v. New York* through *Adair v. U.S.* to *Adkins v. Children's Hospital*, the last a 1923 case invalidating the constitutionality of a minimum-wage law in the District of Columbia as an undue interference with the liberty to contract, Holmes protested against the use of the doctrine and all such "general propositions of law" to decide "concrete cases." But his protest stemmed from a general proposition of his own: "the scope of state sovereignty" was "a question of fact." [57] By this phrase Holmes meant that governmental interference with individual liberties was permissible in circumstances in which that interference could be shown to be grounded on some rational basis or tied to the achievement of some important public purpose. Whether it could be so shown or so tied was a matter of quasi-empirical proof, proof of the seriousness and rationality of the legislature's purpose. The importance and seriousness of a given purpose varied with time, but the test of its rationality was majority sentiment. A majority might behave irrationally, however, and not every interference with liberties was justifiable. The mere fact that legislation infringing individual rights furthered a public purpose did not prevent judicial inquiry into its reasonableness. Such inquiries, however, could only be made on an *ad hoc* basis.

Nowhere in Holmes's approach was there an attempt to demonstrate the particular worth of a piece of legislation. He would support a paternalistic statute only to the extent of conceding that an economic or social inequality existed and that the disadvantaged group could fairly convince a majority that the inequality ought to be alleviated. Thus, in his dissent in *Coppage v. Kansas*,[58] a 1915 case that struck down a Kansas statute prohibiting employers from preventing their employees from joining labor unions, Holmes stated that "in present conditions a workingman not unnaturally might believe that only by belonging to a union can he secure a contract that shall be fair to him," [59] but stopped well short of endorsing the value of labor unions.

In contrast to this fatalism and indifference was the righteousness and zeal of Brandeis. Liberty of contract arguments stimulated Brandeis to demonstrate the value of the legislation being challenged. His interest was not so much in exposing the sterility of judicial decisions that reasoned downward from preconceived beliefs as in showing that the preconceptions themselves were unsound in light of the "facts" of twentieth-century life in America. The liberty-of-contract doctrine was inadequate, he felt, not so much because it represented the inappropriate judicial promulgation of a particular economic theory, but because it assumed an equality of bargaining power between employees and employers when it did not actually exist, or because it failed to recognize that, in modern life, considerations of social welfare could transcend the exercise of individual rights.

For Brandeis there were good theories and bad theories, purposes that were noble and purposes that were illegitimate. A Washington statute forbidding employment agencies from receiving fees for their services had been passed in response to a number of "evils" incumbent upon that practice, including waste, inefficiency, and corruption.[60] An Arizona law forbidding the use of injunctions in labor disputes had been partially motivated by the inequitable and heavy-handed use of the practices and by the divided state of public opinion as to its efficacy.[61] A Nebraska statute fixing maximum weights for loaves of bread was attempting to eradicate unfair competition among bakers and frauds on the public.[62]

Brandeis's support for legislative infringements on individual rights, in short, varied with his enthusiasm for the goals envisaged by the legislation. In certain areas of life he believed firmly that persons should be protected against their own self-destructive tendencies, requiring not only moral guidance but a degree of coercion. Consumption of alcoholic beverages was one of these areas. For Brandeis "evil [was] sure to flow from the appetite of men for stimulating liquors." [63] He supported prohibition legislation and, as a judge, he granted to the federal government and the states a wide scope of power to implement it. A provision of the War-Time Prohibition Act of 1918 preventing the sale of liquors in bond was not an unconstitutional taking of property. [64] Congress and the states had power to enact legislation designed to suppress traffic in intoxicating liquors even if that legislation regulated alleged non-intoxicants such as beer and malt liquor. [65] The presence of intoxicating liquor in a car rendered it forfeitable to the government regardless of whether the car's owner knew of the liquor's presence. [66] The amount of liquor dispensed by physicians for medicinal purposes could be limited by Congress. [67]

Brandeis did not apply uniformly his belief that a paternalistic government should protect members of the public against themselves. In the area of free speech he seemed to move, in the course of his career in the Court, toward a stricter standard of judicial scrutiny for regulatory legislation than he advocated in cases involving property and contract rights. Holmes, as well, appeared in free speech cases to be giving greater deference to individual rights than his theory of majoritarian sovereignty would allow.

Free-speech cases in the early twentieth century underscored the anxieties that centered around the place of consensual norms and values in American civilization. Freedom to express dissident and unpopular sentiments had been a traditional American value, part of the nation's revolutionary heritage. But World War I, an increasingly diverse and heterogeneous population, and the international success of alternative ideologies to capitalism and democracy combined to produce a perception that dissident attitudes and values could threaten national security. As the ethnic and cultural heritage of American citizens became more diffuse, pressures for national unity against outside threats increased. The result was a strident reaffirmation of the values and norms that allegedly unified Americans in the face of their disintegration. Dissident speech raised the troublesome problem of defining what beliefs early twentieth-century Americans still held in common.

Holmes came to free-speech cases with an attitude he once expressed by saying "I see no meaning in the rights of man except what the crowd will fight for." [68] There were no such things as natural rights for Holmes, only the right of majorities to impose their opinions on minorities and the correlative right of minorities to

overthrow the majority. But exchange of ideas, in a democratic society, was an essential part of the continual replacement of majorities by other majorities. Little as Holmes believed in the inalienability of free speech, he said, he hoped he would die for it; although
time had "upset many fighting faiths," the "ultimate good desired"
was best achieved by "free trade in ideas." [69]

Holmes thus appears to have accepted, in addition to the "ultimate fact" of force on which governmental power rested, an intermediate basis of legitimacy. In democratic societies, at any rate,
one way in which majorities held power was by convincing citizens
of the rightness of their beliefs. They imposed their views on others
and suppressed dissenting opinions, but they also attempted to justify their own actions. Quite often in America, Holmes believed,
majorities "doubt[ed] [their] power or [their] premises." [70] There
was something about American civilization that lent an uneasy
status to the naked use of power. Holmes did not go on record as
applauding this uneasiness. He took pains, in fact, to stress that
power was the essential rationale for governmental acts. But he
recognized it and built his analysis of free-speech questions upon it.

Holmes began his free-speech decisions by stressing the power in
legislatures to suppress speech and, having established that premise, attempted to work out an accommodation between majoritarian sovereignty and the First Amendment. In *Patterson v. Colorado*,[71] a 1907 decision, he allowed the Colorado Supreme Court
to hold in contempt a man who had published articles criticizing its
motives, announcing in the process that the First Amendment's
protection extended primarily to prior restraints on speech, not to
speech that had been published. In the 1915 case of *Fox v. Washington*,[72] which sustained the constitutionality of a statute punishing
any speech that had a tendency to encourage or incite the commission of a crime, he made no inquiry into the actual consequences of
the speaker's words.

But in *Schenck v. United States* [73] and *Abrams v. United States*, two
1919 cases, he appeared to be moving toward a practical compromise between governmental power and free expresssion, embodied
in the "clear and present danger" test articulated in *Schenck*. The
proper judicial inquiry in speech cases, Holmes maintained, was
"whether the words used are used in such circumstances and are of
such a nature as to create a clear and present danger that they will
bring about the substantive evils that Congress has a right to pre-

vent."[74] Under this test, circulars urging persons subject to the draft to resist conscription could be suppressed and their authors punished, but circulars urging munitions workers to support the Russian Revolution of 1917 were constitutionally protected.[75] The first endangered the American military effort in World War I, since the authors attempted to prevent the government from amassing a fighting force. The second did not have a similar effect, since the United States was not at war with Russia.

The test for clear and present danger was grounded on a paradox that became increasingly apparent, especially as used by Brandeis in cases in the 1920s. The test began with the assumption that free speech was not an absolute right, despite the First Amendment. It endorsed governmental infringement on individual liberties in principle and tolerated specific infringements. But it also set limits on the power of a legislative majority to suppress speech and permitted the judiciary to determine those limits. A court, under the test, could take a free-speech case away from the jury if it decided that the words sought to be suppressed had not in fact created a clear and present danger to majority security. The test could thus be seen, as Brandeis said in *Schaefer v. United States*,[76] as a "rule of reason":[77] a means by which judges scrutinized the rationality of legislative acts. As a rule of reason, it could conceivably be used the way late-nineteenth-century judicial rules of reason had been used—namely, as a means of allowing the judiciary to make substantive judgments on the worth of legislation.

Here Brandeis's confidence in the inherent soundness of his own judgments prevailed over his tendency to interpret the range of judicial powers narrowly. He believed that a careful analysis of the facts of a case could lead one to truth. When the insights generated by an inquiry into facts harmonized with his own predilections, conclusions became irresistible. Once he had drawn conclusions, he was not particularly tolerant of opposing views, nor terribly anxious, as a judge, to allow them much weight. In *Schaefer* he decided that the publication of newspaper articles expressing skepticism about the professed intent of the United States to send troops to Europe was so far from being an immediate danger to the American war effort that "no jury in calmness" could find it such. Accordingly, the test for clear and present danger dictated withdrawal of the case from jury consideration.[78] Similarly, in *Pierce v. United States*,[79] after carefully studying a Socialist Party leaflet that de-

picted the horrors of war and asserted that the Morgan interests
were behind the war effort, Brandeis concluded that it was a mere
expression of opinion that had even recognized its own impotence
in inducing resistance against the war.

In these cases Brandeis was making a gloss on Holmes's test that
Holmes himself was not entirely prepared to accept. Brandeis was
concerned not only with the close connection of the suppressed
speech to the occurrence of a preventable evil, but also with the
seriousness of the evil that might occur. Holmes, in the 1919 cases
in which he had formulated the test, had been interested primarily
in the chronological relation of the speech to the evil. Brandeis
believed that mere chronological proximity was not enough. If the
evil that the speech induced was relatively trivial, the speech should
be protected. In *Gilbert v. Minnesota* [80] a lobbyist was convicted,
under a Minnesota statute prohibiting public speeches against the
war effort, for stating that conscription should be subject to popular vote and that "if they conscripted wealth like they have conscripted men, this war would not last over forty-eight hours." [81]
Holmes voted to sustain the conviction and uphold the statute's
constitutionality; Brandeis dissented. The statute created a blanket
prohibition of public speech against enlistment or in behalf of paci-
ficism, Brandeis maintained. No effort was made to inquire into the
purpose of the speech or to ascertain whether the speaker's remarks
could reasonably be expected to induce others to perpetrate truly
serious evils.

As free-speech cases moved outside the context of World War I,
this difference in focus between Holmes and Brandeis persisted,
even though it did not again result in their casting opposing votes.
In *Gitlow v. New York*, [82] a 1925 case, a Socialist was convicted
under the New York Criminal Anarchy Act of 1902 for advocating
mass strikes and hostile action against the bourgeoisie. Holmes, in
dissenting from the Court's decision sustaining the conviction
against a free-speech challenge, distinguished between the advocacy
of ideas in the abstract, and concrete attempts to induce others to
carry out those ideas immediately. The "redundant discourse" of
Gitlow, he maintained was not "an attempt to induce an uprising
against government at once," but "at some indefinite time in the future." [83]

Brandeis joined this dissent, but his subsequent concurrence two
years later in *Whitney v. California* [84] indicated that he was con-

cerned with the seriousness as well as the imminence of the resulting evil. He read the test for clear and present danger, he said, as meaning that whenever the "fundamental rights of free speech and assembly" were allegedly invaded, a defendant could raise three questions: whether "there actually did exist at the time a clear danger"; whether "the danger, if any, was imminent"; and "whether the evil apprehended was one so substantial as to justify the stringent restriction interposed by the legislature." [85] The first two questions were questions of fact, the third was a question of law. A court could determine that the evil perceived was not sufficiently serious to merit legislative interference with free speech, and so withdraw the case from the jury. The judicial deference to legislative wisdom championed by Brandeis in liberty-of-contract cases did not always apply in speech cases.

Holmes joined Brandeis in his *Whitney* concurrence, but the facts of the case qualified his support. The defendant in Whitney had been convicted under a California criminal statute for participating in the organization of a state Communist Labor Party. The statute prohibited persons from becoming members of organizations that advocated violence as a means of inducing social or political change, and thus attempted to punish those who merely associated with persons who advocated or practiced violence. A majority of the Court peremptorily sustained the statute. Brandeis, however, thought that the statute might be constitutionally defective as applied to Miss Whitney. Her association with Communists, he argued, did not by itself constitute a sufficiently imminent danger to the security of the State of California. But there was other evidence that might have suggested that Miss Whitney and her associates posed an immediate threat to California's security; and thus Brandeis tolerated her conviction. His focus, ultimately, was thus on the imminence of the danger rather than the seriousness of the perceived evil. This focus was consistent with that of Holmes in *Gitlow*.

At the very end of his career, Holmes seemed to have accepted the notion of reversing the presumption of constitutional validity in speech cases. In *Near v. Minnesota* [86] a majority of the Court invalidated a statute allowing injunctions against newspapers that had printed allegedly defamatory material. In the process, the majority, through Chief Justice Charles Evans Hughes, asserted the importance of keeping the press immune from censorship of its publica-

tions and claimed the power to weigh the serious public evil caused
by authority to prevent publication against the evils suppressed by
the statute.[87] In this, the last speech case decided before Holmes's
retirement, he and Brandeis were both members of the majority.
Whether Holmes's acquiescence stemmed from his belief that protection from "prior restraints" formed the core of the First Amendment or whether he had actually endorsed Brandeis's gloss on his
original clear-and-present-danger test is unclear.

Also in 1931 came one of the last liberty-of-contract cases of the
twentieth century, *O'Gorman v. Hartford Ins. Co.*,[88] in which a New
Jersey statute regulating the fees paid to local agents by insurance
companies was challenged as a violation of the Fourteenth Amendment's due process clause. Brandeis, in a majority opinion sustaining the statute, made the familiar analysis of evils and remedies he
had made in earlier liberty-of-contract cases and then invoked the
presumption of the constitutionality of legislative acts to dispose of
the case. Holmes voted with the majority. The entire five-man majority of *O'Gorman*, which included Justices Holmes, Brandeis,
Hughes, Stone, and Owen Roberts, adopted a rule of presumptions
for liberty-of-contract cases differing from that used for speech
cases. Conversely, the four dissenters in *O'Gorman*—Justices Butler,
McReynolds, Sutherland, and Van Devanter—proclaimed the inviolability of freedom to contract, but, as dissenters in *Near*, argued
that legislative attempts to curb speech were presumptively valid.
By 1931 liberty of speech had apparently come to occupy the exalted place once reserved for liberty of contract, while liberty of
contract had been discredited.

Holmes and Brandeis had played an important part in a process
that ultimately led to temporary placement of First Amendment
liberties in a constitutionally "preferred position" over economic
liberties. This development, when it was made manifest by the
Court in 1945,[89] was hailed as a victory for liberalism and a tribute
to the influence of the foremost judicial liberals of the early twentieth century, Holmes and Brandeis.[90] But rather than demonstrating the compatibility of liberalism with Holmes's and Brandeis's interpretations of their office, the liberty-of-contract and
speech cases had unearthed the paradoxical nature of the modern
liberal blueprint for judicial performance.

V

Holmes had taught that ideas and values, whether employed by judges or by others, were not absolutes but products of changing social conditions. Brandeis had taught that the empirical indices of change could be observed and analyzed and that, by this process, public policies could be made responsive to the dictates of contemporary life. Liberalism, as it coalesced into a definable ideology, drew upon both these insights. American society after World War I was marked by a simultaneous collapse of allegedly timeless values and norms and a pervasive need for governmental policies that responded to the newly perceived facts of modern industrial life. To an extent, Holmes helped make palatable a world without consensual norms, while Brandeis sought to show how governmental institutions could intervene to make that world more livable. Each contributed to the belief of modern liberalism that an activist state could provide both security and progress.

But if some strands of the thought of Holmes and Brandeis were harmonious with liberalism, others were not. The dissonance that thus resulted highlighted the uneasy role of the appellate judiciary in the liberal state. Holmes had been a leading late-nineteenth-century intellectual radical. His quarrel with that century's faith in universal axioms had made him an early-twentieth-century juristic reformer, exposing the essential subjectivity of the oracular approach to judging. With his distaste for intuitive judicial decision-making came an exaltation of self-restraint, and in the liberal world of fragmented values judicial self-restraint seemed eminently sensible. Holmes was hence a professional judge for liberals: the "completely adult jurist," to Jerome Frank.[91] But he was no humanitarian. He not only tolerated but actually believed in the principle of majoritarian repression of minority rights. He rejected the notion that free speech was an absolute right as surely as he rejected the inalienability of a liberty to contract. He was indifferent to the civil rights of blacks, Orientals, and aliens;[92] he was often satisfied with summary forms of procedural due process. His clear-and-present-danger test cut both ways: it carved out an area of constitutionally protected speech but also justified widespread suppression of "dangerous" expression. In short, Holmes abjured close scrutiny of repressive legislation as well as of welfare legislation. Hours and wages laws were sanctioned, but so were statutes requiring the compulsory sterilization of mental defectives.

Brandeis, as well, fell short of the paradigm of a liberal judge. Sometimes, as in the wartime prohibition cases, he assumed the presence of a consensus of values on moral issues that liberalism denied, thereby reaching what were perceived as illiberal results.[93] On other occasions his deviance from liberalism exhibited itself in his methods, as in those speech cases where through his gloss on the clear and present danger test he appeared to be endorsing a subjective form of judicial decision-making that the professional canons of liberalism repudiated. Brandeis was a liberal in his result-orientation only to the extent that liberalism endorsed Brandeisian social policies; he was a liberal in methodology only to the extent that judicial self-restraint fostered results that he thought sensible.

The careers of Holmes and Brandeis hence illustrated the tension in judicial liberalism between "right" results and "right" methods. That tension had been implanted in the movement at its origin. The early-twentieth-century critics of "mechanical" jurisprudence objected not only to methods but to results as well. They disliked conservatism in the appellate judiciary as much as they disliked subjective activism. Their critiques assumed that the liberty-of-contract doctrine represented unsound social policy as well as illogical reasoning, and that assumption rested on their own strong perception of the common goals of American civilization. But as the substantive content of consensual American values became increasingly difficult to perceive after World War I, judicial self-restraint took on an expanded meaning. It was not merely a check against wrong-headed subjectivity but also a means by which the judiciary assured that the decisions of the institution best suited to discern and reflect majoritarian sentiment—the legislature—were given their proper weight. Since the state had become a substitute for value consensus, its legislative fiats should be supported as buffers against anarchy.

The concept of an expansive regulatory state rested, however, on the premise that it would be responsive to the needs of disadvantaged minorities. Otherwise the egalitarian and democratic traditions of America would vanish, and liberalism would be synonymous with totalitarianism. The state was permitted to regulate private conduct only to the extent that its regulations were fairly implemented, and also conferred benefits on the disadvantaged that outweighed the costs to everyone else. Not every manifestation of majoritarian sentiment was to be tolerated; some legislative policies were illiberal. The only institution capable of scrutinizing the fairness of legislative activity was the judiciary; hence, judges in the liberal state should use their expertise in interpreting the Constitution to undertake that scrutiny. They should presume legislation to be constitutionally valid, but be prepared to override that presumption.

The harmony of methods and results envisaged by this conception of judicial performance was fated to dissolve in instances where pressure for national solidarity clashed with pressure to vindicate minority rights. The speech cases represented one such instance in which judicial self-restraint did not produce liberal results. Holmes and Brandeis, both of whom, in varying degrees, believed in tolerating legislative judgments and in vindicating free expression, struggled with the dilemma posed by these cases. Their eventual resolution, at least in the *Near* case, appeared to subordinate a liberal methodology to the achievement of liberal results. As a result of that case and other instances in which they seemed to champion the disadvantaged, they were apotheosized as liberals. That apotheosis, however, ignored the differences between them and minimized the inherent contradictions in modern liberalism's mandate for the judiciary. The considerable skills of Holmes and Brandeis— the keenness of their minds, their capacity for eloquence, the coherence of their thought—did not make any easier for them the task of squaring approved liberal results with approved liberal methods of judging. They, at least, were acute enough to see a potential tension between methods and results. Other early-twentieth-century members of the Supreme Court, who opposed modern liberalism in any form, failed to perceive a distinction between judging and vindicating one's social or political preferences. That failure generated another threat to the independence of the American appellate judiciary.

9

The Four Horsemen:
The Sources of Judicial
Notoriety

High achievement has never been a prerequisite for historical importance. If the Warren G. Harding Administration was low in
stature and accomplishment, it has nonetheless been seen as historically significant.[1] In a similar fashion the careers of certain American appellate judges may be seen as important even though their individual accomplishments have been very poorly regarded. A 1972
ranking of Supreme Court Justices listed Willis Van Devanter,
Pierce Butler, and James C. McReynolds as "failures" in the performance of their office.[2] Yet these three men, together with George
Sutherland, composed one of the most significant blocs of judges in
the history of the American judicial tradition: the "Four Horsemen" (as contemporary newspaper accounts called them) who
openly resisted the legislative reforms of the New Deal and thereby
helped precipitate the Court-packing crisis in 1937.

The Four Horsemen play a part in defining the tradition of
appellate judging in America similar to that played by the judges
who decided *Dred Scott* and the *Legal Tender* and *Income Tax*
cases. Through their long series of negative votes on New Deal legislation and the stubborn resistance to change reflected by their
accompanying opinions, Van Devanter, Sutherland, Butler, and
McReynolds tested the limits of appellate judicial power. As in the
three previous controversies, their performance suggested that there

is a point at which the exercise of power by the American appellate judiciary becomes sufficiently offensive to generate open attempts to restrain its use. The mandate given Lincoln in the 1860 election amounted to a rebuff to the Taney Court; the Chase Court was enlarged to secure a reversal of the first *Legal Tender* case; the *Income Tax* decision stimulated passage of a constitutional amendment. The Four Horsemen's efforts to thwart the New Deal resulted in another attempt to enlarge the Court. Judicial performance, in each case, had come to be considered notorious.

In the nineteenth-century cases notoriety had resulted from a single decision that combined an impolitic result with a vulnerable rationale, bringing scorn upon the Court and the appellate judiciary at large. The Four Horsemen's notoriety did not spring from so identifiable a source. It was the product of a combination of personal, jurisprudential, and political factors, in turn affected by the timing of historical events. Four men whose service on the Court had hitherto been a matter of general indifference to the American public suddenly found their attitudes and work products matters of general public interest, to the detriment of their reputations. But although the Four Horsemen came to be labeled notorious almost overnight, the sources of their notoriety spanned decades.

I

Intertwined with the aspirations and accomplishments of three of the Four Horsemen was the presence of William Howard Taft, the most influential figure in the process of selecting federal appellate judges from 1909 until his retirement from the Supreme Court in 1930. Not only was Taft, as President, former President, and Chief Justice, in a position of unparalleled prominence in the appointments hierarchy during those years, he actively intervened, as has no Chief Justice before or since, to promote the candidacies of his friends and to block those of others.[3]

Taft valued congeniality and goodwill above most other things, and consequently had few acrimonious relations with his professional peers. His ideological convictions very often shaped his attitude toward a colleague, but he never let differences on social and intellectual issues override his desire for harmonious personal relations. He feared and disliked Brandeis's ideas and openly opposed his nomination in 1916; he continually complained in private of Brandeis's "radical" views and sinister influence on fellow "dissenters" such as Holmes; and he tried his best to insure that men whom he perceived as being "with Brandeis," men such as Learned Hand or Benjamin Cardozo, would not be appointed to the Court. Yet he wrote to his brother in 1921 that he and Brandeis were "on most excellent terms," [4] and to his daughter, in 1923, that he had come to like Brandeis a great deal. [5]

The surprising affinity between Taft and Brandeis was mainly superficial, although Taft was pleased to find that Brandeis was not uncompromisingly "radical" on every issue. [6] But Taft's insistence on maintaining harmony and team spirit within the Court went very deep. He hated dissenting opinions, wrote very few himself, and made every effort to dissuade others from writing them. In one case in 1923, in which McReynolds had written a majority opinion that provoked dissents from Brandeis and John Clarke, Taft secured a reargument, took over the task of drafting the majority position, asked Brandeis for a memorandum of his views, and produced an opinion that achieved unanimous support. [7] Taft cared passionately about the efficient disposition of the Court's business, vacillating, in his private letters, between discussing the merits of efficiency and the defects of ideology in certain of his colleagues. Holmes, for example, "pull[ed] his weight in the boat," [8] writing his opinions with dispatch and asking for more, and Taft greatly appreciated this. On the other hand, Holmes's "influence was no good on the Bench," since he was "always or generally with Brandeis," and the Court would thus "be well rid of him." [9] Finally, Taft loathed, seemingly above all else, an absence of cordiality in a colleague. McReynolds personified this: he was "selfish to the last degree," one "who seems to delight in making others uncomfortable," a man with "no high sense of duty" and with "less of a loyal spirit to the Court than anybody." [10]

Taft, then, knew what qualities he wanted in a Supreme Court Justice and labored hard, from 1909 on, to find men who possessed them, encouraging others of influence to do likewise. First in his order of preferences was "sound" social views. Taft's jurisprudence was essentially that of Field. He believed in the autonomy of individual property rights; he felt that the Constitution had secured those rights against governmental interference for all time; he held a conception of the appellate judiciary as guardians of the Constitution against encroachments by the uneducated masses and their misguided spokesmen. Living, however, in a later generation, and being a politician as well as a judge, Taft saw the need for some modifications of his views in practice, if only to strengthen their influence. He perceived, for example, that reform in judicial administration, presented as an exercise in modernizing federal court procedure, could also be a means to strengthen the powers of the appellate judiciary, if the new procedures gave the appellate courts increased discretion to control the state of their dockets. He also understood that the nineteenth-century view of judging as law declaration, though sometimes a useful means of justifying unchecked judicial power, was increasingly regarded by his contemporaries as a fiction. "[O]ne would be foolish who would deny," he wrote in 1914, "that [j]udges are men," or "that courts and judges are affected by the times in which they live." [11] Indeed, "useful [j]udges," for Taft, were those who had "tempered [their] views by long political experience." [12]

Once Taft was confident of the soundness, political "savvy," and also the integrity of a given candidate, he sought to satisfy himself as to the individual's ability to meet the demands of the Court's workload. Having reached an affirmative decision on the basis of these qualities, he became relatively indifferent to more conventional considerations, such as political and religious affiliation or geographic distribution. As a Republican President at a time when party affiliations were in the process of realignment, his first appointments to the Court were Charles Evans Hughes, the Republican Governor of New York, Associate Justice Edward White, a Louisiana Democrat, as Chief Justice, and Joseph Lamar, a Georgia Democrat. Each of these men met Taft's primary qualifications and each possessed an additional helpful attribute. Hughes, appointed in 1910, had been a potential rival for the 1912 Presidential nomination; White was one of the ablest members of the present Court, and Taft had resolved to appoint the Chief Justice from among the Justices then sitting; Lamar was a Southerner at a time when Southern representatives were being reinitiated into national office.

Taft had one more available appointment in 1910. Geographic considerations suggested that the nominee be a Westerner, for Justice Brewer's death in March of that year had left no one from west of the Mississippi in the Court. This particular appointment gave Taft the most difficulty. He was less well acquainted with available candidates and their sponsors, and originally had considerable misgivings about the eventual nominee, Willis Van Devanter. Ironically, Taft's fears were realized in Van Devanter's subsequent career, significantly affecting Van Devanter's professional reputation, though not lowering Taft's esteem for him as a colleague, nor greatly affecting Van Devanter's considerable influence on his peers throughout his tenure.

Taft's concern with Van Devanter stemmed from reports, highlighted by a confidential memorandum he received, that Van Devanter had a "dilatory habit in respect to turning out opinions." [13] Taft had received the memorandum sometime in 1909 or 1910, possibly through the auspices of Judge Walter Sanborn, a colleague of Van Devanter on the Eighth Circuit and a competitor for the "western spot" on the Court.[14] The memorandum contained a listing of the numbers of opinions rendered by all the Circuit Courts of Appeals judges in the nation and also an individual study of the Eighth Circuit. Van Devanter ranked low among the circuit judges in the number of opinions he produced, and especially low in contrast to Sanborn, whose output was the highest among all the judges listed. At the same time sources told Taft that Van Devanter was currently behind in his production, so that at one point, in December 1910, Taft remarked to Senator Francis Warren of Wyoming (Van Devanter's chief sponsor) that Van Devanter had apparently not met his share of the judicial workload.[15] This difficulty, Taft later said, made him "seriously hesitate"[16] before selecting Van Devanter. In fact it disposed him to eliminate Van Devanter from consideration. Only the frantic efforts of Warren, who undermined Van Devanter's rivals, and Van Devanter's own strong defense of his position, in which he conceded that he was behind in his work but pleaded the illness of both himself and his wife, saved the day. On December 12, 1910, Taft sent Van Devanter's name, along with those of Hughes, White, and Lamar, to the Senate.

The first of the Four Horsemen, who was to become a close confidant of Taft on the Court and eventually the dominant behind-the-scenes spokesman for the anti-New Deal bloc of Justices, was perceived, on his appointment, as more a technician than an ideologue. Van Devanter was born in 1859 and grew up in Indiana, graduating in 1881 from the University of Cincinnati Law School, where he was exposed, as were countless other students of his gen-

eration, to the ideas of Thomas Cooley. Although he had not publicly expressed the views articulated by Taft in 1894 with respect to
the sanctity of private property,[17] he believed in them. But the
world of ideas held less interest for him than the worlds of business
and politics. In 1884 he moved to Cheyenne, Wyoming Territory,
to take advantage of the opportunities created by his brother-in-
law's appointment as Chief Justice of the territory. Five years later,
having made a local reputation as a railroad lawyer and loyal Republican, Van Devanter was named Chief Justice of the Wyoming
Supreme Court.

At this time Van Devanter first became acquainted with Francis
Warren, with whom he was subsequently to develop a relation that
greatly benefited both men for the next twenty years. Warren, also
a Republican, was elected to the Senate in 1890, the year of state-
hood for Wyoming. Two years later Van Devanter became chairman of the Wyoming Republican Central Committee, and in 1896 a
Republican National Committeeman.[18] Warren remained in the
Senate, barring a short interval between terms in 1893, until his
death in 1929; from 1896 on, he relentlessly promoted Van Devanter. In 1897 Van Devanter was named by President McKinley to
an Assistant Attorney Generalship in the Department of Interior;
in 1903, after securing a high reputation in that office, he was
named by Theodore Roosevelt to a judgeship on the Eighth Circuit.

Little in Van Devanter's early career suggested the well-
developed ideological stance he would later take. In his Eighth Circuit decisions he showed no universal commitment to Field's perspective. In antitrust cases, for example, he alternately supported [19]
and opposed [20] the federal government's decision that it could freely limit the size and scope of property holdings by private enterprises. He upheld the sanctity of the rights of patent holders
against claims that resale price maintenance agreements violated the
Sherman Act,[21] though, once on the Court, he found some resale
price agreements invalid.[22] He continually allowed the contribu-
tory negligence of railroad employees to bar them from recovering
against their employees for injuries they suffered on the job,[23] but
he construed broadly any federal safety statutes designed to protect
railroad workers.[24] He remained, on the eve of his appointment, a
shadowy figure, vaguely associated by some commentators with
railroads or the Republican party [25] but unknown to most.

Ten years after Van Devanter's nomination, Taft again found himself in a position of considerable influence with regard to Supreme Court appointments. Having endured his own decisive defeat in the 1912 election and eight years of the Wilson Administration, he declared himself in support of Harding in 1920 and, after some anxious moments, was rewarded with the Chief Justiceship on White's death in 1921. Once appointed, Taft plunged into the business of refurbishing the Court and the federal bench with the same eagerness he had displayed as President, ignoring any separation-of-powers questions raised by a Chief Justice's active attempts to influence a President in his choice of Court appointees. Working through Attorney General Harry Daugherty, Taft advised Harding on candidates for every Court vacancy that appeared during the Harding Administration, and tried, with less success, to continue this pattern with President Coolidge and his Attorney General, Harlan Fiske Stone. He also kept an eye on the lower federal and state courts, and worried about the growing reputations of Cardozo and Hand.[26]

Taft could not control the actual nominee, merely influence the class of candidates. In one case he had very little influence on a nomination, although he was entirely in sympathy with Harding's choice. On becoming President, Harding had already committed himself to appointing George Sutherland, a former Republican Senator from Utah. Sutherland had been a close consort of Harding in the 1920 campaign and had earlier made a reputation in the Senate as a conservative intellectual theorist with a special interest in law and the judiciary. "Conservative" was a description Sutherland applied to himself.[27] He associated the term with suspicion of majoritarian government, resistance to legislative solutions to social problems, assertions of the primacy of individual civil rights and liberties against the government, and a role for appellate judges as guardians of private rights against the usurpations of majorities.[28] He had developed these views as early as 1895, deriving them largely from reading Herbert Spencer and Cooley.[29] Unlike that of Van Devanter, Sutherland's ideological stance was fully worked out and well known by the time of his appointment. As early as 1909, Taft had recognized Sutherland as "ideally" suited for the Court,[30] and in 1921 he wrote Sutherland that "our views are very much alike."[31]

Sutherland was Harding's second appointment, the first vacancy having been the position of Chief Justice. At the time of Harding's nomination it was noted that several Court vacancies might soon occur, Justices Mahlon Pitney, William Day, Holmes, Joseph McKenna, and Chief Justice White being elderly or in ill health. Surprisingly, however, the next vacancy after White's death in 1921 was created by Justice Clarke's sudden resignation in September 1922. Clarke wrote Taft that he found the "trifling technical character" of his work oppressive.[32] Sutherland was immediately named Clarke's successor and was confirmed unanimously by the Senate, an endorsement not even Taft himself had received.

If Sutherland was a relatively known quantity when he joined the Court, the next Harding appointment, Pierce Butler, a Minnesota practitioner, was not. Butler, however, had three factors in his favor. He was a Catholic, a Democrat, and a friend of Taft. His religious and political affiliations were important because McKenna's impending retirement would leave no Catholic on the Court and because Harding's first two appointments had been prominent Republicans. His friendship with Taft was, of course, invaluable. Beyond those attributes, Butler seemingly had little to offer. His practice in St. Paul had made him well known to the railroad industry and its counsel,[33] but to few other lawyers. He did not approach the political or professional stature of other prospective nominees, such as John W. Davis or Senator Oscar Underwood of Alabama. The press, on his appointment, stressed his anonymity: the New York *World* said that his nomination "came as a complete surprise." [34] He had made no intellectual contributions, held no national professional office, argued only one case before the Supreme Court, and had been publicly identified exclusively as a railroad lawyer. Those who knew him found him a tenacious and resourceful advocate but a predictable and unsophisticated thinker.[35] Yet he emerged rapidly as the leading candidate to succeed Justice Day (who retired in November 1922) and, upon being nominated, was confirmed by the Senate by a vote of 61 to 8.

Butler owed his nomination essentially to the active support of Taft. John W. Davis was Taft's first choice, but when Davis withdrew his candidacy in October, Taft turned to Butler. Taft had known Butler from their mutual service in a 1921 arbitration proceeding involving the acquisition of a railroad by the Canadian government. Butler had represented Canada and Taft had been one of the arbitrators; they had stayed at the same Toronto hotel and had dined frequently together.[36] Near the close of the arbitration Taft was nominated to the Court and celebrated the occasion with Butler. The friendship was formed in propitious circumstances: Taft's memories of one of the proudest moments in his life were associated with Butler's presence. It took little effort for him to write Butler in late October 1922 that "it would delight me to have you on our Bench, and I think it quite within the bounds of possibility."[37]

With the aid of the politically skillful Van Devanter, who had become his closest confidant on the Court, Taft arranged for a show of strength in Butler's behalf. Support from various important groups was secured, including the senators from Minnesota, selected Catholic clergymen, the justices of the Minnesota Supreme Court, and certain prominent lawyers and law professors. Competitors, notably Nelson Phillips, former Chief Justice of the Texas Supreme Court, and Robert van Moschzisker, Chief Justice of the Supreme Court of Pennsylvania, were undermined. On November 23, 1922, Butler was appointed; about a month later he was confirmed.

Butler's appointment brought the third of the Four Horsemen onto the Court. Taft had been mightily pleased by all three nominations. He was temperamentally and ideologically congenial with all, enjoying close personal relations with Van Devanter and Butler and having high respect for Sutherland. The fourth of the Horsemen, however, was a source of real discomfort for Taft. In 1914 Woodrow Wilson had made his first appointment to the Court, naming James C. McReynolds his Attorney General. McReynolds came to his new office with a reputation for being an aggressive enforcer of the Sherman Anti-Trust Act; his nomination engendered some muttering about "radical elements" invading the Court. Once there, however, McReynolds revealed himself as uniformly and uncompromisingly hostile to any attempts to deviate from Fieldian jurisprudence, which he had learned from Professor John B. Minor at the University of Virginia Law School and which he described as a belief in the constancy of fundamental law.[38] He also impressed Taft as "selfish to the last degree," "fuller of prejudice than any man I have ever known," and a "continual grouch."[39] Taft particularly resented McReynolds's open hostility to other Justices, notably Brandeis and Clarke, feeling that this disrupted team spirit on the Court.

McReynolds, Taft said, seemed to delight in making others uncomfortable.[40] He combined a singular narrow-mindedness with a zeal for communicating his antagonisms to others. He disliked, among other things, red nail polish on women and wristwatches on men, rare meat, tobacco, having his portrait painted, any apparent slight on the dignity of the Court, such as whispering from the audience during an argument or improper protocol toward Justices at social functions, insincerity, flattery, dancing, athletics, "un-Americans," and "political subversives." Many things offended him and, once offended, his estrangements were long and total. He refused altogether to speak to Justice Clarke and did not sign Clarke's or Brandeis's retirement letters. The combination of "radicalism" and Judaism in Brandeis was more than he could bear—and later Cardozo and Felix Frankfurter were anathema to him on similar grounds. These attitudes, when coupled with his outspoken criticism of the New Deal, made him the most vilified of the Four Horsemen. In the 1930s, when his opposition to New Deal legislation had become evident, he was called the Court's "greatest human tragedy," the "narrowest, rudest, and laziest man on the bench," a "flauntingly disagreeable character," and a "savagely sarcastic, incredibly reactionary" Puritan anti-Semite.[41]

As a composite, the Four Horsemen were less than monolithic. Two were Republicans and two Democrats; three were Westerners and one, McReynolds, a Southerner. Two, McReynolds and Butler, were aggressive in their personal relations; the other two were relatively amiable. Three of the four had no particular intellectual interests; the fourth, Sutherland, was something of a scholar. Each, at some point in his career, had been involved in a reform movement: workmen's compensation for Sutherland and Butler, public-land management for Van Devanter, trust-busting for McReynolds. Each developed a specialized area of competence as a Justice: Van Devanter was an expert on jurisdictional disputes, Sutherland on wages-and-hours legislation, Butler on rate valuation, and McReynolds on public education. As personalities they were easily distinguishable: Van Devanter was taciturn, persistent, persuasive, and resourceful; Sutherland was alternately remote and gregarious, caustic and gentle, diffident and impassioned; Butler was stubborn, domineering, heavy-handed, blunt, and sanctimonious; McReynolds was irascible, eccentric, austere, and belligerent.

The Four Horsemen were primarily united by the ideological

convictions of their early maturity. They were all born between 1859 and 1866; they had received their education in the 1880s; they had first achieved professional prominence around the turn of the century. Whether Cleveland Democrats or Harrison Republicans, they were men in the mold of Spencer and Field. Thus, the universe was governed by inexorable laws; certain rights were inalienable; the Constitution was an unchanging document; the judiciary was a refuge against the excesses of the populace. They did not resist change so long as it was not accompanied by revolutionary rhetoric; they would suffer tinkering with any of the institutions of government so long as the essential balance of its functions was not disturbed. In the willing company of Taft and Edward Sanford, appointed by Harding in 1923, from that year to 1930 they formed an unchanging majority that calmly resisted a too-rapid extension of governmental powers and solemnly espoused the tenets of oracular judging. Their views, through the 1920, were controversial, perhaps antiquated, but still respectable. Their reputation changed, however, when in the wake of economic depression and social dislocation the nation suddenly abandoned the jurisprudence of the late nineteenth century and they clung stubbornly and aggressively to it. The result was a perception on the four Justices' part that "the Constitution as many of us have understood it . . . has gone," [42] and a corresponding perception by some commentators on the Court that a bloc of Justices existed whose views were, almost overnight, obsolete.

II

In an age where poverty is defined as a social condition rather than a failure of individual initiative and where the extent to which the federal government regulates certain sectors of the economy has become simply a matter of administrative choice, it may be difficult to imagine the shock waves sent through the nation by the collapse of the stock market in 1929 and the ensuing depression. Financial panics and depressions were not new to Americans, but a realization of the interdependence and vulnerability of their economic system was. In the 1890s a depression was ended by the simple fact of a failure of the European wheat harvest. In 1907 a pooling of funds by private bankers prevented the imminent failure of less solvent banks whose demise might have had widespread ramifications for the economy at large. In the 1920s and 1930s, by contrast, the clientele of the stock market had become so diversified and the purchasing power of European nations had so deteriorated that no comparable stopgap solution was possible. When the market crashed, it destroyed countless savings accounts and sharply reduced consumer demand. The American free-enterprise system, by the 1920s, was increasingly consumer-oriented. When consumer credit vanished overnight, there was suddenly no demand for products in America and no other available world market.

The business community, then, could not right itself or look to exports as a safety valve as it had been able to in the recent past. It was too much affected by the securities system of investment and too wedded to the purchasing power of American consumers. The Hoover Administration did not sufficiently recognize these facts and attempted to secure improvement in economic conditions, first, by pronouncements intended to restore public confidence in business and, later, by surrogate devices to pool private capital, such as government loans to banks and insurance companies. These policies had little impact inasmuch as they were unresponsive to the sharply reduced assets of individual consumers. As the Depression deepened in the 1930s, a sense that the free-enterprise system could not solve its own problems became more widespread. Alternative economic philosophies were discussed, from communism to fascism, both of which had been initiated in Europe. The businessman became a figure of pathos rather than a success model; the get-rich-quick spirit of the 1920s turned sour. Government involvement in private economic affairs was increasingly seen as necessary. Classic tenets of American civilization, such as self-help and free competition, were labeled mythologies. Human fallibility became a common theme. Institutions and enterprises were seen as being as impermanent and vulnerable as the individuals who managed them.

In this mood the nation was hardly responsive to a philosophy of government that stressed the autonomy of private rights, especially the right to hold and use property free of governmental interference; that proclaimed the omniscience of law and the innate wisdom of its judicial interpreters; and that insisted that legislative encroachments on the affairs of individual citizens and their corporate enterprises be kept to a minimum. Yet that was the philosophy of the Four Horsemen, as it had been of Field. At another time, that philosophy had harmonized admirably with the expansive, production-oriented economy of the nineteenth century. In the 1930s it was radically out of joint. It resisted social welfare legislation while the class of economically and socially disadvantaged persons in America continued to expand. It opposed governmental control of business while the "business community" appeared increasingly monolithic and increasingly incapable of controlling its own fortunes. It was wedded, by the 1930s, to jurisprudential assumptions that had been exposed and criticized for nearly a generation. It asserted that the Constitution was unchanging in its precepts at a time when pressure for change was acute; it proclaimed a passive, oracular view of judges in the teeth of a modern jurisprudential school that stressed their capacity to "make" law; it remained hostile to legislative or executive experimentation in a period when the President of the United States had described his election as a mandate to experiment at all costs. It was a philosophy clearly inimical to the New Deal, and if the spirit of the New Deal was to prevail, it would have to be discredited.

Symbolic tests of the Court's adherence to that philosophy of government were not long in coming. In 1934 the constitutionality of two Depression-related state statutes was challenged: one, a Minnesota law placing a moratorium on the foreclosure of mortgages, the other a New York law fixing the price of milk. Both were sustained by the Court in 5–4 decisions.[43] In each, Van Devanter, Sutherland, Butler, and McReynolds dissented *en bloc*. They found the Minnesota statute violative of the impairment-of-contracts clause, and through McReynolds, they described the New York statute as having "no reasonable relation to something within legislative power." [44] Their dissents were more than quarrels with the result reached by the majority; they found the techniques by which those results had been reached equally offensive.

The composition of the Court changed with Taft's retirement and subsequent death in 1930. Hughes, who had resigned to run for President in 1916, was reappointed Chief Justice by Hoover. Holmes finally retired, after thirty years on the bench, and was replaced by Cardozo. Owen Roberts, a Pennsylvania Republican who had prosecuted members of the Harding Administration for their involvement in the Teapot Dome scandals and whose political and social views were relatively unknown, succeeded Sanford, who had died suddenly on March 8, 1930, the same day as Taft. As

New Deal legislation came to the Court, two identifiable blocs developed, the Four Horsemen in opposition and, in support, Brandeis, Cardozo, and Stone, whom Taft, to his great regret, had by 1928 come to call "entirely subservient to Holmes and Brandeis." [45] Thus, the life of New Deal programs apparently depended on the votes of Hughes and Roberts.

The first controversial case passed on by the Court in 1935 [46] challenged, among other things, the constitutionality of a section of the National Industrial Recovery Act, which authorized the President to prohibit interstate shipment of oil produced in excess of state production quotas. In an 8–1 decision the Court found the section unconstitutional as an excessive delegation of Congressional power to the Executive. Power to regulate commerce was reserved to Congress, the Court argued. If it were to be delegated to another branch of government, sufficient standards controlling that branch's discretionary actions had to accompany the delegation. The decision, in which Hughes, Roberts, Stone, and Brandeis joined the Four Horsemen, suggested that any piece of New Deal legislation containing delegations of Congressional power to agencies, either executive or administrative, might be vulnerable to constitutional attack.

The breadth of the Court's opposition to this piece of New Deal legislation was surprising. The next group of cases, which tested the power of Congress to devalue gold currency through a joint resolution passed in 1933, produced a somewhat more predictable result. [47] Holders of gold certificates and bonds claimed payment in pre-devaluated gold, maintaining that Congress could not impair the obligations of pre-existing contracts that contained clauses protecting the holders from devaluation. The Court, in its decision, distinguished between certificates and bonds, holding that Congress could affect existing obligations with regard to certificates but not to bonds. It further held, however, that the bondholders had not shown that they were actually damaged by receiving face value for their bonds instead of the pre-devaluated equivalent. Hence they could recover only face value.

The decision produced an outraged extemporaneous dissent from McReynolds, who spoke in open court on behalf of himself, Van Devanter, Sutherland, and Butler. As a result of the decision, McReynolds claimed, "the powers of Congress have been enlarged to such an extent that no man can foresee their limitations." The refusal of the government to meet its obligations in pre-devaluated gold was "horrible dishonesty." "Shame and humiliation" were upon the Court that had sanctioned the scheme.[48] Later McReynolds was to say that he had not wanted to deliver the dissent in the *Gold Clause* cases, "but the others were insistent." The experience, he said, "took a good deal out of me." [49] Wanting, however, "to attract sharp attention to the true situation," [50] McReynolds agreed to have his remarks published in the *Wall Street Journal*.

Following the *Gold Clause* cases, the Four Horsemen embarked on a course of undeviating resistance to any legislation they could identify as inconsistent with their philosophy of government. This included federal statutes delegating power to executive officers; [51] federal social welfare legislation such as the Railroad Retirement Act of 1934, which provided pensions for railroad employees; [52] federal laws conferring tax subsidies or other special benefits on disadvantaged groups; [53] federal legislation fixing prices or regulating hours and wages; [54] legislation making the federal courts available for bankruptcy proceedings of municipalities; [55] and state legislation providing minimum wages for women,[56] and providing unemployment compensation.[57] In each of these cases they had the support of at least one other member of the court, usually Justice Roberts. In each case they disrupted the social and economic planning ventures of the New Deal.

In the election campaign of 1936 President Roosevelt was silent on the Court's opposition to his programs, but others quickly identified the Court as a center of anti-New Deal sentiment. Roosevelt's decisive victory could have been interpreted as a mandate for Court reform, and in February 1937 the President announced his celebrated plan to "pack" the Court with additional Justices in the event that sitting Justices who had reached age seventy did not retire. Since only Roberts, Stone, and Cardozo were under seventy in 1937, the plan would have given Roosevelt six additional appointments—enough, when added to the existing bench, to secure a majority apparently sympathetic to the New Deal. The plan's weakness as a political stratagem was that it chose to ignore differences in social philosophy between the Roosevelt Administration and the Court and to emphasize "neutral" factors such as age and workload instead. Although this avoided partisan debate on the Court's decisions, it linked Justices Brandeis and Hughes (both over seventy), with the Four Horsemen and provoked Hughes to make an impassioned defense of the Court's efficiency. The plan hence came to be perceived as an attack on the institutional integrity of the Court rather than as a protest against obsolete interpretations of the Constitution, and that perception was eventually fatal to its implementation.

The covert message of the Court-packing nonetheless reached Justice Roberts, whose decisive role in changing the course of Court decisions in 1937 led one commentator to call him "the perfect personification of the chanciness of government by judges" and "the most powerful person in the United States." [58] Sometime in January 1937, when a case testing the constitutionality of a Washington state minimum-wage statute—essentially similar to the New York statute invalidated during the preceding past term—was argued before the Court and voted on in conference, Roberts changed his position to sustain the statute. Roberts's vote predated the president's announcement of his Court-packing plan in February. It has been alleged [59] that Hughes, anticipating or perhaps knowing of the plan, had persuaded Roberts to uphold the Washington law. The Court's decision was announced in March and hailed as an index of a changing posture toward the New Deal. In it the Court not only maintained that freedom of contract—a means of invalidating the New York statute—appeared nowhere in the Constitution, it moreover stated that "superven[ing] economic conditions" compelled a "fresh consideration" of the utility of social welfare legislation.[60] In the light of those conditions, the Court argued, the New York decision was no longer good law, and the 1923 *Adkins v. Children's Hospital* [61] decision, invalidating a District of Columbia minimum wage law, was discredited.

During the same term the new Court majority moved to extend its impact. It sustained the constitutionality of the Wagner Labor Relations Act, which guaranteed the right of collective bargaining to workers in interstate commerce.[62] It asserted, in a related case, the right of newspaper employees to organize in unions.[63] It prohibited the use of injunctions against picketing employees, even if the purpose of the picketing was to coerce an employee to join a union.[64] And in perhaps the most far-reaching set of decisions of the 1930s, it sustained the old-age benefit and unemployment compensation provisions of Alabama's [65] and the federal government's [66] social security laws, thus clearing the way for the imposition of social insurance programs.

All these decisions were reached over the protests of the Four Horsemen. In the Washington minimum-wage case Sutherland, for the group, stated that the only means of implementing wages and hours legislation was through constitutional amendment. In the labor relations cases McReynolds and Sutherland reaffirmed the autonomy of private employers to hire and fire on whatever terms they chose. In the picketing case Butler dissented for himself and the other three; in both social security cases the Four Horsemen dissented wholly or in part. Realizing that his hour had come, Van Devanter became the first Justice to receive the benefit of the new statute allowing Justices to retire at full pay by announcing his intention to leave the Court at the end of the 1936 term.

With Van Devanter replaced by Senator Hugo Black of Alabama, the Court continued to tolerate of New Deal experiments, while the remaining three Horsemen continued their protest. Justice Roberts, underscoring his changed attitude, upheld a marketing quota provision of the 1938 Agricultural Adjustment Act, even though it seemed to regulate production no less than had the first Act, which he had declared unconstitutional.[67] The Court validated a municipal bankruptcy statute virtually indistinguishable from one it had struck down in 1935;[68] demonstrated its support for federal legislation regulating utilities;[69] indicated more sympathy for administrative regulation by allowing agencies to correct their own procedural errors without the necessity of court intervention;[70] and suggested that in the future it would not usually exercise a strict scrutiny of economic regulatory schemes drafted by state legislatures.[71]

Sutherland, Butler, and McReynolds continued to resist these trends, each increasingly alone as his confreres passed on. Sutherland retired in January 1938; Butler died in November 1939; McReynolds retired in February 1941. In McReynolds's last years he stood, one critic wrote, "like the boy on the burning deck amidst what obviously appears to him to be the imminent destruction of the old constitutional system."[72] Only Sutherland escaped the crisis of 1934–36 with his reputation intact. He had so eloquently articulated the theoretical underpinnings of Fieldian jurisprudence that his opposition to the New Deal seemed on a higher level. Although more of his opinions have been overruled than those of any other Justice, he has been treated, thus far, more charitably than have the other Horsemen.[73]

There has been a certain irony in the classification of the Four Horsemen as "failures." They were remarkably successful at resisting change past the point where it seemed inevitable. Their success underscores the variety of ways in which a Justice can achieve a position of real influence on the Supreme Court. Van Devanter found writing so difficult that he could barely turn out five opinions a year, but he came to conference with his ideas well developed and his arguments marshaled, thus possibly securing votes before any writing began. Butler was not always adept at the niceties of an argument, but could be counted on to maintain his views with firmness and resolution. McReynolds was often offensive and rarely congenial, but was endowed with the single-mindedness and passion of a zealot. Sutherland could be counted on to grace a seemingly reactionary position with appeals to time-honored American values. When the Four Horsemen saw their conception of the Constitution coming under attack in the early 1930s, they moved to consolidate their views, meeting Friday evenings before the Saturday conferences so that they might secure and present a united front. Their single-mindedness enhanced their power. In a Court at a crossroads point in its history, they were confident in their understanding of what the Constitution said and what a judge could do under it.

III

The Four Horsemen were seen as notorious because their uncompromising resistance to change exposed the mythic character of their jurisprudence. They believed, and maintained, that the Constitution was intended not to change with time, that its strictures against governmental regulation of the economy were permanent, and that its exaltation of the judiciary as a buffer for property rights was one of the fundamentals of American political thought. But by the 1930s it had become painfully obvious that these interpretations were in need of modification. History had shown the Constitution capable of change through means other than by amendment. The origins of a negativist interpretation of the Constitution, which emphasized its limitations on the power of legislatures, had not appeared until after the Civil War. Judges had not always protected property, nor had the kind of property they protected always been the same. A link between, on one hand, the value of freedom to transact one's business without governmental interference and, on the other, an implicit conferral of power on judges who used their office to safeguard that value, had not been forged until late in the nineteenth century. The link had itself been the product of a new interpretation of the Constitution that harmonized with new economic conditions. Why should this particularized view, with its distinctive historical origins, be frozen forever in time?

The social climate that engendered the New Deal reinforced the need for an adaptive theory of the Constitution and a conception of judging as an exercise in political innovation. The Four Horsemen, having implicitly accepted judicial glosses on the Constitution in a late-nineteenth-century context, sought to deny that glosses were permissible in the 1930s. Their protest against innovative judging revealed itself as a preference for one set of economic and social views over another. It was not compelled by the nature of the Constitution or the function of the judiciary, despite the Four Horsemen's claims to the contrary. The old conundrum that Holmes had propounded for late-nineteenth-century mechanical jurisprudes returned to plague Van Devanter and his colleagues: Who is to say that the Constitution is designed to favor the majoritarian thinking of one generation over that of another? Trapped by this argument, the Four Horsemen had only two choices, to declare openly their philosophical commitments or to retreat to mechanical jurisprudence. Opting for the second course, they made the theory of oracular judging appear to be a fiction.

Thus, as the Four Horsemen came to be perceived as notorious, the oracular conception of the appellate judiciary passed into oblivion. That theory had died hard. Marshall had impressively articulated it, Shaw had shaped it to the conditions of mid-nineteenth-century life, Field had demonstrated its usefulness to particularistic late-nineteenth-century goals, Taft and his colleagues had salvaged it despite an open challenge from Holmes. The Four Horsemen participated in its demise, with their sometime ally, Justice Roberts, unwittingly caricaturing its canons of judicial decision-making in the *Butler* opinion. "When an act of Congress is appropriately challenged in the courts as not conforming to the constitutional mandate," Roberts wrote in *Butler*, "the judicial branch of the Government has only one duty—to lay the article of the Constitution which is invoked beside the statute which is challenged and to decide whether the latter squares with the former." [74] The passive role painted for the judiciary by this description was so patently bogus, in the face of fifty years of active resistance on the part of the Court to legislative experimentation, that it undermined the credibility of the oracular theory and its attendant conception of law as a body of timeless principles waiting to be discovered. Hughes had said, twenty years before the stock market crashed, that the Constitution is what judges say it is; few were willing to refute that observation after the Court-packing crisis.

Realism was the jurisprudence most congenial with the New Deal. Judges were human, motivated in their decisions by individual subjective prejudices. [75] The Court-packing plan was consistent with Realism, since its advocates assumed that an individual's social and political views were sufficiently discernible to allow others to predict how he would vote as a judge, and that votes, not reasons, determined the path of constitutional law. For Realists the Four Horsemen merely exposed the dangers of the judicial selection process. Their presence was offensive not because they shaped the Constitution to fit their preconceived views—all judges did that—but because those views were out of touch with contemporary conditions. The remedy was not to eliminate judicial glosses on the Constitution—those were inevitable—but to change the Court's personnel. Viewed in this light, American constitutional history had been a series of minor Court-packing plans. Jackson had chosen Taney to replace Marshall; the Court had been expanded to reverse the first *Legal Tender* decision; a series of indistinguishable property-conscious Judges had been appointed by indistinguishable property-conscious Presidents from the Civil War to the 1930s, excepting only those dissenters (Holmes, Brandeis) appointed by unorthodox Presidents (Theodore Roosevelt, Woodrow Wilson). The final proof of the validity of Realism, in the minds of its supporters, was Roberts. As he changed his mind, so changed the meaning of the Constitution.

But if the Four Horsemen were for some a testament, however unpleasant, to the "reality" that judges made law, they were for others a justification for building additional contraints into the process of judging, so that Realism was not an invitation for judicial arbitrariness. The actions of the Court in the 1930s appeared so

transparently political, and the reasoning of many decisions so tor-
tured, that critics began to ask whether any stature remained in the
judicial branch of government. Although Realists were prepared to
admit that the Court was a political institution, the combination of
political consciousness and inept reasoning seemed to threaten the
integrity of the judiciary. Thus were the seeds of yet another jurisprudential school inadvertently planted by the Four Horsemen.
This school was built on the assumption of the Realists that judges
"made" law, but went beyond to suggest that political and social
predilections were only one component of judicial decision-making.
Another and more important component was the articulation of
those predilections in a manner that secured general acceptance of
the position advanced and thereby legitimated the desired result.
The attention of this school was directed primarily at the reasoning
process of opinions. As critics, its members were less interested in
where a judge came out than in how he got there. Implicitly, in this
emphasis, the role of institutional constraints in judging was revived. Reasoning was a means by which the judge communicated
the fact that his preferences were more than idiosyncratic. His
reasons demonstrated that his choices transcended his own biases to
rest on values held by large segments of the American public.
When a judge properly reasoned in this manner, he demonstrated
that he was more than an individual voice; he became a repository
of social wisdom. He was constrained, in a democratic society, by
his own analytical powers. He was required to make reasoned
rather than arbitrary decisions precisely because his office gave him
the opportunity to exercise arbitrary power.

The gradual emergence of this approach to appellate decisions
and the consequent decline in the influence of Realism came well after
the last of the Four Horsemen had left the Court. But the Four
Horsemen had been more than the last representatives of the oracular theory of judging. They had also provided a powerful counterargument to Realism, for they showed how easily the judiciary
could perpetuate obsolete social views. Ironically, they thought of
their jurisprudence as one of constraints—the constraints of tradition, definiteness, and permanency that they saw embodied in the
Constitution. Their attributed notoriety, in the final analysis, came
from a failure to perceive, or at least to admit, that the Constitution
contained ambiguities, not absolute truths, and that the process of
judging was one of temporarily choosing among competing princi-

ples more than one of declaring the law for all time. By this failure they invited critics to find them misguided on their first principles: expounders of the perfect symmetry and unity of a jurisprudence whose time had passed.

10

Hughes and Stone: Ironies of the Chief Justiceship

The catchphrase "first among equals" both reveals and obfuscates the role of the Chief Justice of the United States Supreme Court. The Chief Justice is a person with one vote in conference and one mind with which to make his presence felt. Often, though not always, his colleagues are his intellectual superiors, and sometimes Associate Justices dominate a Court, as with the Chase Court and to a lesser extent the Waite and Fuller Courts. Relations among those who occupy the office of Supreme Court Justice are shaped by the pride in self and status that accompanies the possession of that office. No member of the Court can fairly think of another as his subordinate, nor expect to be so perceived by his colleagues. In addition, the internal rituals of the Court reflect, to an extent, an institutional attempt to foster feelings of equality. Notes and memoranda are exchanged, critical comments are made, independence is asserted, heated discussion is anticipated, strength of character and conviction is valued even among antagonists. The Chief Justice presides, to be sure, over arguments, conferences, and other functions, but he also listens and defers and yields.

The Chief Justice can thus be said to be "among equals," and members of the Court—especially Chief Justices—have suggested that the "firstness" of the office is merely perfunctory and ceremonial. But this has not been true since Marshall's tenure. The office of Chief Justice has carried with it a special influence, an extra dimension of power, added opportunities to make one's mark in history. Among the perquisites of the Chief Justiceship is the possibility of leading a Court in more than formal ways. Not all Chiefs have chosen to exercise this kind of leadership, and some have tried and failed. But the possibility remains attached to the office. Marshall not only bequeathed a general legacy of judging to the Justices that followed him, he also left a special legacy to his successor Chiefs, a legacy that included a tradition of unanimity in Court decision-making, a sense of the delicate and ambivalent political position of the Court in the processes of American government, and a custom of forceful executive leadership in the Chief Justice. Marshall had built this legacy in numerous ways, among them his substitution of an opinion by the Court for the customary seriatim opinions; his insistence that members of the Court not engage openly and actively in partisan politics; his assignment of important opinions to himself or to Story, his trusted delegate; his subterranean efforts to disseminate his ideas beyond the courtroom and to vindicate his positions against attack.[1]

I

None of Marshall's nineteenth-century successors was able to preserve intact the combination of personal and political influence he passed on to them with his office. Taney was more permissive toward dissent and somewhat less astute as a political statesman. He dominated his Court to a lesser degree than did Marshall and saw it lose stature as a repository of political wisdom. Chase was embroiled in the *Legal Tender* controversy almost immediately after taking office and failed to divorce his office from his Presidential ambitions, thereby losing the respect of his colleagues. Waite fought cheerfully and not always unsuccessfully against the apparent inevitability of Field's ideas, but became increasingly overshadowed. Fuller came to the office with ordinary intellectual talents and little professional reputation, and managed to remain obscure even though he was regularly in sympathy with the majority views of his Court.

The strong Chief Justice apparently returned with the twentieth-century appointments of White and Taft. Holmes had felt that, next to himself, White was the finest intellect on the Fuller Court.[2] Not a man to change his mind in the face of opposition, White did not shrink from attempting to exercise influence over others. Taft, for his part, came to the office with experiences and lines of communication that no previous Chief had ever had. But two changes coinciding with the advent of the twentieth century were, in separate ways, to limit the power of both White and Taft. First, the business of the Court was to grow to the point where the Chief Justice's administrative duties took on a new dimension. Second, the Court developed a reputation as a leading source of resistance to social change.

At the opening of the 1870 term the Court had 636 cases listed for decision. Five years later, Congress passed the Judiciary Act of 1875,[3] which expanded the jurisdiction of the federal courts to include "federal question" disputes and a full range of diversity-of-citizenship cases, when the alleged damages exceeded $1000. The effect of this Act was to increase greatly the Court's docket.[4] In addition, from 1866 to 1889 direct review to the Court was expanded, encompassing civil rights,[5] patents,[6] jurisdictional questions,[7] and habeas corpus petitions.[8] Furthermore, the practice of lower federal judges of certifying questions for guidance by the Court was eliminated by statute in 1872,[9] and in its place the Court was authorized to review on appeal cases in which federal circuit court judges had evidenced differing views.

In 1891 Congress passed the Everts Act,[10] which attempted to meet the problem of overcrowded Court dockets. The Act created three-judge circuit courts of appeals as intermediaries between the federal district courts and the Supreme Court, and restricted the means of appeal to the Court by introducing discretionary certiorari power, through which the Court could decline to hear selected cases if a given number of Justices felt that the case was not of sufficient importance. Denial of a certiorari petition meant that the decision of the Circuit Court was upheld. The certiorari power, however, did not extend to all cases, and between 1891 and 1925, when another Congressional statute [11] attempted to reduce the Court's workload, the docket continued to expand. Major increases in population, a more extensive governmental administrative apparatus, and other less perceptible factors accounted for this trend. By the time of Taft's tenure the certiorari power was seen as the Court's principal means of keeping abreast of its work.[12]

White's Chief Justiceship showed the increased importance of administrative ability in the Court's presiding officer. Fuller was "extraordinary" as an administrator, according to Holmes. "He had the business of the court at his fingers' ends; he was perfectly courageous, prompt, dedicated. He turned off the matters that daily call for action easily, swiftly, with the least possible friction . . . and with a humor that relieved any tension with a laugh." [13] Holmes thought these qualities helpful but trivial. Others, such as Charles Evans Hughes, found them more important.

Hughes came on the Court in 1910, at the same time that White was named Chief Justice. Later Hughes was to remember White's habits of stating cases imprecisely at conference, offering virtually no suggestions as to how to dispose of each case, and allowing discussion to ramble. [14] During White's tenure the Court was not clear about how to make use of its new certiorari power and suffered from a haphazard management of its docket. It might begin a term behind in its work, then allow more important cases to be pushed ahead, so that it often ended in June with a backlog of over a hundred undisposed cases. [15] The experience taught Hughes a lesson he was to put into practice: an efficient, well-organized Chief could not only manage his docket but increase his power in the process.

Taft succeeded at administration where White had failed. He helped push through Congress the Judiciary Act of 1925, which reorganized the federal courts and put teeth in the certiorari power. During his tenure the practice of assigning to each Justice a law clerk (first called a secretary) to help with certiorari petitions and other research was adopted generally. He pressed his colleagues to keep up with their workload. He asserted himself, in his own genial fashion, in conference. But the very sources of Taft's strength were also sources of weakness. He cajoled and pressured his brethren toward unanimity and consistency in their decisions and took pride in the regular triumph of his views, but he unwittingly painted for the nation a picture of the Court as a monolith of reaction, asserting the beliefs of the late nineteenth century in a changed world.

The leadership patterns of White and Taft indicated means by which twentieth-century Chief Justices could exercise or fail to exercise leadership. The first means, of ever increasing importance, was through administration of the Court's internal business. Faced with a massive docket, armed with a research staff and the certiorari power, entrusted with the duty of organizing and presiding over conferences, allotted the increasingly important task of summarizing the work to be taken up at a conference, the Chief Justice could shape the Court's business in a fashion convenient to himself, thereby making administration an exercise in maintaining power and perpetuating of influence. A second means was through scholarly exchange. The Chief continued to be among equals, but enjoyed the privilege of stating his views first and voting last. An accomplished administrator could combine the first two means through careful selection of items for the agenda and sophisticated presentation of viewpoints affecting each item.

The third means was through political influence. Taft had been an artist at one sort of political involvement, but other, more symbolic options were open—e.g., speeches before professional groups, cultivation of an imposing manner of presiding over the Court, development of subtle but effective lobbying with Congress for accoutrements, an interest in the response of the nation's press to Court decisions. In each of these areas the twentieth-century Chief Justice was better suited to exert influence than any of his colleagues. He stood for and could shape his Court.

In the light of such opportunities, the careers of two prominent twentieth-century Chief Justices, Charles Evans Hughes and Harlan Fiske Stone, were fraught with ironies. The ironic cast of their respective Chief Justiceships came from the fact that performance expectations engendered by the image of each man on his confirmation as Chief were unrealized. Neither Hughes nor Stone can be said to have failed as Chief Justices. Their experience simply did not materialize as they and others expected it to. Their reputations were not necessarily damaged by the experience, but they were altered. Their tenures reveal the complexity and uncertainty of the process of holding the office of Chief Justice of the Supreme Court.

In Hughes's case the central irony concerned his management of his office. It appeared at the time of his nomination that no man had ever come to the Chief Justiceship better suited to perform its duties. Hughes was the embodiment of the modern Chief Justice. He was conspiciously efficient, ideologically receptive to progress and reform, aloof from partisan politics, of immense public stature, with wide-ranging contacts in all branches of government and influential sectors of private enterprise, possessed of superior qualities as an intellectual technician, and experienced as a Supreme Court Justice. If ever an individual seemed matched to the needs of an office, it was Hughes: the modern Chief for a Court adapting itself to New Deal America. And yet under Hughes the Court first isolated itself from the mood of the nation, then painfully and embarrassingly embraced it, revealed itself as being polarized and rancorous, saw its autonomy and even its composition threatened, and lost its aloofness from politics. Hughes himself was not responsible for most of these difficulties, but he was powerless to alleviate them and may even have exacerbated them.

In the case of Stone the ironies were strikingly different. Upon his appointment to the Court as an Associate Justice, Stone became a marginal member of the Taft majority. Yet before long he found himself increasingly quarreling with that majority's premises, and, on the Hughes Court, siding with those Justices who supported New Deal experimental legislation. Eventually this group itself became a majority, one apparently committed to sympathetic treatment of the policies of the Roosevelt Administrations. In short, Stone became Chief Justice of a Court whose personnel increasingly supported positions he had held under fire and seen vindicated. Yet under Stone the new majority fell out among themselves, both personally and ideologically, so that the expectations of the nation—as expressed by the nation's press—of a new "liberal" monolith were dashed into fragments.

As in the case of Hughes, some of Stone's difficulties seemingly arose from factors over which he had no control. Fragmentation of the "liberal" Stone Court came in part from the fact that the issues confronted by the Court at the onset of the New Deal were somewhat different from those it would confront in the 1940s. Justices who agreed, for example, on the general principle of judicial permissiveness toward economic regulation might not agree on specific extensions of that principle, especially when those extensions affected institutional balances in a federalist system of government.[16] Fragmentation was related also to the consideration of altogether novel issues, such as the role of civil liberties in a society dominated as never before by statutory and administrative regulation. But it came as well from Stone's style of leadership. He was not able to coalesce his Roosevelt appointees into a majority that articulated a consistent, rounded philosophy of constitutional interpretation, although he had seemed, by reason of his acknowledged skills, his symbolic role in preceding Courts, and his strong and likable personality, eminently capable of such an achievement.

Both Hughes and Stone underwent experiences that symbolized

the ironies of their tenures. The unassailable, nonpartisan Hughes went hat in hand in 1937 to argue for the perpetuation of a nine-man Court before a Senate Committee. Stone, the Justice who had seen more of his dissents become majority positions than any other Justice in the Court's history, delivered as the last opinion of his life a dissent from one of those new majority decisions.[17] The position he had once espoused and the Court now adopted was, he maintained, no longer good law.

II

Hughes was an extraordinary person, it seemed, almost from the moment he was born. As a child his health was frail and his contacts with others minimal, but his intellectual powers were fearsome. A photographic memory, combined with an internalization of his parents' maxim to "be thorough in all you undertake,"[18] enabled him to excel in undergraduate classes at Madison College (now Colgate University) and Brown University, at Columbia Law School, and on the New York State bar examination, where he received the highest possible score.[19] For all his working life Hughes retained his obsession with thoroughness and his great capacity for amassing and organizing details. During his early career as a practitioner in New York, where he entered a partnership with Walter S. Carter and Paul D. Cravath, two founding fathers of modern Wall Street practice, Hughes mastered German and the intricacies of the sugar beet industry for one case so that he could cross-examine German engineers in connection with breakdowns in the operation of a sugar beet factory designed in Germany.[20] He could, one of his law clerks said, "read a paragraph at a glance, a treatise in an evening, a roomful of papers in a week";[21] he could also retain what he read to a remarkable degree. In this respect Hughes was an ideal investigator of complex businesses, such as the New York State gas utilities and insurance industry or the aircraft industry in World War I, or the armaments industries in the 1920s.

Hughes was an ideal early-twentieth-century investigator and administrator in two other respects. Like many others who saw themselves as "progressives," Hughes made a fetish of efficiency.[22] In his view, modern America had grown complicated and technocratic almost overnight, and hence careful, thorough management of private and public enterprise was essential to prevent disorderly and wasteful growth. His zeal for efficiency harmonized with his own intellectual abilities. His talents lay in sifting, organizing, and marshaling pieces of evidence rather than in imaginative or creative thought.[23] He associated efficiency with objectivity and nonpartisanship, two qualities he and numerous others of the time valued in public service. Moreover, as he matured he saw efficient administration as a means of acquiring and holding power.

The second quality that endeared Hughes to early-twentieth-century reformers was his combination of moral fervor and personal aloofness. Hughes's strong religious antecedents survived in his adulthood as a strong sense of duty. He had been filial toward his parents, despite his not opting for the ministry, as they had wished; likewise he was loyal to the perceived obligations of the offices he held, and he invariably interpreted them in moral terms. This meant rigid nonpartisanship as referee, arbitrator, investigator, or judge; strong commitment to social justice through efficient administration as Governor of New York; a certain forced buoyancy and conviviality coupled with Calvinistic patriotism as a Presidential candidate. In playing these various roles, Hughes seemed to hold something back. To those around him he appeared unapproachable, austere, and cold, and his career as an elected official may have suffered accordingly. But despite his concern that the public regarded him "as a human icicle,"[24] his aloofness may well not have been a disadvantage. He personified the reformer who was above politics, the man immune from corruption and special influence, committed only to the ideals of honest government, efficiency, and progress. In addition, detachment from the privileges and favors of his offices allowed Hughes to appear as a genuine public servant whose constituency was not the professional politicians but the people. This was a position he took seriously and an image he thought consonant with reality. "I am," he said during his tenure as Secretary of State, "counsel for the people of this country."[25] In other roles his assumed aloofness was a positive advantage. Felix Frankfurter said of Hughes as Chief Justice that he "acted on the realization that aloofness is indispensable to the effective discharge of the Supreme Court's functions."[26]

Hughes tried to appear human, and succeeded with some of his closest acquaintances. A shipmate on a European voyage found him "friendly and genial" rather than the "cold, detached, self-centered individual" he expected; [27] Holmes thought him "funny" and not altogether rigid in his "nonconformist conscience"; [28] Justice Roberts described him as "considerate, sympathetic, and responsive"; [29] Frankfurter felt him whimsical, genial, and mischievous. [30] His wife and children regularly received warm tributes of admiration and affection from him. [31] Others, however, persisted in thinking him remote. Herbert Hoover, one great admirer, said that he had "no instinct for personal friendship that I ever could discover." [32]

Hughes's personal characteristics so dominated his social attitudes that his ideological views resist characterization. He joined strongly held, quasi-religious convictions with a general desire to be thought of as a political moderate. So long as he appeared consistent to himself, he was not particularly concerned with how his actions were characterized by others, caring only that his views did not isolate him. He came to the career of judging with deep beliefs about the close connection between efficiency and justice. If persons in authority performed their tasks in an impartial and careful fashion, he reasoned, they would effectively serve the welfare of their constituents. "The more we study the problems of organization and method and appreciate the necessity of improvements in these respects," he wrote in 1931, "the more sensible we are that such improvements can serve only to clear the way for the essential judicial service which no unit of mechanization can supply." [33] Effective management and organization bred stability, stability was a necessary component of progress, and "growth and progress are the law of our nature." [34]

In some respects Hughes, as a judge, appeared to be a link to the Founding Fathers. [35] He believed that the structure of American government rested on delicate balances, such as that between individual autonomy and the demands of governing institutions, that between competing sovereign powers, federal and state, that between the respective branches of government, and that between the intentions of the framers and the open-ended content of the commerce, due process, and equal protection clauses. He tried to adapt this system of balances to an industrial, urbanized, polyglot society without essentially disturbing its equilibrium. This entailed a series of trade-offs. The commerce clause need not prohibit all forms of state taxation, [36] but it did prohibit some; Congress could regulate instrumentalities not used solely in interstate commerce, so long as they affected that commerce,[37] but sometimes factual investigations revealed that they did not affect it.[38] Administrative agencies could constitutionally make an independent, final determination of facts necessary to their decisions,[39] but a court, on review, could make its own factual determinations if the agency's action had adversely affected property rights.[40] Government infringements on civil liberties should be carefully scrutinized [41] and vigorously checked,[42] but not all libertarian interests were to be protected,[43] and the due process clause gave no greater safeguards to civil liberties than it did to property rights.[44]

The theme of moderation suggests itself in Hughes's balancing efforts and in certain of his public statements, such as his insistence in 1932 that judges "escape the errors of . . . extreme constructions" in constitutional adjudication.[45] But although Hughes liked to be thought of as a moderate, he was not, either temperamentally or ideologically. He was nervous, intense, and compulsive. He took long vacations to avoid undue mental strain; he abandoned smoking and adopted a regular routine of exercise as a defense against frequent headaches. He believed that a judge should "[do] his work in an objective spirit," [46] and, further, that a methodical analysis of the facts and issues in a case would result in an "objective" solution. When he had arrived at that solution, he regarded it not as a compromise or an exercise in political discretion, but as the correct result. He did not, in short, think of himself as being moderate, but as being right. Rightness and moderation were linked only because he perceived the Constitution's framers as having been moderates.

Yet Hughes attempted, as Chief Justice, to associate himself and his Court with the principle of moderation. He was himself inclined to strike balances and make fine factual distinctions in interpreting the Constitution, so that in being "moderate" he was often merely arguing for his own position. In addition, his Court was split into opposing factions whose presence Hughes wanted to conceal as much as possible from the public. Finally, as an administrator Hughes was committed to the principle of power maintenance through efficient and full use of management techniques, which in his case were substitutes for ideological compromises. The second and third of these comments require elaboration.

The Hughes Court was confronted with pressures for social change of an almost unprecedented magnitude. Not since the period of the Chase Court had the nation's social and economic

theories been in such turmoil; not since the Taney Court had the
consequences of Court involvement in political issues seemed so
grave; not perhaps since the Marshall Court had the Court's future
appeared so precarious. In addition, the Court's personnel appeared
singularly ill-equipped to respond to these pressures beyond merely
reflecting them. Between 1931, the year of Hughes's nomination,
and 1937, when Van Devanter resigned, the Court's composition
remained virtually fixed, Benjamin Cardozo replacing Holmes in
early 1932. In the same timespan Hoover was replaced by F. D.
Roosevelt, voting patterns were dramatically realigned, the capitalist system seemed close to collapse, Fascism and Communism entered expansionist phases in Europe, and the social programs of the
New Deal were launched. In the midst of this turmoil stood nine
Justices, only one of them under sixty when Roosevelt assumed office and only one of them graduated from law school in the twentieth century. It is remarkable that during these first six years any
of the Hughes Court Justices was capable of responding sympathetically to the proposed redistributions of political and economic
power that came before them. Those proposals were designed to
respond to the exigencies of what to the Justices must have seemed
a startlingly new world.

Brandeis and Cardozo were able to embrace some of the early
New Deal schemes because their interpretation of judging was in
some respects a passive one, and, to a lesser extent and in varying
degrees, because they were politically sympathetic to social experimentation in behalf of disadvantaged persons. Stone's enthusiasm
for the social welfare legislation was more subdued, and his conception of his office requires separate treatment. Stone's view, did,
however, enable him to tolerate some New Deal legislation, even
though he had once said that "abstract or social justice as a test for
the correctness of judicial decisions is absolutely without value." [47]
Consequently he often voted with Brandeis and Cardozo in the
Hughes Court, and was perceived by others on that Court as a
member of a faction, and by commentators as a "liberal" or a "Roosevelt" Justice.

For the first six years of the Hughes Court, between the Four
Horsemen and Brandeis, Cardozo, and Stone—who came to have
pre-conference meetings just as the Four Horsemen had their Friday night sessions—were Owen Roberts and Hughes. The thorn-
iest issues of those years involved the scope of Congress's com-

merce and taxing powers, a secondary issue being the extent to which Congress could delegate those powers to administrative agencies. The Four Horsemen held views, especially as to taxing and delegation, entirely consistent with late-nineteenth-century canons of constitutional interpretation and rigidly inimical to the New Deal. They added to these beliefs varying degrees of distaste for Roosevelt and his perceived philosophy of government, approaching the apoplectic in McReynolds. The Three Musketeers (as Learned Hand called Brandeis, Cardozo, and Stone [48]) were not so consistently inclined to support the New Deal as their antagonists were to oppose it, each having his own concerns about excessive delegations of power, bigness in government, or "double" taxation. But the mere fact that they supported the New Deal at all was enough to alienate them from the Four Horsemen. Roberts and Hughes, meanwhile, strove to maintain an intermediate position in strikingly different ways.

Roberts, who had been comfortable enough as counsel for the Pennsylvania Railroad and as a special prosecutor of the Harding Administration scandals, seemed in a daze on the Court. He would react to cases in political terms, then search for a jurisprudential position to justify his vote. Seizing on a theory of appellate judging, he would articulate it, doing it and himself a disservice in the articulation, and see it abandoned by his colleagues. After originally showing an inclination to support state regulatory legislation, Roberts began to show concern about a similar stance by the federal government. He was with a "New Deal" majority in the Gold Clause cases, [49] but then wrote an opinion for the Court denying that Congress had any power to pass compulsory pension legislation for railroad employees. [50] After the Railroad Pensions case, Roberts swung sharply against the philosophy of the Roosevelt Administration. Of eighteen cases involving government regulation of the economy in the 1935 term, he sustained the government's position in only three. [51]

Having felt the sting of academic criticism for his efforts, [52] Roberts then reacted to the Court-packing controversy by voting differently in two nearly indistinguishable cases in the 1937 and 1938 terms. He cast his lot, during the crisis, with the Roosevelt sympathizers, voting to sustain the National Labor Relations Act, which granted workers the right to organize and bargain collectively; [53] to uphold a Wisconsin statute prohibiting injunctive interference with picketing; [54] to uphold state [55] and federal [56] social security legislation; to sustain the revised Agricultural Adjustment Act of 1938; [57] to sustain a municipal bankruptcy statute [58] (although he had opposed a similar one two terms past [59]); and to allow government subsidies to public utilities. [60]

With the Court transformed by five new appointments between 1937 and 1939, Roberts altered his stance. He now decided that a too-swift overruling of previous precedents was jurisprudentially unsound, upsetting expectations on the part of persons whose conduct was guided by the Court's decisions. This position was a curious one for him to take in the light of his sudden transformations in the 1937 and 1938 terms, but he expounded it with considerable emotion. In one 1944 case distinguishing earlier precedents, Roberts said in dissent that the Court's opinion made the law "not a chart to govern conduct but a game of chance; instead of settling rights and liabilities it unsettles them." [61] In another, which in his opinion differed from the precedent it failed to follow by "not a fact . . . except the names of the parties," Roberts claimed that the Court's change of views "tends to bring adjudications of this tribunal into the same class as a restricted railroad ticket, good for this day and train only." [62] He suggested that since the bar, the lower courts and the public would be so confused by the sudden changes, the Justices should consider announcing ahead of time that they would change their minds on an issue the next time it was presented. [63]

However strong Roberts's commitment to institutional consistency, clear guidance, or literalism in constitutional interpretation, he was never able to shake the image of a Justice with vacillating social views and only a dim perception of the complexities of his job. He seemed, in his person, to associate moderation with fuzzy-mindedness. In contrast, Hughes associated it with aspirations to dominance.

Immediately on becoming Chief Justice, Hughes set out to meet the problem of increasing pressure on the Court's docket. He did this primarily through skillful use of the certiorari power. When certiorari petitions came to the Court, Hughes took it upon himself to read and summarize them all, weeding out some as easily disposable. The ones so designated went on a separate list before the Saturday conference. In conference Hughes attempted to average about three and one-half minutes for discussion of each certiorari petition, and since his preparation far exceeded that of the other justices, his views on petitions were seldom challenged. The result of Hughes's use of the certiorari power was not always, however, a restriction of access to the Court. As an example, he expanded the Court's scrutiny of *in forma pauperis* petitions to the point where habeas corpus arguments by prisoners became an important portion of the Court's docket.

Hughes used similar administrative techniques in the internal consideration of major cases. He came to the Saturday conference prepared to the hilt, opened discussion of each case with a short but comprehensive review of its issues, barely tolerated debate, and actively discouraged requests for more time to study or reflect on an issue. Some of his colleagues mocked his zeal for efficiency and order; others saw his practices as attempts to impose his views on others. Brandeis recalled ironically that the Saturday conferences lasted six hours and that Hughes did all the talking.[64] In Frankfurter's opinion Hughes saw the conference not as "a debating society" but as "a place where nine men do solos." [65] Stone believed that discussion of cases on the Hughes Court should have been "much fuller and freer." [66] President Roosevelt, who had misgivings about Hughes, was reported to have believed that he used his authority to steer the course of debate in conferences for the purpose of sowing discord among New Deal sympathizers.[67]

In fact, Hughes was far more interested in preventing the exposure of divisions within the Court, and in identifying himself with the least controversial position possible, than in seeing "conservative" or "liberal" views triumph. He continually strove to maintain the appearance of unanimity and nonpartisanship in Court opinions. If he believed the sentiments he expressed in 1928 that "unanimity which is merely formal, which is recorded at the expense of strong conflicting views, is not desirable in a court of last resort," [68] as Chief Justice he no longer believed them, or did not practice them. He took pains to assign opinions in such a way as to blunt the identification of any Justice with a partisan position. He sought to secure widespread support for moderate draft opinions. He filled his own opinions with careful distinctions intended to distinguish contrary precedents without overruling them. He rarely dissented, and he urged swift disposition of highly controversial cases, such as *Powell v. Alabama*,[69] one of the "Scottsboro Boys" cases, in order to cut down the amount of public attention focused on the Court.

The results of Hughes's drive for influence or authority through moderation were ambiguous. Despite his efforts, he was not able to influence any members of the Court to accept his jurisprudential views, with the imperfect and sporadic exception of Roberts. This was partly because Hughes's jurisprudence represented something of a balance between the Fieldian views of the Four Horsemen and the reformist stance for the judiciary advocated, in differing ways, by the Three Musketeers. Hughes offered no real alternative to either position, but simply blended them in an *ad hoc* fashion. Thus on occasion he was more capable of securing individual votes than philosophical conversions at large. Hughes's internal influence was also lessened, paradoxically, by the strategies he used to enhance the Court's stature. One Justice found that his technique of making decisions through a meticulous comparison of the facts of the case before the Court with those of arguably applicable precedents sometimes produced meaningless distinctions.[70] Another felt that Hughes was "unduly emphasizing keeping the dockets clear as against the quality of the clearing." [71] Hughes's administrative skills were frequently employed to the disadvantage of others: Justices were asked to write on a subject they did not enjoy,[72] or to write an opinion not squarely in keeping with their general inclinations; Justices' views were summarily dismissed or suppressed in discussion; Justices' strategies were outflanked by Hughes's sheer preparedness and forcefulness—in the words of Justice Robert Jackson, Hughes "look[ed] like God and talk[ed] like God." [73]

However much Hughes saw his task as one of minimizing and concealing tension among his colleagues, there is evidence he may have stimulated it. Though he may have tried to lead his Court on a narrow path out of the nineteenth century and not too far into the twentieth, there is evidence that the Court led him, staking out the poles as if on a magnetic field and drawing him this way and that. A dominant Chief Justice like none since Marshall, he could dominate in only minor ways. When he tried to achieve through administration what he could not through jurisprudence, he lost some of the harmony he sought.

Yet one hesitates to view Hughes as a captive or a victim of events. Another type of person fated to be Chief Justice in the Hughes Court might have accomplished far less and tarnished his reputation far more. Hughes, after all, overcame the Court-packing crisis (if he did help precipitate it), presided over a vast change in theories of constitutional adjudication without seeing his Court lose its identity, and successfully initiated administrative reforms to deal with the greatly increased business of the modern Court. Although he was not faultless as an administrator, he was far more adept than his successor, Harlan Stone. Although he had no well-rounded theory of judicial performance and no genuine consistency in his decision-making, he was dedicated to the preservation of an ideal for the Court—as a detached, impartial, efficient, dignified, and just institution—and he did not, at a time when myths were being exposed and idols shattered, make a mockery of that ideal.

III

In the last years of the Hughes Court there developed what might have seemed to the Chief Justice an example of history's perversity. Cases testing the limits of governmental control over the economy receded in importance as the Court's new majority coalesced in an unaccustomed attitude of broad tolerance toward regulatory legislation. Older suspicions of the constitutionality of administrative agencies vanished; the new major concerns of administrative law involved questions about the proper allocation of functions between courts and agencies.[74] Civil liberties issues began to receive serious attention for the first time in more than a decade, and some members of the Court began to doubt its apparent decision not to interfere with the determinations of legislatures if those determinations infringed on human rights.[75] Hughes had been least comfortable with the transition from the nineteenth century to the twentieth in the area of property rights; he could not bring himself to a ringing affirmation of the value of administrative regulation of private enterprise. But he had been a consistent supporter of civil liberties.[76] Had such cases been the meat of the New Deal Court he might have been able to exercise a Marshallian kind of substantive leadership.

As it was, the task of leading the new Court majority of the 1940s devolved on Harlan Stone. At a time when the Court was in

one of its most expansive, ebullient phases, Stone was committed to
a view of appellate judging that emphasized the unique role of the
judiciary in American government and the limitations on judicial
power implicit in that role. In a period when many members of the
Court appeared to share, in a surface way, predilections and values,
their Chief Justice was a man accustomed to looking beneath the
surface even if the search revealed new areas for disagreement. Although changes of personnel, the impact of the Court-packing plan,
and a shift of focus had produced strong expectations of a harmonious, active, reformist Court in the 1940s, the new Chief Justice was
a man who, for all his personal charm, had an administrative style
calculated to encourage dissent, disrupt harmony, and fragment reformist impulses.

Stone sought balance in his intellectual life as in his personal life,
but sought it with a certain passion and fierceness. He had grown
up in a spartan, enterpreneurial environment where economic scar-
city was a fact of life, and flush times an enticing dream. Once out
of that world he indulged himself in comforts of leisure, such as
fine wines and the arts, while retaining a sense that affluence ought
not to breed extravagance and that love of pleasure ought not in-
trude on good health. Unlike Hughes, Stone was not a compulsive
worker, nor remote in his personal contracts, nor lacking in humility. Like Hughes, however, he was tenacious in his views and confident of his intellectual powers. He probed to the heart of issues
until satisfied that he saw the value conflicts they revealed. He then
refused to rest in those conflicts, but pressed on to make a choice,
or to learn why he, as a judge, should not choose. In the course of
these inquiries he was not distracted by those who believed the
search futile or excessively time-consuming or impolitic, and he
rarely abided their counsel, even though he invited it.

The coexistence in Stone of humility and pride, open-mindedness and stubbornness, intemperance and a yearning for balance
made him interpret leadership roles in a distinctive way. He was
impulsive and sometimes indiscreet in stating his views on issues,
and might on occasion, after "sober second thought," [77] modify
his position, thereby giving a simultaneous impression of intellectual honesty and political naïveté. He was reluctant to assume leadership, declining the post of editor-in-chief of his college newspaper
and even refusing to accept the deanship of Columbia Law School;
but he might be persuaded to assume such leadership. He did not

avoid positions of power if he felt that he could hold them and maintain his independence. He would abandon a leadership role, however, if he felt compromised on a principle. Nicholas Murray Butler, President of Columbia University in the early twentieth century, periodically attempted to influence the development of the Law School during Stone's tenure as dean (1910 to 1923). Butler's actions, such as comments in an annual report to the Board of Trustees that "legal education has fallen into ruts . . . and been treated . . . too little as a matter of education," [78] invariably piqued Stone, who believed that Columbia Law School had gained in stature during his deanship. Finally in 1923 Stone had had enough of the ambitious Butler and "the petty bickerings which go on in the life of a university," [79] and resigned. His primary motivation, however, was the principle of institutional autonomy: the Law School of which he was dean was not to tolerate judgments made by persons outside the legal profession.

Nonetheless, despite his independence, stubbornness, honesty, and fidelity to conviction, as Chief Justice Stone gave an impression of vacillation and indecisiveness. Two different elements of his character combined to produce this image. The first was his philosophy of judging, which, paradoxically, was more fully and carefully developed than that of any Chief Justice since Marshall. The second was his reluctance to see himself, despite his role as first among equals, as superior in any sense to his colleagues on the Court. The two elements are discussed separately.

For a man who was to become identified with the use of the judicial office to insure the continuance of social experimentation in America, Stone exhibited, in the years before his appointment to the Court, a singularly negative attitude toward that proposition. Not only did he believe, as he said in 1912, that abstract or social justice as a test for the correctness of judicial decisions was without value, he even supported attempts on the part of courts to resist experimental legislation. He defended, for example, the *Ives v. South Buffalo Ry. Co.* [80] decision, in which the New York Court of Appeals invalidated a 1910 state workmen's compensation statute, to the dismay of, among others, Roscoe Pound and Benjamin Cardozo. Stone felt, as the *Ives* Court had, that workmen's compensation should come through "the orderly process of constitutional amendment"; [81] that "social justice may mean anything, and therefore, as a basis of judicial description, means nothing"; [82] that "the unfit do survive in fact and perpetuate their species to become sources of weakness to the social structure"; [83] and that the task of appellate judges was "to ascertain whether the facts proved in the case" were "controlled by rules of law which may be found in the precedents." [84] In taking these positions, Stone identified himself, in the eyes of a contemporary, as an opponent of "adherents of sociologic[al] jurisprudence who would make judicial decisions in regard to large public questions depend upon the fallible and sometimes hasty human sciences of sociology and economics." [85]

With time, however, Stone's resistance to the use of social theory as a test of the effectiveness of judicial decisions began to erode. During his deanship at Columbia he became involved in the early stages of the American Law Institute's promulgation of Restatements of Law, whose purpose was, he said, to "state in detail and with precision accepted rules and doctrines, eliminating or modifying the rule or doctrine not supported by reason or adapted to present-day social institutions and needs." [86] He began, at the same time, to argue that "in declaring law the judge must envisage the social utility of the rule which he creates." [87] By 1938 he was prepared to concede that he probably did not agree with much of what he had said in 1915 about the relation of courts to their social context. [88]

Yet a consistent thread ran through Stone's early-twentieth-century writings about judging. He believed that the law was an evolutionary process, that common law adjudication reflected its evolutionary character, and that therefore the common law model of decision-making, which in Stone's view produced change through continuity, and reform through order, was the single most appropriate method for the appellate judiciary. Stone had at first rejected theories of social justice as apt criteria for evaluation of judicial performance, as he found them speculative and irrelevant to the rules and doctrines judges declared. As he became persuaded that those theories did, however, play a part in determining how socially useful an existing common law doctrine was, he broadened his concept of common law adjudication to embrace them. Significantly, he looked upon currently-held beliefs not as a counterweight to adjudication but rather as part of the evidence weighed by the common law method. On the Court, he began to question altogether the idea of law declaration by judges. The common-law model, he saw, allowed some judicial lawmaking in the sense of making delicate political adjustments between competing social values. He thus moved from the conceptualist jurisprudence Holmes had attacked in *Lochner v. New York* to a position not unlike that of Holmes, and finally to one that went beyond Holmes in the degree of creativity and political compromise it tolerated in courts.

Stone's judicial philosophy, in its mature form, attempted to accommodate personal flexibility with institutional constraint. He believed that Supreme Court Justices, particularly but not exclusively in the area of constitutional law, should have a certain freedom to ignore or modify precedents if faced with unanticipated exigencies that made suspect the continued viability of such precedents. On the other hand, he believed that Justices should be prepared to justify their modifications by appeal to reason, so that a decision to change the state of the law appeared to have been made on other than *ad hoc* grounds. Stone's trade-off, then, was between pragmatic accommodation and fidelity to an institutional ideal of rationality, consistency, and transcendence of the immediate. Once the judiciary was given a power to interpret the Constitution, Stone believed that it necessarily had a certain freedom to change the meaning of constitutional language with time or find statutory language offensive where it had once been tolerated. But judges could not exercise such power without a sense of the institutional and intellectual limitations that accompanied it.

Stone identified these limitations primarily with certain techniques of appellate judging. He attempted, as he said, to "[mark] out, as cases arise, step by step, the line between the permitted and the forbidden, by the process of appraisal and comparison of the experiences of the past and the present." [89] This meant a search for a narrow rationale by which to distinguish a new case from a seemingly troublesome precedent, while not overruling that precedent. It also meant, however, the avoidance of *ad hoc* judgments, requiring that some rationale of intermediate generality accompany even the most delicate distinctions. Analytical techniques represented a search for the overriding purposes of laws. Purposes could be found, in cases involving statutory interpretation, in the words and actions of legislators; in constitutional cases, in the language of the Constitution itself, as disclosed through judicial interpretation; [90] and, on occasion, in an obligation in the judiciary to make delicate political choices when conditions required them and no other branch of government had made them.

Stone's effort to articulate different standards for judicial review of legislation in accordance with the character of the interest invaded was part of his general theory of judging. That effort has often been associated with a footnote in Stone's opinion in *United States v. Carolene Products*, and with his dissent in *Minersville School District v. Gobitis*. In those cases Stone suggested that the presumption of constitutionality for legislation might be given a narrow scope where civil liberties interests, as distinguished from economic interests, were infringed. This distinction, however, was only part of Stone's general attempt to identify occasions on which a legislative decision to curtail individual rights, whether economic or civil, had been made without an effective "political restraint." [91] Examples included statutes where the economic interest involved was out-of-state,[92] and statutes curtailing the civil rights of a small and powerless minority. The absence of an effective political restraint, for Stone, invited closer judicial scrutiny of legislation. In such cases the judiciary frankly placed itself in a quasi-legislative position and weighed the importance of the values protected and infringed by the legislation in question. That position he made tenable by singling out in the Constitution certain rights deserving of special protection. If the political process would not protect those rights, the judicial process should.

Stone's view of judging, for all its analytic subtlety and power, did not have a happy effect on the members of his own Court. It failed, of course, to satisfy any of the Four Horsemen so long as they remained in service. More important, it was not fully accepted, on different grounds, by any of the Roosevelt appointees. In the 1940s three issues surfaced that had not received much attention in the earlier years of Stone's tenure: legislative discrimination against the civil rights of blacks, legislative or administrative suppression of civil liberties in a wartime context, and legislative promotion or restriction of the powers of labor unions. In a loose sense, "liberalism" in the 1940s was identified with sympathy for each of the three groups whose interests were being affected. Yet the "liberal" Stone Court divided in a variety of ways on these issues.

The personnel of the Stone Court from 1941 to 1946 was heavily identified with the Roosevelt Administration, and yet revealed the diverse character of Roosevelt's political constituency. Stone, Roberts, and Harold Burton (who replaced Roberts at the very end of

Stone's Chief Justiceship), were the only non-Roosevelt appointees. Three of Roosevelt's nominees were academics: Felix Frankfurter, William O. Douglas, and Wiley B. Rutledge (former dean of the State University of Iowa Law School). Two were practitioners and government servants: Stanley Reed and Robert Jackson, each of whom had been a Solicitor General under Roosevelt. Two more, Hugo Black and James Byrnes, had been senators from Southern states; and the last, Frank Murphy, had been the Governor of Michigan and a Roosevelt Attorney General. Their diverse backgrounds, when coupled with strong personal conviction, were not conducive to jurisprudential harmony, however much they might be identified with one political party or President. Stone himself noted in 1942 that "any high expectations that the Justices of the newly reorganized Court would have minds with but a single thought and hearts that beat as one were speedily dissipated." [93]

In civil rights cases involving blacks, for example, Stone ran into markedly different kinds of difficulties with his fellow judges. In a 1941 case, *United States v. Classic*, [94] Stone used his method of searching for overriding constitutional purposes to find that a primary election was an essential part of the voting process, giving voters a constitutional right to an honest court. He also found that dishonest state officials could be prosecuted under the Civil Rights Act of 1870, even though primaries were not in existence when the Act had been passed. The latter finding offended Justices Douglas, Black, and Murphy, who felt that the Act was not sufficiently specific to allow prosecution. The *Classic* case was a harbinger of things to come. Stone's protection of one set of individual rights was seen by civil libertarians on his Court as an infringement on another set.

Classic plunged Stone into difficulties of a different kind with Roberts. In *Grovey v. Townsend*, [95] a 1935 opinion written by Roberts and joined by Stone, the Court had characterized voting in a primary as a privilege of party membership rather than a constitutional right. *Classic* put that characterization in jeopardy. For Stone, precedents were persuasive only if the principles they represented were sound. He did not, however, enjoy square overrulings of recent precedents. He failed even to mention *Grovey v. Townsend* in *Classic*, although he was prepared to follow through the implications of his *Classic* opinion for it. When the case of *Smith v. Allwright*, [96] testing the constitutionality of all-white primaries in Texas, came before the Court in 1944, Stone privately took the position that

Classic had overruled *Grovey v. Townsend*, but encouraged Justice Reed to write an opinion that stopped short of saying that.[97]

Such subtleties were too much for Roberts, who was embarrassed by the fact that he had joined Stone in *Classic*. He attacked Stone's view of precedent, maintaining that "not a fact differentiat[ed] [*Grovey*] from [*Smith v. Allwright*] except the names of the parties." The *Allwright* case, which provoked Roberts's railroad ticket analogy, symbolized his increasing dissatisfaction with Stone's philosophy of judging. For him it destroyed a sense of "consistency in adjudication"[98] and was disingenuous to boot. A year after *Allwright* came down, Roberts resigned from the Court.

Stone's attempt to strike a measured balance between flexibility and restraint in wartime civil liberties cases proved to be equally offensive to some of his colleagues. Five justices of the Stone Court—Black, Douglas, Murphy, Rutledge, and, from a different perspective, Jackson—were notably sensitive to alleged violations of civil liberties. One measure of their commitment was the belief, held by the first four, that all the procedural safeguards of the first eight Amendments to the Constitution were incorporated into the due-process clause of the Fourteenth Amendment, serving as checks against the actions of the states as well as against those of the federal government. Another example of their commitment to civil libertarianism came in cases testing the wartime scope of government power to restrict individual rights. In such cases, although they could not entirely agree among themselves, they clashed with Stone.

The wartime civil liberties cases in the Stone Court illustrate the difficulties of achieving judicial consensus on politically explosive issues. Throughout World War II Stone sought to articulate a position that tolerated discretionary decisions by the military yet protected civil liberties. He believed that the Constitution did authorize the substitution of military tribunals for civilian courts in times of national emergency, but he also believed that it underscored the importance of keeping civilian courts open and available wherever possible. The occasions on which military courts and martial law prevailed were matters for the judiciary to decide, since the Constitution allowed Congress and the Executive "to authorize martial law in appropriate cases."[99] If martial law prevailed, traditional civil liberties guarantees could be infringed. Otherwise, the guarantees applied even to wartime enemies of the nation.

Difficulties for the Stone Court congealed in *In re Yamashita*,[100] in which a military commission convicted a Japanese general for war crimes without granting him the acceptable procedural safeguards of a civilian court. Army lawyers for Yamashita, appealing on habeas corpus to the civilian courts, raised two questions: whether the power of the commission to try Yamashita was subject to judicial review, and whether the commission's mode of conducting its proceedings was similarly subject. Stone's majority opinion answered the first affirmatively and the second negatively. The second answer alienated Murphy and Rutledge. In Rutledge's view, judicial review on habeas corpus required scrutiny of possible Fifth Amendment violations by the tribunal. Murphy felt that the absence of procedural safeguards in war crimes trials required not only civilian scrutiny but even a revamping of the system of military justice.

Meanwhile Stone had run into problems in maintaining support for his views on the scope of military discretion to confine the activities of Japanese residents of the United States. Here he retained the vote of Black, who was able to subordinate his interest in fair procedure to his patriotism, but he offended, in various ways, Douglas, Murphy, Rutledge and Jackson. *Hirabayashi v. United States*,[101] a 1943 decision, tested the constitutionality, in the face of a right to travel, of a military order establishing a curfew for U.S. citizens of Japanese origins. Sustaining the order, Stone attempted, for a majority that included Black and Jackson, to distinguish between military judgments about the dangerousness of certain ethnic groups in wartime and more general ethnic discriminations. Such general discriminations were "odious to a free people whose instructions are founded upon the doctrine of equality";[102] the specific instances were justifiable if made on the reasonable belief of those "charged with the responsibility of our national defense" that a genuine threat to national security existed.

Douglas, however, suggested that disloyal Japanese, rather than all Japanese, were the objects of the curfew order, and hence some mode of judicial review should exist whereby an individual Japanese could show that he had been singled out unfairly as a threat. This position invited countless habeas corpus petitions in the federal courts and was therefore disruptive of the efficiency of the war effort. Stone could not shape his majority opinion in *Hirabayashi* to accommodate Douglas without losing other votes; Douglas ended up writing a concurrence. Meanwhile Murphy and Rutledge worried about the wide discretion given to military officials by Stone's opinion, and concurred separately.

In short, the delicate balances on which Stone's view of civil liberties in wartime rested made his approach too vulnerable to political emotions to serve as a doctrine for the Court in the 1940s. In *Korematsu v. United States*,[103] a 1944 Japanese internment case, and *Duncan v. Kahanamoku*,[104] a 1946 case testing the scope of the power of military courts in Hawaii, Jackson, Murphy, Rutledge, Douglas, and finally Black came to find Stone's flexible definition of the discretionary powers of the military too threatening. The majority opinion in *Korematsu*, written by Black and joined by Stone, justified the exclusion of Japanese from selected areas on the West Coast because the process bore "a definite and close relationship to the prevention of espionage and sabotage." For Stone and Black the test was whether an acknowledged discretionary power in the military had been reasonably exercised. Rutledge voted with the majority in *Korematsu*, but Jackson decided that wartime cases inevitably involved untoward violations of civil liberties, and suggested that the Court not entertain them.[105] Murphy called *Korematsu* a baldfaced attempt to legitimate racism.[106]

By the date of the *Kahanomoku* case Black, Douglas, Murphy, and Rutledge had decided that the time had come to impose strict limits on the war power. In an opinion declaring that civilians in Hawaii could not be tried in military courts despite the presence of martial law, those four Justices, through Black, called the American system of government "the antithesis of total military rule." [107] Stone disagreed, reaffirming his view that martial law could be applied in "those cases where it [was] needful in the interest of public safety and good order." [108]

In the wartime incarceration cases and other wartime civil liberties cases,[109] Stone repeatedly tried to decide on the narrowest possible grounds, to preserve a measure of doctrinal consistency and to face hard political decisions while seeing "that the emotions of war are kept out of the courtroom." [110] Much of the time he maintained a majority for his viewpoint, but he almost never escaped without an inflammatory concurrence or dissent. His approach conceded too much for some of his colleagues and not enough for others. It was too flexible to satisfy one set of justices and too moderate to suit another. The wartime civil liberties cases did pose problems of delicate balancing, but few of the members of Stone's Court really wanted to balance. They were either fervent patriots and warhawks or zealous defenders of minority rights or, as in the case of Black and Douglas, they were converts from the first position to the second and found it difficult to find accommodation.

If the civil liberties cases of the 1940s were a testing ground for Stone's approach to interpreting the Constitution, labor cases of the same decade tested his approach to statutory interpretation. He resolved these controversies by ascertaining the primary purposes of the relevant legislation involved. On the Hughes Court he had tolerated the presence and the potentially expansive jurisdiction of the National Labor Relations Board, but had refused to make it a foil for organized labor.[111] His primary interest was reading the National Labor Relations Act[112] so as to effectuate what he thought to be its central purpose: the creation of even-handed administrative machinery through which labor and management could negotiate their differences.

As the NLRB evolved, its rulings exhibited an increasing sympathy with the views of labor unions. This raised two difficulties for Stone. His apprehensions about unchecked union power were renewed, and he became concerned about the emergence of administrative construction of a statute, as he thought this could be used to circumvent the statute's primary purposes. As NLRB cases moved from inquiries as to whether unions possessed any power, to questions about the scope of their power, Stone sought to restrict what he thought were indiscriminately pro-union constructions of the Act on the part of the NLRB. He was somewhat frustrated in this effort by his own earlier efforts. He had been a leading supporter of labor on the Hughes Court. Now Justices on his own Court, such as Black, Douglas, and Murphy, seemed anxious to tolerate any pro-union decision. Previous suggestions by Stone[113] that Congressional statutes protected unions from unfair discrimination were converted into justifications for wide union power to coerce unsympathetic employers.[114] Once again, Stone felt, a search for moderation and restraint, based on fidelity to statutory language and a gradualist approach to change, had been converted into a politicized crusade.

Stone's theory of judicial performance was better suited to the Hughes Court than his own. It emphasized political accommodation and stressed the limitations on judicial lawmaking, allowing change while confining it. It grounded its rationale not on factual distinctions, as had the Hughes approach, but on a subtle understanding of the relations between governing institutions. As such Stone's theory enabled the Court to avoid being imprisoned by the set of social attitudes exhibited by the Four Horsemen while not appearing entirely result-oriented in its decisions. Once a new militancy emerged on the Court in the 1940s, however, Stone's view became a restraining influence, in terms of both end results and implicit assumptions about the power of judges. Those more deeply committed to substantive change than he were impatient with his belief that judicial creativity functioned only in a limited institutional ambit.

Stone's theory of judicial performance was not, however, the sole or perhaps even the primary cause of fragmentation in his Court. Of equal or possibly greater significance was his view of leadership. His humility, independence, and distaste for open personal confrontations combined to make him uncomfortable with Hughes's approach to the Chief Justiceship. Moreover, Stone was disinclined or reluctant to attempt to convert others to his views. The Stone Court was not one molded by the preferences of its Chief. Although Stone set the tone for his Court, it was a tone that deemphasized conventional leadership.

Stone's pre-Court career, especially his deanship at Columbia Law School, had suggested that he would be reluctant to assume positions of leadership, loathe to cloak himself in the status perquisites of an office, publicly deferent to the views of others, yet at the same time fiercely independent and prepared to relinquish power for the sake of a belief. In addition, those years had indicated that, when thwarted, Stone inclined to retreat from controversy, but that he nonetheless tended to communicate his antagonisms privately in a manner that was less than discreet.[115] Each of these characteristics reappeared on the Court. Once Chief Justice, Stone rapidly abandoned Hughes's practice of summary dispositions of cases in conference. As an Associate Justice he had characterized Hughes's technique as one of "greatly over-elaborating the unimportant details of [a] case and disposing, by ipse dixit, in a sentence or two, of the vital question." [116] He encouraged full discussion and debate in conference, viewing his function as not unlike his new role as chairman of the Judicial Conference of the United States: "to focus discussion . . . without being too much of a

Czar." [117] He stated his own views with diffidence, allowed himself to be freely interrupted, and invariably granted extensions for more time to consider an issue. [118]

For all his open-mindedness and deference to his colleagues' views, Stone, once he had staked out his own position, was stubborn and vocal in its defense. Justice Reed recalled him as "an indefatigable proponent for the position he had reached, an ardent advocate and a forceful writer for the ground that he deemed solid." [119] Stone regarded the Court's internal debates as intellectual exercises. He found them stimulating, rarely took offense at one advocating views counter to his, borrowed ideas from others freely, and enjoyed the process of sharpening or trimming a position through the exchange of memoranda. To the extent that Hughes had identified leadership with detachment and "objectivity," Stone altered that conception. To him influence on the Court was equated with the soundness and firmness of one's intellectual views and the degree of one's persuasiveness. By this criterion, Justices as diverse as Van Devanter and Brandeis won his admiration, and others, such as Frankfurter and Rutledge, with whom he often had a sympathy of views, did not.

Stone carried over to the workings of the Court the sense of balance that marked his philosophy of judging. He traded off efficiency in the handling of the docket against "full exposition" and "painstaking consideration" of issues before the Justices. He was interested in unanimity and shaped his majority opinions to achieve it, but he believed that "differences of opinion in the court . . . should be fully expressed." [120] He felt that a Chief Justice should be "fired by a passion for the prompt and faithful performance of the work of the Court," but that he was only a "titular leader among equals." [121] He believed that conflict, paradoxically, bred detachment: "a considered and well-stated dissent" was "a manifestation in its best sense of the common effort of judges to develop law dispassionately." [122] And while he "dreaded [personal] conflict," as Jackson said, and sometimes "feared action that would bring it about," [123] he also believed that legal doctrines should "be exposed to the most searching examination and criticism." [124]

Stone's combination of personal diffidence and intellectual combativeness, when commingled with the vibrancy and contentiousness of others on his Court, formed a catalyst for divisiveness. Stone had to contend as Chief Justice with at least four Justices—

Black, Douglas, Frankfurter, and Jackson—of high intellectual ability and marked strong-mindedness and persistence, and three others—Roberts, Murphy, and Rutledge—who could on occasion become perversely or militantly doctrinaire. Only in Justice Reed did Stone have a colleague amenable to persuasion and largely amiable about it.[125] During his tenure as Chief Justice, Stone endured, among other things, an early expression of the longstanding quarrel between Black and Frankfurter, in which Black wrote a concurrence whose sole purpose was to attack a Frankfurter dissent;[126] the celebrated dispute between Black and Jackson over Black's failure to disqualify himself in a case argued by his former law partner;[127] and an awkward series of internal bickerings among the Justices over the writing of a retirement letter to Justice Roberts, who had alienated almost all his colleagues by the time of his resignation in 1945.[128] Some commentators concluded that this divisiveness earned the Stone Court "less popular admiration and respect than any previous Supreme Court has enjoyed within the memory of living men."[129] Others, however, believed that the Court between 1937 and 1945 was one of the greatest in American history.[130]

IV

The office of Chief Justice of the United States Supreme Court is not that of an ordinary Justiceship, although Stone may have so conceived it. It contains an internal political dimension with which each occupant is forced to come to terms. Internal politics on the Court is not politics in the conventional sense, but it is more than mere "administration," as that word is commonly used. A Chief Justice, above all his colleagues, seeks to convey a sense, as Stone put it, that the Court is "greater than the individuals who happen for the moment to represent it."[131] He attempts to communicate to the public an impression that harmony prevails among the Justices, that intellectual honesty is admired, that reason triumphs over irrationality and partisanship, that pettiness is at a minimum and statesmanship predominant. He is forced, at the same time, to deal with personal antagonisms, political differences, disingenuousness, artifice, and estrangement.

A continually dissenting Chief Justice is not a Chief; he does not lead his Court. When he does not dissent, he must assign an opinion; no other member of the Court is faced so frequently with that delicate political exercise. When important cases are handed down, there is pressure on the Chief to speak for the Court, and additional pressure—if the case has major social ramifications—to secure unanimity or a clear majority for his viewpoint. On explosive occasions, therefore, he is put in the position of being an agent of compromise and an apostle of harmony.

The position of Chief Justice thus requires both intellectual power and political acumen, and in an abstract sense both Hughes and Stone possessed these skills. Nevertheless, because of the interaction of their personal styles with the context, both personal and historical, in which they operated, neither was able to use them to best advantage. Hughes's formidable intellect and mastery of administrative techniques appeared as arbitrariness, heavy-handedness, or pedantry. His commitment to preserving the autonomy and integrity of the Court occasionally undercut his political strength, or further polarized an easily divided Court. The remarkable subtlety and sensitivity of Stone's conception of his office sometimes created the image of one who abdicated leadership when controversies were heated, while his humanness and gregariousness served dissension and encouraged conflict. There is much to admire in Hughes and Stone as intellects, as public officials, and as human beings. Both may have achieved a certain greatness as Chief Justice, but it was a greatness tinged with irony. Their experiences demonstrate the fortuitousness of the process of leading the Supreme Court and the potential vulnerability of any occupant of the Chief Justiceship.

11

Personal versus Impersonal Judging: The Dilemmas of Robert Jackson

With the death of the oracular theory of judging, two emerging jurisprudential perspectives placed contradictory sets of pressures on the twentieth-century appellate judiciary. One perspective emphasized human limitations (such as irrationality and bias) on judges, assumed that judges made law, encouraged the judiciary to acknowledge candidly those "realities," and implicitly conveyed a skepticism about the permanency of values or truths, in law or elsewhere.[1] The second, building on the insights of, while responding to the potential nihilism of the first, emphasized institutional limitations. It attempted to limit the influence of judicial bias and judicial lawmaking through methodological techniques that recognized the limited and distinctive role of the American judiciary. It began with a recognition that law was not a body of discoverable truths, but nonetheless attempted to define law as more than the aggregate of the biases of officials. Ultimately, this perspective defined law as a process, with its own internal limitations on the conduct of judges and other lawmakers.[2]

The thrust of the process perspective was methodological in the sense that judges were encouraged to transcend their biases through the use of analytical reasoning. Those (primarily academicians) who shared its assumptions believed that a thorough and balanced articulation by judges of the competing issues at stake in a case would produce a rational solution whose justification lay in the technique of analysis that derived it. In the context of the 1940s and 1950s this set of beliefs had substantive ideological and political implications as well. It was designed in part as a counterweight to the implicit moral relativism of "realistic jurisprudence," [3] which became linked with totalitarian threats to American civilization. [4] As the value of national solidarity increased in importance during World War II and the Cold War, the distinctive features and shared beliefs of American society were reaffirmed. As part of this reaffirmation, rationality, democratic ideals, and law were interfused. Judging came to be seen not only as an exercise in reason but also as a means of implementing the historic values of a democratic society, a society in which law was more than the fiats of governmental officials. [5]

The judicial career of Robert Jackson, who was appointed to the Supreme Court by Roosevelt in 1941 and remained there until his death in 1954, mirrored the contradictory jurisprudential impulses of the times. Jackson openly rejected the oracular theory and maintained a vividly personalized and "realistic" approach to judging. At the same time he strove to develop a theory of adjudication that emphasized the importance of internalized constraints on judges. He recognized the substantive implications of his approach and sought to redefine traditional American values, such as libertarianism or egalitarianism, in the light of an enhanced interest in national solidarity and security. Confronting competing pressures, he sought accommodations of one to the other. Although his solutions were idiosyncratic and not particularly influential, they helped frame central issues for the American appellate judiciary in the decade immediately after his death.

Three features of Jackson's judicial career have particular relevance to the role attributed to him above. One was his style, which was an index not simply of literary inclinations but of character traits and social values as well. Another was his efforts to redefine the proper relations between individual citizens and the state in post-war America. A third was his view of the role of law and lawyers in American society, from which he derived his attitudes toward judging.

I

"In his case," Felix Frankfurter observed in a memorial tribute, "the style was the man." [6] To a degree unusual in their profession, Frankfurter believed, Jackson's judicial writing revealed his thoughts and feelings. In contrast to Frankfurter himself, Jackson rarely seemed to be searching for the proper "judicial" stance or tone in his opinions. Instead, he appeared capable of expanding the stylistic range of opinion writing to accommodate his human reactions. As Holmes had done, and most of his predecessors had not, Jackson entertained with his style. Quips such as "If it is interstate commerce that feels the pinch, it does not matter how local the operation which applies the squeeze" [7] filled his opinions. In such moments the distance between judges and mortals was suddenly shortened; charm became a counterweight to pomposity. The assorted "Jacksonisms" [8] of his opinions reminded his audience that, for him, judging was not sharply distinguishable from other public performances, and that in all such ventures he was to retain his individuality.

For Jackson, then, style was more than a blending of temperament with role. It was a means by which the self pierced through roles to communicate at a more personal level. This conception of uniqueness and worth in oneself was a core value for Jackson. He was, as he said repeatedly, an individualist, both temperamentally and philosophically. Individualism meant a variety of things. It was associated with a thirst for competition ("I was never a crusader. I just liked a good fight"). [9] It served to identify financial security and generalist law practice with independence. It manifested itself in a flashy style of dress or in an affinity for Emerson ("Self-reliance, self-help, and independence of other people I believe to be the basis of character and essential to success"). [10] It produced a small businessman-entrepreneur bias on economic issues, and was the source of dissenting views on politics ("The great difficulty with the conservative class in this country is that they've lost their guts. The American industrialist has just ceased to be an individualist. . . . Instead of an old-fashioned liberalism, the liberals have tended to collectivism and communism. . . . Both groups . . . lack imagination and constructive thinking." [11]) Individualism had been, in Jackson's eyes, the creed of his ancestors and the motif of his locality; it was a counterbalance to the mass society he saw America becoming.

Jackson's individualism decisively affected his professional relations. It motivated him to develop a law practice in Jamestown (New York) that was distinguished by the diversity of its clientele. The only corporate client that Jackson's firm persistently serviced was a locally owned business, the Jamestown Telephone Corporation, which was fighting to preserve its independence in the face of encroachments by the Bell System. Beyond that, Jackson represented, among others, a streetcar company, a bank, striking members of a labor union, and occasional accused murderers. General practice, he believed, made lawyers "harder to dominate" and kept them from being "hired men." [12] Not one of Jackson's clients (he guessed) contributed as much as five per cent to his gross income, but his practice nonetheless "laid the foundation of financial independence which is an important asset in public office, relieving one of fear of loss of office and contributing a general sense of security." [13]

Once consulted on a problem, Jackson felt, a lawyer "usually dominated the matter, no matter who the [client] was." [14] Lawyering brought independence and power, but also a sense of self-worth. This was because law was a necessary ingredient of civilized living, a cementing force in a society of individualists. It functioned, fundamentally, as a means of accommodating competing claims and resolving disputes. A lawyer's skills were largely practical and his orientation was basically pragmatic. He succeeded in his profession primarily through careful preparation, persuasiveness, common sense, and sound judgment. But he could feel satisfaction beyond the immediate victories of his clients, in doing his part to minimize friction and to maintain order in society. Receptiveness to the needs and wants of individual citizens was essential in America; but since individual claims were so diverse, some measure of social organization was required. A good lawyer could function as an honest broker between individual persons and the institutions whose purpose it was to maintain that organization. Law was hence both a process of harmonizing competing desires and a "rule" of civilized conduct. A lawyer stood for the maintenance of both.

In fostering the latter attitude in the mind of his clients, a lawyer needed to develop within himself an impersonal, detached attitude toward potentially provocative situations. A practitioner needed to separate his sense of appropriate tactical behavior from his perception of what his clients wanted, so that he could give "sincere advice" instead of telling a client "exactly what he wanted to hear." [15] A judge, especially, ought to be "a man that didn't let the personalities on either side interfere with his deciding the case. . . . The interpretation of the law ought to be as impersonal as possible." [16] When one "[put] on a judicial robe," Jackson said, "psychological change" was required. One needed "to get into an attitude of deciding other people's controversies, instead of waging them." After being appointed to the Court he acknowledged that some judges were never able to adapt themselves to this change in perspective, and he was not sure that he had. [17]

Here as in other places Jackson understood himself. His self-esteem, zest for personal combat, ambition, and fear of being compromised—manifestations of his individualism—made his transition from private practitioner and government lawyer to judge a painful and imperfect one. He had admired or gravitated toward strong personalities—notably Hughes, Roosevelt, and Henry Morgenthau—before becoming a judge, and even his abiding ambitions could not always temper his zeal to meet strength with strength. Harold Ickes once said of Jackson that "he is far from aggressive, but disposed to accept what comes along without really fighting for a different result . . . , [and] more of a lawyer than an aggressive leader." [18] But these comments were made in the context of Jackson's apprentice relations with Roosevelt, who had in 1937 encouraged Jackson to run the next year for Governor of New York, who had appointed him Solicitor General in 1938 and Attorney General in 1940, and who had intimated that he would name him to succeed Hughes as Chief Justice. [19] While Jackson was consistently deferential to Roosevelt, he was to no one else, including Morgenthau, who had first brought him to Washington in 1934 as General Counsel to the Bureau of Internal Revenue. [20] On the Court he encountered more strong personalities, such as Stone, Douglas, and Black. Buoyed by the achievement of independence, he did not suppress his differences.

In debate Jackson utilized the talents that had made him appear to a fellow advocate in Jamestown as "wickedly brilliant." [21] He personalized issues and poked fun at opposing Justices' views; [22] he filled his opinions with devastating similes and pejorative meta-phors. When pressed, he revealed the internal politics of the Court [23] and on occasion seemed to suggest that partisanship was its lifeblood. One such occasion was his impassioned attack on Justice Black in 1946. This attack, which came in the form of a cable from Nuremberg, Germany, where Jackson was serving as chief prosecutor at the war crimes trials, was the culmination of a series of earlier confrontations dating back to Jackson's appointment to the Court in 1941.

In a 1942 case, *United States v. Bethlehem Steel Corporation*,[24] Jackson, who had worked on the case as Solicitor General, disqualified himself, then saw his position repudiated by the Court in a Black opinion. In 1944 and 1945 two cases [25] came to the Court involving the effect of the Fair Labor Standards Act on contracts between mine workers and their employers. In both cases the workers were represented by Crampton Harris, a former law partner of Black's. In both instances a majority of the Court read the Act favorably for the workers. Both decisions ranged well beyond the collective bargaining context to announce a comprehensive policy with regard to overtime benefits in the mining industry. Jackson objected to the decisions as being overbroad and politically inspired.

The Jewell Ridge Coal Corporation, the defeated party in the second case, subsequently petitioned the Court for a rehearing on the grounds of Black's close connection with Harris. In June 1945, denying the petition for the Court, Jackson emphasized that disqualification questions were matters for decision by individual Justices, rather than the Court, and that this was the sole ground for denying the petition. Subsequently Jackson temporarily left the Court to participate in the Nuremberg Trials.

While Jackson was in Nuremberg a petty dispute arose among the Justices over the wording of a letter to Justice Roberts on his retirement. Stone had included in his draft of the letter (whose tone was polite but not effusive) the phrases "brings to us a profound sense of regret that our association with you in the daily work of the Court must now come to an end," and "you have made fidelity to principle your guide to decision." [26] In accordance with custom, Stone routed the draft to Black (by now the senior Associate Justice) for his signature. Black suggested deletion of the two phrases, the only ones that could be interpreted as an endorsement of Roberts's performance as a Justice. Stone responded to Black's suggestion by inviting Black to write his own draft and submit it to the remaining Justices. Black merely forwarded Stone's draft, with his deletions, adding a note that Stone "had me sign it first in order to save time." [27]

Frankfurter, who had learned of Black's objections privately from Stone, reacted by criticizing Black for implying that Stone's original draft was no different from Black's revised version. Frankfurter refused to sign the revision and pressed Stone to circulate the original draft—which Stone eventually did. Black reacted by repeating his refusal to sign the original and withdrawing his own draft. There matters stood at the end of August 1945. Meanwhile, in mid-August Jackson, who had been sent Stone's original draft and had signed it, received a letter from Stone describing Black's objections. Jackson responded by saying that "the deletions leave the letter so colorless that it would be best to omit the letter entirely," and refused to sign a letter "that deliberately omits the only sentence that credits [Roberts] with good motives." [28] A poll of the other Justices, however, revealed that all six were prepared to sign Black's version,[29] leaving only Jackson, Stone, and Frankfurter in favor of the more generous letter. Stone ultimately issued no letter at all, announcing Roberts's retirement orally in court in October 1945, with the Black draft as his text.[30]

The letter incident heightened Jackson's sense that the Court had become factionalized, with Black at the head of a faction and Frankfurter and himself in opposition. Isolated in Nuremberg, he felt vulnerable to attack from his colleagues. He had consulted none of the Justices before accepting the Nuremberg appointment and knew that Stone deeply disapproved of it. In January 1946, he offered to return temporarily to the Court in April to facilitate the discharge of business, but Stone ultimately suggested that a temporary stay would be counterproductive.[31] In the midst of this atmosphere, Stone suddenly died on April 22, 1946, and Jackson was prominently mentioned as his successor. In the last days of April President Truman consulted Hughes, then eighty-four and in the fifth year of his retirement, and Hughes apparently recommended Jackson.[32] Meanwhile some Jackson supporters, fearing that his absence from Washington would hurt his chances, suggested that he return to America for Stone's funeral. Jackson, who was at a critical stage in the Nuremberg proceedings, refused. Later he said, "I wouldn't have asked Harry Truman for a commitment as to the Chief Justiceship any more than I would cut my head off." [33] There is little doubt, however, that Jackson coveted the office and felt that he was entitled to it.

Between Hughes's meeting with Truman at the close of April and the nomination of Fred Vinson as Chief Justice on June 6 an anti-Jackson campaign was launched [34] by persons identified by Jackson with the Black faction. [35] Drew Pearson announced in a radio broadcast that Black had told Truman that he and another Justice would resign if Jackson were appointed to the Chief Justiceship. [36] On May 15, 1946, a newspaper columnist, Doris Fleeson, repeated that Black threat and revealed some of the debate in conference over the rehearing petition in the *Jewell Ridge* case. She referred to the antagonism between Black and Jackson as a "blood feud" and asserted that Black had perceived Jackson's suggestion that he disqualify himself as "an open and gratuitous insult, a slur upon his personal and judicial honor." [37] Jackson, who received notice of the Pearson and Fleeson accounts in Nuremberg, believed that the columnists' sources were members of the Court and that the purpose of the stories was to discredit his candidacy. He responded by preparing a public statement describing in detail his role in the *Jewell Ridge* disqualification controversy.

On June 10, four days after Vinson's appointment, Jackson released to the press a communication to the chairmen of the Judiciary Committees of the House and Senate. In it he characterized the Fleeson account of the *Jewell Ridge* rehearing debate as detrimental to "the reputation of the court for nonpartisan and unbiased decision," declared that insinuations that the debate represented "a mere personal vendetta among justices" were "utterly false," and insisted that his differences with Black involved questions not of "honor" but of "judgment as to sound judicial policy" in disqualification matters. [38]

Jackson then gave a full account of the *Jewell Ridge* conference debate. The question debated, he maintained, was whether the Court should summarily deny the petition for rehearing or cite its lack of power, as an institution, to pass on disqualification issues. "Justice Black," Jackson said, "insisted on a mere denial to his participation. . . . Neither I nor the other [dissenting] justices . . . wanted to lend our names to [that option]." In conference, Jackson revealed, he had argued that the Court should discuss the disqualification issue in denying the petition for rehearing, whereupon

"Mr. Justice Black became very angry and said that any opinion which discussed the subject at all would mean a declaration of war." Then, Jackson continued, "I told Justice Black in language that was sharp but no different than I would use again that I would not stand for any more of his bullying and that, whatever I would otherwise do, I would now have to write my opinion to keep self respect in the face of his threats." As to the principle he regarded as being at stake in the debate, Jackson asserted that "however innocent the coincidence of these two victories at successive terms by Justice Black's former law partner, I wanted the practice stopped. If it is ever repeated while I am on the bench I will make my *Jewell Ridge* opinion look like a letter of recommendation by comparison." [39]

The attack on Black and the skirmishes that preceded it revealed the contradictions within Jackson. He was proud but ambitious, politically astute but quixotic, at times morally uncompromising, at other times pragmatic. He took the political squabbles and maneuvers of judging as a given, and yet at the same time identified the judiciary with detached nonpartisanship. He strove to impose his personal views of proper judicial behavior on his colleagues, but often these views stressed the limitations on judicial power. Jackson's interpretation of his office implied the coexistence of two sets of counteracting characteristics in appellate judges. They were human beings, capable of pride and spitefulness and arrogance and disingenuousness in their relations. But they strove to be symbols of the nobility and impartiality and transcendence of law, which was composed of more than the sum of human passions and prejudices. Jackson believed in the latter ideal of judges as much as he acknowledged the former characteristics. Yet he conveyed the humanness of himself and his colleagues so sharply that he seemed to be living proof of the unattainability of his own standards for judicial performance.

Jackson's style was a self-representation in that it conveyed a lofty vision in pungent terms. The terms themselves distracted from the vision, just as Jackson's dapper appearance distracted contemporaries from his basic indifference to social pretensions. He demythologized his office with his candor and his wit. When a Justice of the Supreme Court could announce "I have never discovered that disregard of the Nation's liquor taxes excluded a citizen from our best society and I see no reason why it should banish an alien

from our worst," [40] some of the solemnity of the appellate judiciary
peeled off. When the same Justice could confess, "I see no reason
why I should be consciously wrong today because I was unconsciously wrong yesterday," [41] the mysterious art of following precedent had been given a human dimension. But when the jurisprudence of that Justice was oriented toward eventual distinctions
between the behavior of judges and that of other persons, or between law and mere power, stylistic strengths became weaknesses.
Candor became a counterweight to dignity; pithiness an antidote
to reverence, and Jackson the man became a difficulty for Jackson
the judge.

II

When Jackson joined the Court in 1941, the established tradition of
judicial tolerance toward legislative attempts to regulate the economy had taken on a new meaning. The tradition had arisen in the
context of state statutes affecting private economic interests. The
questions debated by the White and Taft courts in this area had
primarily involved largely the permissible scope of state power to
regulate private enterprise in the face of the due process clause.
Once the liberty-of-contract doctrine was discredited, state regulatory legislation flourished. But almost simultaneously with this development came a reorientation of the locus of economic regulation
and a new spate of problems. With the New Deal the federal government emerged as a regulatory force, and after the Four Horsemen's attempts to resist this change had been overcome, two
regulators—the states and the federal government—began an uneasy coexistence. The Stone Court had to address itself to the
implications of this coexistence and, consequently, had to re-ex-
amine the meaning of federalism in the post-New Deal economy.
An essential issue for the Stone and subsequently the Vinson
Court was whether a spirit of judicial permissiveness toward state
economic regulation could be maintained in the face of the increased presence of the federal government.

This issue was complicated by a potentially new meaning for the
commerce clause in modern America. Marshall had used the commerce clause to create an area of plenary federal power, but
Congress had generally not exercised that power, so that a judicial

decision declaring that the federal government pre-empted an area
of the nation's economy had usually left the area free from regulation altogether. Only in the early twentieth century did extensive
federal regulation appear, in the form of directives from newly-
created independent regulatory agencies; and these directives did
not receive full-blown support in the courts until the Court-packing
crisis. By the time of Jackson's tenure, however, recognition of federal power in a particular area implied affirmative control of the
economy in that area rather than unexercised potential control.
Commerce clause questions became problems in distinguishing between types of regulation as much as between regulation and its absence. Federalism, therefore, became identified with a modern rationale for a nationally oriented economy, in which attempts by
states to regulate private enterprise were seen as inimical to broader
national considerations.

The new meaning of federalism implicitly revived a role for the
judiciary that had become increasingly dormant in the early twentieth century. Passivity toward legislative experimentation in the
area of economic regulation had allowed federal appellate judges to
avoid posing as advocates of any particular approach to economic
questions. They were simply considering the permissible scope of
state regulation, not passing on its wisdom. But the presence of an
alternative federal regulatory forum not only changed the ground of
constitutional debate from the due process clause to the commerce
clause, it forced an evaluation of the comparative worth of nationally and locally administered regulatory systems. In considering
the limits of state power to regulate the economy, judges were
asked to become economic theorists. An old bugaboo for the judiciary was thus reborn. Against a legislative act was pitted open-
ended constitutional language; judges were invited to give substantive content to the language by interpreting it to compel a result
consistent with a particular social or economic theory. Yet the judiciary, as Holmes and his followers had believed, was a peculiarly
inappropriate instrument for promulgating social and economic
views.

A dilemma for the post-New Deal Court was thereby raised.
How could the judiciary adopt an approach to regulatory questions
consistent with increased federal participation in the economy,
without putting itself back into the vulnerable position of advocating a particular point of view? Jackson faced this problem squarely

in his decisions in cases involving government regulation, and attempted an ingenious solution. He conceded to the judiciary an intermediate power to interpret open-ended constitutional concepts, such as "commerce," "due process" or "equal protection," so as to achieve practical solutions to contemporary problems. Yet he insisted that judicial interpretations be sufficiently broad and general in their applicability to reflect popular sentiments rather than to attempt to influence them. For Jackson, in the area of economic regulation, as elsewhere, an appellate judge could make law, but only if in the process he conveyed his ultimate subordination to it.

As a member of the Roosevelt Administration, Jackson had labored to achieve legitimacy for the proposition that federal regulation of the economy was constitutionally permissible and desirable. His concern in that effort was with defining the scope of federal power to control private enterprise more than with marking out the precise boundaries between federal and state regulation. In an opinion written a year after his appointment, Jackson indicated that he viewed the commerce clause as giving virtually unlimited power to the federal government to regulate private economic activity.

The case (*Wickard v. Filburn* [42]) involved the constitutionality of a federal statute authorizing the Secretary of Agriculture to impose quotas on wheat production and to prescribe penalties for excesses. A penalty was imposed on Filburn, an Ohio farmer who claimed that he used his wheat crop for home consumption as well as for marketing. Counsel for the Department of Agriculture, mindful of older Supreme Court decisions defining "commerce" narrowly, argued that the statute purported to regulate only marketing. Jackson dismissed this argument. Filburn's decision to consume some of his own wheat, he maintained, affected interstate commerce in the sense that it could be said to constitute part of a collective decision by a class of persons. That decision, taken at large, had an impact on the supply of wheat; it was spurious to pretend otherwise. The statute, as applied to Filburn, was therefore a legitimate exercise of Congressional power to regulate commerce, a power extending to matters indirectly as well as directly affecting its flow.

The views Jackson expressed in *Filburn* suggested that state efforts at economic regulation whose effect was to curtail potential federal powers might prove troublesome to him. Congress, he argued, might not choose to exercise its powers in a variety of areas, thereby inviting states to fill the void. Judicial toleration of regulatory state legislation might, under such circumstances, defeat one of the purposes of the commerce clause, uniformity of economic conditions throughout the nation. If Congress took no action because state restraints were "individually too petty, too diversified and too local to get [its] attention," the "practical result" would be "the suffocat[ion], and retard[ation] and Balkaniz[ation] [of] American commerce, trade, and industry." [43] Jackson was concerned that "the reaction of [the] Court against . . . excessive judicial interference with legislative action" might lead it to "rush to other extremes," [44] namely indiscriminate toleration of any action taken by state legislatures in the area of economic regulation. Judicial responsibility under the commerce clause, in this view, was different from that under the due process clause. "The excessive use for insufficient reason of a judicially inflated due process clause to strike down states' laws regulating their own internal affairs" was illegitimate. Invocation of the commerce clause "to keep the many states from fastening their several concepts of local 'well-being' into the national commerce" was "a wholly different thing." [45]

In taking the view that the judiciary could assess the economic impact of state regulation prior to Congressional intervention Jackson was associating himself in a limited way with a discredited view of the judiciary as a barrier against legislative excesses. In a case decided before Jackson came on the Court, Justice Black had announced his conviction that "judicial control of national commerce—unlike legislative regulations—must from inherent limitations of the judicial process treat the subject by the hit-and-miss method of deciding single local controversies upon evidence and information limited by the narrow rules of litigation." [46] The judiciary being incapable of creating "integrated national rules" [47] for the protection of interstate commerce, Black argued, the matter should be left to Congress. Premature judicial intervention only signified for Black, as he said in a 1949 dissent from a Jackson opinion, "an instinctive hostility to any governmental regulation of 'free enterprise.'" [48]

Jackson met this attack by recourse to his distinction between intermediate and ultimate judicial power. The commerce clause was capable of a variety of interpretations. It could fairly be analyzed by judges with reference to the practical results its use fostered. Deciding whether a state regulation "affected" interstate commerce, and if so, whether "directly" or "indirectly," was a traditional judicial inquiry. If it produced different results at different times, that was because economic conditions changed. Freedom in the judiciary to interpret broad constitutional language such as "commerce" to secure pragmatic accommodations to changed circumstances was not illegitimate if judges were faithful to original constitutional purposes. And Jackson saw a clear purpose for the commerce clause. "There can be no doubt," he wrote in the year of his death, "that in the original Constitution the states surrendered to the Federal Government the power to regulate interstate commerce. . . . They did so in the light of a disastrous experience in which commerce and prosperity were reduced to the vanishing point by states discriminating against each other through devices of regulation." [49] This original meaning ultimately ensured that the judiciary would in the future be unable to impose its views on the commerce clause insofar as such views ran counter to those of the framers. Ultimate impotence justified intermediate power. Since the "philosophy that the federal interstate commerce power should be strongly supported" [50] was a bedrock of the Constitution, judges in their interpretive role could flesh out the implications of the commerce clause in given situations.

Given this mandate, Jackson felt, judicial suspicion of "impingement of the states upon that commerce which moves among them" [51] was entirely warranted. Arkansas could not require a permit for the transportation of liquor through the state.[52] New York could not prevent a Massachusetts milk dealer from obtaining part of its supply from farms within New York State.[53] New Jersey could not place a tax on the storage of coal whose ultimate destination was outside the state.[54] Neither Maryland [55] nor Iowa [56] could enact compensating "use" taxes on sales by out-of-state business to local residents. Utah could not enact an inheritance tax on an out-of-state transfer of shares of stock in a railroad incorporated in the state.[57] In short, "the desire of the Forefathers to federalize regulation of foreign and interstate commerce" stood "in sharp contrast" to "their jealous preservation of the state's power over its internal affairs." [58]

Federalism, for Jackson, was thus a doctrine that could justify both local and national primacy, depending on the emphasis of the framers. In matters of economic regulation Jackson detected a firm original intention to allow Congress and individual entrepreneurs to work out their economic relations for themselves. Thus federal regulation of commerce-related matters should be anticipated and the ambit of federal regulatory power could be very broad. But the free flow of private trade and investment—the maintenance of an unrestricted "national market"—was also thought desirable. Where Congress had not acted, it had exhibited a tacit preference for the national market, not a desire to shift regulatory power to the states. This had been the original meaning of economic federalism. In the period of Jackson's tenure, with its greater emphasis on legislative regulation, that meaning had enhanced significance. "It is more important today than it was then," Jackson wrote in 1954, "that we remain one commercial and economic unit and not a collection of parasitic states preying upon each other's commerce." [59]

III

State primacy in certain areas, however, was also inherent in the framers' vision. Federalism dictated, for example, a measure of judicial deference to the states in their efforts to maintain security and order within their boundaries. Herein Jackson was faced with difficulties in the area of civil liberties. The framers, he believed, had begun with the assumption that human rights ought to be free from governmental control. But the government against which rights were held they had identified as the federal government rather than the state, and they had also recognized that on occasion human liberty had to give way to the preservation of social order. Formalized restrictions on state usurpations of individual liberties had come only with the Reconstruction Amendments. All this suggested the possibility of a double standard for protection of civil liberties, whereby the federal government was restrained to a greater degree than the states from intruding on rights. But if this were so, was not the abstract inalienability of human rights sharply reduced in practice?

In his civil liberties decisions Jackson struggled to find a set of principles that would satisfy these separate insights. He occasionally characterized Bill of Rights guarantees as absolutes. "The very purpose of a Bill of Rights," he declared in 1943, "was to withdraw certain subjects from the vicissitudes of political controversy, to place them beyond the reach of majorities and officials and to establish them as legal principles to be applied by the courts." [60] In such instances his theory of ultimate judicial impotence served him well. In protecting Bill of Rights freedoms, judges acted "not by authority of our competence but by force of our commissions"; history had "authenticate[d]" a function for the Court "when liberty [was] infringed." [61] The judiciary had only to declare the fundamentality of the right being protected and its consequent immunity from governmental infringement. In cases testing the scope of the Fourth Amendment's protection against illegal searches and seizures, Jackson expressed similar sentiments. He felt that "uncontrolled search and seizure is one of the first and most effective weapons in the arsenal of arbitrary government"; [62] he found the Fourth Amendment a safeguard of human dignity and self-reliance. [63]

But Jackson was quick to emphasize the context in which usurpations of civil liberties had taken place, and mindful of countervailing values that might justify usurpations in specific instances. He tolerated restrictions on free speech if they protected tranquility [64] or prevented disorderly conduct [65] or fostered harmony in race relations. [66] He allowed members of the American Communist Party to be convicted under a criminal statute for conspiring to teach the necessity of overthrowing the United States government, even though no showing had been made that an overthrow was an imminent result of their teaching. [67] He permitted coerced confessions in major crimes, [68] indicated that he would tolerate roadblocks and searches as a means of tracking kidnapers, [69] and in general opposed attempts to use the due process clause to give criminals "new and unprecedented opportunities to re-try their cases, or to try the prosecuting attorney or their own counsel." [70] Although he once stated that "security is like liberty in that many are the crimes committed in its name," [71] he accepted as a reasonable trade-off the denial of procedural safeguards for the criminally accused to allow the police not to be "forced to stand by helplessly while those suspected of murder prowl about unmolested." [72]

On balance, Jackson found clearer answers in the Constitution on questions of economic regulation than on issues involving government restrictions of civil liberties. Federalism, with the passage of time, seemed more intelligible as an economic philosophy than as a social one. A national free market was as meaningful in the 1950s as it apparently had been to the framers, but the language of the Bill of Rights seemed elusive in its simplicity when re-examined in the

light of Reconstruction, an official police force, an international
Communist conspiracy, rapidly changing attitudes toward religious
privileges and race relations, an expanded governmental intelligence
apparatus, and the legacy of two World Wars. The overriding constitutional principles being cloudy and double-edged, Jackson retreated in civil liberties cases to practical accommodations between
the competing values of liberty and order. On the Stone Court his
approach became a counterweight to militant libertarianism; on the
Vinson Court it became an aid to those who tolerated curtailment
of civil liberties when national security was allegedly involved.[73]

IV

In a variety of ways Jackson's views on the proper function of the
judiciary ran counter to those held by the influential Justices of his
tenure. To the extent that such Justices as Black and Douglas perceived an obligation in governmental institutions to aid disadvantaged persons and supported results that were consistent with that
perception, Jackson's attitude diverged from theirs. He believed in
"liberal legislation," he said in 1948, as long as it was "conserva-
tively construed." [74] He did not think it appropriate for judges "to
seize the initiative in shaping the policy of the law, either by constitutional interpretation or by statutory construction." [75] At the end
of his life he attacked the "cult of libertarian judicial activists" on
the Court whose attitude, he felt, "encourage[d] a belief that the
judges may be left to correct the result of public indifference to
issues of liberty." [76] In two areas especially, Jackson's differences
with Black and Douglas on this point produced opposing votes:
labor relations and civil liberties. Black and Douglas regularly voted
to construe the Fair Labor Standards Act and the National Labor
Relations Act in ways sympathetic to labor unions; Jackson
frequently disagreed.[77] After World War II, Black and Douglas
took a virtually uncompromising stand in behalf of protection for
civil liberties against usurpations by federal and state governments; [78] Jackson's view disclaimed this stance for an approach that
asked the Court to "temper its doctrinaire logic with a little practical wisdom" lest it "convert the constitutional Bill of Rights into a
suicide pact." [79]

Jackson's clashes with Black and Douglas underscored the fact that his conception of appellate judging was too delicately poised between intermediate activism and ultimate restraint to satisfy his colleagues on the Stone and Vinson Courts. Stone's theory of judging rejected distinctions between intermediate and ultimate stages in judging. He simply acknowledged that the judiciary was sometimes forced to make hard choices between competing social values with no guidance from history. Stone's belief that judicial activism was permissible where an interest being invaded had no effective recourse to the political process assumed a freedom in the judiciary to decide the scope of its own power. Jackson found that assumption untenable. Frankfurter, in contrast, did not deny Jackson's belief that judges were ultimately impotent as social policy-makers, but claimed that they could not even function in a policy-making capacity at intermediate levels. When Jackson maintained in a 1942 opinion that judges could "legislate" in unraveling a "jurisdictional snarl" involving a taxation issue, Frankfurter found the remark offensive. It "disregard[ed]," he asserted, "the role of this Court in our Constitutional system since its establishment in 1789." [80] Yet Frankfurter, for all his efforts to avoid functioning as an architect of social policy, came to scrutinize the constitutionality of legislation through an accommodation process—not unlike Jackson's—in which competing interests and values were balanced. What Frankfurter could not abide was Jackson's open confession that a choice not to subordinate one's personal preferences for the judgments of a legislature was still a choice, with political implications.

The responses of Jackson's colleagues highlighted the central tension in his approach to judging. He insisted that judges could respond to the exigencies of practical problems while at the same time basing their resolutions on principles of law that transcended merely pragmatic judgments. His involvement with the Nuremberg trials reflected this dual sense. Stone and also Frankfurter criticized his participation in the trials as threatening to the stature of the judiciary. The outcome of the trials was foreordained, they argued; for Jackson to lend his office to the prosecution suggested that the Supreme Court could be identified with what Stone called a "high-grade lynching party." [81] Others on the Court were said to have expressed concern with Jackson's participation in Nuremberg for different reasons, either because he did not establish an overwhelming case against leading Nazis or because he had accepted the job of Chief Prosecutor to advance his own political career.[82]

Jackson, however, believed that Nuremberg could illustrate the capacity of law to serve as a force for social cohesiveness. The trials, if carefully conducted, could legitimate desired results—the execution of enemies to the American nation and the repudiation of a way of life they personified—and also demonstrate the inherent fairness and justice of the Anglo-American adversary system. As prosecutor, Jackson was both an advocate for the destruction of Nazism and a servant of the legal system under which that destruction was being attempted. He could not expect to achieve vindication of the positions he advocated unless the system, through its evidentiary rules and procedural safeguards, affirmed them. Trying the Nazi criminals in a court of law, Jackson felt, was worth the conceded risk of failing to convict them. "The world yields no respect to courts," he had said prior to his Nuremberg appointment, "that are merely organized to convict. . . . You must put no man on trial before anything that is called a court . . . if you are not willing to see him freed if not proven guilty." [83]

In his remarks as prosecutor, Jackson stressed the two levels of his approach. His case was "hard and uncompromising." Defendants were characterized individually as "venomous vulgarian," "half militarist and half gangster," and "the greatest and cruelest slaver since the Pharaohs of Egypt." [84] Their conduct was pictured as "a dreadful sequence of aggressions or crimes . . . the destruction of all that was beautiful and useful in so much of the world." They were "living symbols of racial hatreds, of terrorism and violence, and of the arrogance and cruelty of power." [85] Yet at the same time the task of the trial was to "draw the line" between "just and measured retribution" and "the unthinking cry for vengeance which arises from the anguish of war." The Nazis had not distinguished between law as a tool of power and law as an emblem of "the moral sense of mankind"; [86] that was all the more reason for keeping that distinction sharply in focus at Nuremberg.

Jackson believed that his participation in the Nuremberg trials had been the "most important, enduring and constructive work of [his] life." [87] He took the notion of a "rule of law" seriously: properly administered, law could be a repository of "detachment and intellectual integrity" that fulfilled "humanity's aspirations to do justice." [88] It could also be a guide for practical conduct, a vehicle for facilitating business arrangements, a method of reconciling value conflicts, a forum for vindicating human rights, and a process

through which the virtues of rationality and civilization could become dominant. Yet Jackson as a judge was never quite capable of
conveying the sense that law could have an existence apart from the
workings of its agents. As an advocate, whether in Jamestown,
Washington, or Nuremberg, he had attempted to adopt partisan
stances without giving the impression that he had surrendered his
independence or integrity. He was a lawyer, not a hired man, and
in suggesting the difference between the two he helped distinguish
law from power or partisanship. But on the Court he somehow
failed to personify the detachment he tried to achieve at Nuremberg. He was at his most effective as a judge, paradoxically, in the
use of adversary skills, ridiculing the positions of Justices who opposed him, or restating an issue in vivid but sometimes polemical
terms.

Consequently Jackson was himself a counterargument for his
belief that judges could wield power at one level only to yield it at
another. His puncturing of fictional doctrines, his candid discussions of his own thought processes, his recognition that judges
"legislated" whether they supported or opposed the actions of legislatures, his open squabbles with his colleagues, his use of humor,
sarcasm, and irony in his opinions—all these created the impression
of a human being whose personal passions and prejudices had not
been lessened by his becoming a judge. Yet Jackson's approach to
judging rested on a premise that at some point in the decision-making process subordination of individual will to institutional imperatives was required. The approaches to economic regulation and
civil liberties that he took were, in this sense, not his but those of
the framers of the Constitution. They were compelled not by personal predilection but by a legacy of eighteenth-century social and
economic policies. Jackson was so much the modern judge, however, breaking down the mystique of his office, that his deference
to eighteenth-century views seemed out of joint. One was tempted
to ask whether the framers' economic theories were not Jackson's in
disguise, and whether a distinction between the intermediate and
ultimate stages of judging really existed.

There were those, however, who took seriously Jackson's effort
to characterize judging as an exercise of both power and humility,
and who accepted his premise that law could simultaneously function as a process for adjusting conflict and a rule of civilized conduct.[89] If Jackson's influence in the Stone and Vinson courts was

more that of gadfly than that of intellectual leader, his theory of judicial performance did not atrophy after his death. In a society increasingly marked by legislation, Jackson's theory freed the judiciary from an utterly passive stance toward the actions of legislatures; in times when competition between the federal government and the states had revived, it reasserted the framers' belief that American government rested on balances between the powers of the states and those of the nation; in a world where judges no longer merely discovered law, it refused to concede that law was therefore synonymous with the dictates of judges. As debates about the proper function of the judiciary focused increasingly on means to achieve a satisfactory balance between creative leadership and fidelity to institutional constraints, Jackson's view offered itself as an intellectually respectable model, made less controversial, perhaps, by its eventual dissociation from its architect.

12

Cardozo, Learned Hand, and Frank: The Dialectic of Freedom and Constraint

Throughout the early and middle years of the twentieth century, jurisprudential dilemmas of the kind confronted by Jackson and other Supreme Court Justices were experienced also by appellate judges of the lower federal and state courts. Although lower court judges heard far more private law cases and had far fewer opportunities than Supreme Court Justices to interpret the federal Constitution, they too felt the pressures swirling about the demise of oracular judging.

Although those pressures were still unresolved and keenly felt as late as Jackson's tenure, they had originated in the late nineteenth century. As early as the 1870s a skepticism had arisen about the validity of universal principles whose truth could not be empirically demonstrated. This insight, symbolized by Holmes's *The Common Law* (1881), and first confined to a handful of intellectuals, interacted with the numbing effects of World War I, which seemed to symbolize the simultaneous collapse of "gentlemanly" codes of behavior, a hierarchical society, and the martial virtues, to produce a value crisis of major proportions.[1] One side effect of the crisis, previously discussed, was an intense questioning of the absolutist character of moral truths. Two others of a more academic nature were criticism of formalistic methodologies based on *a priori* postulates and growing intellectual support for the proposition that the only "reality" was that which was empirically observable.[2]

The attacks on and the eventual repudiation of the oracular theory of judging may be traced to the same sources. The oracular theory was challenged and eventually discarded because it assumed the existence of unverifiable fixed truths in an intellectual climate in which that assumption was no longer credible. Once a conception of judges as oracles was discarded, however, the vulnerability of the autocratic judiciary in a democratic society became evident. If judicial decisions were not merely declarations of finite truths, but were something resembling the personal views of judges, they had to be justified on different intellectual grounds.

In response to this need the jurisprudential theories previously alluded to—Sociological Jurisprudence, Realism, and Process Jurisprudence—emerged in a consecutive sequence from the 1900s through the 1950s. Sociological Jurisprudence insisted that decisions be grounded in empirical observations of changing social conditions and thereby replace pseudologic with "experience." [3] Realism, which drew on the contributions of Sociological Jurisprudence but ultimately deviated from it, assumed that judging was as illogical and idiosyncratic an exercise as any other form of decision-making by human beings and sought to reduce its irrationality by developing, through empirical observation, methods of predicting court decisions.[4] Process Jurisprudence, reacting to Realism's apparent fatalism toward unchecked judicial power, attempted to build institutional constraints back into adjudication and to identify rational judging with an awareness of the discrete functions of the judiciary and other branches of government.[5] No longer, then, was the twentieth-century appellate judge an oracle; he was, depending on the theory advanced, primarily a social engineer, or a "hunch player" [6] who understood and trusted his instincts, or a craftsman in the "reasoned elaboration" [7] of justifications for his power.

These developments, stretching over more than fifty years, produced an ambivalent stance for the twentieth-century appellate judge, a stance that reflected recognition that judges were human as well as an attendant sense of the possibility that a judge could use his office to promote values in which he believed. At the same time this stance conveyed the importance of continued identification of judging with the values of impersonality, impartiality, and rationality. A judge had opportunities for creativity; at the same time he had obligations and constraints that bound those opportunities.

Jackson's interpretation of judging centered on the question as to what extent a judge dedicated to the ideal of impersonality could personalize his office. The interpretations of Benjamin Cardozo, Learned Hand, and Jerome Frank centered on a related question raised by Hand in a 1933 radio address: How far was a judge free in rendering a decision? [8] The question was intended to incorporate the several facets of the twentieth-century judge's role: a human being, a member of contemporary American society, a representative of a special type of governing institution, an heir to a tradition of decision-making that emphasized independence and accountability, individuality and self-limitation.

During their careers, Cardozo, Hand, and Frank made prime contributions to an understanding of the dialectic of freedom and restraint in the appellate judiciary. In certain respects they were particularly well-situated to make that contribution. For the great part of their collective judicial careers, they were judges on appellate courts of intermediate status, reviewing the decisions of inferior courts in their system but bound to follow judgments of the United States Supreme Court. Cardozo served on the New York Court of Appeals for eighteen years, from 1914 to 1932. During that time he made a national reputation as a judge and wrote his most influential extrajudicial works, including *The Nature of the Judicial Process*. His short subsequent career on the Supreme Court, which ended with his death in 1939, paled by comparison. Hand served for fifteen years as a federal district court judge, then for thirty-seven on the United States Court of Appeals for the Second Circuit. Frank's only experience as a judge consisted of his sixteen years as Hand's Scond Circuit colleague. For most of their judicial lives Cardozo, Hand, and Frank wrote their opinions with the awareness that they were both free to overrule decisions that came to them yet required to have their opinions possibly subjected to further scrutiny.

Moreover, Cardozo, Hand, and Frank held judicial office during a time of profound and rapid social change, in an environment that magnified the scope and pace of that change. When Cardozo first took office, the status of the automobile industry in American society was indeterminate; Cardozo himself helped clarify it. By the time of Learned Hand's death in 1961, two world wars and a world-wide depression had been weathered, and radio, television, travel by airplane, and the computer had become features of American life, each headquartered in New York City. No judge operating in such an atmosphere could fail to perceive the implicit pressure upon the law to be responsive to changing social conditions.

The combination, perhaps, of the New York environment, the status of their courts, and their own intellectual powers moved Cardozo, Hand, and Frank to produce judicial and extrajudicial literature of considerable quality and influence. They distinguished themselves among early-twentieth-century American appellate judges in their attempts to create jurisprudential stances to accommodate the contradictory pressures of modern judging. For them judicial decision-making meant neither assuming complexities out of existence nor being defeated by them. Rather, it meant trying to unravel such complexities until the social trade-offs they represented were revealed. Each man had his own method for dealing with the necessity of balancing what Hand called "incommensurable" values.[9] Although the relative soundness of their methods is largely a question of individual taste, each man clearly distinguished himself in his effort. Together the three added a dimension of intellectual sophistication to the American judicial tradition.

I

Cardozo's family history might have been chronicled by Edith Wharton or Louis Auchincloss. His ancestors were Sephardic Jews, longtime residents of New York, successful businessmen, educators and patriots,[10] a closely knit and intermarried clan. Relatives sat on the board of Columbia University, held judgeships, were patrons of the arts and generally carried out the rituals of New York's upper class, whose anti-Semitism did not extend to prominent Sephardic Jews who could trace their American citizenship to the eighteenth century. Three years after Cardozo's birth in 1870, the position of his family was severely shaken by the implication of his father, Albert Cardozo, a judge of the Supreme Court of New York, in a probe of the Erie Railroad's bankruptcy proceedings. The elder Cardozo resigned to avoid impeachment, having apparently acted with impropriety in the appointment of a receiver for the railroad, and having, on other occasions, allowed immigrants to acquire citizenship illegally. He had also assigned a large share of his authorized appointments as a bankruptcy referee to one of his nephews. His resignation dishonored the Cardozos and created in his son Benjamin a lifetime mission of restoring the family name.[11]

Cardozo grew to maturity in an environment marked by intrafamily trials and tensions. His mother died when he was nine and his father six years later, leaving a depleted inheritance to be divided among six children, only two of whom were potential wage earners. He was raised by his sister Ellen, who combined, throughout his life, the roles of mother, confidant, and companion, and Cardozo confided once to a cousin that he would never marry because he "could never put [Ellen] in second place."[12] From his college days at Columbia, where he was described as antisocial and clannish,[13] to his years on the Court of Appeals in Albany, from which he wrote Ellen with great regularity,[14] Cardozo demonstrated a singular preoccupation with private family affairs. For over twenty years before 1913, his life consisted primarily of work with his brother Albert's law firm and its successors, and of family gatherings, at which he often played piano duets with Ellen. He appeared to some contemporaries as "congenitally shy" and "monkish in his habits."[15] Learned Hand said that he "never wanted anybody to penetrate into his inner life."[16]

Yet Cardozo's mission of restoration dictated that to some extent he seek public contacts and even covet public attention. In this task he proved remarkably adept, despite his reclusive tendencies. He continually managed to charm those with whom he came in contact. His shyness projected itself as modesty, his reserve as calmness and poise, his tendency to enjoy and indulge in flattery as graciousness and civility. He appeared, to observers, as a man of "rare courtesy," with a "nobleness and lofty exaltation of spirit," who possessed "extraordinary charm and infinite benevolence of character"; a "saintly character," who was "sweet, gentle, modest, and ever considerate."[17] Even those who displeased him were given little cause for offense. "Cardozo," maintained Learned Hand, "could handle the scalpel . . . but perfectly painlessly so that the subject would not know he was being dissected."[18]

Cardozo's self-effacement and charm masked his ambition but did not eradicate it. In 1913, after considerable success as an ap-

pellate litigator, he was proposed as a candidate for a judgeship on
the New York Supreme Court. Here was a dramatic opportunity to
bury his father's ghost; and although Cardozo publicly maintained
that he would not participate in the campaign, he worked carefully
and astutely behind the scenes [19] and was elected. A month later he
was named to the Court of Appeals, and his public career was
launched. While a judge, he combined a tendency to cherish his
privacy with intermittent forays into the public eye, each undertaken with a certain coyness. He initially declined an invitation to
give the Storrs Lectures at Yale in 1921, protesting that he had
nothing to talk about, but subsequently realized that he could describe how he went about deciding cases, and produced *The Nature
of the Judicial Process*.[20] He allegedly resisted pressure from those
who sought to have him nominated to the Supreme Court to replace Holmes, and upon being nominated complained bitterly
about having to leave Albany. Nonetheless, he did not decline the
invitation when it came.

The reconciliation of Cardozo's private self with his public
image was not effectuated without some strain. His unpublished
college essays reveal a concern with the depersonalizing effects of
thwarted aggression and repressed passions, as well as the emotional demands communal living made upon individuals.[21] Those
close to him saw occasional snatches of bitterness and self-pity.
Nicholas Murray Butler, one of his teachers at Columbia, referred
to him as "desperately serious"; [22] Learned Hand spoke of his "very
deep skepticism" and tendency to "shy away from a commitment"; [23] George Hellman, his authorized biographer, referred to
"channels of affection, even perhaps of married love" that were
"consciously barred" by Cardozo's family loyalties.[24]

Cardozo's surface affect—gentle, ethereal, humble, lavish in his
praise of others—did not adequately convey his skepticism, ambition, bitterness, and tendency to evaluate others critically. To an
extent he must have worn a mask in public, his graciousness and
charity representing defenses against overly intimate contact with
others. His judicial opinions exhibited a similar quality, and were
at times close to being disingenuous. But he did not deceive himself. His theory of the proper exercise of the judicial function candidly admitted that on many occasions a judge found himself free
to shape the course of the law, yet might choose to mask that
freedom of choice in the traditional techniques and canons of his

profession. That kind of artifice, for Cardozo, was not hypocrisy or dishonesty but simply good sense. It strengthened rather than undermined respect for the judiciary.

The state of mind in which Cardozo initiated his investigations into the nature of appellate decision-making was characteristic of his time and place. He saw the "perpetual flux" of his immediate environment; he recognized that "nothing [was] stable, [n]othing absolute, [a]ll fluid and changeable." [25] Yet at the same time he confessed to a "yearning for consistency, for uniformity of plan and structure," for "a larger and more inclusive unity in which differences will be reconciled and abnormalities vanish," finding in himself an "intellectual craving" for "symmetry of form and substance." [26] To fashion a rule that settled one case, then to expand it, through logical progressions, to the point where it covered countless similar cases was enormously satisfying. Not only was the process analytically and conceptually tidy, it gave the professional constituents of appellate judges—the bar and its clients—clear guidelines for the future conduct of their affairs.

But the law, like modern civilization, was pitted with anomalies and irregularities. Logical symmetry took a judge only so far. Historical anachronisms dominated the law of real property, their earlier logical significance obscured by time. The legal steps that created an estate in fee simple could not be distinguished from those that created a life estate by any process except an appeal to history. Yet the procedures were part of modern estate planning. Another source of logical anomalies was the incorporation into the law of the customs and practices of a trade, such as the proliferation of different types of securities, with the attendant creation of new rights and responsibilities in the law of secured transactions. In deciding a controversy involving the exchange of securities a court could not ignore the role played by custom, whatever it thought of the logic of a particular business practice. Finally, logic sometimes conflicted with equity and justice. One might begin with the traditional premise that private property rights should be protected from governmental usurpation. Expanded to its logical outcome, this premise forbade state regulation of railroad rates, since the substitution of a state-imposed rate for a "market" rate was surely an interference with the right to free enjoyment of the fruits of private ownership. In the absence of regulation, however, railroads tended to set discriminatory rates, making it more costly for certain classes of persons to use their facilities, and denying some classes the use altogether. At times the resultant inequities proved so offensive to the general public that sound policy required a partial retreat from the original premise.

For Cardozo the appellate judge's task, most broadly defined, was to seek an accommodation between the values embodied in symmetrical logic and the competing values manifested by any anomalies. In his extrajudicial writings he proposed several means by which this accommodation might be sought. One employed a distinctive methodology for appellate decision-making; another made use of a refinement of that methodology, one that emphasized the role of broad overriding purposes and goals in American society. Still another flowed from an eventual recognition of the inadequacy of any one method of decision-making in solving the complex value choices that judging required.

In *The Nature of the Judicial Process*, a work that established him as one of the leading jurists of his time, Cardozo described a method of decision-making that would enable appellate judges to respond to simultaneous pressures for continuity and change. Both stability and progress were contemporary goals, Cardozo believed, the question being how to ensure their coexistence. The answer lay in a selective use of four distinct methods: philosophy, emphasizing logical symmetry; history, anachronistic vagaries; tradition, the customs and practices of a trade or business; and sociology, the social policies behind legal rules. The first three methods were associated with particular areas of the law. Logical analysis took care of the ordinary run of appellate cases, in which matching precedents to new facts was all that was required; "a page of history was worth a volume of logic" [27] in areas (such as real property) where ancient procedures had survived; trade practices dominated the law of commercial transactions. The fourth method "was always in reserve": when other methods conflicted, it served as an "arbiter" between them. New conceptions of the responsibility of private property-holders had created "new restraints upon ancient rights" [28] in which contemporary logic clashed with history. The question in such instances was whether "a paramount public policy" prevailed over "certainty and uniformity and order and coherence." [29] Judicial appeal to contemporary social values helped resolve that question.

Cardozo's audience, mindful of the dramatic value shifts taking place in early-twentieth-century America, hopeful yet skeptical about progress, unsure of the roles history and tradition were to play in the modern world, reacted to his book with great enthusiasm. After the author's first lecture at Yale University the auditorium was overflowing; at its conclusion he received a spontaneous standing ovation.[30] The book has become a classic of legal education, and is continually recommended to aspiring law students on the perhaps dubious ground that "it still possesses the same validity and vitality . . . as it did when published." [31] The appeal of the work was that it represented a compromise between oracular and nihilistic judging. The four methods—really classification devices—retained a conceptualistic approach familiar to the late nineteenth century. At the same time, Cardozo conceded that judges made law, albeit in a limited sense. Since the methods—even that of sociology—were intended as restraints on the judge, Cardozo could face the fact that he was not an oracle without appearing to be a tyrant.

The success of *The Nature of the Judicial Process* created a market for Cardozo's further reflections on his function. In two additional series of lectures, *The Growth of the Law* (1924) and *The Paradoxes of Legal Science* (1927), he refined his thinking. *The Growth of the Law* focused on the problem of choosing between alternative methods of decision-making. In a case in which traditionally protected practices were being rescrutinized in light of a new calculus of social values, a judge had the option of employing the methods of history and custom or the method of sociology. His choice, Cardozo maintained, should rest on an understanding of the purposes each method served as well as on a determination as to which purposes more accurately approximated the current ends of society. Law, in Cardozo's view, was continually growing, and its growth was "conscious" in that it reflected "the attainment of the moral end" as embodied in "legal forms." [32] By searching for purposes in the law and testing its decisions with reference to perceived ends, judges could make a more intelligent balancing of the competing values cases presented.

The argument advanced by Cardozo in *The Growth of the Law* assumed the existence and intelligibility of shared social purposes and goals. This was a large assumption, especially in the light of the sense of value disintegration perceived by many of his contemporaries in the 1920s. With the publication of *The Paradoxes of Legal*

Science Cardozo exhibited some doubts about this premise. He rejected the concept of continual progress, asserting that the law changed over time but did not necessarily grow. He rejected, in addition, two implications of his earlier works—the belief that morality could be said to have a fixed content, and the ideal of law as a science. Judicial decisions ought to reflect contemporary moral values, to be sure, but one generation's morality was not necessarily another's. A fourfold classification of methods for appellate decision-making was a helpful analytical device but not a scientific formula. The judicial calculus was "precarious," consisting of "little compromises and adjustments, the expedients of the fleeting hour." [33] No method or approach could dispel uncertainty; paradoxes lay at the heart of social organization. A judge could not achieve any ultimate reconciliation of stability with progress. His function was "not to transform civilization" [34] but to make a "timid and tentative approximation" of currently cherished values. [35]

Cardozo's interpretation of his office, then, juxtaposed a private craving for certainty and predictability against a public acceptance of the complexities of modern life. Although he believed that "where conflict exists, moral values [were] to be preferred to economic and economic to aesthetic," [36] and that morality had a core of timeless substantive content, he stopped short of imposing these beliefs on his constituents. His style was rather to lay bare the competing elements in a case and then to make it appear as if their clash had been resolved by someone other than himself, either in principles of law laid down by his predecessors or in the actions of a legislature. He was candid in revealing the problems he faced, but in solving them he retreated behind conventional techniques of judicial subterfuge—of which he was a master. His retreat was motivated less by a desire to deceive than by a fear that if the sovereign prerogative of choice were truly his alone he would not know how to make it. The judiciary's arsenal of craft techniques was his barrier against that fear. It allowed him, said Learned Hand, to appear inflexible once he had arrived at a decision, although he had agonized in the process of reaching it. [37]

II

With Cardozo there was a continual layer of gentility between him and the contemplation of social disintegration and personal despair.

If he was not completely the saintly, ethereal figure some saw him as, he had at least enough commitment to the ideals of nobility and purity to have merged those qualities in his public image. Learned Hand, by contrast, had no particular fear of the horrors and brutalities in life and no illusions about his own saintliness. At one level this made him a less artful judge and a more accessible person than Cardozo. Yet in his own fashion he was remote and distant, with his own areas of self-consciousness and self-doubt.

Throughout his life, but especially in the eminence of his later career, Hand had the gift of public charm. Like Holmes, he could inspire his professional audience with an unforgettable pithy phrase, usually a metaphor rather than a epigram. Life was "a dicer's throw"; reason "a smoky torch." [38] Hand was more versatile than Holmes in his appeal, however. He could sing a stanza of Gilbert and Sullivan, tell a ribald story, mock a dialect, or serve as the voice of God in an Archibald MacLeish play. He was a clubman, a figure on the banquet circuit, an academic lecturer, a speaker at patriotic public ceremonies, a commemorator of his fellow judges. He never failed to notice the nuances of these different roles; the tone of his remarks was always appropriate. Even on the most delicate occasions during his tenure as Chief Justice of the Second Circuit, he knew how to charm. Writing to Judge Charles Clark at a particularly trying time in the latter's career, Hand said: "We all get the feeling that we are beating our wings ineffectively in the void, and I know of no way to prevent that mood coming on us from time to time. I should like to say, however, for whatever it may be worth, that we all think of you as one of the outstanding judges on the federal or any other bench. . . . Courage, mon ami, le Diable est mort." [39]

Yet Hand's singular charm and great zest for companionship were in part products of a private tendency toward introspection and even melancholia. He did not like to be alone, an old friend once said: he was "a man of moods," and good conversation cheered him. [40] As an undergraduate at Harvard, he described himself as being "just on the fringe" socially: "all his friends got into clubs and he did not." He wondered, much later in his life, whether he had not been "kind of a sissy." [41] He was not comfortable or successful as a law practitioner, either in Albany, where he worked from 1896 to 1902, or in New York City, where he practiced until his 1909 appointment to the United States District Court for the Southern District of New York. [42] His father and grandfather had been judges; there his talents seemed best suited, he said, for he "thought with his fingers." [43]

But judging was not without its uncertainties and disappointments. First was its close identification, in early twentieth-century New York, with state and national politics. Hand owed his district judgeship to the overtures of Charles C. Burlingham, one of the kingmakers of the New York bar, who was also influential in Cardozo's campaign for the New York Supreme Court in 1913. Through Burlingham and George Wickersham, Attorney General under President Taft, Hand received his first appointment. Three years later, in the 1912 election, he publicly supported Theodore Roosevelt and the Progressive Party against Taft. In 1913, he ran for the New York Court of Appeals on the Progressive ticket, did not campaign, and was soundly defeated. The alienation of Taft produced by this series of events redounded to Hand's considerable disadvantage, for Taft (as has been noted) exercised veto power over major federal judicial appointments during the Harding and Coolidge administrations. In 1922 Hand, still a district judge, was proposed to Harding as a Supreme Court candidate, but Taft, remembering Hand as "a wild Roosevelt man and a Progressive," suggested that he would be a divisive force on the Court. [44]

This legacy of political animosity combined with other circumstances to deny Hand a Supreme Court nomination all his life. He managed to secure promotion to the Second Circuit in 1924, again with the aid of Burlingham; but Taft's presence kept him from further consideration for the Court until 1930. He was then twice denied nomination by the fortuity of geography, two other able candidates, Cardozo and Charles Evans Hughes, also being residents of New York. By 1942, at age seventy, he seemed finally destined to succeed. Felix Frankfurter, who had lobbied long for Hand's nomination, was instructed by President Roosevelt to prepare a statement announcing it. At the last minute, however, Roosevelt backed down, embarrassed by his own Court-packing arguments, which had emphasized the advanced age of the then current justices. [45] Thus Hand, despite a growing national reputation, remained on the Second Circuit. "For about 20 years or so," he said late in his life, "every time I went to Washington . . . I said, 'Oh, wouldn't it be wonderful if I got on the Supreme Court.' " [46] By the end of his career he had put aside both the hope and the subsequent disappointments. Only vestiges of his feelings occasionally surfaced, as when he asked President Kennedy in 1961 to "promote those best qualified in the lower levels [of the federal judiciary] when you can." [47]

Despite these and other smaller frustrations, which occasionally provoked outbursts of temper in the courtroom,[48] Hand, like Holmes, had the fortune to live long enough to be made fully aware of the high esteem in which he was held. As early as the 1920s, before he joined the Second Circuit, Holmes had urged his appointment to the Supreme Court; [49] in 1925 Cardozo put Hand in "a little group of two or three" judges who were "pretty close" to "my idol" Holmes in his esteem; [50] Justice Stone lobbied for Hand's appointment to the Court in the 1930s; [51] Felix Frankfurter, a consummate promoter, boosted Hand incessantly for thirty years. In 1946 Hand was termed in *Life* Magazine "the spiritual heir of Marshall, Holmes, Brandeis and Cardozo." [52] In a tribute issue of the *Harvard Law Review* a year later he was called "unquestionably first among American judges." [53] In proceedings commemorating his fiftieth year of judicial service in 1959, Frankfurter called him "the greatest master of English speech on the bench since Holmes laid down his pen." [54] Others paid tributes to Hand, as they had to Holmes, such as are rarely paid to the dead and almost never to the living.

Yet the stature of Hand has recently been questioned. The intermediate status of his court and his "restraintist philosophy" of judicial review, it has been argued, made his impact "less than his reputation would lead us to expect." [55] His reputation has been seen as "mostly myth": "he was great because he was reputed to be great." [56] This assessment of Hand raises once more the question of the sources of an appellate judge's image in history. To an extent the reputation of an appellate judge is a function of the sociological or political implications of the results he reaches, and as such changes with time.[57] In addition, insofar as a judge reveals the philosophical foundations of his approach to decision-making he becomes vulnerable to changing fashions, since activism and self-restraint rise and fall in public esteem. Finally, the legal questions of dominant interest for most educated Americans have been constitutional questions, and the opportunities of an intermediate appellate court to render major decisions on constitutional issues are extremely limited. As Hand once wrote Stone, "The most futile job I have to do is to pass on Constitutional questions. Who in hell

cares what anybody says about them but the Final Five of the
August Nine of which you are one?" [58]

But the sources of Hand's eminence were more varied than those
of most judges in comparable positions. His notable longevity on
the bench gave him the opportunity to write in a number of areas
and thereby tended to counteract the limited reach of his court.
The crowded, varied docket of the Second Circuit, the skill of the
New York City bar, and the high quality of his judicial colleagues
resulted in the regular presentation of complex issues whose ramifications were thoroughly perceived and articulated. The economic
and intellectual importance of the New York environment meant
that his decisions on normally arcane subjects, such as patent law,
could take on national significance. The originality and clarity of
his writing style served to widen the audience for his opinions, and
his versatility as a public speaker expanded his popular impact. Finally, his theory of judicial performance, imperfectly described as a
"restraintist philosophy," encouraged creativity as much as it
checked it. His criticism of judicial activism was reserved for constitutional cases, and his advocation of a limited interpretation of
judicial power in that area associated him with an influential body
of early-twentieth-century jurisprudential thinkers, including
Holmes and Brandeis. Only very late in his life did his philosophy
of judging appear to isolate him from current events.

Hand began thinking about the intellectual process of judging
by, as he said, looking the grey rat in the eye.[59] Civilization was a
thin layer covering the anarchistic and brutal tendencies of humanity. Beneath its surface "the murderer lurk[ed] always not far . . .
to break out from time to time, peace resolutions to the contrary
notwithstanding." [60] Social gains came "with immeasurable waste";
conflict was normal; the path of history was "strewn with carnage."
And there were no eternal guiding principles for social conduct: the
Absolute was mute. All man could do was grope through trial and
error, trying to "shake off the brute" and keep the social order he
had created from disintegrating.[61]

There was a certain comfort in this acceptance of man's limitations. Wisdom, Hand felt, emerged as the "false assurance[s]" of
human omniscience and omnipotence vanished. "[G]entle irony,
friendly skepticism," and open-mindedness were the appropriate
moods in which to assess the worth of man's attempts to organize
his society.[62] There was little hope of human perfectibility, he felt,

and little assurance of progress, but some indication that, at least in democratic societies, individuals tended to tolerate each other's needs and to make accommodations with conflict rather than exacerbate it. This "spirit of moderation" [63] was not always evident, nor were attempts of accommodation always triumphs of reason, but despair was premature. So long as one did not expect too much from efforts to make life in America more civilized, one could find some solace in those efforts.

These perceptions could be useful to the work of American appellate judges, who had, Hand believed, some responsibility to contribute to "civilization" and also some power to dictate the ways in which individuals were to conduct their affairs. Judicial wisdom came, for Hand, with a dual realization. First, a judge could not ignore the powers of his office. "The law" was not always clear, and inevitably in interpreting it a judge mingled his own sense of the appropriate rules of social conduct with already existing sanctions. To the extent that his own glosses on prior cases and statutes were accepted, a judge was free to "make" law. Second, on the other hand, governing in America was a reciprocal process. Although "the law" was synonymous with the commands of government officials, those officials were charged with the duty of expressing the common will. The common will, however, was difficult to discern, largely because of the inability of human beings to articulate, or even to know, what values they shared with each other. Thus the judge was "in a contradictory position . . . pulled by two opposite forces." [64] He had to try to interpret "the common will expressed by the government" even in those circumstances when it was virtually indecipherable, trusting that his analytical powers and instincts would produce an acceptable formulation. But he could not merely "enforce whatever he [thought] best." [65]

In walking this delicate line of creativity and restraint Hand was guided by his original judgments about mankind and civilization. He began with three paradigm situations. Where the judge had emerged as a declarer of the common will of the people, as expressed in law, ample room for judicial creativity existed; common law cases were the best example. Where the legislative branch of government had articulated the common will through a statute, the judge was bound to interpret that statute in conformity with the legislature's intentions. And where two sets of potentially conflicting declarations existed, such as a statute and the United States

Constitution, or where the specific intent of a legislature could not clearly be determined, a judge was forced to balance the expertise of his office against the institutional limitations on it.

Hand refined these paradigms in the light of his social perceptions. Given that the common will was so difficult to discern and articulate, great caution had to be exercised in following its apparent mandates. The more specific the mandate, the greater the confidence one could have that it truly expressed the desires of the people. The more general it was, the less valuable it became in this capacity. In the case of specific mandates, the judge was required to "loyally enforce" [66] the dictates of the legislature. Where the only mandate that existed was that of an implicit delegation of power to judges to enact "authentic bit[s] of special legislation," [67] the judge was only constrained by the canons of his profession, the people having agreed to be guided by judicial expertise. In the intermediate situations of statutory and constitutional interpretation, the generality of the mandate determined the appropriate judicial response.

Some provisions of the Constitution were "specific enough to be treated like other legal commands": they prescribed clear limitations on the jurisdiction of courts or the power of legislatures and were simply to be obeyed. Other provisions were of intermediate specificity. Their application to an individual case could be determined by "look[ing] to their history and their setting with confidence that these will disclose their purpose." [68] Still others, however, such as freedom of speech and freedom of press, due process of law, and equal protection of the laws, were so general that they ceased to be commands and became merely "moral adjurations." [69] "[N]ot definite enough to be guides on concrete occasions," [70] they could only be used by the judiciary as a check on legislative activity in situations in which evidence indicated that a piece of legislation represented "nothing but the patent exploitation of one group whose interests [had been] altogether disregarded." [71] There the due process or equal protection clauses might come into play; but such occasions, Hand felt, would be very infrequent, for the fact-finding powers of courts were limited and usually not capable of amassing much evidence about internal legislative affairs. Judicial review of legislation under the general provisions of the Bill of Rights thus was extremely limited.

A comparable restraint did not always exist in situations involving statutory interpretation in the absence of a constitutional provision. If a statute was of intermediate specificity, judges should attempt to ascertain its general purposes and to reason from these assumed purposes to the specific question of application they faced. In this class of cases the judicial function was analogous to that of interpreting similar constitutional provisions. If, however, the statute was very broadly drafted, Hand viewed it as an invitation to the courts to "do what you think is right"—namely, "take the conflicting values and probabilities and make the best guess you can." [72] General statutory language thus invited judicial creativity; general constitutional language dictated restraint. In the former case the public had implicitly indicated a preference for judicial rather than legislative guidance. In the latter, it had merely made "admonitions of moderation" [73] to the legislature.

Hand's view of the proper function of the judiciary places him in an anomalous position in the history of twentieth-century jurisprudence. In the early years of the century his insistence that judges were free, within limits, to be creative identified him with Holmes, Pound, Cardozo, and other critics of both mechanical jurisprudence and what Hand called the "dictionary school" [74] of literalist statutory interpretation. At the same time his position on judicial review of the constitutionality of legislation was compatible with that advanced by Holmes and glibly identified with liberalism. But whereas his fellow members of "the race of giants" [75]—Holmes, Brandeis, and Cardozo—all died before World War II, Hand lived on into the 1960s, to confront the Warren Court and see the meaning of judicial liberalism apparently change. Suddenly, close judicial scrutiny of the impact of legislation on equal protection and due process rights became a "liberal" response. Hand saw, in the light of these developments, a virtual repudiation of his thesis by legal scholars and jurists. In 1964, three years after Hand's death, Judge Charles Wyzanski wrote that "[his] thesis has not yet been supported by a single eminent judge or professor." [76]

Believing that tolerance and moderation were virtues, Hand was well suited to bear this isolation. Believing, as well, in man's insatiable appetite for social panaceas, he may have viewed the current of opinion that rejected his positions as further evidence of man's persistent attempts to shake off the brute. If he could not accept Warren Court activism intellectually, perhaps he understood it emotionally: liberty and democracy, after all, were values he cherished despite their limitations. What he insisted upon, finally, was that judges take concepts like "equality" and "the common will," explore them, and come to see them for what they were—catchwords for a whole set of complex and ambiguous phenomena. Sometimes this process of exploration gave rise to delicate judicial choices and a balancing of values that were hard to weigh. Sometimes that choice had to be faced and made, at other times it had to be delegated to another arm of government. The process, however, was what judging was all about. Explaining it to others was the "honest craft" of his profession, in which Hand delighted.[77] Grounded in the unresolvable complexities of modern life, it yet held out a hope that the judiciary could help maintain the persistence, if not the permanence, of civilization.

III

In his discussions of freedom and restraint in the judiciary, Hand had rejected "two extreme schools" [78] of jurisprudence. One was the dictionary school, the other a school that argued, he said, "that a judge should not regard the law; that this has never really been done in the past, and that to attempt even to do it is an illusion." Rather, Hand continued, the judge according to this second school "must conform his decision to what honest men would think right, and it [was] better for him to look into his own heart to find out what that is." [79] The school thus caricatured was Realist Jurisprudence. One of its American founders, Jerome Frank, came to be Hand's colleague on the Second Circuit. Neither Hand nor Frank substantially changed his view during his tenure together, and the institutional limitations on judges so important to Hand remained partially illusory for Frank. If anything were to limit a judge's freedom to make law, Frank thought, it should be a sense of the personal sympathies and antipathies that led him to irrational conclusions, but even those, if candidly set forth, could become part of a reasoned opinion. Yet, despite this divergence of positions, Frank told Hand that "no one else I've ever known has excited in me such admiration and affection." Hand was Frank's "model as a judge": [80] to sit with him was "an inestimable privilege, a constant source of education." [81] Hand, for his part, wrote Frank's widow after his death in 1957 that "we . . . agreed about the real values of life, much as we often differed about the ways and means." [82]

The intellectual combativeness and close personal involvement manifested in his relations with Hand was characteristic of Frank's professional encounters. He was continually anxious to encounter new ideas and remarkable in the speed with which he could absorb them; and yet he greeted them with skepticism and often quickly cast them off. He relished conversation and debate and was judged by many of his acquaintances to be an exceptionally stimulating companion,[83] but he tended, especially in print, to caricature opposing positions and to engage in personal attacks on those he criticized. He was capable of undiscriminating hero worship and also of unbalanced enmity. Persons he had savagely attacked in his writings found him friendly and engaging in person. Judge Charles Clark, who clashed continually with him in correspondence during their service on the Second Circuit, said that Frank "never seemed to harbor permanent spite of any form whatsoever" and doubted if Frank "realized how heavy was the impact of his intellectual blows." [84]

The presence or absence of certain characteristics in others set off emotionally charged reactions in Frank. He could not bear intellectual dishonesty, duplicity, or self-delusion; conversely, he greatly admired skepticism, candor, and detachment. His heroes, such as Holmes, Hand, Aristotle, or Lord Halifax, took no refuge in dogma, legal or otherwise. They could face hard truths (men were not angels, legal rules were fictions, judges were inevitably biased, social conflict was inevitable) and build a philosophical stance that incorporated them instead of wishing them away. By contrast his villains, who included Edward Coke, Plato, and Christopher Columbus Langdell (Dean of Harvard Law School from 1870 to 1895 and founder of the case-method approach to legal education), were immature or unscrupulous neurotics who imposed their own obsessions on others in the form of one-sided or disingenuous theories. Coke, for example, was "a nasty, narrow-minded, greedy, cruel, arrogant, unsensitive man, a time-serving politician and a liar who, by his adulation of some crabbed medieval legal doctrines, had retarded English and American legal development for centuries." [85]

The extent to which Frank personalized his assessments of the ideas of others is illustrated by his changing attitudes toward Cardozo. In 1930 Frank published *Law and the Modern Mind*, the culmination of an intensive three-year exploration of the relations of the behavioral sciences to law, including a six-month stretch during which Frank underwent psychoanalysis. *Law and the Modern Mind* asserted, among other things, that the persistent attachment of lawyers and judges to rules or principles of law perfectly illustrated Freud's insight that a childhood desire for security and certainty was retained in adults. Legal rules and principles, Frank argued, were artificial, fungible entities manufactured for the purpose of rationalizing predetermined results. Judging, an intuitive, idiosyncratic, flexible process, was being presented as if it were systematic, depersonalized and formal. This presentation, resting upon the childish wish that law could be made certain and predictable, was wholly mythical.

At the time *Law and the Modern Mind* appeared, jurisprudence in America was in ferment. As noted, a long line of criticism of "mechanical" decision-making had appeared, and Holmes, Pound, Learned Hand, and Cardozo, among others, had made separate contributions to the development of an approach that Pound loosely termed "sociological" jurisprudence.[86] This approach emphasized the dual responsibility in judges to preserve continuity and to respond to change. Various decision-making strategies were proposed through which this responsibility could be met, including Cardozo's fourfold classification of methods.[87] In *The Paradoxes of Legal Science*, Cardozo had suggested that although the values of continuity and change still framed judicial choices, no one method of decision-making could insure success in the balancing process of adjudication. On some occasions, he conceded, the judge's choice was merely intuitive.[88] This insight found support in a 1929 article by another judge, Joseph Hutcheson, who argued that "the intuitional faculty" was "essential . . . to great judging." [89]

While drawing on the contributions of sociological jurists in *Law and the Modern Mind*, Frank dissociated himself from them. He agreed with Hutcheson, he said, that judging was largely intuitive, but he rejected any intimation of the sociological jurists that it could be made otherwise. He saw their interest in the preservation or promotion of continuity in the law as simply a manifestation of the collective desire for certainty that he was exposing. Any method directed at the attainment of that end was ill-conceived. Cardozo, then, generated an ambivalent response in Frank. "His writings [have] been of inestimable value," Frank wrote in *Law and the Modern Mind*, "in making possible realistic thinking about law." But his "yearning for the absolute" gave Frank pause.[90]

As Frank's view of the judicial function coalesced after 1930, he found himself increasingly estranged from Cardozo. Frank identified himself with Realist Jurisprudence in 1931,[91] and Cardozo openly criticized the Realists in a 1932 address to the New York State Bar Association. The crux of the quarrel was over the place of "certainty and order and rational coherence," [92] as Cardozo put it, in the law. Cardozo read some Realists, including Frank, as saying that the elements of randomness and chance always predominated in adjudication, and that therefore principles and rules were meaningless aphorisms. If this reading was fair, Cardozo maintained, Realism was "a false and misleading cult." [93] Indeterminacy was surely present in judge-made law, he felt, but it was only one of several ingredients in the cauldron. The value of certainty was another of these ingredients, and it often prevailed, to conform the law with established customs or the plain and unquestioned dictates of contemporary morality.[94] To assert that it was merely a childish fiction was to give a distorted picture of the process of judicial decision-making.

Frank responded to Cardozo's critique in two ways. He refined his own thinking and found that in some respects he and Cardozo were not, after all, at loggerheads. In 1948, for example, he divided "realists" into two groups: "rule-skeptics" and "fact-skeptics." Rule-skeptics, he claimed, "resembled Cardozo in that they had little or no interest in trial courts, but riveted their attention largely on appellate courts and on the nature and use of the legal rules." Some rule-skeptics, however, "went somewhat further than Cardozo as to the extent of the existent and desirable power of judges to alter the legal rules." Fact-skeptics, of which he was one, were primarily interested in trial courts. They traced "the major cause of legal uncertainty to trial uncertainties." So "far as appellate courts and the legal rules are concerned," Frank argued, "the views of the fact-skeptics as to existent and desirable legal certainty approximated the views of Cardozo . . . and many others not categorized as 'realists.' " [95] This description of himself vis-à-vis Cardozo was bizarre, since he had clearly been a "rule-skeptic" in *Law and the Modern Mind* and had never at any time "approximated" Cardozo's position on legal certainty.

The other way was to attack Cardozo personally in an oblique and unfortunate fashion. In 1943, under the pseudonym "Anon Y. Mous of Middletown," Frank wrote a critique of Cardozo's style. In it he advanced the thesis that Cardozo, in response to personal pressures, had adopted the disguise of "an 18th Century scholar and gentleman" and that his style, "imitative of 18th Century English," was a manifestation of that persona. Cardozo had, Frank claimed, "translated himself into a past alien speech environment." One of Cardozo's "selves or persons," Frank surmised, "was that of an educated Englishman engaging in imaginary conversations with Charles Lamb or Dr. Johnson." [96]

Frank's perception that Cardozo's affect and manner served as devices to shield him from his public contacts was shared by others who knew Cardozo well. "Very few," Hand said of Cardozo, "have ever known what went on behind those blue eyes." [97] But Frank chose to caricature his insight. He accompanied quotations from Cardozo's opinions with editorial comments. He claimed that in using "elaborate metaphors" [98] Cardozo "was opposing the national genius of the [American] language," which "tends to the use of plainer materials and towards a simpler cut." [99] He suggested that Cardozo's "ornaments" were "annoyingly functionless," and he maintained that his style was designed to flatter his readers "that they are sharing in English upperclass virtues." [100]

The anonymous Cardozo essay was vintage Frank. His intuitions about others were often perceptive and his characterizations imaginative. But he frequently incorporated those perceptions into the set of ideas that currently interested him, so that his judgments on his contemporaries, especially in print, took on an ideological or even a polemical tone. In the Cardozo essay, for example, he began with a suggestion that Cardozo preferred to use his lawmaking powers covertly rather than openly and that this illustrated a personal use of masks and disguises in his public contacts. But he rapidly converted that suggestion into a crusade for "plainness" in judicial writing and an argument against yearning for the "unattainable . . . absolute in law." [101] The result was an effort that offended many readers of the essay and somewhat embarrassed Frank.[102] Yet Frank, characteristically, never retracted his position. The last year of his life, in an article on Learned Hand, he repeated, nearly verbatim, many of the observations he had made on Cardozo fourteen years earlier.[103]

Despite his tendency to polarize debate, caricature the views of his critics, and conduct intellectual exchange at an awkwardly personal level, Frank was a compassionate and gregarious man who enjoyed making and having friends, was sensitive to criticism, and found it difficult to view his close acquaintances with critical detachment.[104] He could, as in his relations with Charles Clark, carry on a series of correspondence debates in which his remarks were often biting, even acrimonious,[105] and then write (to Clark), "Somehow you seem to have obtained the impression that I'm antagonistic to you. Through some fault of mine, I got off on the wrong foot with you. I'd like to start again." [106] By and large, he maintained cordial relations with those whom he saw regularly on a face-to-face basis; at a greater distance he had more difficulty. His most rabid hatreds were reserved for those, like Coke, whom he never met and never could. As long as he was able to think of people as personifications of values or ideas that he found distasteful, he could criticize them with abandon; as soon as he met them, some of his intellectual anger dissipated.

The provocative tone of Frank's writings was characteristic of the jurisprudential school he helped found. The Realists, especially when they first perceived themselves as having a group identity, had the zeal and dogmatism of any collection of persons who believe they have found truth. The "realities" of lawmaking, particularly by judges, had been revealed to them; they had no patience with those who slavishly maintained the fictions of the past. They saw, as had others in the 1920s, the collapse of traditional moral values in America, but the lesson they drew was that morals and ethics were relative terms, not absolutes. They seized on Holmes's deliberately caricatured picture of law as the predictions of what courts did in fact, and used it to create a technique of "institutional analysis" through which the "real" factors controlling the decisions of governmental office could be studied empirically.[107] Stripping away the "rationalizations" in judicial opinions, they revealed the subjective values that lay beneath. In the process they perceived the manipulation of "paper" rules of law to produce desired results, and discovered the "real" rules of judicial decision-making, whose significance became clear "only after the investigation of the . . . behavior" of judges.[108] Armed with these insights, they set out to reorient American jurisprudential thought.

Frank's particular contribution to Realism was his psychoanalytic theory of the judicial function. The process of judging, he argued, began with tentatively formed conclusions rather than with the discovery of rules or principles of law. In writing an opinion the judge reasoned backward from results: legal principles served as "formal justifications—rationalizations—of [predetermined] conclusions." [109] The crucial factor in judging was the biases of the judge whose sympathies or antipathies influenced the way he heard evidence, the importance he placed on particular facts, and, eventually, his determination of the result. The "law" a judge announced was therefore "really" a manifestation of his own value judgments, concealed by "verbal contrivances" whose function was to give an illusion of harmony and continuity. Being humans, judges came to believe in their own fictions, so that they not only claimed that "announced rules" were "the paramount theory in the law," they also became convinced that the values of uniformity and certainty were of great importance and could be "procured by uniformity and certainty in the phrasing of rules." [110]

A realization of the psychological dimensions of the judging process could, in Frank's judgment, lead to a more realistic and "progressive" approach to adjudication. If judges "c[a]me to grips with the human nature operative in themselves," they could begin to abandon the fantasy of a perfect, consistent, legal uniformity for a sensible skepticism. [111] Frank suggested two devices to aid in this process—the use of experts to aid judges in their fact-finding efforts, and the use of "the best available methods of psychology" [112] as a means of revealing to judges their own biases.

Frank's insight that judicial decision-making was rooted in subjective preferences led him to argue that judges should have freedom and power to function as creative lawmakers. So long as a judge knew that he could not be detached, he did not have to be. So long as he understood that "facts" were manipulable pieces of data rather than symbols of truth, he could choose the facts he wanted to emphasize. And so long as he understood the role of value preferences in judicial decision-making, he could interpret his function as one of enlightening the public as to the importance of certain social values. In Frank's view judges, like other governmental officials, could be seen as members of an elite that drew on its special expertise to educate its constituents. If judges understood that "law" as an abstract entity neither prohibited nor required anything, they could make decisions that, for example, secured special treatment in the courts for economically or socially disadvantaged persons. Thus, skepticism could nurture paternalism, and realist jurisprudence could harmonize with the social goals of the New Deal.[113]

The jurisprudential theories of Frank and Hand, then, started with similar assumptions but ended with divergent views of the judicial function. Hand and Frank both believed that legal doctrines contained elements of myth and fiction and that these elements should be exposed; that subjectivity was an important element in the judicial process; that no aid to judging, or indeed to living, could be found in philosophical, moral, or religious absolutes; and that judging could fairly be described as an attempt to weigh unquantifiable values. But they drew different inferences from these assumptions. For Hand the presence of bias in the judge engendered a search for detachment, which he equated with wisdom. For Frank a judge did not have to be detached if he knew that detachment was ultimately unattainable. Common morality, as a workable entity, was elusive for both men, but Hand nonetheless preferred a dim approximation of it over his own intuitions, while Frank thought that it could be ignored altogether if contrary to the views of "ethical leaders." [114] In general, Hand's sense of the idiosyncratic and intuitive nature of judging engendered a conviction that judicial creativity should be curtailed as much as it was encouraged, whereas the same perception in Frank led him to believe that the primary check on the judge need only be his own self-awareness.

The iconoclastic views expressed by Frank might have seemed incompatible with judicial service. But he had been an early and enthusiastic supporter of Roosevelt and the New Deal, serving as General Counsel to the ill-fated Agricultural Adjustment Administration and later as Counsel to the Reconstruction Finance Corporation and Chairman of the Securities and Exchange Commission. In 1934 he called himself and fellow "experimental" jurisprudes "humble servants to that master experimentalist, Franklin Roosevelt." [115] Roosevelt, for his part, admired Frank and had a highly politicized view of the office of judge. Hence, when a vacancy appeared in the Second Circuit in 1941, Frank was given the appointment, which was a presidential prerogative. One commentator likened the choice of Frank to that of a heretic for a bishopric in the Catholic Church.[116]

IV

The major opportunities for Cardozo, Hand, and Frank to operationalize their respective attitudes toward freedom and restraint in judging came, of course, in the decision of cases. They were fortunate in being able to serve on courts of considerable stature and significance. To the Second Circuit and the New York Court of Appeals came significant pieces of litigation, argued by members of one of the leading bars in the nation, involving sizable sums of money and energy and reflecting the rapid pace of social and economic change in twentieth-century urban America. Like the Supreme Court, and unlike many lower appellate courts, the New York Court of Appeals and the Second Circuit provided its members with a diversity of material and abundant opportunities for visibility and prominence.

During Cardozo's eighteen years on the Court of Appeals the traditional common-law framework in which American state appellate judges made their decisions confronted the momentum of mature industrialization, which transformed economic and social relations in the early twentieth century. Older descriptions of the rights and responsibilities of participants in industrial enterprise appeared increasingly inadequate in their modern setting. The doctrine that employees assumed all the risks of dangerous jobs seemed troublesome when the employees in question had no other employment options. The theory that manufacturers of dangerous products were responsible only for the safety of persons who had contracted to buy the products appeared to make little sense if the products were regularly used by third-party consumers. As industrial enterprise expanded, millions of persons came to be affected by it, even though their connection with the actual processes of product manufacturing and distribution was peripheral or nonexistent. Once injured, either physically or economically, they came to be perceived as victims of industrial progress, a perception that generated lawsuits asking that courts expand the remedial coverage of the common law to include these new potential beneficiaries.

A conventional piece of wisdom about the common law system of adjudication is that a court may not grant an injured party relief unless it can base that result on some existing principle of substantive law. Even in a so-called case of first impression, a court, if it is to create a new remedy, must subsume that remedy under the articulation of a new common law doctrine. Thus, where social change creates grievances that a pre-existing body of legal doctrine has not anticipated, a common law court has to decide whether, reasoning by analogy, the existent body of doctrine can fairly be stretched to cover the new grievance. If it decides that the questions presented by the new grievance are too novel or unique to sustain such a stretch, it has, in the conventional view, only two options. It may announce, as a matter of substantive law, that the aggrieved party is not entitled to relief, or it may refuse to entertain the grievance by asserting that doctrinal change of such magnitude should be made by the legislature. It may not, in this view, allow the aggrieved party relief while conceding that the logic of pre-existing doctrine mitigates against that result. To do so would be to replace a durable impersonal body of common law principles with intuitive individual notions of justice in a given case.

Cardozo developed his theories of judicial performance within the confines of this attitude. Believing, by and large, that common law judges were permitted to "make" law only through reasoned interpretations of previously received doctrine, he attempted to show in his opinions that any changes his court made in substantive law stemmed from the adaptability of previous common law principles to new situations. Believing also, however, that common law courts should be responsive to social or economic change, he tried to avoid denying an aggrieved party relief simply because previous generations of courts had not envisaged the complainant's predicament. The strains engendered by these simultaneous beliefs motivated Cardozo to search for a means of making novel results appear to be the logical products of established doctrines, so that changes in the common law seemed to underscore common law continuity.

Cardozo made this search his mission as a jurist and his art as a judge. His national reputation, which stemmed primarily from his common law decisions on the Court of Appeals, was founded on his ability to make his innovations seem the natural, almost inevitable consequence of past decisions. This achievement was grounded on his skill in analyzing common law precedents. Faced with a series of arguably relevant prior decisions, each with its own factual circumstances, he could extract from them a general principle of law linking them to the case before him. Often that principle allowed him to extend the common law's remedial coverage; sometimes it gave him a point where coverage could be cut off. Many times the principle was itself a distinction between some types of cases and others; where it was, the distinction invariably illuminated the position of the case he was considering. On occasion, Cardozo's analysis was not altogether candid. He could deemphasize or ignore contrary evidence and make distinctions without differences. But he was not result-oriented in his decision-making; rather, he recognized competing values and agonized over choices between them. If many of his results promoted progress, as his colleague Irving Lehman observed, his justifications for them were often, Hand noted, "tentative, at times almost apologetic." [117]

Cardozo's most influential common law opinions came in the areas of torts and contracts. The ferment in those areas during his years on the Court of Appeals symbolized the increasingly industrial and commercial character of the New York environment. The traditional negligence calculus of tort law, which conditioned liability on "fault" defined in terms of duties of reasonable care, was reexamined by Cardozo's court in the fact of changing approaches to the problem of industrial accidents. In contracts, an existing series of technical, formal requirements affecting the creation of contractual obligations was reconsidered in the context of the complicated commercial transactions taking place in twentieth-century New York.

In both areas Cardozo's opinions changed the state of the law by reshaping existing doctrines, but the changes did not appear dramatic, nor was the reshaping process easily perceived. In torts, Cardozo initiated, over a period of time, a new approach to one aspect of the negligence calculus. It was clear, as courts came to consider negligence cases in the latter half of the nineteenth century and the early twentieth, that although the violation of a standard of reasonable care was a prerequisite for liability, not every violation resulted in a holding of liability. In particular, the courts appeared reluctant to hold negligent defendants responsible for remote or bizarre consequences of their acts. Considerable difficulty had arisen, however, in converting this common-sense reluctance into doctrines of law. Courts had emphasized the closeness of the relation between the plaintiff and defendant, borrowing contract terms such as "privity," or they had asked whether the defendant's negligence "caused" the plaintiff's injury. In both instances they encountered linguistic snarls, for some injured persons, though not in a direct contractual relation with a defendant, were known by him to be relying on his careful conduct, and, alternatively, endless chains of causation could be constructed linking remote injuries to negligent acts.

Cardozo shifted discussion in this portion of the law of negligence to inquiries about the anticipation of risks. If the result that generated a negligence suit was one that came within the foreseeable ambit of risks created by the defendant's failure to meet a standard of reasonable care, Cardozo maintained that the defendant should be found liable. The class of persons injured and the type of injury suffered were subsumed in the term "result." One asked whether the defendant could reasonably be expected to anticipate that his careless act would create a risk of this result. Using this approach, Cardozo found that a manufacturer of motor cars had a duty to make a careful inspection of the cars' wheels, and that this duty extended beyond the car dealers "in privity" with the manufacturer to the ultimate purchasers of the cars.[118]

In another case,[119] however, he used the same analysis to prevent recovery against the Long Island Railroad by a woman injured while standing on the platform of a railroad station. In that case a passenger, racing to catch a moving train, was helped onto the train by two guards employed by the railroad. In the process the guards knocked loose a package the passenger was carrying which, unbeknownst to them, contained fireworks. The package fell to the ground and exploded, setting off vibrations which caused a set of scales on the station's platform to fall on the woman, who was sitting near the scales some distance from the train tracks. In determining the railroad's liability to the woman, Cardozo stated that "the risk reasonably to be perceived" defined "the duty to be obeyed." Risk was "a term of relation": here the relation of the woman's injury to the carelessness of the guards was too remote to allow a finding that they should have anticipated that their negligence would inflict that particular injury. Cardozo sought in his analysis to relate a defendant's carelessness not only to the type of injury that had occurred but to the class of persons injured. The term "risk" encompassed both considerations.

Risk analysis did not fundamentally reorient tort law but merely shifted some of its emphasis. It invited courts to ask cost-benefit questions, considering the degree of difficulty in anticipating and preventing certain types of risks and the social desirability of various enterprises, such as railroads. These kinds of questions marked a departure from the previous metaphysical ones. Asking whether a result was within a set of risks may have seemed to be very similar to asking whether a careless act was the "proximate cause" of an injury, but there was a subtle difference. The new set of questions prepared the way for courts to consider which segments of society were best suited to bear the costs of risky enterprises. Such considerations have led to attacks on the negligence calculus itself: the fault standard, it is said, is an inefficient means of shifting or spreading costs.[120] Cardozo, however, intended to retain the fault system, merely wanting to make it more responsive to the conditions of modern industrial life.

In contracts, as in torts, Cardozo made few sudden changes in doctrine, but his opinions suggested a changed judicial perspective. He de-emphasized formalities and literal readings of contracts, finding, on occasion, implied promises where explicit ones were lacking.[121] He disregarded the requirement of consideration for a promise in certain cases in which the promise had been "justifiably" relied upon, while retaining it in general usage.[122] He scrutinized the circumstances under which contracts were made and broken to see if performance was absolute or conditional, sometimes giving greater weight to unforeseen events than to the language of the original agreement.[123] He interpreted the statute of frauds and the parol evidence rule liberally, believing that neither should "be pressed to the extreme of a literal and rigid logic." [124] In general, except perhaps for his treatment of certain consideration cases,[125] he made no innovations in the substantive law of contracts, but rather sought to induce judges to read agreements with more flexibility and common sense. "The law," he argued in one contracts case, "has outgrown its primitive stage of formalism when the precise word was the sovereign talisman, and every slip was fatal." [126]

The most intriguing aspect of Cardozo's judicial service, however, was his approach to writing opinions. Methodology was his chief concern as a jurisprude and his special art as a judge. *MacPherson v. Buick*, one of his earliest and best-known opinions, reveals the strengths and limitations of his method. The *MacPherson* case, noted earlier, presented the question whether the Buick Motor Company was liable to one Donald MacPherson for injuries he suffered when a wheel of his Buick collapsed. Buick claimed that it was not in privity with MacPherson, since he was a consumer rather than an automobile dealer. An old precedent,[127] involving a mail coach in

England, had held that a supplier of coaches was not liable to third parties not in privity with it for injuries resulting from defects in the coaches caused by the supplier's negligence. But the precedent appeared shaky. New York cases had created an exception to it for "inherently dangerous" instrumentalities, scholars had attacked it, and automobiles had the potential to travel at much greater speeds and submit their occupants to much greater risks than did carriages. Despite these developments, the New York Court of Appeals had reaffirmed the "privity" rule only eight years before the *MacPherson* case was heard.

Cardozo began his opinion in *MacPherson* with a characteristic technique: statement of the operative "principle" of law that governed the case. But the principle, he found, was not that of no liability absent privity but of liability absent privity in certain circumstances. The principle, then, rested on a distinction. If the instrumentality used by the defendant was "inherently" dangerous, privity was not required; otherwise it was. The distinction was illustrated by *Thomas v. Winchester*,[128] a case imposing liability on a defendant who had carelessly mislabeled a poison bottle. *Thomas v. Winchester*, Cardozo claimed, had laid "the foundations of this branch of the law, at least in this state." [129]

A successive series of cases, Cardozo maintained, had attempted to apply the *Thomas* principle. The first two cases had held that no liability existed absent privity. They illustrated for Cardozo "a narrow construction of the [*Thomas*] rule." [130] The next two demonstrated "a more liberal spirit." [131] They had applied the *Thomas* holding against a manufacturer of an improperly constructed scaffold and against the manufacturer of a defective coffee urn, both of whom were sued in behalf of injured third parties. The court had apparently failed to distinguish between "inherently dangerous" objects and other objects, and Cardozo turned this error to his own advantage. Coffee urns and scaffolds were not inherently dangerous, as were poison bottles. They became destructive only if imperfectly constructed. Hence, the two cases might "have extended" the *Thomas* holding, Cardozo stated, to "imminently" as well as "inherently" dangerous instrumentalities. "If so," he maintained, "this court is committed to this extension." [132]

Thus *Thomas*, not the English carriage case, was transformed into the "foundation of this branch of the law" rather than being denominated a special exception of the privity rule. *Thomas v. Winchester*,

Cardozo argued, "became quickly a landmark of the law . . . ; there has never in this state been doubt or disavowal of [its] principle." [133] He cited three additional cases in which the *Thomas* holding had been followed: a builder of a defective building, a manufacturer of an elevator, and a contractor who supplied a defective rope were all held liable for injuries to persons outside privity with them. These cases, Cardozo felt, demonstrated a "trend of judicial thought." [134]

Cardozo thus interpreted precedents so as to prepare the way for a further extension of the *Thomas* exception, but his goal was even more ambitious. He wanted the exception to swallow up the privity rule in *MacPherson*-type cases. To achieve this end he sought to buttress the public policy foundations of a new definition of a manufacturer's duty to persons to whom it had supplied hazardous products. Seizing on the dictum in an English opinion [135] that a duty of ordinary care, irrespective of contract, could be imposed on manufacturers, Cardozo argued that the "tests and standards" created by that dictum were, "at least in their underlying principles," the tests and standards of the common law of New York. If the nature of a product was such that it was reasonably certain "to place life and limb in peril" if carelessly made, Cardozo announced, the product was "a thing of danger." If a manufacturer of this kind of product knew that it would be used "by persons other than the [immediate] purchaser," without further tests, then the manufacturer was under a duty to make it carefully "irrespective of contract." [136]

Hence, "the principle" of *Thomas* was "not limited to poisons . . . and things of like nature." [137] It encompassed all instrumentalities that met the tests of "dangerousness" as formulated by Cardozo. The nature of automobiles "[gave] warning of probable danger if their construction [was] defective." The Buick Motor Company knew the danger, "knew that the car would be used by persons other than the buyer" [138] and was therefore liable for the damages suffered by MacPherson. As for the English carriage case, "[p]recedents drawn from the days of travel of stage coach do not fit the conditions of travel today. The principle [of "dangerousness"] does not change, but the things subject to the principle do change. They are whatever the needs of life in a developing civilization require them to be." [139]

The *MacPherson* opinion reveals the nature of Cardozo's artistry.

He announced in the opinion that a definition of the duty of a manufacturer "emerge[d] from a survey of the [New York] decisions." In actuality, the definition arose from the English judge's dictum and Cardozo's unexpressed belief that the New York decisions extending *Thomas* were groping toward the position expressed in the dictum. By the time that Cardozo came to apply his definition of a manufacturer's duty to the situation in *MacPherson*, the reader had the impression that the definition had long existed in New York, even though it had not previously been articulated. But this was not the case. The *Thomas* case itself reaffirmed the privity rule, while creating a special exception; the coffee urn and scaffold cases appear to have been decided on equity grounds related to their special facts; and the Court of Appeals had followed the privity rule in a 1908 case involving an exploding glass bottle.[140] In *MacPherson* Cardozo employed the method of sociology, which underscored the "needs of a developing civilization" for a means of recourse against negligent automobile manufacturers, as a counterweight against the method of logic. He was, as he said in *The Nature of the Judicial Process*, "testing and sorting . . . considerations of analogy and logic and utility and fairness." He was assuming "the function of a lawgiver,"[141] but he gave the impression that he was simply acting as a traditional common law judge, reviewing precedents and applying them to the case before him. With Cardozo the line between art and artifice was blurred. His opinions, like his public stances generally, contained levels of candor and deceptiveness. His intuitions were sound, but he rarely revealed their existence.

The period of Cardozo's tenure on the Court of Appeals marked the end, in a sense, of traditional common law adjudication in America. Since 1931, when he was appointed to the Supreme Court, even state appellate judges no longer serve primarily as interpreters of case law established solely by their predecessors. Partial codification of the common law, through federal or state statutes, has taken place in nearly all major substantive areas. In contracts decisions, courts are now aided by the Uniform Commercial Code; for questions involving property relations, state statutes or housing ordinances modify ancient common law rights; for torts questions, workmen's compensation statutes, and, increasingly, no-fault accident insurance programs prevail. The common law of crimes, of course, has been extensively altered by statutes. This codification is by no means complete, but it has significantly affected the function of the appellate judge, who now allocates a sizable portion of time to the interpretation of statutes.

While Cardozo was making a national reputation as a traditional common law judge, Learned Hand, over a similar time span, was enhancing his own reputation by pioneering the modern judicial approach to statutory interpretation. Hand recognized very early in his career [142] that although statutes would make a great impact on twentieth-century lawmaking, their presence would not necessarily restrict judicial creativity and freedom of choice.

His theory of statutory interpretation, as previously noted, rejected the view prevalent in the late nineteenth century that courts could go no farther than the "ordinary" or "plain" meaning of words in a statute, so that, for example, independent contractors were not covered by legislation directed at "employees." But it also rejected readings that substituted for "what the government did not say" things a judge thought "it ought to have said." [143] Hand's approach sought to achieve a middle ground between the perspective of mechanical jurisprudes and that of realists by use of the concept of statutory purpose. A judge began with statutory language, but refrained from interpreting it too liberally or ignoring it altogether. Instead, he examined it as a manifestation of the general purposes of the statute, the broad social policies the legislature "intended" to implement. Where specific statutory coverage of a situation was lacking, Hand deduced coverage or its absence from an application of the general statutory purposes to the particular situation. [144]

This theory assumed, of course, that a court was capable of determining the primary purposes of a statute. That assumption seems to have been easier for Hand to make than for some other judges. Although he was not indifferent to popular enthusiasms and hatreds, he was somewhat detached from them, and was neither a partisan nor an ideologue. Once he saw what a legislature wished to achieve, he was not apt to be captivated or offended by the end it sought. Conversely, he was not inclined to find a purpose where none existed, simply to protect the interests of a favored group. He believed that most legislative purposes, being accommodations of values, bore a presumption of legitimacy. So long as legislative words were capable of interpretation at all, he reasoned, a search for purpose would not be fruitless.

How did the judge proceed, then, when called on to interpret a statute? First, by looking at the language in its specific applications; then, if those seemed inappropriate, in its more general sense. When the meaning of general language in the context of the litigation before the court remained imprecise, the search for statutory purpose began.[145] In this search Hand reasoned by constructing alternative interpretations of language, each producing different results, then asking which result would best conform to the general intent of the legislature, insofar as he could determine it through examination of the statute as a whole.[146] If he could not satisfactorily determine purpose by this method, he turned to further aids, including the legislative history of the statute or administrative interpretations of it. But he did not seek out those aids without first deciding for himself which of the alternative meanings, and consequently which result, was most consistent with his impression of the general purpose. Legislative history and administrative interpretations of a statute only served to test the validity of his tentatively formulated hypotheses.[147]

Hand's theory required judges to maintain the delicate balance between creativity and restraint that he associated with wisdom in the judiciary. It not only assumed that statutory purpose could be found, but that all the intellectual ingenuity exercised in searching for purpose and applying a general intent to unanticipated specific situations could operate in the service of the legislative purpose alone. If the judge's alternative interpretations of the statute were to receive more weight than expressions by legislators or interpretations by agencies, the judge needed to remain neutral toward the political implications of the legislative purpose. Otherwise his own views on the wisdom of legislation might affect his construction of the statute, since he knew that his reading of purpose would be decisive in a doubtful case. He could be creative in interpretation, then, only to the extent that he refrained from an evaluation of the worth of legislation. Hand recognized this dilemma. "On the one hand," he wrote, the judge must not enforce what he thinks best; . . . on the other he must try . . . honestly to say what was the underlying purpose expressed." Nobody does this exactly right, Hand said; "great judges do it better than the rest of us." [148]

In his statutory interpretation decisions, Hand demonstrated that he was not merely one of "the rest of us." He twice brought maintenance workers who were not specifically designated beneficiaries of the Fair Labor Standards Act under its coverage, once where the

tenants of the building in which the workers operated were manufacturers and once when they were administrators.[149] He refused to
deem a corporate reorganization a "tax-exempt entity" under the
Internal Revenue Code when the sole purpose of the reorganization
was to reduce taxes.[150] He dismissed a literal reading of the Trading With the Enemy Act of 1917, which would have barred all
creditors' claims to alien property after the outbreak of World War
II.[151] And, in his next to last year on the bench, he read the federal
Copyright Act as protecting textile pattern designers against "deliberate copyists" of their patterns.[152] Statutory interpretation cases
did not by any means form the bulk of Hand's judicial labors; he
left his impact on numerous other areas, from patent law [153] to free
speech.[154] But in one sense they were his most representative, for
they illustrate most clearly the theory of judging that influenced all
his efforts. One of his colleagues said that he achieved "perhaps his
greatest mastery" [155] in matters of statutory interpretation; "mastery" in Hand was appellate judging at its finest.

   If Cardozo revealed his approach to judging most clearly in torts
and contracts cases, and Hand in exercises in statutory interpretation, Frank's area of special interest and concern was criminal procedure. Here his philosophical inclinations undoubtedly stimulated
his strong interest in the subject matter. He believed, in a general
way, in the obligation of the state to upgrade the quality of its citizens' lives. He looked favorably on social welfare legislation; he
supported direct governmental intervention to correct inequalities
and promote the values of fairness and justice; he sympathized with
the lot of disadvantaged persons and saw their plight as one of society's responsibilities. In addition, he felt that evidence used as an
"objective" foundation for judgments by governmental officials
could be manipulated; he was hence continually skeptical about the
fairness of allegedly neutral and impartial procedures. His paternalism merged with his "fact-skepticism" to produce a highly charged
response to cases involving the procedural rights of criminal defendants. "In all too many [criminal trials]," he maintained, "the prosecutors utilize unjust techniques to obtain convictions of men
who may be innocent." To disregard "courthouse injustices to
the humble, obscure man," he felt, was "to disregard that which
renders a democratic society distinctly antitotalitarian."[156]

   One of the questions of greatest interest for followers of Frank,
after his 1941 appointment to the Second Circuit, was how his Real-

ist stance toward judicial decision-making would affect his judicial performance. By the early 1940s he had already begun to modify some of the implications of his work in the 1930s, notably its apparently relativistic approach to morals and ethics.[157] He continued this modification in articles throughout the 1940s and 1950s, conceding that precedents and rules, especially in appellate decision-making, had more weight than he had originally ascribed to them.[158] He never, however, abandoned his commitment to the notion that judging was not a formal, detached process but an informal and impassioned one, susceptible of coloration by value judgments.

Nothing in the body of a lawsuit, then, was neutral for Frank. "Facts" were as manipulable as rules or precedents or principles. A judge's sense of justice necessarily affected his attitude toward the use of all legal procedures and processes, no matter how technical or mundane. Law enforcement techniques, rules of evidence, regulations for the incarceration of criminals were inherently susceptible of critical evaluation on ideological grounds. There were, to be sure, some institutional limitations on appellate judges. Frank accepted, for example, the canon of *stare decisis*, although he did not rigidly adhere to it.[159] But these constraints did not prevent the judge from being an uncompromising advocate of the social values he cherished, provided he acknowledged the limits on his powers and openly revealed his attitudes.

Frank therefore regarded the liberalization of rules of criminal procedure, to do justice to "humble, obscure [men]," as a legitimate performance of his function. This interpretation of his office foreshadowed an interpretation subsequently advanced by a majority of the Supreme Court during Earl Warren's tenure as Chief Justice. Under this view the appellate judiciary could closely scrutinize the conduct of law enforcement officials, both in and out of court, to determine whether the accusatory procedures they employed against criminal suspects were, in a broad sense, fair and just. The traditional deference of the judiciary to the discretionary powers of other branches of government, according to this view, vanished when constitutional guarantees of fair procedure were involved. State and federal rules of criminal procedure needed to conform to constitutional fairness and justice.[160]

Frank's approach to criminal procedure cases was not precisely like that subsequently adopted by the Warren Court majority, primarily because the expansive view of Bill of Rights freedoms developed by members of that Court was not in full-blown existence during the years of Frank's service on the Second Circuit.[161] Although Frank was concerned that criminal procedures not infringe upon the constitutional rights of defendants, his specific interest in preserving Bill of Rights freedoms was subordinated to a more general interest in preventing injustices in the process by which criminal suspects were indicted, tried, and convicted.

The central difficulty in that process, Frank felt, was that law enforcement officials possessed an ability to exercise almost complete control over the use of evidence relevant to the crimes under consideration. They could, by virtue of their power to incarcerate persons accused of crimes, deprive those persons of access to others who might help them defend themselves; they could put psychological or even physical pressure on them to reveal important information. Since Frank doubted the objectivity of "facts," this inequality of position greatly troubled him. He worried aloud [162] about criminal convictions of innocent persons; the fact that crimes had to be proven beyond a reasonable doubt did not altogether dispel this fear. As an appellate judge, operating on only a printed record, Frank felt incapable of truly understanding what had happened in a criminal prosecution. In order to "sleep well" [163] he wanted some means of satisfying himself that the process, at all stages, had been fair to the defendant.

A chronological history of Frank's criminal procedure opinions, many of which were dissents, reveals his interest in scrutinizing every instance where a law enforcement official could use his powers to manipulate evidence. One major example was the use of pressure on defendants to compel them to reveal information despite their Fifth Amendment privilege against self-incrimination. In a 1942 case [164] Frank protested the use of the contempt power against persons who had testified as to the elements of a crime but refused to admit the details. Sentencing them to jail for this refusal, he maintained, made a mockery of the privilege by forcing the defendant to either admit incriminating evidence or go to prison, an unfair dilemma. Another example of injustice, in Frank's view, was the absence of legal representation at trial for criminal defendants. Without the advice of counsel, defendants could be tricked or bullied into incriminating themselves, or the jury could be permitted to draw dubious inferences from the evidence. Anticipating the

Warren Court by twenty years, Frank declared in a 1943 case that the Sixth Amendment required trial counsel for all criminal defendants unless the right had been fairly waived.[165]

Throughout the 1940s Frank continued his search for justice in criminal proceedings. In two cases in 1945 he began a series of assaults on the use of hearsay evidence in conspiracy trials and continued an earlier attack on the so-called "harmless error" rule as employed by the Second Circuit. The out-of-courtroom testimony of one conspirator had been deemed admissible as evidence in the subsequent trial of another; Frank maintained that this violated the general prohibition against hearsay evidence. The crime of conspiracy itself, he felt, was excessively vague and "fraught with danger to the innocent." The admissibility of hearsay evidence compounded the dangers.[166]

Frank's harmless-error position in the cases was a crystallization of an insight he had first articulated in 1943: the Second Circuit was simply calling a technical deficiency in the trial proceedings "harmless" when a majority of judges felt that, on balance, the defendant was guilty.[167] The proper means of treating such deficiencies, Frank argued, was "to reverse where error [had] been committed, regardless of [the judges'] belief in guilt or innocence, unless [the judges] conclude[d] that in all probability the error had no effect on the jury."[168] Using this test for harmless error, Frank voted to reverse convictions in one case in which a defendant's Italian nationality had been commented upon in a trial that took place while the United States was at war with Italy,[169] and in another in which a prosecutor had released information to newspapers during the course of a trial.[170] The aim of Frank's test for harmless error was to reflect the more stringent standards of proof in criminal trials by foreclosing an appellate court from deciding that an error was "harmless" merely by determining that it was more probable than not that the criminal defendant was guilty. Preponderance of the evidence was a civil standard of proof; Frank felt it should not be introduced, *sub rosa*, into criminal cases.

Frank also expressed in the 1940s a concern about the extensive discretionary power given prosecutors in introducing evidence before a grand jury. A case came before the Second Circuit in which the prosecution, seeking an indictment, had presented to the grand jury a confession obtained through physical abuse. The prosecution argued that the confession, concededly inadmissible at trial, could nonetheless be used to secure an indictment. Frank called this "an astonishingly callous argument." A wrongful indictment, he felt, "often works a grievous, irreparable injury to the person indicted . . . ; [f]requently the public remembers the accusation and still suspects guilt, even after an acquittal." [171] He maintained that prosecutors should be barred from using any illegally obtained evidence in indictment proceedings.

The indictment case also illustrated Frank's interest in protecting criminal defendants from coercion or harassment by law enforcement officials. He expressed this concern in several contexts in the 1950s. Long delays before arraignment of a prisoner rendered a confession obtained during the delay inadmissible. [172] Even the slightest use of entrapment techniques by police officers was illegal. [173] The privilege of self-incrimination extended to witnesses at grand jury proceedings. [174] A witness could refuse to answer non-incriminating questions if they were interspersed with incriminatory ones. [175] The use of concealed eavesdropping devices by narcotics agents violated the Fourth Amendment's prohibition against unreasonable searches and seizures. [176] "The test of the moral quality of a civilization," Frank wrote in 1955, "is its treatment of the weak and powerless." [177]

In only one area was Frank less than passionately concerned for the rights of criminal defendants: cases involving violations of national security. Here Frank's sympathy for the disadvantaged clashed with the strident patriotism he came to advocate in the 1940s and 1950s. Frank's zealous championing of the values and institutions of American civilization was motivated partially, no doubt, by articles in the late 1930s linking realist jurisprudence with totalitarianism. [178] In attempting to refute his critics, Frank may also have set out to convince himself of his patriotism. If so, he succeeded, at least to the point of tolerating some infringement of Fifth Amendment rights in cases involving national security interests. [179]

Frank's most celebrated national security case was *United States v. Rosenberg*, [180] in which Julius and Ethel Rosenberg were convicted of violating the Espionage Act of 1917 and sentenced to death. Frank, writing for the Second Circuit, affirmed the conviction, despite his dislike of capital punishment and despite the fact that the government had, at trial, introduced evidence of the Rosenbergs' membership in the American Communist Party. One might reasonably infer, Frank wrote, that "an American's devotions to another country's welfare" might make him "more likely to spy for it than other Americans. . . . [T]he Communist label yields marked ill-will for its American wearer." [181] Thus, patriotism and the atmosphere of the 1950s helped reverse Frank's general presumption that criminal defendants tended to be treated unfairly. But the Rosenberg case remained in his consciousness. The year of his death he published a book depicting the lives of innocent persons who had been wrongly convicted of crimes. [182]

V

The experiences of Cardozo, Hand, and Frank, when added to those of the major figures on the Supreme Court from Holmes through Jackson, demonstrated the dramatic reorientation of American appellate judging in response to the intellectual and cultural ferment of the early twentieth century. Cardozo and Hand, in different ways, tried to retain and revive the longstanding canon that judges were never truly free to decide in accordance with their personal views. They converted metaphysical constraints—those derived from an eighteenth-century conception of law—to methodological constraints derived from an early-twentieth-century approach to governance. Frank's angle of vision was different still. For him freedom in judges was a profound "reality," and constraints were primarily personal rather than institutional. For him oracular judging had not died; it had only existed as a collective fantasy.

The jurisprudential ferment attendant upon the abandonment of oracular judging did not radically upset the delicate balances that had previously characterized appellate judging in America; it merely changed their intellectual context. Whether law was thought of as a brooding omnipresence, a social science, the fiats of officials, or an "on-going, functioning, purposive process," [183] American appellate judges still functioned as autocratic officials in a democratic society; still labored to maintain an image of impartiality and detachment while operating in a highly politicized atmosphere; still looked outside themselves for justifications for their decisions, even though their decisions may have been personally motivated. Although the cultural milieu in which judging took place underwent profound changes in the twentieth century, the core elements of the tradition nonetheless endured.

13

Rationality and Intuition in the Process of Judging: Roger Traynor

Cardozo, Hand, and Frank had spanned in their careers successive crises of legitimacy for the twentieth-century appellate judiciary. To recapitulate: the first crisis was that of "mechanical" jurisprudence, in which the oracular theory of judging was discredited by its identification with outmoded social and political attitudes. Cardozo attempted to respond to this crisis by developing a theory of judging that retained a nineteenth-century conceptual framework but made that framework responsive to social change. He employed the characteristic constructs of oracular judging—fixed principles, time-honored precedents, received doctrines—but sought to show their ability to expand or contract under the pressures of time and circumstance.

Cardozo's response, which paralleled that of Hand in his early career, was inadequate for those who were prepared to question the sanctity of any sort of conceptualist judging. If rules, principles, and doctrines were fictions, and precedents merely examples of judicial lawmaking, all vestiges of oracular judging should be eliminated and the appellate judge should start afresh, with empirical observation and a candid awareness of his own predilections serving as his only relevant source materials. But the destructive effects of Realism on surviving remnants of oracular judging precipitated a second legitimacy crisis, illustrated by the Court-packing controversy. If the "rules" of law were discredited, what was left except the arbitrary judgment of officials? How was law thus a cementing force in society, a repository of moral values or national beliefs? How, at another level, were certainty and predictability to be fostered by appellate judging? Frank grappled, not always successfully, with such questions.

In response to the second crisis a process theory of judging emerged, in which analytical reasoning and institutional self-consciousness combined to limit judicial choices to those that could be competently made and rationally justified. But despite the process theory's responsiveness to the social and intellectual climate of America in the late 1940s and the 1950s, it did not forestall the appearance of yet another potential legitimacy crisis. A central message of the process theory was that judges should confine their involvement with social issues to those areas susceptible to reasoned analysis by a court. Some social problems did not admit of rational judicial solution. They were "political" or "legislative" in their nature; no "neutral principles" existed by which they could be judicially resolved.[1] The constraints on judicial activity fashioned by the process theory suggested that explosive social issues might remain unresolved, if they were not capable of "judicial" consideration, when another branch of government did not attempt to resolve them. But when such issues were perceived as involving individual rights, the process theory appeared to clash with one of the American judiciary's historic functions: that of protector of rights and liberties. Thus, in the 1950s and 1960s pressure mounted for a judicial vindication of individual rights in cases where other governmental institutions had been indifferent to them, despite the absence of impeccably rational justifications for the vindication. An intuitive sense of fairness and justice, where individual rights were concerned, became a counterweight to rationality.[2]

Each of the twentieth-century judges thus far considered was forced to confront one or another of the above crises. Learned Hand, in the course of his fifty years as a judge, was involved with each. At various stages of his judicial life Hand was a critic of oracular judging, a skeptical observer of Realism, and a sounding board against which adherents of the process theory tested their ideas. At the very end of his career, Hand, who had always conceded the role of intuition in judging, sharply dissociated himself from efforts to make constitutional interpretation an intuitive exercise.[3] Hand's ubiquity and longevity were not typical, however; other judges, in addition to Cardozo and Frank, may be identified with one of the crisis periods. The Four Horsemen confronted the first, only suggesting the possibility of the second. Jackson functioned primarily in the context of the second. As for Hughes and Stone, the timing of their service required that they face both the first and second crises, thus adding to their already considerable burdens.

Roger Traynor, who served on the California Supreme Court from 1940 to 1970, developed his approach to judging in response to the third crisis of legitimacy. A firm advocate of the process theory, Traynor nonetheless saw its limitations as a vehicle for promoting the values of fairness and justice. Convinced that rationality was the essence of judging, Traynor nonetheless did not suppress his intuitions, believing that he could articulate reasoned justifications for them.

If New York, with its long preindustrial history, its successive waves of immigration, its tradition of commercial dominance, and its rapidly changing patterns of enterprise and communication, had invited reflection by its leading appellate judges on continuity and change in the law, California was also a source of stimulation. California, too, suggested the problem of harmonizing past with present, but more acutely, for the state had come to maturity almost overnight. The provincial state Supreme Court on which Field had served was but one step, at least in his person, from impressionistic frontier justice; Traynor's Court confronted the complex litigations of a modern industrial and commercial society. Only about seventy-five years separated the two institutions. The earlier Court bequeathed a legacy of case law to the later, dramatizing the pressure placed on *stare decisis* by rapid social change.

California's most rapid growth took place during the years after the philosophy of modern liberalism had become acceptable. Not only were economic and social discrepancies perceived as problems, affirmative governmental action to relieve them was expected. Social planners came increasingly to favor legislative solutions to the problems they perceived; statutes proliferated in California. A relatively sparse body of common law, inadequate to meet an apparent need for increased governmental planning, had created a climate favorable to legislative activity; and as legislation fostered problems in statutory interpretation, the California judiciary was forced to expand the range of its activity.

The California appellate judiciary in the years of Traynor's tenure accordingly faced the recurrent task of defining its role as a contributing institution to the "welfare state" [4] system of government. In this task, apparently, it was handicapped by the ominous contrast between its previously limited range of activity and the massive array of legal problems engendered by modern California life. The corpus of legal doctrine created by the California Supreme Court prior to 1940 had been of average size and scope for a moderately populated, predominantly rural state in an age of quiescent government; suddenly California became one of the nation's most populous and most urbanized states, with attendant growth pains. Under the prodding of the Warren Administrations from 1940 to 1952, the California legislature had responded to demographic changes with a variety of pieces of social service legislation. State agencies were created, statutes proliferated, affirmative government became a feature of modern California life.

The interaction of massive growth and affirmative governmental action altered fundamentally the character of California jurisprudence. A need was created for a body of judge-made law that could coexist with the proliferating social problems and legislative responses of the 1940s, 1950s, and 1960s. Judicial decisions, in this context, needed to be modernized, so that they could be responsive to the social conditions of contemporary California life; to be generalized, so that they could function as guidelines for conduct in an increasingly complicated world; to be synthesized, so that they could function as uniform rules rather than *ad hoc* judgments; to be deprovincialized, so that they no longer reflected the parochial anomalies of California's frontier past.

Roger Traynor's judicial career can be seen as an effort to meet the foregoing needs and thereby transform the position of the appellate judiciary in California government. In the course of this effort Traynor established a model for judicial performance that extended beyond the boundaries of his state. His model assumed that judges were lawmakers and found activist, innovative judging compatible with that assumption. It replaced traditional distinctions between branches of government with a theory of governance in which activity by one branch could stimulate activity by another. It enlarged the scope of appellate judges' prerogatives and expanded the audiences at which their opinions were directed. It emphasized the dependence of judging on rationality and disinterestedness, but stressed that making choices between conflicting social values or policies was a basic aspect of judicial decision-making. If California was a testing ground for governmental theories of modern liberalism, Traynor was an architect of a judicial role compatible with the activities of the modern liberal state.

I

Although Traynor's most significant response to the demands of time and place came in his technique of judging, he also proved responsive in personal ways. In believing that courts had "a creative job to do" upon finding "that a rule has lost its touch with reality and should be abandoned or reformulated to meet new conditions and new moral values," [5] Traynor was asking the judiciary to act as public spokesmen, not unlike elected officials. This posed the familiar Realist dilemma: how was bias to go unchecked in the absence of political restraints; what was to keep judicial formulations of a society's value choices from being mere statements of a judge's own inclinations? Traynor's solution was embodied in the terms disinterestedness and rationality. Judges were "uniquely situated," he felt, "to articulate timely rules of reason." They enjoyed a "freedom from political and personal pressures and from adversary bias," a "long history of high public service." Their "environment for work" was "independent and analytically objective"; their task was "keeping the underlying body of the unwritten general law . . . 'rationally consistent within itself [and] rationally related to the purposes which the social order exists to serve.' " [6] They knew that "one entrusted with decision . . . must also rise above the vanity of stubborn preconceptions . . . , that he must severely discount his own predilections," that he must "realize how essential it is . . . that he be interested in a rational outcome." [7]

To this conception of judges as aloof, independent, rational beings one might respond, as did unreconstructed Realists [8] in the years of Traynor's service, that judges could not remain immune from political pressures, that preconceptions and predilections hardened with the process of opinion-writing, that analytic objectivity was elusive, or that many "rational" outcomes were possible. Yet Traynor himself made a strong case for the proposition that disinterestedness and rationality were attainable ideals. He achieved this, primarily, by burying himself beneath a layer of official discourse, so that he could write controversial opinions in a tone of relentless impersonality or describe his objectives as a judge in a series of elusive metaphors.

An example will illustrate. In *Escola v. Coca Cola Bottling Co.*,[9] a case arising from injuries sustained by a waitress when a defective soda bottle broke as she carried it from its case to a refrigerator, Traynor suggested an innovative treatment for defective-products cases in the California common law of torts. His treatment rested on an imaginative interweaving of twentieth-century developments in torts and contracts; it relied on policy judgments rather than legal doctrines; it was original with Traynor. Yet it was presented, like Cardozo's decision in *MacPherson v. Buick*, as though it were the inevitable result of a thorough canvass of the law of defective products; an impersonal, rational solution that any "analytically objective" judge could have reached. One had the sense, on reading the opinion, that a straightforward inquiry into the economics of the soft-drink industry had revealed an obviously efficient and equitable means of allocating the costs of injuries from defective products. If absolute liability for defects were placed on the soft-drink manufacturer, the manufacturer could then insure against injuries and distribute the cost of his insurance among his consumers. Yet that allocation scheme represented a major change in the law of defective products and, once adopted, necessitated a recalculation by California manufacturers of their cost of doing business.

The primary doctrinal change made by Traynor in *Escola* was to fuse an expanded concept of negligence in the products liability area with developments in the law of sales. Cardozo and other judges in the early twentieth century had succeeded in imposing on manufacturers a duty of care for defects in their products, a duty extending beyond immediate purchasers. Ordinary users, like the waitress in *Escola*, could sue manufacturers for negligence even though they had received the product from someone else in the chain of distribution. Meanwhile, the concept of an implied warranty of fitness and merchantability had emerged in contract law. Sellers were considered to have warranted to buyers that their products would not be defective in ordinary use, and sellers could

be sued for damages should the products prove unsafe. No showing
of negligence on the part of the seller was necessary for the buyer
to recover; in turn the seller, if a retailer, could recover against the
manufacturer on a warranty theory without proving negligence.[10]

Traynor combined these two developments in *Escola* to create the
doctrine of an absolute liability in tort on the part of manufacturers
for injuries caused by their defective products. The doctrine represented, he maintained, a substitution of public policy imperatives
for common-law fictions and gimmicks. It was "needlessly circui-
tous" to use exceptions to the standard negligence calculus, such as
the device of *res ipsa loquitur*, which under certain conditions relieved plaintiffs of the burden of affirmatively proving negligence,
to "impose what is in reality liability without negligence." [11] It was
equally unnecessary to maintain the double litigation required by
the warranty model. Injured consumers should be able to base their
actions "directly on the manufacturer's warranty." [12] The warranty
of the manufacturer to the consumer rested "on public policy," although "the courts [had] resorted to various fictions" to rationalize
extending it that far.[13] Such fictions were no longer necessary once
"the warranty is severed from the contract of sale between the
dealer and the consumer and based on the law of torts as a strict liability." [14] Once that was done the justification for abandoning sales
law and negligence theory in the defective products became clear.
If defective products found their way into the market, "it is to the
public interest to place the responsibility for whatever injury they
may cause upon the manufacturer," since he was "best situated to
afford . . . protection" against the risks of injuries.[15]

The triumph of *Escola* was the apparently irresistible simplicity
of its logic. Traynor was able to convey a sense that the result was
inevitable once one thought through the purposes of allocating risk-
bearing among the participants in a chain of distributing merchan-
dise from manufacturer to consumer. The party best suited to bear
the risks of defective products on the market was the manufacturer,
since he alone could make an empirical determination, through testing, of how risky the product was likely to be at each point in the
distribution chain, and then weigh the related cost of his insurance
against the financial benefits to be derived from making the product
available to the general public. Strict liability made that calculus an
open one, since fault was no longer an issue. The manufacturer
bore the cost whether he could have prevented the risk from being

created or not. With one stroke the doctrines used by sales and negligence law to extend a manufacturer's liability to remote consumers were recast: one suddenly saw that their purpose all along had been risk allocation. Traynor appeared as the objective analyst. Once the area of products liability was approached from this perspective, nearly anyone could see the rational solution. But Traynor had himself created the perspective. He had synthesized the parallel developments in sales law and negligence law; he had articulated the policy justifications for imposing absolute liability on the manufacturer; he had contrasted his social accountant's logic against the fictions of past courts; and he had reached a result that seemed intuitively just.

The *Escola* approach to products liability, which was eventually adopted by all of Traynor's colleagues,[16] was not simply an exercise in substituting one sort of reasoning for others. It asked manufacturers of potentially defective products—and as the case law developed, this included nearly any product—to reorder their thinking about liability for consumer injuries. A negligence standard invited them to plan to avoid liability by showing, in the courts, that they had not acted carelessly. This meant expert witnesses, constant litigation, release forms, investigations of the activities of victims who brought claims against them. The strict liability standard invited them to consider changing their thinking. Absent a showing that a "defective" product had been used in an unreasonable way, they were forced to bear the costs of the injuries that this product caused. Avoiding liability was thus perhaps less efficient than spreading or shifting its costs through insurance and higher wholesale or retail prices. This proposed recalculation was an extensive one, giving new meanings to what Traynor had called the "cost of doing business." Traynor had been aware of *Escola's* implications in this regard. "The manufacturer's obligation to the consumer," he commented, "must keep pace with the changing relationship between them." [17] His opinion had not merely underscored the changes in that relation, as it implied, but had stimulated them as well. He had functioned as an economist and a policymaker, although his tone suggested that he was merely an impersonal judge.

The jurisprudential point of *Escola* was to suggest that careful analysis would yield a result that could be identified not with the presuppositions of the judge who reached it but with the more dispassionate and durable values of rationality and common sense. The judge, in this view, was simply a mouthpiece for the rational policy choices of his time. Although he no longer "found" the law, he made law by "finding" public policy. Traynor recognized, however, that the process of judging was more complicated; that preconceptions interspersed themselves with logic in a way that could make one judge's "rational" solution quite different from another's. In his efforts to articulate the way he performed his function, he implicitly communicated the intuitive dimensions of judging, primarily through the use of metaphors in his descriptions of the judicial process.

In a 1961 address at the University of Chicago Law School Traynor came closest, perhaps, to an articulation of the limits of "objective analysis" in judging. Finding "acceptable rational alternatives" for the disposition of a case did not enable a judge to avoid the choice between them, Traynor said; and there was an obligation to avoid making that choice an arbitrary one. A decision would "not be saved from being arbitrary merely because [the judge was] disinterested"; he could not "remain disoriented forever, his mind suspended between alternative possible solutions." A "value judgment as to what the law ought to be" was required; an "interest in a rational outcome" at some point became channelled into "an interest in a particular result." But the result needed to be justified, and there the value of rationality became apparent. In searching to articulate his reasons, the judge drew on the aggregation of scholarship and common sense about him. Result-orientation was "no more than the final step toward reasoned judgment." [18] The judgment was the judge's, but the reasoning somehow more than his, the embodiment of the consensual attitudes of his environment.

The last step of this process was the one Traynor found hardest to describe. Indeed, he refrained from describing it with any precision. The step did not solve the problem of reconciling an obligation on the part of judges to reason their way to decisions with the necessity of making value choices, because the impression that a judgment was "reasoned" rather than "arbitrary" could be created by the judge. A result, in a close case, was not an inevitable logical necessity. Reaching it was often, as Traynor said, an exercise in "professional skill . . . and legal imagination." [19]

At this stage, then, an allegedly rational process came to be conveyed in metaphors. A judge took care "that when the chips are

down, they have fallen into the right places." [20] He "looked beyond
. . . disintegrating trees along judicial trails" to "the oaks from
little peppercorns growing" and "placed a contemporary case
within the sheltering ambit of contemporary live oaks." [21] He undertook "reclamation" of the "badlands" in a "realm of reason." [22]
He attempted "careful pruning," on which the "vigorous
growth" [23] of the law depended. He tried to "synchronize" into the
common law "the unguided missles launched by legislatures" [24]
without "shield[ing] wooden precedents from any radiations of for-
ward-looking statutes." [25] He "work[ed] away" at "fine interweaving." [26] He performed "the close work of imposing design on fragments of litigation, dealing . . . with the bits and pieces that blow
into [his] shop on a random wind." [27] In such statements Traynor
communicated a sense that judging was ultimately an art, resisting
precise characterization. The statements also served to distract his
audience from himself to the craft of his profession. In thinking
about the metaphors, one had no clearer picture of their creator.
He seemed to personify the characteristics he sought in judging: detachment, intellectualism, impersonality, rationality.

II

But Traynor's judging nonetheless revealed his personal sympathies
and inclinations, which were highly intellectualized. In particular,
Traynor created for himself a sophisticated theory of decision-making that attempted to fuse the institutional value of rationality
with his own intuitive preferences. His theory contained a reinter-
pretation of older characterizations of the technique of judging,
the development of an alternative technique more harmonious with
a model of affirmative government, and a re-evaluation of the place
of the judiciary in the modern process of lawmaking in the light of
that technique's implications.

Traynor began thinking about the methodology of judicial decision-making by noting the legacy of attitudes he had received on
becoming a judge in 1940. Looking back over time, he noted a persistence of "formulism"—a "vision of the common law as a completed formal landscape graced with springs of wisdom that judges
needed only to discover." [28] Formulism, though it had "been discredited by its cumulative inadequacies and distortions," continued

"to haunt our own time." [29] Its presence was felt in two related cults of judicial behavior: reluctance to abandon precedent, and insistence on a sharp separation between the "lawmaking" functions of the legislature and the "maintenance" functions of courts. The two cults were united in the conventional belief that "whatever incidental law courts create they are bound to maintain unless the legislature undertakes to unmake it." [30] Hence, courts perpetuated "ill-conceived, or moribund, or obsolete precedents" on the ground that their action enhanced the stability or predictability of the law [31] and represented proper deference to their superiors.

Traynor's reading of history revealed, however, that those canons had not always been followed in practice. The "greatest judges of the common law" had "steadily made advances," taking "an occasional dramatic leap forward . . . in the very interest of orderly progression." Holmes and Brandeis had "cleared the way for a liquidation of ancient interpretations of freedom of contract that had served to perpetuate child labor." Cardozo had "moved the rusting wheels of *Winterbottom v. Wright* to one side to make way for *MacPherson v. Buick Motor Co.*" [32] In the realm of statutory interpretation, creativity was also discernible. Early in the history of common law, judges had coined the phrase "equity of the statute," [33] which became a device by which they could avoid unjust results produced by a literal reading of statutory language. Moreover, judges found statutory rules "a source for analogous [common law] decisions." [34] In short, alongside the "recurring grotesqueries in the evolution of law" [35] produced by blind adherence to precedent and false distinctions between the work of courts and legislatures was a counter-tradition of significant judicial participation in lawmaking on a variety of fronts.

Buoyed by this tradition of judicial innovation, Traynor set out to identify it with order and rationality. He noted the gaps between outmoded legal rules and their application, both by courts and by juries. Courts resorted to fictions, such as lost grants, to further property settlements. [36] Juries in negligence cases imposed liability without fault through saving doctrines such as last clear chance or *res ipsa loquitur.* [37] The purpose of these efforts was to "achieve a rough justice by circumventing rules long out of tune with community values." [38] Such tendencies, though necessary, undermined respect for the process of adjudication. The solution was to reform the rules themselves. If a strict liability standard for torts was more suitable to "our ultra-hazardous age," the courts should make the change openly, and "thereby impose uniform operation of the law." [39] In lieu of "magic words" [40] that had lost their meaning, "tried and half-true formulas," or "antiquated compositions," [41] judges should "create some fragments of legal order out of disordered masses of new data." [42] In a judicial universe where the sharpness of syllogisms was liable to rust with time, adherence to rules that had lost their practical effectiveness was foolish. In 1926, while a law student, Traynor had condemned the perpetuation of an ancient rule of property despite its being "universally condemned as entirely without reason or common sense to support it." [43] Thirty-five years later he noted that the rule "still eke[d] out a precarious existence," and likened those courts that followed it to "that pack rat who hoards what is familiar to him, regardless of its value, and spends his energies to protect it at all costs." [44]

Traynor was motivated by these occurrences to search for judge-made rules that could be based on rational grounds and applied in a uniform fashion. His search proceeded in stages: a compilation of current sources from which a rule could be derived; an attempt to articulate the rule as a principle of general applicability; finally, an assessment of the consequences of the first two stages for the place of the judiciary in the larger process of lawmaking. By the last stage Traynor was prepared to concede that although "the mechanical logic grounded in old forms of action" had ceased to be a "quality control" for judging, no "model of rational methods" had supplanted it, "a tradition of reasoning on a noble plane" [45] had not yet been achieved.

Since he believed that judicial rules could not be rationally based if they did not conform to contemporary intellectual premises and social values, Traynor sought out "environmental data" [46] to supplement the traditional source materials of his profession. Such data, which were distinguishable from "the selected litigated facts presented to the court" by necessarily partisan counsel, could be gathered "through independent research" in the customs and practices of business, in scholarly treatises and law review articles, in the recent decisions of other courts. In their marshaling of data, appellate judges ought not to be confined to the evidence supplied them by litigators. Their "very independence" developed in them an ability to "detect latent quackery in science or medicine, to edit the swarm spore of social scientists, to add grains of salt to the fortune-telling statistics of the economists." They could inform themselves on matters beyond the facts of a particular case, and, when reliable data were lacking, "construct . . . environmental assumptions." [47]

In practice Traynor relied heavily on academic theorists to supply him with supplementary insights. Academicians had "the freedom . . . to differentiate the good growth from the rubbish," to "mark for [judicial] rejection the diseased anachronism." [48] In contracts Traynor drew on Arthur Corbin [49] and Samuel Williston; [50] in torts, William Prosser; [51] in conflicts of law, Brainerd Currie; [52] for an overview of administrative law, Walter Gellhorn, Kenneth Culp Davis, and Louis Jaffe.[53] In most instances he used scholarship as authority for the proposition that an older, judge-made rule needed revision as being analytically unsound or unresponsive to current conditions.

A final source of data consisted of actions by the California legislature. Here Traynor devised an ingenious theory of the use of statutes in common-law cases. The traditional separation of legislative lawmaking from judicial interpretation, he believed, was simplistic. In actuality, courts and legislatures had a symbiotic relationship, each drawing on the actions of the other. Legislatures passed statutes whose applicability to specific situations was uncertain; courts undertook the applications; legislatures revised the courts if they found a specific application offensive. Alternatively, statutes supplied, by analogy, common-law rules: when a case was "not governed by a statute," a court was "free to copy an appropriate model in a statute." [54] For example, when the California Probate Code provided detailed rules for administration of testamentary gifts by executors, but failed to include in its coverage administration by guardians, Traynor created a common law rule for guardians by analogy to the executor provisions of the statute.[55] Once created, the judicial rule took on "a life of its own"; it could "serve as a model . . . for successive judge-made rules." [56]

Traynor's partnership theory of legislative-court interaction led him to reject some traditional maxims of statutory interpretation. Like Hand, he deplored the "dictionary" approach to statutory language: "The words of a statute . . . are no longer at rest in their alphabetical bins . . . ; they challenge men to give them more than passive reading, to consider well their context." [57] As with Hand, Traynor made his basic inquiry in statutory interpretation "What purpose did the legislature express . . . ?" [58] Courts, in his view, ought to prevent "erratic omissions or errant words" [59] from defeating legislative purpose. Legislative silence, in this vein, did not always mean approval. The maxim that the failure of a legislature to repudiate an erroneous judicial interpretation of a statute meant that the legislature had incorporated that interpretation into the statute was for Traynor a "fiction." Legislative silence was "much more likely to mean ignorance or indifference" than "applause." [60] Courts should not be barred from re-examining their own statutory interpretations merely because they had been ignored by a legislature.

Judicial reliance on unconventional source materials exposed another myth about appellate judging: that "policy" was "a matter for the legislators to decide." [61] Traynor's approach was predicated on the notion that since there was always an area not covered by legislation in which judges needed to revise old rules or formulate new ones, policy considerations were "appropriate and even . . . basic" to their decision-making. His use of extralegal materials assumed that judicial "responsibility" connoted "far more than a mechanical application of given rules to new sets of facts"; it included also "the recurring choice of one policy over another in . . . the formulation of new rules." [62] Judicial decisions were responses to current social problems; lawmakers should reflect contemporary value choices rather than isolate themselves from them. That was the whole point of searching for clues outside the law books.

Despite his skepticism about maxims, formulas, and other "magic words," Traynor did not deny that courts had an obligation to articulate their decisions in general terms. The fact that judge-made rules became obsolete was a reason to avoid their indiscriminate perpetuation, he maintained—but not a reason to avoid formulating them at all. Appellate courts needed to "frame their opinions with enough perspective to guide others in comparable fact situations." [63] They had an obligation to articulate "guiding principles." [64] Their decisions had to "allay the suspicion of any man in the street who regards knowledge of the law as no excuse for making it." They also ought to "afford conscientious lawyers an ample basis of predictability for purposes of counseling and determining when to litigate." [65]

But if rules should be grounded in the environmental conditions and assumptions of a society at a specific point in its history, and

consequently might change with time, how could a judge insure
that they would serve as guideposts for social planning in more
than the most ephemeral sense? Here Traynor entered the "neutral
principles" controversy of the 1960s, which had been stimulated by
Herbert Wechsler's insistence that courts rest their decisions "on
reasons . . . that in their generality and neutrality transcend any
immediate result that is involved." [66] No one could quarrel,
Traynor felt, with an obligation in appellate courts to generalize
their results, or to base their decisions on reason. But the phrase
"neutral principles" sounded "pure and simple" to "a judge who
confronts problems ridden with impurities and complications." It
smacked of "magic words." Such principles were "hardly to be
found in briefs" and not always in academic treatises. [67]

For Traynor, however, the primary difficulty with the neutral-
principles theory was not in the elusiveness of its central phrase,
but in its assumption that generalized legal rules could be durable.
Its advocates apparently believed that judges could "somehow walk
out of themselves and record a distilled impersonal judgment yet
stay close enough to common people to gain their acceptance." [68]
These assumptions were sticking points for Traynor, for they ignored the inability of courts to predict the likelihood that rules they
formulated would survive the moment of their articulation. In
Traynor's jurisprudence judge-made rules responded to the contemporary environment; no one could tell how that environment
might change. Even though it might seem reasonably clear to a
court that a legal concept seemed destined to expand, judges had
"no way of divining a concept's optimum tolerance for expansion at
a given moment in a given situation." [69] Rules, in this sense, could
never be "principles" if that term connoted permanency, any more
than policy choices could ever be "neutral."

Traynor's theory of judging, in short, blended a belief that empirical observation, personal disinterestedness, and intellectual integrity could insure that appellate decisions were grounded in rationality, with a sense that those decisions, if properly made, were
ultimately subservient to the dictates of history. He differed from
Holmes in that he did not read the inevitability of social change as
compelling fatalism in the judiciary. A competent judge's reasoning, he felt, could be more than merely an articulation of the "felt
necessities" of his time; it could be a guideline for continued
change. Active judicial participation in change, through an innova-

tive reformulation of rules and doctrines, could insure that the process of lawmaking remained orderly while it evolved. Policy choices were in one sense dictated by the environment, but in another sense made by judges. The manner in which they were made could make a difference. "Well-tempered" judges could "stabilize the explosive forces of the day," do "everything within their power of reasoning to make each day in court lead constructively to the next one and to set an example approaching what a civilized day could be." [70]

Certain implications for a court's role in the process of lawmaking followed from the above. Whenever possible, Traynor preferred to retain decision-making power in courts rather than in juries, since he believed that judges had greater capacity for formulating orderly and intelligible rules. He dismissed as unrealistic the "arbitrary line" between questions of "fact" and questions of "law." The questions overlapped, he felt, and the distinction should not be used (as it had been on occasion in torts) to deny a court the power to set forth a standard for negligence or to confine appellate judicial review to matters of "law." [71] He rejected the image of the branches of government as "those of a hatrack, fixed and therefore incapable of movement." [72] Courts not only made law, they made policy; they were partners of the legislature, interacting with it in a variety of ways. Similarly, courts interacted with administrative agencies. Traynor supported active judicial review of agency decisions even if they were purportedly grounded in "expertise." Technical appraisal by an administrator in a specialized field was insulated from review, but not opinions of agency officials on matters "that should as much be within the ken of judges." [73] Finally, Traynor recognized the extent to which modern lawmaking institutions "interact[ed] in countless ways with powerful private groups." [74] Understanding the expectations and practices of these groups was another obligation of courts. This responsibility, however, gave rise to a power in judges to insure that these groups did not in their own decisions arbitrarily infringe on the rights of individuals. [75]

The accepted premise that judges made law, then, created for Traynor an obligation on their part to make law in a rational and orderly fashion, but this obligation itself conferred power on the judiciary to expand the scope of its prerogatives, since judicial decisions were a prime source of rationality in the legal process as a whole. An area illustrating this line of reasoning was the retroactive application of new judge-made rules of criminal procedure. Traynor conceded that new rules expanding protection to criminal defendants in the 1950s and 1960s had not been "discovered." They represented a policy choice to restrict the ability of law enforcement officials to abuse their discretion. Expanded procedural safeguards, however, meant increased opportunities for incarcerated criminals to challenge their confinement on the ground that they had not been afforded a full measure of protection. Retroactive application of new criminal procedure rules therefore suggested that countless criminals might be turned loose upon the public.

Traynor approached the problem by equating the automatic retroactivity of new judge-made rules of law with the oracular theory of judging. If judges merely *found* the law, "new" law was law for all time but had simply not previously been discovered, and hence, retroactive application was required. But if judges *made* the law, and especially if in the process they based their judgments on a perception of current conditions, they could adjust the retroactive scope of their decisions to meet contemporary social needs. If retroactive application of criminal procedure rule changes resulted in a wholesale freeing of incarcerated criminals, this negative value could become part of a judge's calculus. Prospective application of innovations in criminal procedure (which Traynor advocated) [76] was thus in keeping with his perception of the way judges functioned in modern America. If prospectivity suggested freedom in the judiciary to make policy choices openly, those choices, after all, were attempts to construct rational responses to the demands of the environment in which judges functioned.

The thrust of Traynor's approach to judging was thus to carve out a wide area of lawmaking power for the judiciary, but to equate effective use of that power with the constraints of rationality. The judge could substitute himself as a lawmaker for juries or legislators or administrators if he exemplified in his decisions social awareness, intellectual openness, and powers of analysis. These qualities gave his decisions the measure of rationality that they needed to be accepted. In making law the judge was synthesizing and organizing the insights of others. His primacy was justified by an exhibited dependence on outside contributions.

The delicate reciprocity between judicial power and restraint envisaged by Traynor's technique of adjudication appeared to ignore a difficulty raised earlier. If judges could, by imaginative use of extrajudicial sources, retain for themselves a number of problems traditionally entrusted to other lawmaking branches, what prevented techniques of craftsmanship from being a means of concealing bases for decision rather than of revealing them? Could not a judge decide on intuitive grounds, then express his preference in terms that suggested a greater amount of impersonality and detachment than he in fact had?

The implicit answer to this inquiry, for Traynor, was that in a sense the original motivations of the judge did not matter. If a judge took the time and effort to reason his judgments through, to justify them by means of broadly based social and intellectual appeals, his original intuitions became secondary to his own articulated reasoning processes. The significance of a result was indistinguishable from the reasons given in connection with it. If the reasons were vulnerable to attack, so was the result. Conversely, a potentially upsetting result, in the sense of one that dramatically changed the state of the law, was less troublesome if the reasons advanced for it were sound. Judicial innovations were thus no less troublesome than alterations in the law of other branches, provided they were rationally based. Reason remained for Traynor a nearly objective concept. He felt that one could easily distinguish what was rational from what was arbitrary; that one could subsume one's intuitions in an analytical exegesis.

III

The confidence that Traynor placed in the innovative capabilities of the judiciary was exemplified by his own contributions to numerous cases of substantive law. In torts—perhaps the area of his widest impact—he pioneered in the development of strict liability in defective products cases; [77] undermined the defense of immunity, whether charitable,[78] sovereign,[79] or family,[80] in negligence actions; exposed fictional distinctions in the law defining the responsibilities of a landowner for accidents on his property; [81] and helped create the new tort of intentional infliction of emotional distress.[82] In contracts he went beyond the contents of documents to gather information about and assess the practical impact of the agreements they signified, and was not deterred in his search by

rules limiting a court's consideration of extrinsic evidence [83] or
traditional limitations on the fact-finding abilities of courts.[84] Once
having secured ample information, he attempted to piece together
the reasonable expectations of the contracting parties and weigh
these against the policy implications of one outcome or another.[85]
He did not take literally legislative requirements that contracts be
in writing,[86] nor was he reluctant to discard the formalities of offer
and acceptance in allocating responsibility for business losses between general contractors and subcontractors.[87] He voided contracts, however, on occasions in which one of the parties had not
been authorized by the legislature to enter into the type of agreement in question.[88] In short, his approach de-emphasized formalities in the face of immediate practical considerations.

In real property, Traynor discarded or reformulated older decisions setting forth requirements for the delivery of a deed of title,[89]
adverse possession of land,[90] the recognition of security interests in
real property transactions,[91] the remedies of a landlord on forcible
entry of his property by a tenant,[92] and the remedies of a seller
against defaulting purchasers of land.[93] The thrust of these decisions was to break down stringent rules by altering them to fit the
context of particular sets of real property transactions. In civil procedure, similarly, Traynor discarded the rule of mutuality, which
had insisted that when a person attempted, in a later litigation, to
invoke an earlier judgment against another, he could make use of
the first judgment only if he himself was bound by it.[94]

In a case where the administrator of a will attempted to sue a
bank for unauthorized payment of money in the will to a beneficiary, the bank invoked an earlier judgment of a probate court that
the payment was authorized by the will. The bank, however, had
not been a party in the probate court, although the administrator
had. The mutuality rule therefore prohibited the bank from using
the probate court judgment to prevent the administrator from subsequently suing it. Traynor took the occasion to reject the mutuality rule outright and substitute a test that focused on the issues
resolved in the first adjudication (were they "identical" with those
presented in the second?), the occurrence of a "final judgment on
the merits" in the first adjudication, and the presence of the same
party or his contractee in both suits.[95]

Despite Traynor's status as a state judge, he was able to make innovations in constitutional law through his consideration of analo-

gous issues in the California constitution and his interpretation of the implications for the states in any changes in federal criminal-procedure rules. In 1948, for example, Traynor struck down a California anti-miscegenation statute on equal protection grounds,[96] anticipating a Warren Court decision [97] by sixteen years. Two years earlier he had invalidated the California Syndicalism Act as applied against officers of the American Civil Liberties Union who had refused to swear that they were not members of subversive organizations.[98] In later cases he protested against a loyalty oath's being made a condition of tax-exempt status,[99] and Communist Party affiliation's being made the sole basis for discharge of an employee.[100]

Likewise in criminal procedure Traynor found his views congenial to the innovative stance of a majority of the Warren Court. After holding, in 1942,[101] that the Fourth Amendment's prohibition of the use of illegally acquired evidence in criminal trials did not apply against the states, Traynor reversed his position in 1955 [102] and subsequently expanded protection for criminal defendants against illegal searches and seizures, including searches of a home without uncoerced consent or a warrant,[103] and searches incident to "felony" arrests where the arresting officer knew only that a felony had been committed.[104] His changes, however, were not always favorable to criminal defendants. In the course of reconsidering standards for police conduct in the late 1950s and the 1960s, he created rules that justified arrests on observation of a defendant's behavior [105] or reasonable searches even before arrests.[106] He also expanded the discovery rights of prosecutors against defendants despite the Fifth Amendment's requirement that persons accused of crimes not be compelled to incriminate themselves.[107]

Two other substantive areas deserve attention in this brief review of Traynor's innovations: conflict of laws, and taxation, both of which were fields of special interest for him. Conflict of laws, because of its abstract, conceptual character, gave Traynor a stark opportunity to criticize mechanical rules and formulate functional ones of his own; taxation offered him a chance to apply as a judge views that he had first developed as a law professor. The "conflicts" field was dominated originally by dichotomies between questions of "substance" and questions of "procedure," or by rigid rules such as the rule that territoriality defined the primacy of competing state laws.[108] After an early struggle to work within the framework of

these concepts [109]—in which he increasingly questioned their usefulness—Traynor eventually abandoned them altogether, first in a
contracts case [110] and then in a tort case. [111] In their place he substituted an analysis that compared and evaluated the respective interests of the states affected. Sometimes this analysis produced a bona-
fide conflict between competing state interests; when this happened, another policy, such as that facilitating commercial transactions among the states, could be used to resolve the conflict. [112] On
many other occasions investigation revealed no real interest on the
part of one state and a substantial interest on the part of another, so
that a "false conflict" could be said to exist. Interest analysis in
conflicts lead ultimately to a consideration of the social policies
promoted by choosing a legal rule of one state over that of another.
That was the kind of inquiry Traynor attempted to make in all his
decisions. Rules were meaningful only to the extent that they reflected rational policies derived from a responsiveness to social conditions.

If conflicts was perhaps Traynor's most congenial field in the latter portion of his career, taxation had originally been his compelling
interest. While teaching law at Berkeley, he recognized that expansion of governmental activity required additional taxation, and that
the welfare purposes of affirmative government would be subverted
if tax obligations were not equitably allocated. [113] He gave particular attention to state taxation of national banks, publishing a series
of articles on the subject [114] and participating in a 1933 revision of
the Bank and Corporation Tax Act, which reflected his views. [115]
He also sat on legislative committees to redraft tax statutes for
sales, personal income, motor vehicle licensing, corporation income, and fuel consumption. He served as administrator of the California sales tax in the 1930s, and in 1937 as tax advisor to the U.S.
Treasury Department. All the while he taught courses in taxation
at Berkeley in which, as one of his students observed, "the quality
of mercy . . . dropped as the gentle rain from heaven upon the
Sahara." [116]

The function of appellate judges in tax cases often consists of
supplying operational meanings, in varied contexts, to statutory
language. This requires fine verbal distinctions that have practical
significance. Traynor was equal to that task. The phrase "source of
income" invited a distinction between a tax applied directly to net
income and a tax on franchises measured by net income. [117] Lease-

holds on land exempt from taxation were "real property" for the purposes of the property tax laws.[118] "Full cash value" was defined as arm's-length market value under ordinary conditions.[119] Liquor licenses were not "intangible personal property." [120] And "goods in transit," immune from taxation, embraced out-of-state goods temporarily stored in San Francisco while awaiting shipment to Hawaii during wartime.[121]

IV

Despite the continually innovative character of Traynor's judicial performance, despite his receptiveness to affirmative governmental action, and despite the fact that many of his changes in the common law of California broadened the opportunities of aggrieved persons to seek redress in the courts, conventional political characterizations are no more helpful in illuminating his stance than they are for Story, or Shaw, or Cooley, or Doe. Traynor was, though not universally, a "liberal" judge if the term signifies receptiveness to change, or interest in the plight of disadvantaged persons, or, as previously used in this study, a commitment to the management of society by professionals. But calling him a liberal does not clarify his attitude. Of greater importance is his methodological approach to judging. Traynor regarded results as simply a logical consequence of a satisfactory technique of analysis, the final steps of a reasoned judgment. In his most significant opinions, such as *Escola*, *Muskopf v. Corning Hospital District* (in which he discarded the doctrine of governmental immunity), or *Reich v. Purcell* (in which he abandoned the "place of the wrong" rule in multistate conflicts cases), his results were difficult to classify in ideological terms, though his methodological approach was consistent and distinctive. In each case Traynor focused on a conventional judge-made rule or doctrine, identified its working difficulties, repudiated it, and substituted for it a rule of his own derived from extrajudicial sources as well as from the ordinary materials of the appellate judge.

Traynor's technique of decision-making emphasized that judging was not an exercise in declaring rules but a process of weighing varieties of evidence in search of a rational solution. Effective judicial "laws" underscored the rationality of the process by which they were made, rather than the content of their language. Effective lawmaking by appellate courts gave them freedom to revise their own decisions without abandoning their allegiance to rationality. Here Traynor's starting assumptions about judging were thrown into sharp relief. The "primary internal characteristic of the judicial process" was that it was "a rational one." It was "based on reasoning and presupposed[d]—all antirationalists to the contrary notwithstanding—that its determinations [were] justified only when explained or explainable in reason." [122]

More than any appellate judge of his time, Traynor witnessed a dramatic change in the social context of his decisions. If American society in the years between 1940 and 1970 became increasingly complicated, heterogeneous, consumer-oriented, diversified, and dominated by the presence of institutions of government, California was at the crest of those trends. No state in the nation had developed so rapidly. None of comparable size and population had undergone such massive changes after omnipresent government had become tolerated in American society.

Traynor's contribution, in these terms, was to develop a theory and a technique of judging that proved responsive to the symbolic experience of California life. As the process of distributing products from manufacturers to consumers became altered with the advent of supermarket economics, Traynor reoriented tort law to reflect that alteration. As purchasing power widened so that more uneducated or uninformed persons entered into contracts, Traynor recognized that arm's-length bargaining based on complete information was often a fiction, whether in commercial ventures or in the sale of homes. As governmental institutions demonstrated their capacity to injure persons as well as to aid them, Traynor saw the undesirable consequences of immunities. As more and more persons crossed state lines in their occupational and leisured pursuits, Traynor perceived that territorially-based conflicts rules needed re-examination. And as legislatures made laws with increasing frequency, created agencies to administer them, and looked to courts to clarify their meaning in specific instances, Traynor resolved that a theory of government that emphasized rigid boundary lines between governing institutions was unrealistic.

Like other judges of his time, Traynor's perceptions of the imperatives of social change were intuitive, and doubtless the results he reached brought him emotional as well as intellectual satisfaction. But for Traynor the promotion of substantive policies in a judicial opinion was easily distinguishable, if the opinion was properly crafted, from the individual bias of the writer. The identification of law as a process and of appellate judging as an intellectual effort to keep the process in smooth working order focused discussions of judicial decision-making on reasons rather than on results. Reasons, in fact, subsumed results; process subsumed substance; result-orientation was merely one stage in the progression toward a reasoned judgment. A social policy was promoted not because of its emotional appeal to the judge but because, after careful examination, it emerged as a rational and intellectually defensible resolution of a current conflict.

In the context of American society after World War II, a society widely perceived by scholars as being unprecedented in its complexity and interrelatedness,[123] the notion of law as an integrated, impersonal, rationally-based process was appealing. Process Jurisprudence framed divisive value conflicts in an orderly institutional structure that resolved them; it allowed some freedom for governing officials to shape law to changing conditions, but confined each branch of government to the tasks it could perform most rationally. Process Jurisprudence thus suggested the restoration of balance and harmony in government at a time when extremes of behavior were out of fashion and consensual American values were being reaffirmed. It also identified law and legal institutions with the social assumptions of modern liberalism by providing an apparently non-partisan technique of implementing affirmative governmental action.

Yet the dichotomy between the process of reasoning and the substantive results that process yielded remained a central element of American appellate judging in the 1950s and 1960s. Despite the timeliness of Traynor's approach, views such as his did not sweep the field. Pressure for legal change, especially with respect to the rights and interests of minorities, combined with inertia on the part of legislatures to create a fruitful climate for the open judicial espousal of substantive values. In their fervor to respond to this need and their sense of the importance of the values themselves, influential judges began to eschew intellectual niceties for ringing affirmations of the rights and privileges of American citizenship. In their affirmations results transcended reasons, and process was only a means of conveying substance. While in his opinions Traynor was able to achieve a delicate fusion of substantive change and methodological consistency, of intuition and rationality, in other judges those goals became self-opposing, engendering the jurisprudential controversies of the Warren Court.

14

The Mosaic of the Warren Court: Frankfurter, Black, Warren, and Harlan

Over the course of American history, the practice of identifying an incumbent Supreme Court with the figure of its Chief Justice has produced analytical difficulties. Personifying the Court in its Chief may exaggerate the influence of certain holders of that office, as in the Chase Court. It may suggest a flavor to the Court that in fact it does not have: the Stone Court, typically, did not reflect the jurisprudential views of its Chief. It may invite political characterizations that lead to erroneous assumptions, such as that the Taney Court signified a sharp break from the Marshall Court. Or it may suggest that the Court's history falls into neat chronological phases, synonymous with each change in Chief Justice. This is often not the case: transitions from Waite to Fuller and from Fuller to White, for example, produced no major alterations in the Court's stance.

The practice has some utility, however, as a shorthand device for indicating the opportunity available to each incoming Chief Justice to encourage, through personal and intellectual leadership, the development of a collective jurisprudential viewpoint among his colleagues. No Chief, not even a Marshall, can expect to make a Court's attitude synonymous with his own; none can hope to achieve unanimity on a very high percentage of issues; none, not even a Hughes, can expect by force of personality and intellect to impose fully a style of decision-making on his fellow justices. Judging at the Supreme Court level is too individualized, independent, and prideful an activity for such expectations to be realized. Challenges nonetheless come with the succession to the Chief Justiceship, the challenge of extracting unity from diversity, that of supplying channels for intellectual energies, and that of giving a loosely identifiable cast to the institution. The designation "Warren Court" is an apt one in the sense that its Chief attempted to meet those challenges. Earl Warren invested his Court with a discernible character, if not necessarily a coherent jurisprudence.

I

The unity of the Warren Court did not suppress its diversity, but was merely superimposed upon that diversity. If one analogizes the creation of an intellectual identity for a Court to the creation of a cultural identity for a nation, the Warren Court was not a melting pot but a mosaic. Its dominant Justices retained their distinctive points of view, harmonizing with one another only sporadically and superficially. No individual emerged as its intellectual leader during the sixteen years of Warren's tenure; several powerful figures stood in trenchant opposition or in uneasy coexistence. No theory of constitutional interpretation or judicial performance captured the Court; instead, much of its energy came from a clash of competing jurisprudential attitudes.

Despite this clash, a generalized pattern of behavior came to mark the Warren Court. The pattern may be described as a momentum toward an increasingly broad definition of the rights attaching to American citizenship. It was no more precise than that. The Court, as a unit, did not draw clear distinctions as to eligibility for these rights or as to the class of government officials compelled to respect them. Abstract statements were made about the rights extending to "all Americans"; yet certain rights clearly did not so extend, and others extended beyond citizens to aliens. Similar comments were voiced about the broad responsibilities of all government officials—whether federal or state, administrators or legislators, bureaucrats or law enforcers—to protect citizenship rights, although in practice the obligations of these categories of officials were differently defined. In short, although the Warren Court as a whole revealed itself as increasingly inclined to recognize new citizenship rights or to protect those already extant, its individual Justices could not arrive at any broad collective decision about what rights they wanted protected against which sorts of persons in what specific contexts. The Warren Court's concern for rights was abstract and growing: its breadth and momentum, rather than its precise content, gave the Court its character.

The social and institutional values around which the Warren Court cohered were markedly broad and abstract. The Justices, to a man, accepted the principle that affirmative governmental action to meet the problems of disadvantaged persons was a necessity in mid-twentieth-century American society. Their quarrels were over methods of implementing the principle—especially with regard to the role of the judiciary—rather than with its general validity. The Warren Court Justices believed also in the inevitability of social change and were generally optimistic about the American people's ability to better themselves in the process of responding to changing conditions. Beyond this abstract belief, however, they rapidly diverged: some justices tended to equate "the people" with their elected or appointed representatives; others came to find representative government not always responsive to popular needs.

The Warren Court in the aggregate also accepted the notion that U.S. government was in some sense paternalistic, and they did not insist on participatory democracy in its pure forms. They quarreled, however, over the institutional implications of paternalism. In general, some held a vision of a paternalistic Court scrutinizing the other branches of government to insure that their processes afforded full protection to the people's rights; others identified paternalism primarily with other branches of government and sought to restrict the class of wards protected by the Court. Finally, the Warren Court was unified behind a broad sense of patriotism, and its participants shared a faith in the unique worth of American society and a commitment to its preservation. They differed, however, in their interpretation of the imperatives of patriotism in specific instances, some equating it with preservation of human rights more than with maintenance of national unity or security, others reversing this balance; some exhibiting a fidelity to models of government employed by the American nation at its origin, others suggesting that the American experiment implied that those models were to change with time.

Although the core values of the Warren Court were abstractions, they were not all-embracing political shibboleths. Alternative view-points had been articulated and widely accepted during the course of American history. The Founding Fathers had exhibited little confidence in the ability of the masses to govern themselves; some believed that even a government made up of the people's represen-tatives was not a sufficient buffer against the excesses of the mob. For a good part of the nineteenth century the theory that a govern-ment governs best which governs least was influential: paternalism was "odious," and affirmative government action offended against the laws of the universe. Patriotism was a recurrent value, but had in previous decades been linked with certain attitudes, such as racial and ethnic discrimination, that the Warren Court largely deplored. The shared values of the Warren Court Justices, in short, were those of modern liberalism. Life in America was assumed to be composed of complex patterns of change and affected by a loss of consensual values; victims of an industrializing society were identified, and an active, benevolent government of professionals was invested with the tasks of meeting current needs and serving as a force for social cohesiveness.

Stating the credo of modern liberalism underscored its internal ambiguities. It had, as indicated earlier, a commitment to profes-sionalism. One of its purposes was to insure that the programs of affirmative government would be conceived and managed in a man-ner sufficiently sophisticated to respond to the complexities of mod-ern life. Achievement of this goal seemed to require a careful evalu-ation of the roles and functions of governing institutions so that the agencies of government did not overlap one another or venture into areas where they had no expertise, and so that the decision-making procedures of the separate institutions responded to the needs of their different constituents. The logic of this approach appeared to mandate a limited role for the judiciary as an agent of affirmative government. Judges had little access to current empirical data, and the data they did receive was skewed by the adversary process. They were not, by and large, representatives of the people, and their nonpartisan status insulated them from the waves of current opinion; hence, for them to pose as social theorists raised dangerous questions of unchecked judicial tyranny. Holmes's model of a pas-sive judiciary, refined by Brandeis and Stone to tolerate judicial in-volvement where expertise could be acquired or where legislative attempts at social ordering had produced woefully inefficient or unfair side effects, harmonized with this thrust of modern liberalism.

Another purpose, however, was to give aid to the casualties of industrial and urban progress. As individual initiative came to be seen as inadequate, and as social and economic powerlessness came to be perceived as threshold barriers to upward mobility, paternalistic governmental action was regarded as the chief means of ameliorating the social condition of disadvantaged persons. The "freedom" of a market economy proved to be one-sided; political action, in the form of social welfare legislation, emerged as the remedy. By accident, the Holmes model of institutional performance interacted with this humanitarian thrust of liberalism, since many of the legislative innovations he declined to scrutinize were designed to subordinate economic freedom to the needs of the disadvantaged. Brandeis's decisions exemplified more starkly the policy dimensions of a passive theory of judicial performance in the early twentieth century. On the relatively few occasions when an experimental piece of state legislation served an antihumanitarian purpose, such as suppressing the rights of expression of a political or ethnic minority,[1] Brandeis asked himself whether the evil that the legislation was designed to eradicate was sufficiently noxious to justify the statute's regressive thrust.[2] His calculus in such cases smacked of substantive due process, anathema to advocates of a passive judiciary.

In the Stone and Vinson Courts tensions between the professionalist and humanitarian impulses of modern liberalism were evident. Celebrated cases of the 1930s, 1940s, and early 1950s—such as the flag salute controversies [3] (in which the Stone Court overruled itself within a three-year time span [4]), cases involving racial discrimination in colleges,[5] in primary elections,[6] and in housing,[7] or the clashes between free speech and national security [8] after World War II—can be seen as struggles in harmonizing judicial passivity with humanitarian impulses. In those decades a shifting number of justices, despite their voiced opposition to substantive due process, came to favor judicial intervention in behalf of minorities whose civil rights and liberties had been infringed by states or the federal government. No detailed rationale for this intervention was formulated: it seemed to rest on an unexpressed commitment to substantive values. In the second flag-salute case, Justices Douglas and Black indicated that although they remained "reluct-[ant] to make the Federal Constitution a rigid bar against state regulation of conduct thought inimical to the public welfare," on certain occasions the "application" of that "sound" principle was "wrong." [9]

The doctrinal struggles of the pre–Warren Court years were manifestations of a more fundamental issue: What were the costs and benefits of a substantive judicial commitment to modern liberalism? Herein lay the origins of a central theme of the Warren Court, the conflict between the professionalist and humanitarian strands of the modern liberal impulse. From one perspective the history of the Warren Court may be seen as a clash between these strands in the context of an expanding judicial definition of citizenship rights. Although the Warren Court Justices began with shared assumptions as to the role of government in modern American, as well as a generalized commitment to the social ends—efficiency, humanitarianism, equality of economic opportunity, equal treatment before the law—of modern liberalism, they soon exhibited major disagreement over the methods of achieving these ends, especially as they affected the role of the Court. In the course of the debate, professionalism and humanitarianism were expanded into jurisprudential postures that might be represented by the terms "process" and "substantive liberalism."

Process Jurisprudence, as noted above, accepted lawmaking in judges but confined it to limit areas, emphasizing the antidemocratic character of the judiciary and the inability of judges to achieve detailed technical expertise. A passive model of judicial performance was thus part of its tenets. In addition, Process Jurisprudence emphasized the complexity of post–World War II American society and the proliferation of government agencies, and attempted to match governmental institutions to the areas they were best prepared to supervise and the problems they were most suited to resolve. Lawmaking became an exercise in affirmative governmental action of a specialized and confined sort. Governing institutions could be aggressively innovative so long as they remained in their ambits of competence. Catchwords and catchphrases described specialized institutional skills: courts were "disinterested" and their judgments "reasoned"; legislatures were "representative of popular opinion" and could "canvass a wide spectrum of views"; the executive was "efficient"; administrative agencies were "flexible" and "expert." An integration of specialized governing institutions produced the hybrid, pragmatic social ordering of post–New Deal America.

As new problems surfaced, their character was defined, the appropriate institution for their solution identified, the process of affirmative government set in motion, and the limitations on each unit of government once more underscored. The smooth functioning of the process became the overriding goal. The general implementation of social values transcended the particular content of the values. The process theory was hence integrated with modern liberalism: it assumed the necessity of positive governmental action and sought to provide jurisprudential guidelines to make that action effective.

The impact of process liberalism on the Warren Court was manifested primarily in a set of limitations on judicial performance. Such limitations included a requirement that the Court decide only mature and full-blown controversies; an obligation on its part to avoid deciding "political" questions; an insistence that it justify its decisions by appeal to intelligible legal principles, or, if no principles emerged, refrain from deciding altogether; an indentification on the part of Justices of their own biases, with a view to achieving the proper mood of detachment; a preliminary classification of controversies as suitable for "judicial," "legislative," "executive," or "administrative" decision, and their consequent allocation to the appropriate branches of government, with the judiciary recognizing its own limited jurisdiction. Justice Frankfurter, on his retirement in 1962, described the obligations of process liberalism for a judge. It required, he said, the "pertinacious pursuit of processes of Reason in the disposition of controversies," a pursuit identified with "intellectual disinterestedness in the analysis of the factors involved in issues that called for decision," which decision was in turn a product of "rigorous self-scrutiny" in the judge "to discover, with a view to curbing, every influence that may deflect from such disinterestedness." [10]

But what if a judge believed that some values did not compete with others, but invariably superseded them? What if he perceived American society as being grounded on fundamental guaranties of citizenship and could point to the Constitution as declaring those guaranties? What if he further believed, as had Marshall and Story, that some values were embedded in the fabric of American society in addition to being alluded to in specific constitutional provisions? Could not his balancing process regularly affirm those values against the competing claims of other values in accordance with their fundamental social importance? Could not the claims of disadvantaged persons be seen in this context, so that judicial responsiveness to them was simply a recognition of the primacy of egalitarianism and libertarianism in America, which compelled the eradication of social and economic inequalities? Was not the humanitarian impulse of modern liberalism thus part of a historic tradition in America, a tradition that defined the meaning of the nation? If so, why should this impulse be subordinated to any judicial conception of the currently appropriate process of social ordering—a conception that was, after all, itself a value judgment?

Therein lay the Warren Court's competing theories of judging: the sophisticated models of process liberalism against the straightforward imperatives of substantive liberalism. Originally conceived of only as different methodological techniques, these theories took on broader implications in the latter years of Warren's tenure. Since process liberalism fostered caution in the judiciary and deference to the judgments of other governmental institutions, it served as a brake in the momentum of substantive liberalism in areas where legislatures, agencies, and the executive were taking no action. An example was the issue of whether state legislatures should be reapportioned on a population basis. If the judiciary, terming that question "political," declined to compel reapportionment, then it allowed a system of unequally weighted representation to persist, since no other unit of government had shown an inclination to change the existing system. The demands of process liberalism thus harmonized, in this instance, with counteregalitarian values; judicial inaction perpetuated the power of rural areas in state legislatures.

As humanitarian impulses gained momentum in the Warren Court, techniques of process liberalism became vehicles for the maintenance of countervailing values, such as the autonomy of law enforcement (against increased protection for criminal suspects), freedom of association (against equal access to facilities by all races), or federalism (against uniform courtroom procedures across the nation). Since espousal of the Warren Court's humanitarianism required change in all of these areas, process liberalism became identified with political conservatism. To argue, on professionalist grounds, for confinement of the Warren Court's jurisdiction was often to advocate resistance to sweeping social change.

Seventeen justices served in the Warren Court, so that describing only a few of them as predominant invites difficulties. In terms of the themes of this chapter, however, four Justices were of special importance: Felix Frankfurter, Hugo Black, Earl Warren, and John Harlan. Frankfurter and Harlan, on one side, and Black and Warren, on the other, were the most influential representatives of the theories of process and substantive liberalism. Frankfurter and Black represented polar positions in the first stage of this controversy, which ended with Frankfurter's retirement in 1962 and in which the conflicts were more methodological than political. Harlan and Warren, along with Black, played significant roles in the second stage, which lasted until Warren's retirement in 1969 and in which the original debate metamorphosed into something resembling an ideological confrontation. At stake in the debate was more than the delineation of proper techniques of opinion-writing or even the designation of social values deserving of judicial implementation; at stake was the viability of the process theory of appellate judging.

II

An important dimension of the Warren Court was its sensitivity to the implications of status. This Court numbered among its influential Justices three men—Black, Douglas, and Warren—who had seen poverty in their youths, who identified with persons of low social and economic status, who remained indifferent to or suspicious of inherited wealth and social position, whose philosophy of government was a leveling one, and yet who were upward-mobile in their own lives and not uncomfortable with the possession or maintenance of power achieved through individual initiative. Another member—Harlan—reflected a fundamentally different perspective. He was conscious of his own elite social and intellectual status and interested in maintaining civilized standards and in protecting the social order from anarchistic impulses. Many issues considered by the Warren Court had status implications, since many of the persons whose rights the Court vindicated—prisoners, blacks, industrial laborers, migrant workers—were identified with low socioeconomic standing.

The presence of Frankfurter was richly suggestive of this theme. Frankfurter was himself upward-mobile, a German-Jewish im-

migrant from New York's Lower East Side with a lifelong fascina-
tion with public figures—such as Henry Stimson, Franklin D. Roosevelt, Holmes, and Hand—with aristocratic backgrounds. But
Frankfurter's heritage encompassed academic and intellectual traditions, and his conspicuous success in the American educational system gave his upward mobility a special flavor. He emerged from
Harvard Law School in 1906 proud of his Jewishness but determined to enter the Wasp-dominated world of Wall Street practice,
a firm supporter of the democratic bias of American civilization but
a member of and apologist for the Eastern intellectual meritocracy.

In his later career these patterns continued. He spoke dispar-
agingly of special privilege and economic imperialism,[11] but limited his classes at Harvard Law School to students of high academic
standing. He participated enthusiastically in the elitist apprenticeship system of the legal profession, in which conspicuously high
grades at a national law school created a series of opportunities—law review staff membership, judicial clerkships, positions
on law faculties or with large urban law firms—for a narrow strat-
um of candidates. In the 1930s, by virtue of his numerous contacts, tireless energy, and seemingly endless capacity for promoting
the candidacies of those whose qualities struck him favorably,
Frankfurter was a nerve center of the apprenticeship network. He
helped choose the clerks of Holmes, Brandeis, and Learned Hand;
he served as a conduit between Harvard graduates and Wall Street
firms or government agencies; he secured research assistantships at
Harvard for Supreme Court clerks who had a potential interest in
teaching; he wrote joint articles with promising law students as a
means of exposing them to the process of academic publication. In
his mind this patronage served a noble end, the perpetuation of an
elite based on merit rather than on privilege, and hence compatible
with democratic ideals.

Frankfurter reconciled intellectual elitism with democracy
through the notions of paternalism and social responsibility. He
believed that the masses needed opportunities to achieve elite status, but that they could recognize those opportunities only if educated by an elite. Public-mindedness was the obligation attendant
on one's rise in the meritocracy. The expertise and elite status
achieved in reward for surviving the competition of the educational
system was to be used to prepare the way for other entrants. American citizens had the capacity for self-improvement, and even self-

government, Frankfurter believed, if shown the proper techniques; those techniques were to be conveyed to them by elite leadership.

In his vision of a paternalistic, responsible, expert elite channeling the innate wisdom and virtue of the masses into constructive and noble tasks, Frankfurter was representative of a group of early-twentieth-century thinkers who called themselves "progressives" and who thought that popular sovereignty and elitism were as easily reconcilable as humanitarianism and professionalism.[12] Progressivism had its greatest meaning for Frankfurter in a concern that elites use their privileged status to further rather than block mass participation in education and politics. Out of this concern evolved his conception of the limited role of the Supreme Court.

During the first twenty years after Frankfurter's graduation from law school, while he was supporting standard Progressive policies such as scientific management,[13] organization among laborers[14] and the "Wisconsin idea" of state-university cooperation,[15] as well as championing the 1924 Presidential candidacy of Robert LaFollette,[16] the Supreme Court was demonstrating a persistent, if not universal, hostility to the kind of experimental humanitarian legislation that Progressives supported. Aroused by Court invalidation of wage-and-hour legislation, Frankfurter began to question the justifications for such power. Although he first viewed the problem as simply one of personnel, so that a "Court dominantly composed of Holmes and Brandeis and Learned Hand and Cardozo"[17] would be acceptable even if omnipotent, he came, on reflection, to frame the question in an institutional perspective. If the Court functioned as a "revisory legislative body,"[18] it sapped the independence of legislatures and "mutilat[ed] the educative process of responsibility."[19] Judicial negation of legislation under the due process clause was unsound regardless of the worth of the legislation, inasmuch as it deterred the masses from participating in government and thereby deprived them of opportunities for self-education and public service. The Court should no more attempt to "guarantee toleration"[20] by invalidating legislation with a religious bias than it should attempt to protect economic privilege by striking down minimum wage laws, since the values of humanitarianism and efficiency could be fully instilled in the population only through education and direct political participation.

Many types of elitism were possible in Frankfurter's ideal polity, but the judicial variety had to be of a peculiarly negative kind.

Courts had to use their power to restrain themselves so that other branches of government, as being better forums for public education, could expand the range of their activities. A strong Presidency could provide "brave and clear-sighted leadership"; [21] administrative agencies could supply necessary expertise; legislatures could serve as vehicles of "public scrutiny" and report "alert public criticism." [22] Cooperation among the branches of government and symbiosis between the intelligentsia and the masses could insure continual progress.

Such were the views Frankfurter held upon his nomination (by Roosevelt) to the Court in 1939. Two years earlier, Black had joined the Court holding remarkably similar beliefs. Although Black's boyhood environment was less intellectually charged and his professional training less formal than Frankfurter's, the two men shared a sense of the incomparable value of self-education. Frankfurter's education, although wide-ranging in its scope, had had an institutional structure and a substantive focus; Black had for the most part created his own program. He had attended college and law school in Alabama and developed an interest in history and classical civilization in addition to law, but once out of the academic situation he channeled his interests, and his reading became more systematic. Before his election to the Senate in 1926 he was said to have had nightly sessions in which he and a law partner read aloud from Gibbon; [23] to have devoured selections on Thomas Jefferson; [24] and to have devised reading lists for himself. [25] Once a Senator, his access to books widened with the proximity of the Library of Congress, and he began to follow reading programs, such as Will Durant's 1929 selection of "One Hundred Best Books." [26]

Black's reading selections indicate that he read purposively and self-consciously. He invariably preferred reacting to a book independently to accepting another's evaluation. Once a book made an impression on him, he reread it often, underlining passages, making marginal notations, and occasionally supplying his own index. [27] His selections tended to expand, but also reinforce, his own attitudes. Tacitus, Livy, and Thucydides showed him the degradation of human liberties by tyrannical governments; Plutarch, the complexities and deceptions in human relations; Macaulay, the egalitarian tradition in Anglo-American history. Edith Hamilton's *The Greek Way* described the origins of democratic thought in ancient Greece; Vernon Parrington, Charles Beard, and Claude

Bowers presented American history from a perspective unsympathetic to vested privilege; Saul Padover's *To Secure These Blessings* and Leon Whipple's *Our Ancient Liberties* dramatized the exalted status of the rights codified in the American Constitution; Joseph Baldwin's *The Flush Times of Alabama and Mississippi* reminded him of the wild-and-woolly, unromantic environment of his youth.[28] For Black, education through reading meant independence, self-analysis, and finally wisdom; through reading the recurrent qualities of human nature and the inevitable links between past and present were revealed.[29] One could, through self-education, develop and distill a working philosophy.

Black's education led him to embrace, in his pre-Court career, some of the values supported by Frankfurter. One theme of his reading had been the negative effects of privileged status and concentrated power. He saw his heroes, among them Jefferson, Jackson, Lincoln, and Brandeis, as champions of the common man.[30] His law practice in Alabama had handled a significant amount of personal-injury litigation and labor disputes. He believed in the unionization of labor and welcomed the Roosevelt Administration's identification with labor movements. Consequently he regarded judicial utilization of the due process clause to nullify wage-and-hour legislation to be as inappropriate as had Frankfurter.

In 1924 Frankfurter had said that "the due process clause ought to go";[31] seven years later Black declared in a Senate speech that the Court had no power to pass on the reasonableness of state or federal legislation under the due process clause.[32] Black as a lawyer and Senator shared Frankfurter's preference for legislative over judicial solutions to social problems, since a legislature, in his view, had a better opportunity to reflect the needs of the average man. Finally, Black and Frankfurter were united in their enthusiasm for Roosevelt. Both saw the Roosevelt Administrations as progressive and humanitarian, favoring the common man over vested interests. Both strongly believed in active, paternalistic government with a leveling bias; both regarded unregulated giant industries as oppressive forces; both had a certain faith in the virtue and good sense of the mass public. Both were regarded on their appointments to the Court as "liberals" whose voting records would reflect the position of the Roosevelt Administration.

Although none of these characteristics augured the deep differences that would ultimately develop between the two men as

Justices, there were other qualities that presaged the alienation to come. One was personal style. Frankfurter was a bundle of nervous energy: garrulous, effusive, intense, enthusiastic, fond of debate for its own sake. In court and in conference he lectured counsel or his colleagues, interrupted the remarks of others, and "buttressed straightforward argument [with] anger, scorn, sarcasm, and humor." [33] These qualities made him, especially to his numerous friends, a delightful conversationalist and a stimulating companion. To others he appeared pretentious, feisty, tiresome, or petty. Although generous in his appraisal of others and unabashed in his communications of friendship, Frankfurter thrived on controversy: a no-holds-barred intellectual debate, he felt, could bring the antagonists closer to one another. As a judge he felt a responsibility to submit issues to a full and thorough exploration, so that reasoned solutions might emerge. He did not believe in consensus or compromise until an issue had been thoroughly articulated and explored, and he was not interested in dispatching business promptly or in joining a majority opinion if he felt that his position had not been fully aired.

Frankfurter's impulsiveness and effusiveness sometimes made him indiscreet. [34] By contrast, although Black rivaled Frankfurter in the strength of his views, he made an effort to be diplomatic in his collegial relations. When pressed, Black did not shrink from controversy, but he avoided open confrontation where possible. During his long career he became embroiled in several incidents of public concern, of which the *Jewel Ridge* disqualification dispute with Jackson was only one, and in most instances his response to attacks on him was a calculated silence. [35] He took pains to be gracious and civil to his fellow Justices. He valued charm and kindness in acquaintances; he did not like rancor and was not easily provoked. He was quick to make up his mind on issues, and disinclined to change it. He proceeded to the solution of problems in his own idiosyncratic fashion, seeking the counsel of few save his clerks and rarely inviting debate on propositions he had thoroughly considered. Self-contained, private, impatient with detail, largely indifferent to debate as an intellectual exercise, he was, in these respects, the antithesis of Frankfurter.

The differences between Black and Frankfurter ultimately went well beyond personal characteristics. When Frankfurter was appointed to the Court he had a well-developed theory of the judicial function, seeing himself as the heir of Holmes, Brandeis, Cardozo, and Stone, the architects of a passive model of appellate judging. Frankfurter's conception of his office, however, did not precisely match the conceptions of any of the others. He was less indifferent to the substantive content of legislation than Holmes, and his self-restraint was sometimes anguished, as in the flag-salute cases. He was not so much inclined as Brandeis to give civil liberties a higher priority than economic rights; he tried to be scrupulously indifferent to the character of the interest a statute invaded. He was less openly moralistic than Cardozo, although his conscience was sometimes shocked; [36] he continually attempted to subordinate his personal sympathies and animosities to the dictates of his office. Although he recognized with Stone that the Court inescapably made choices between competing values and was thus involved in American politics, he was slow to find necessity for Court intervention even when the recourse of a minority to the political process seemed to be unavailable. By drawing on the contributions of his four precursors and developing shadings of his own, Frankfurter created a consistent and wide-ranging philosophy of adjudication: his particular version of passivity, articulated in virtually unchanging fashion during his twenty-three years on the Court.

Black brought no philosophy of such breadth and depth with him to the Court in 1937. If he did evolve a pattern in his decisions throughout the 1930s and 1940s, it was that of support for values he believed in, even in the face of apparent historical or institutional limitations. Hence, he resisted judicial scrutiny of legislation that regulated business [37] or other property rights,[38] delegated broad power to administrative agencies to oversee the securities market [39] or labor negotiations,[40] and restricted the activities of minority groups in wartime.[41] He tolerated judicial scrutiny, however, where free speech was concerned,[42] although not universally.[43] He joined a 1937 opinion holding that all the Bill of Rights guaranties did not extend as against the states,[44] and he allowed state restraint-of-trade laws to prevent picketing.[45] On the other hand, he invalidated a city ordinance prohibiting announcements from sound trucks.[46] In sum, in his early career Black balanced interests, choosing one over another on an intuitive basis.

By the late 1940s, however, Black showed signs of abandoning this stance for one revealing a more abstract and integrated philosophy of adjudication, at least in the area of constitutional law. Outside that ambit he persisted in older habits; he had been the friend of maritime and industrial workers and small businessmen before coming on the Court, and he continued to be so as a Justice, manifesting his friendship through favorable statutory construction.[47] When interpretations of the Constitution were involved, however, Black developed his own comprehensive and internally consistent theory of judging. In practice it served as an alternative to the passive model, although it was predicated on the responsibilities and duties of judges rather than on their powers.

Black's theory was uniquely his own, the culmination of his self-education. It began with the assumption (reinforced by his reading) that human nature was unchanging, and thus that principles of conduct established by one era could serve as guides for the next. Just as Plutarch yielded insights into current social relations, so could the Constitution be a guide to contemporary affairs. But the Constitution was more than a source of conduct of Americans, it was *the* source. It had been elevated to a position of dominance by the very structure of American government; it was a blueprint for all time. Its words were explicit limitations on the power of governmental institutions and explicit grants of rights against the state. Judges had a responsibility to follow its commands, but no power to make glosses on them. They were servants of the document, but their power in that subservient capacity transcended that of all other branches, for constitutional imperatives prevailed over all other lawmaking efforts. The judiciary could do no more than apply the meaning of the Constitution, and certainly could do no less.

In the intellectual context of Black's first decade on the Court, this view could be seen as purposive. Its emphasis on the literal meaning of constitutional language precluded pouring substantive content into the due process clause; indeed, Black's view apparently rendered invalid any judicial "balancing" of rights in the interpretation of a clause in the Constitution. At the same time Black's position seemed to compel a broad-ranging, "absolutist"[48] reading of the Bill of Rights provisions that conferred rights against the government. Since many of these provisions codified support for values that Black had long believed in, calling them absolutes precluded their being "balanced" against a countervailing interest, such as national security or law enforcement. The chief analytical difficulty with this position was that the Bill of Rights was directed at the federal government, not at the states, and hence its scope was relatively narrow. Black solved this problem for himself when, in a dissent in *Adamson v. California* (1947),[49] he announced that the due process clause of the Fourteenth Amendment incorporated against the states all the Bill of Rights guaranties. His reading of the Fourteenth Amendment in *Adamson* was not a gloss, he argued, but a product of historical research.[50]

Difficulties remained for Black if his theory of constitutional interpretation was viewed as a purposive enterprise. He had gone on record as deploring judicial glosses on Constitutional language; hence he seemed committed to the notion that the Constitution gave protection to individuals only in those areas where its framers had explicitly granted protection. This meant that attempts by the Court to expand the ambit of constitutional language could be viewed as intolerable usurpations of power. Certain areas, especially, presented problems: activities, such as wiretapping and eavesdropping, that could be said to come within the meaning of a Bill of Rights clause ("search and seizure") but had not been explicitly considered by the framers; activities, such as sexual relations among married couples, whose regulation by governmental institutions seemed offensive but which had received no explicit protection from regulation in the Constitution; and activities, such as poll tax requirements, which were clearly tolerated by the framers but which over time came to be perceived as inimical to egalitarian traditions in American society. These areas were troublesome for Black because they invited conflict between the specific values he wanted to protect and the superordinate value of judicial fidelity to the literal meaning of the Constitution.

Black reconciled these difficulties through two devices that came teasingly close to contradicting each other. The first device was to adopt Marshall's view of the Constitution as a document whose core meaning was not to change with time, but whose language could be interpreted as expansively as it could endure. Protected "speech" could include types of speech (broadcasts from sound trucks)[51] that the Founding Fathers had never anticipated. The "literal" words of the Bill of Rights could be given a "liberal" judicial reading. By this technique the relevance of the past to the present was underscored; an eighteenth-century document could thrive in the mid-twentieth century. The phrases of the Constitution could be read in light of its over-all design. If a particular provision was intended to reflect the original importance of a social value such as liberty or equality, a judge could anticipate that the extension of that provision's coverage to unforeseen sets of circumstances would be consistent with the original purposes of the Founders.

Black's first reconciling device was intended to give judges a small amount of freedom from history; his second was to confine them within it. The words of the Constitution, he believed, were barriers to judicial initiative. Speech, whether libelous [52] or obscene,[53] was protected to the fullest, but conduct that served a communications function, such as picketing [54] or sitting-in,[55] was not. Only unreasonable searches and seizures were constitutionally prohibited, given the language of the Fourth Amendment,[56] but the Fifth Amendment prohibited absolutely compulsory self-incrimination.[57] No right of privacy was mentioned in the Constitution; hence judges could not create one.[58] Poll taxes as prerequisites for voting, however anti-egalitarian and therefore undesirable, were not forbidden by any constitutional language.[59] Where the scope of a provision's reach was not clear, judges ought to appeal to history, not to current social impulses. If those appeals produced inconvenient answers, such as the fact that corporations were not intended to be included in the Fourteenth Amendment's definition of "persons," [60] judges ought not to ignore or discard them. Otherwise, the supremacy of the judiciary became a surrogate for the supremacy of the Constitution.

A delicate tension between the powers and limitations of the judicial branch of government thus characterized Black's philosophy of constitutional adjudication, as it had Marshall's. Judges were permitted to scrutinize the activities of other branches of government, and to intervene to modify or abrogate governmental action, precisely because they were not acting for themselves. The duty to follow the dictates of the Constitution had become a source of power. The determination of whether that duty compelled intervention remained a judicial one, but the standards used in the determination process were so clear and straightforward that glosses could barely creep in. Only in those instances in which the meaning of a word or phrase—"liberty" in the Fourteenth Amendment, for example—was not clear from the body of the Constitution itself, thus inviting a judicial foray into history, did substantive judging re-enter Black's calculus. On these occasions he used history purposefully, to promote values in which he believed.[61] On balance, however, he was prepared to make interpretations that did not reinforce his own views—he thought birth control laws deplorable, for example, but nonetheless could not find power to invalidate them—to maintain the consistency of his theory.

As with Frankfurter, the original motivation for Black's theory of constitutional adjudication was probably a response to concrete events. Frankfurter had appropriated the passive model of judging in the context of the invalidation by the Taft Court and the Four Horsemen of legislation he supported. From the polemical position that the due process clause "ought to go," he had moved to a theory of judging designed to strip the clause of substantive content. Similarly, Black had responded negatively to the Vinson Court's apparent indifference toward government intrusions on civil liberties,[62] but felt himself precluded from reincarnating substantive judging, through the due process clause or any other means, to support the rights he thought were being unduly circumscribed. His mature philosophy of constitutional adjudication provided a solution to this dilemma: judges could protect the rights of minorities because a literal and liberal reading of the Constitution compelled it.

Black's theory, in its developed form, thus provided a full-blown alternative to that of Frankfurter. It by-passed questions about the proper allocation of power among governing institutions by simply asserting that if the Constitution had declared rights against the government, the judiciary had an obligation to enforce them. A calculus based on language replaced one based on process. Instead of asking what interests were competing in an issue of constitutional adjudication, one asked whether the rights allegedly invaded by an act of government were enumerated in the Constitution as subject to its protection. If one answered this question affirmatively, questions of process became irrelevant. Governing institutions had to accommodate themselves to the protection of these rights, whether the task was inefficient, whether interests of their own were invaded, and regardless of the offensivenesss of the persons whose rights were invaded. Frankfurter's stress on properly limiting the reach of the antidemocratic judiciary was a matter of complete indifference to Black, since he felt that the judiciary's reach never exceeded the Constitution's. Since the Constitution was in principle a democratic document and since judges were bound by its strictures, judicial tyranny was impossible if constitutional

interpretation was properly carried out. Only if what Black caricatured as the "natural law–substantive due process–fundamental fairness" school of judging prevailed could the Supreme Court become
a threat to democracy.

Black's theory had bowed to process liberalism by positing that
the role of the judiciary in constitutional interpretation was essentially a constrained one. But its implications pointed in another direction. By compelling judicial action where the Constitution
required it, and by permitting the judiciary to determine the ambit
of the Constitution's reach, Black's theory invited a renaissance of
substantive judging. Black himself confined judicial involvement
strictly; another judge, less interested in Black's literalism and more
in his mandate for compulsory judicial action, might find Black's
theory useful in other respects. A judge with those inclinations
joined the Court with Earl Warren's appointment as Chief Justice
in 1953.

Little in Warren's background augured his eventual prominence.
His family's financial security was dependent on the whims of the
Southern Pacific Railroad, which laid off Warren's father without
notice. He had been encouraged to pursue an education, but had
not been conspicuous in his academic performance. When he graduated from the University of California Law School at Berkeley in
1914 he did not have a wide range of employment opportunities,
and his first job in law practice eventually proved unbearable. At
thirty-four he was a deputy District Attorney in Alameda County.
His first state-wide office was not attained until he was forty-seven,
when he was elected Attorney General of California. Fifteen years
later he was Chief Justice of the United States, having been a successful Governor of California, a candidate for U.S. Vice President, and a serious Presidential contender. Reminiscing, his acquaintances attributed his success to intangibles, not to the power
of his intellect, the charismatic qualities of his leadership, or the
adroitness of his political maneuvering. He seemed to have succeeded by virtue of characteristics long thought incompatible with
public office: integrity, nonpartisanship, honesty, humanity. He
appeared to have acquired prominence and power simply by being
a good man.[63] It all seemed too mythic to have actually occurred.

There was, of course, more to Warren than his surface affect. He
had an extraordinary ability for making people like him; he could
remember names, size up acquaintances, put others at ease. He had

a strong ideological distaste for influence and corruption, and thought of himself as beholden to none, his morals untarnished. He inspired others, partly through an intuitive eloquence, partly through a certain domineering attitude. He was a genial companion but did not reveal his private thoughts; he held out his hand to the world, but retained his reserve. He tolerated no disloyalty or disingenuousness in an employee, and surrounded himself with persons whom he perceived as trustworthy and dedicated. He could be stubborn and self-righteous; he was not above trapping an opponent or summarily dismissing one who had affronted him. His grudges and animosities were longstanding; he remained outwardly unmoved by public abuse but bore in his mind the images of his attackers.

He had an intuitive sense of California politics, and his ability to avoid exposing himself on controversial issues was marked. He enjoyed power and knew that its use could serve to expand its scope; he liked executive action and disliked delegating responsibility. When pressed, he resorted to face-to-face confrontation, for here his blend of geniality, stubbornness, shrewdness, and decisiveness made him a formidable opponent. He came to the Court with no judicial experience, limited exposure to the world of ideas, no easily characterizable social attitudes, and no evidence of literary talent. But he did not come, as some thought he had, to be a ceremonial, conciliatory, middle-of-the-road Chief Justice. He came, rather, imbued with self-confidence in his ability to persuade others, possessed of a strong belief in the worth of active government, secure with power and unafraid of controversy, and eager, as in the past, to make his influence felt. The fact that initially he had no well-developed philosophy of judging was in his case of no consequence; he had instead a well-developed philosophy of governing.

The atmosphere on the Court that Warren joined in the summer of 1953 was marked by two significant realities: the estrangement of the mature philosophy of Frankfurter from that of Black, and the specter of the school segregation decisions, which had first reached the Court in 1952. Internal security and criminal procedure cases of the late 1940s and the 1950s had demonstrated the incompatibility of the Frankfurter and Black positions—federalism, limitations on the scope of judicial power, and countervailing values of law enforcement or national solidarity were simply irrelevant to Black when Bill of Rights freedoms were being infringed. Black had quarreled with Frankfurter over the general incorporation of Bill of Rights guaranties in the due process clause of the Fourteenth Amendment,[64] over specific examples of incorporation in the criminal procedure area,[65] and over the availability of First Amendment protection to advocates of Communist Party doctrine.[66] In two of these cases the opinions of one Justice were directed at the views of the other. Black deplored what he called in another case "substitution of this Court's day-to-day opinion of what . . . is fair and decent for . . . Bill of Rights guaranties"; [67] Frankfurter, for his part, attempted to show that his adversary was engaging in "warped construction of specific provisions of the Bill of Rights." [68]

At the core of the dispute, insofar as it had become personalized, was a memory from the past. In Black's early years on the Court, Chief Justice Stone, concerned that Black's approach to judging was too politicized, had invited Frankfurter to advise Black discreetly on the historical limitations on the judiciary. Frankfurter, never one to resist an opportunity to educate others, had complied.[69] One can imagine the effect on Black, who valued his independence, had a full measure of pride, and intended to work out his jurisprudential views for himself. By the 1950s Black had solidified his stance and become interested in converting others.[70] In his mind he had moved beyond Frankfurter's intricacies to see the mandate of the Constitution in sharp relief. He invited others to share his vision, while Frankfurter continued his own efforts at conversion. The natural beneficiary of this joint wisdom was Warren, affable and seemingly open-minded, inexperienced in the fine points of Constitutional interpretation, and potentially malleable.

The school segregation cases presented this jurisprudential controversy in terms Warren could appreciate. A special ingredient of Frankfurter's jurisprudence was cautious judicial participation in politically sensitive areas. When the Court first considered re-examining the separate-but-equal principle of *Plessy v. Ferguson* [71] in the context of public schools, Frankfurter sought to avoid a final decision; Black voted with Douglas, Burton, and Minton to overrule *Plessy*.[72] The case, *Brown v. Board of Education*, was not decided that term; it was set down for reargument during the following term. Vinson's death and Warren's appointment in the summer of 1953 meant a new composition for the Court and the possibility of a different result in the *Brown* case. Warren was hence in a position of particular significance in the reconsideration of *Brown*.

Not only was he a new member with unknown views, he was also a national politician with his fingers allegedly on the pulse of American society.

The critical political question in *Brown* was not whether the system of separate educational facilities should prevail—for all signs pointed to increasing Court animosity toward artifacts of racial segregation, especially in the area of schools.[73] The question rather was whether an adequate rationale for reversing *Plessy v. Ferguson* could be found so that the South would comply with the decision. Over this issue the Black and Frankfurter views seemed in potential conflict. For the Court to find that a system of segregated schools violated the equal protection clause, a finding was necessary that the separate sets of schools were not "equal" in fact. This involved an empirical inquiry by the Court into local "political" conditions, the very sort of practice that Frankfurter's jurisprudence cautioned against. That inquiry was justified, however, if one read, with Black, the equal protection clause as an inexorable mandate. The Constitution insisted that laws equalize educational opportunities, and the judiciary was bound to implement that principle by ascertaining whether or not it had been subverted in a given context.

The rationale for overruling *Plessy* was thus apparent: separate-but-equal schools violated the equal protection clause if they did not in fact provide equal educational opportunities. But that rationale was very broad and abstract, rested on the Court's taking notice of empirical data, and made the Court a watchguard of local conditions. Nonetheless, Warren endorsed the rationale and secured unanimity for it. Frankfurter, ultimately no less sensitive to racial discrimination than any other Justice on the Warren Court, joined the opinion in *Brown*. But he retained his concern about the political wisdom of the decision, and the phrase "all deliberate speed"—the standard for compliance with *Brown*—was his suggestion.

The *Brown* decision was a symbolic event in shaping Warren's approach to his office. If he came to the Court with a history of less than total sympathy with the interests of racial minorities,[74] he unburdened himself of that with *Brown*. His longstanding beliefs that government should be responsive to the people at large, not to special interests, was transposed into an image of an energetic court protecting the rights of all Americans, especially the downtrodden and disadvantaged. His moral indignation over corruption and dishonesty metamorphosed into an undeviating interest in the abstractions of fairness and justice, and a conception of law as inexorably linked with ethics. He retained the impatience with legislative insensitivity or inactivity that had surfaced during his gubernatorial years in California, substituting judicial action for executive action in instances in which a legislature had been indifferent or inimical to human concerns.

Warren extended the *Brown* principle of judicial intervention to support the rights of minorities in numerous other areas of American life, coming to view that extension as a mission to help the Constitution reach the people. In the course of this excursion he was continually touched by the same impulse of patriotic duty, moral outrage, pride, and compassion that had moved him in *Brown*. He was willing to face controversy and suffer abuse for the rightness of his cause; he reached beyond the academic critics of his methods to the public beneficiaries of his acts.

Like that of Black, Warren's jurisprudence gained momentum with time. If Black's overriding principle of adjudication was fidelity to his conception of the Constitution, Warren's was fidelity to his interpretation of the rights inherent in American citizenship. Warren started tentatively, his early decisions constraining such rights as much as they affirmed them.[75] After the two *Brown* cases he began to take a more expansive view. Fishing expeditions by the House Un-American Activities Committee into the private lives of persons suspected of having Communist sympathies outraged him, and he initiated what was to become a persistent practice of issuing ringing affirmations of individual freedoms and scathing condemnations of the activities of those who would infringe them.[76] Buoyed by a change in membership of the Court in the early 1960s, he expanded his horizons, encouraging judicial reform of legislative apportionment, criminal procedure, Church-State relations, antitrust laws, labor relations, and the boundaries between the federal government and the states.

Although Warren's positions dovetailed with those of Black in many areas, the views of the two Justices ultimately diverged. Black's theory allowed for some extensions of the literal commands of the Constitution, but it was essentially based on constraint. The judge could do no more than the Constitution permitted, whether he wanted to or not. Warren did not feel similarly confined. He, too, interpreted his role as that of enforcing the Constitution's mandates, but he was also prepared to enforce mandates that appeared not from a reading of the constitutional text but from analogy to it. He analogized the constitutional requirement of procedural safeguards in criminal cases to disputes between private parties,[77] and he determined that the Fifth Amendment empowered the Court to write precise codes of conduct for police in their relations with criminal suspects.[78] On occasion he also declined to confer the full protection of the Constitution on persons whose conduct outraged him, such as panderers of obscene literature [79] or gamblers.[80]

Pressed to its logical outcome, Warren's jurisprudence appeared to make the humanity and integrity of judges themselves the only check on judicial power. It de-emphasized the complexity of the process of judging and emphasized the substantive importance of values at stake in a case. Over and over again Warren stressed that the Constitution embraced the small and helpless, the disfranchised, disadvantaged, and discriminated-against. His perspective was openly humanitarian and just as openly antiprofessional, almost contemptuous of the niceties of a legal argument when fundamental American beliefs called out to be affirmed.

At the high tide of its momentum in behalf of citizenship rights, and especially in the person of its Chief Justice, the Warren Court dramatically portrayed the contrasts between process and substantive liberalism. Having once invaded an area hitherto felt to be inappropriate for judicial appraisal, the Court seemed to gain confidence, even in the face of adversity, and invaded another. In some areas, such as civil rights, it seemed in a race with Congress to outlaw notorious practices.[81] Confident of the rightness of its governing principles, it minimized or discounted analytical barriers. In the process it revealed itself as having a distinctly ideological character.

With this revelation the Warren Court majority became exposed to the ancient attack that they were simply using their office to propound their own social views. But the attack in this instance had a different slant from that made on the Four Horsemen in the 1930s. The Warren Court reforms had run with the tide of ideas in postwar America rather than against it; contemporary definitions of equality, liberty, fairness, and justice were difficult values to oppose. Hence critics of the Warren Court majority argued that the difficulty with its premises was not that they were misguided but that they were simplistic. The Court's code words, the argument ran, concealed complexities and ambiguities, thereby endangering delicate balances in the process of living and governing in modern America.

John Harlan came to personify this criticism of the Warren Court majority. In Harlan's hand the two-pronged character of the criticism became clear. It was based both on the methodological canons of process liberalism and on a substantive quarrel with the majority's value orientation. Harlan's approach did not precisely resemble that of Frankfurter, a justice to whom Harlan had ascribed "a fierce determination to keep his own ideologies and predilections out of the decision of cases." [82] Harlan did not always make a similar effort. His ideological stance, however, was a counter-stance, not so much affirming particular values as suggesting that the momentum of Warren Court egalitarianism was trampling on interests and ignoring attitudes deserving of respect. Harlan's position, in its maturity, represented a blending of standard caveats about the unrestrained exercise of judicial power that had characterized one strand of twentieth-century jurisprudence since Holmes, and his own personal suspicions of substantive liberalism. He added another dimension to the inner controversies of the Warren Court: he asked not only whether a given innovative result had been reached by proper judicial methods but also whether it was sound philosophically. His views, especially when contrasted with those of Warren, signified the eventual incompatibility of the professionalist and humanitarian impulses of modern liberalism.

The substantive dimension of Harlan's jurisprudence was shaped by his instinctive social inclinations and by the ideological atmosphere of the Warren Court. If a populist tinge marked the Warren Court's consciousness, so that legal issues came to be perceived as struggles between "haves" and "have nots" or between vested interests and the common man, then Harlan's orientation offered a stark contrast. He had been born to wealth and status, educated at Princeton and Oxford, and assimilated into the upper strata of the New York bar. If the Warren Court showed an increasing sympathy for the rights of persons accused of crimes, Harlan had seen the other side of law enforcement, serving under Emory Buckner in the U.S. Attorney's office in the 1920s and as General Counsel to the New York State Crime Commission in the 1950s. If the Warren Court could be said to be suspicious of big business, Harlan had given longstanding counsel to members of the Dupont family.[83] If the symbolic journey of certain Warren Court Justices from the environments of their youth to Washington had been filled with reminders of poverty and oppression, Harlan's had encompassed the accustomed way-stations of a respected member of an intellectual and social elite. In contrast to the other influential Warren Court Justices, Harlan could not be said to have experienced the stings of arbitrary injustice, whether based on ethnic prejudice or on the lack of family income.

Harlan's social background was not the sole determinant of his judicial vision, but it may have made him less passionate about those inequities in American life whose very presence outraged some of his fellow Justices. Thus, when the Warren Court majority embarked on its reform crusades, Harlan may have been less inclined to ignore analytical obstacles because his sympathies were enlisted less in the cause. In this vein, Harlan's stance could fairly be identified as conservative. American civilization, despite its egalitarian premises, had been fraught from its origin with social and economic inequalities and had not reflected participatory democracy in its governing institutions. The momentum of the Warren Court was toward a re-examination of practices that deviated from those egalitarian ideals; in resisting this momentum Harlan was allying himself with a longstanding tradition of resistance to mass equality. He was conservative, in the context of the Warren Court, to the extent that he embraced its humanitarian and egalitarian goals less regularly and less sweepingly than the majority.

If Harlan began his examination of the social problems coming before the Warren Court with such inclinations, he did not end the inquiry with them. Instead he created an approach that harmonized Frankfurterian assumptions about the role of the judiciary with a substantive critique of what he called "unrestrained egalitarianism." [84] Perhaps the most representative example of his approach was in his linking of the framers' theory of federalism to judicial self-restraint. That linkage required some redefinition of terms. The theory of federalism, in Marshall's day, emphasized national as opposed to state power, and Marshall had used it to justify active judicial scrutiny of the actions of state government. Marshall's interpretation resembled that of the Warren Court majority, envisioning for the national government a broad mandate that was to be implemented by the federal judiciary. The principal difference between the Marshall Court's and the Warren Court's theory of federalism was in the effects: the former served to protect private rights from any sort of governmental control, the latter, to simulate affirmative governmental action.

Harlan's federalism more closely resembled that of Holmes, Brandeis, and other architects of the passive model of judging, in that it stressed balances between state and federal sovereignties and called for judicial tolerance of experimental legislation by the states. This was, of course, the reverse of Marshall's interpretation. Judges were to suffer state regulation of private enterprise rather than actively oppose it. Federalism stood not for the primacy of national power but for emphasis on the two-tiered character of American government. In the early years of the twentieth century this version of federalism insulated state experimental legislation in economic areas; in the Warren Court years an emphasis on distinctions between state and federal government attempted to serve a different purpose, insulating the states from the increasingly stringent checks on governmental activity demanded by the Warren Court's expansive reading of the Bill of Rights.

Thus the concept of federalism, which Marshall had identified with plenary national power, Taney with concurrent sovereignty, Holmes, Brandeis, and Frankfurter with state experimental legislation, and Jackson with expanded national regulation of the economy, came to serve yet another purpose for Harlan: a justification for the preservation of values infringed by bold judicial definitions of citizens' rights. One such value was law enforcement: the application of a literalist view of Bill of Rights protections against the states hampered indigenous state efforts to prevent crime and violence. Another was grass-roots democracy: rigid mandates affecting the representativeness of local government stifled experiments in governmental organization. Still another value (and linked to the second) was that of allowing the states to function as laboratories for social planning. A fourth was the privacy and autonomy of the individual citizen, federalism serving as a barrier between such citizens and the continually expanding federal bureaucracy of postwar America by reducing units of administration and helping to keep government entirely removed from a range of private affairs. By linking federalism to these values, Harlan sought to demonstrate that the egalitarian momentum of the Warren Court was not a necessary good; that humanitarian gestures sometimes trespassed on individual rights.

Superimposed on the values that Harlan identified with federalism were all the canons of Process Jurisprudence: judicial detachment and disinterestedness; a limited lawmaking role for the elitist judiciary; a search for "principled adjudication," which for Harlan meant an adequately broad rationale in an opinion, to serve as a clear guide in deciding future cases; a presumption in favor of adherence to precedent so as to promote clarity and stability in the law, even when a prior decision was found to be distasteful; emphasis, in opinion writing, on careful exposition of the facts, marshaling of the arguments on both sides, and full-blown statement of reasons for a decision; the fostering of harmony between lawmaking institutions by deference to the actions of administrative agencies and legislatures wherever possible; and self-conscious, methodical, and articulate balancing of competing social values in circumstances where the Constitution required such weighing. In all these respects Harlan resembled Frankfurter, but his angle of vision was somewhat different. For Frankfurter these tenets defined his role. His paramount goal as a judge was adherence to them rather than to the promotion of any set of social values. Harlan asked what results this adherence tended to produce and noted that in the context of the Warren Court it often produced resistance to judge-initiated reforms. On occasion, Harlan acknowledged that he was as comfortable with the policy implications of his stance as he was with its methodological underpinnings; in a rare instance he abandoned process liberalism altogether in order to promote substantive values; at other times, however, he complained that the dictates of process liberalism prevented him from reaching humanitarian results. In short, Harlan recognized the substantive elements of his judicial calculus and, in a small number of contexts, gave them free play.

III

Such, in rough outline, were the views of the four figures who stood out most prominently in the mosaic of the Warren Court. They can be seen as forming symbolic confrontations: Frankfurter's consummate process liberalism against Black's highly individualized blend of formalized restraint and active championing of individual freedoms; Warren's energetic substantive liberalism—in some respects a logical extension of Black's views—against Harlan's version of process liberalism, in which substantive conservative values were occasionally affirmed. The confrontations were more abstract than concrete, since heated jurisprudential debates, even among the four, were exceptional in the ordinary course of the Court's judicial business. Tendencies were nonetheless revealed in individual decisions, and it was possible to discern phases in the Court's history. In the first phase, from Warren's appointment to Frankfurter's retirement, process and substantive liberalism marked out an uneasy coexistence, their ultimate incompatibility not entirely clear. In the second phase, from Frankfurter's departure in 1962 to Warren's retirement in 1969, substantive liberalism continually gathered momentum to the point where differences between the views of Warren and Black became strikingly apparent, and process liberalism, in Harlan's hands, was seen as compatible with substantive conservatism.

Three cases serve to illustrate the first phase: *Trop v. Dulles*,[85] *Poe v. Ullman*,[86] and *Baker v. Carr*.[87] *Trop v. Dulles* was decided in the context of anti-Communist hysteria in the 1950s, which placed high priority on the values of patriotism and national solidarity. In the name of those concerns an ample degree of government scrutiny of the lives and careers of citizens had been tolerated, in the Supreme Court as well as elsewhere. In a 1954 case, for example, the Court, in a 6–3 decision, allowed New York State to suspend the medical license of a physician who declined to produce records of an anti-Fascist organization to which he belonged.[88] Warren had joined the majority in that instance, but by 1958, when *Trop v. Dulles* came down, he had become indignant at inquisitorial or repressive practices in the name of loyalty or national security.[89] The *Trop* case was for him another such example.

Trop and a companion case, *Perez v. Brownell*,[90] tested the constitutionality of sections of the Nationality Act (1940), which provided for loss of American citizenship in specified instances. In *Perez* a citizen had voted in a Mexican election; in *Trop* another citizen had deserted the Army in wartime. Both had been expatriated as a consequence. The Court split on the two cases, finding that Congress, pursuant to its implied power to regulate foreign affairs, had authority to strip away citizenship as a consequence of voting in a foreign election, but that it had no authority to expatriate for desertion. Frankfurter wrote the majority opinion in *Perez* and dissented in *Trop;* Warren dissented in *Perez* and wrote for a plurality in *Trop;* Black voted in each case with Warren, Harlan in each case with Frankfurter. *Trop* was the more significant case of the two for the breadth of Warren's opinion and the controversy it engendered.

Warren had, in his *Perez* dissent, indicated that he was not prepared to tolerate any attempts on the part of the federal government to impose loss of citizenship. He maintained that citizenship was "man's basic right," the "right to have rights," and that it was "not subject to the general powers of the government." [91] Citizenship, in his view, could be only voluntarily relinquished. The Act of 1940 had, he believed, merely attempted to describe certain acts—such as voting in a foreign election—that might give rise to the inference that a person had voluntarily relinquished his citizenship. But voting could not alone create the inference; the voting would have to be "at the behest of a foreign government to advance its territorial interests." [92] This had not been shown in *Perez* and was not actually required by the Act; hence the Act was overbroad and defective as applied to the citizen in *Perez.* For Warren the issue was crystal clear: the Court had an "imperative . . . duty" to protect "the fundamental rights" of American citizens under the Constitution. [93] By conferring citizenship on all persons residing in the United States, the Fourteenth Amendment had raised an absolute bar to governmental efforts to take away that citizenship; and the Court was compelled to enforce that bar.

The difficulty with Warren's position, in practical terms, was that only he, Douglas, and Black accepted it in its pure form. The other six Justices conceded a power, albeit limited, in Congress to expatriate under certain circumstances. The question, then, was whether desertion, the "voluntary" act in *Trop,* was sufficiently different from voting in a foreign election to preclude Congressional exercise of its authority to expatriate. Justice Whitaker, who had questioned the scope of the expatriation power in *Perez,* and Justice Brennan decided that it was, producing five votes for disallowing expatriation. Warren then sought to articulate a rationale for the decision.

Warren's opinion was characteristic of his approach. He began with an impassioned statement of what he believed to be the controlling principle in the case; the statement, taken in context, was entirely dictum. Citizenship, he declared, was "not subject to the general powers of the National Government," and therefore could "not be divested in the exercise of those powers." [94] The deprivation of citizenship was "not a weapon that the Government may use to express its displeasure at a citizen's conduct, however reprehensible that conduct may be." On "this ground alone," [95] Warren asserted, *Trop* should be decided; but for that proposition he had only three votes.

Next, Warren confronted the critical challenge that his opinion faced—that of stating "why the action taken in [*Trop*] exceeds constitutional limits, even under the majority's decision in *Perez*." [96] Here two principal strategies were available to him, and his choice between them was revealing. One strategy was to attempt to distinguish (as Justice Brennan was to do in his concurrence) between rational governmental exercise of the power to regulate foreign affairs (which had occurred in *Perez*) and the attempted exercise of power in *Trop*. Expatriation in *Trop* was concededly based on the war power and not on the power to regulate foreign affairs. It was intended to maintain discipline in the armed forces by deterring desertion. In Brennan's view other such deterrents existed, whereas expatriation bore "only a slight or tenuous relation" [97] to the war power. Expatriation being an extraordinarily harsh remedy for desertion, and other remedies existing, it was therefore not a means "reasonably calculated to achieve [the] legitimate end" of waging war. [98] The section of the Nationality Act providing for expatriation as a consequence of desertion therefore offended the Fifth Amendment.

Warren did not choose this option, with its emphasis on technical niceties. Rather he defined the constitutional question raised by the desertion provision as being "whether or not denationalization may be inflicted as a punishment." [99] To support his position he had to show that expatriation of American citizens was different from deportation of foreign nationals, held by the Supreme Court not to constitute "punishment"; [100] that the purpose of expatriation was to punish rather than merely "to prescribe rules governing the proper performance of military obligations"; [101] and that expatriation for desertion was a punishment that violated the Constitution. This he did in the most sweeping and summary fashion. The deportation of aliens, he said, was incident to the government's sovereign power to regulate the naturalization of foreigners; no such sovereign power over its citizens existed, since the people were sovereign. The provision was penal rather than regulatory in that it "prescribe[d] the consequences that will befall one" who failed to abide by military regulations; thus the purpose of "taking away citizenship from a convicted deserter" was "simply to punish him." [102] The question therefore became whether this punishment was "cruel and unusual" within the meaning of the Eighth Amendment.

Here Warren faced his greatest analytical difficulty. The Court was then conceding that the death penalty was not cruel and unusual punishment: the Rosenbergs had been executed only five years previously. How was denationalization of a citizen a fate crueler than death? It was so, Warren maintained, because it involved "the total destruction of the individual's status in organized society"; it was "more primitive than torture," because it destroyed "for the individual the political existence that was centuries in the development." [103] For these and other reasons denationalization was "offensive to cardinal principles for which this Constitution stands." The Court's role in Constitutional cases of this type, Warren maintained, was clear. The meaning of the Eighth Amendment could change with "the evolving standards of decency that mark the progress of a maturing society." [104]

An interesting aspect of Warren's opinion in *Trop v. Dulles* was the extent to which it showed the influence of Black while at the same time revealing differences in focus between the two Justices. Warren's view of constitutional adjudication in *Trop* was Blackian in its assertion of the absolute primary of an enumerated constitutional right, its lack of sufferance for balancing that right against countervailing values such as national security, its impatience with fine statutory distinctions in the light of constitutional imperatives, and its posture for the judiciary of enforcing the mandates of the Bill of Rights. But there was no appeal to history. The deportation precedents were summarily dismissed, the death penalty analogy placed "to one side," the legislative history of the Nationality Act characterized as "equivocal." The emphasis was rather on the "realities" of the case. Expatriation for desertion was a punishment, not a regulation, because it occurred after the act of desertion itself; it was a "cruel" punishment because all the nations of the civilized world deplored and decried the condition of statelessness. It was, in short, a violation of the Constitution because any decent-minded, humane judge could read the Constitution and see that it was.

This judicial interest in "decency" and "progress"—at least in the type of situation raised by *Trop*—was regarded by Frankfurter as outside the scope of the Court's prerogatives. He began the relevant portions of his dissent in *Trop* with some characteristic admonitions. "Judicial power . . . must be on guard against encroaching beyond its proper bounds." Judging required "rigorous observance of the difference between limits of power and wise exercise of power." It was "not the business of the Court to pronounce policy" or to "giv[e] effect to its own notions of what is wise and politic." The Constitution had "not authorized the judges to sit in judgment on the wisdom of what Congress and the Executive branch do." [105] These caveats set the stage for an opinion deferential to the power and judgment of Congress. Congress could "deal severely with the problem of desertion from the armed forces" under its war powers; the rights and privileges of citizenship imposed correlative obligations, such as compulsory military service; there was a "rational nexus" between refusal to serve in the armed forces and Congressional withdrawal of citizenship. [106]

Warming to his task, Frankfurter quarreled with Warren's "punishment" theory of the cases. "Simply because denationalization was attacked by Congress as a consequence of conduct that it had elsewhere made unlawful," he argued, "it does not follow that denationalization is a 'punishment.' " [107] Nothing on the face of the Nationality Act or in its legislative history supported that inference. And "to insist that denationalization is 'cruel and unusual' punishment" was "to stretch that concept beyond the breaking point." Constitutional "dialectic" that "seriously urged that loss of citizenship is a fate worse than death" was "empty of reason." [108] Nor was Warren's belief that the condition of statelessness was universally deplored sound, since "many civilized nations" had imposed loss of citizenship for "indulgence in designated prohibited activities." [109] Nor were denationalized citizens necessarily subject to inhumane treatment; and in America aliens enjoyed "very substantial rights and privileges" under the Constitution. In short, "the awesome power of this Court to invalidate [Congressional] legislation" needed to be "exercised with the utmost restraint"; [110] and this was a case for deference.

Two interpretations of patriotism and two approaches to constitutional adjudication clashed in *Trop*. Warren's patriotism identified American citizenship with the possession of rights against the government, the supreme right being to possess and retain citizenship status. Frankfurter's no less intense patriotism identified citizenship with obligations such as service to one's country in a time when its existence was being threatened. Warren's conviction that the right to be an American citizen was beyond the power of any government official to curtail had led him to a vigorous scrutiny of Congress and a free-wheeling use of statutory and constitutional language in support of that conviction. Frankfurter's approach had begun with an orientation toward the cautious use of judicial power rather than the impassioned vindication of human rights, and ended with a series of arguments intended to justify judicial deference to Congress in the circumstances of *Trop*. Giving substantive content to citizenship had been Warren's primary purpose; maintaining fidelity to the delicate process of constitutional adjudication had been Frankfurter's.

Harlan had silently joined Frankfurter in *Trop v. Dulles*, but *Poe v. Ullman* showed that his numerous pairings with Frankfurter concealed differences in approach. *Poe v. Ullman* attempted to test the constitutionality of a Connecticut statute prohibiting the use of contraceptive devices by married couples, even when conception could be shown to constitute a potential threat to the health or life of the woman. The issues involved were troublesome, analytically as well as politically. The statute had been passed under a police-powers rationale, that the Connecticut legislature was protecting the morals of its citizens by preventing them from interfering with the creation of human life. It was being challenged as a violation of the Fourteenth Amendment, but no clear violation of a constitutional "liberty" was apparent. The Bill of Rights said nothing about a right to bear children under the terms one wished, or a right not to bear children at all. The legislation, however, was offensive, in that it purported to regulate the private lives of married persons with regard to matters that hardly seemed the concern of government. Its enforcement raised a series of constitutional problems, since one could not easily imagine state officials making random checks in the homes of Connecticut residents to insure that contraceptives were not being used in sexual relations. Affirmance of the statute put the Court on the side of public censorship of highly private affairs;

invalidation forced it to find an adequate constitutional rationale and involved it in religious controversy.

These factors suggested that the Court might be well advised not to decide the merits of the case, especially since attitudes toward the use of birth control devices were in a state of flux in the early 1960s, when *Poe v. Ullman* was argued. A way to avoid decision existed: the Connecticut statute had been enforced only once in eighty years, to compel closing of public clinics dispensing birth-control information.[111] This suggested that the persons claiming that the statute infringed their interests were in no actual peril of being prosecuted under it. Primarily on this basis a majority of the Court dismissed the case for failure to present a substantial controversy justifying the immediate adjudication of a constitutional issue. Frankfurter wrote for a plurality, which included Warren. Black dissented, stating only that he believed that the constitutional questions should be reached and decided. Harlan wrote a massive dissent in which he took issue with Frankfurter on the question of justiciability and then went on to find the statute unconstitutional as applied to married persons.

The nub of the debate centered on Frankfurter and Harlan, but the positions of Black and of Warren were not devoid of interest. Black had little patience with the web of doctrines used to avoid a full-blown decision of a constitutional issue: standing, mootness, ripeness, the "political question" doctrine, the "case and controversy" requirement, and other "passive" devices.[112] He was prepared to decide constitutional cases whenever possible, since his theory of constitutional adjudication provided him with clear and enduring solutions. Warren, often eager for an opportunity to affirm a constitutional right, was not so in *Poe v. Ullman*. He believed in government censorship of morals, as other decisions indicated; he believed also in the privacy of married life. Later he was to find the same Connecticut statute unconstitutional (and Black was to vote to sustain it).[113] But in 1961 Warren was not prepared to declare himself on the issues in *Poe v. Ullman*, and he welcomed Frankfurter's disposition.

Justiciability was an important ingredient in Frankfurter's version of process liberalism. Since the Court was compelled to write thorough, analytically sound, carefully crafted opinions, and since the process of constitutional adjudication required a delicate balancing of competing values and reasoned debate of the relevant issues, the precious time of Justices should not be wasted on trivial or abstract controversies. Frankfurter tirelessly campaigned to limit the Court's jurisdiction to a relatively few selected cases so that it could do full justice to those it decided, thereby marking out the areas of its competence with precision and giving clear guidance to the bar and the lower courts. That effort largely failing, he resorted to passive devices, which he identified with "the historically defined, limited nature and function of courts" and "the fundamental federal and tripartite character of our National Government," [114] to keep the Court from "entertain[ing] constitutional questions in advance of the strictest necessity." [115]

In his relatively brief plurality opinion in *Poe v. Ullman*, Frankfurter simply called attention to the absence of enforcement of the birth control statute in Connecticut and then strung together previous cases denying justiciability on a variety of grounds. The only ground that seemed truly germane to the case at hand was that Connecticut had not enforced the statute, thus "depriv[ing] these controversies of the immediacy which is an indispensable condition of constitutional adjudication." [116] Of the appellants in *Poe*, the two married women were not sufficiently adversely affected by the statute to merit adjudication of their claims, and the third, a doctor who had given them birth control information, had no "realistic fear of prosecution." [117]

Harlan disagreed with Frankfurter's sense of the impact of the statute. He maintained that the plurality opinion was grounded essentially on the fact that on only one occasion in more than seventy-five years had the statute been used as a basis of prosecution, and that the other grounds asserted for limited justiciability were merely window dressing. He then argued that the one prosecution could be seen as a major deterrent to noncompliance with the statute, since the prosecutor had said in the context of that case that "any person, whether a physician or layman, who violated [the statute] must be expected to be prosecuted and punished in accordance with the literal provisions of the law." [118] The "very purpose" of that prosecution, he asserted, "was to change defiance into compliance," and the purpose "may have been successful." [119] Indeed, Harlan believed, "all that stands between [the complaining parties in *Poe*] and jail is the legally unfettered whim of the prosecutor." [120] The threat of prosecution tended to "discourage the exercise of the liberties of these appellants, caused by reluctance to submit their freedoms from prosecution . . . to the discretion of the Connecticut prosecuting authorities." [121] The deleterious effect of the statute was not "chimerical," [122] but was "present and very real"; [123] hence, the Court ought to take jurisdiction and decide the merits of the case.

Implicit in Harlan's justiciability argument was his feeling that the constitutional rights allegedly infringed in *Poe* were substantial and deserving of judicial protection. This was, he said, "the core of [his] disagreement with [the Court's] disposition" [124] of the case. Harlan's deviation from Frankfurter revealed that the canons of process liberalism, although important for Harlan, were not always ends in themselves. Where their use served as a counterweight to the affirmance of values he cared deeply about, he was occasionally prepared to abandon them. In these rare instances he was prepared to accept a role for judges as glossators of constitutional language that included giving substantive content to clauses such as the due-process clause of the Fourteenth Amendment. His opinion in *Poe v. Ullman* made ingenious use of this glossing power.

The first step in Harlan's discussion of the constitutionality of the statute challenged in *Poe* was to set forth a governing "framework of Constitutional principles" in which his reading of judicial powers and responsibility under the due process clause was made explicit. The standard for judicial review of state legislation under the clause was normally whether the legislative action could be said to have a rational basis, but where "fundamental" liberties were involved, the standard was stricter, embracing the means of implementing the legislation as well as its underlying purposes. In determining whether a legislative act had violated the due process clause, the judiciary did not limit the meaning of the clause to "a guarantee of procedural fairness," [125] nor did it define "due process" as embodying only those specific restraints on the government enumerated prior to the passage of the Fourteenth Amendment. Due process was "a discrete concept which subsists as an independent guaranty of liberty . . . more general and inclusive than the specific provisions" of the Bill of Rights.[126] The judiciary should give a general meaning to the clause, remaining attentive to "the balance which our Nation . . . has struck between . . . liberty and the demands of organized society." [127] The term "liberty" in the due process clause was "a rational continuum" that embraced "a freedom from all substantial arbitrary impositions and purposeless restraints." [128]

The judicial obligation in *Poe v. Ullman* was therefore to weigh the substantive implications of the due process clause against the social purposes served by the implementation of the Connecticut statute. In this balance, two inquiries were essential: whether the due process clause, given its expanded meaning, embraced the conduct that Connecticut sought to regulate—namely, the use of artificial contraceptives by married couples; and whether, if that question was answered affirmatively, the Connecticut statute constituted, in its operation, a justifiable use of state police powers.

Defining the judicial task in these terms allowed Harlan to proceed to the next crucial step in his opinion, defining "liberty" in the due process clause to include the use of contraceptive devices by married couples. To create this definition he analogized from other constitutional provisions, and conceded that his finding did not rest on any explicit language in the Constitution. The "liberty" offended by the statute was "the privacy of the home in its most basic sense," [129] a condition protected implicitly by the Third Amendment, prohibiting soldiers from being quartered in homes, and by the Fourth Amendment, forbidding unreasonable searches and seizures. From these provisions Harlan drew the meaning that the Constitution, as interpreted by the Court, protected "the privacy of the home against all unreasonable intrusions of whatever character." [130]

But could not the State of Connecticut nonetheless seek to insure the "moral soundness" of its citizens? Was not a decision by the state legislature to prevent Connecticut citizens from interfering with the process of human birth grounded on a moral choice that could be rationally justified, and thus constitutionally permissible, even though it infringed on individual rights? Here Harlan distinguished between the soundness of the moral judgment made in the statute (which judgment he conceded might withstand scrutiny) and the choice of means used to implement that judgment. Connecticut, he maintained, was "asserting the right to enforce its moral judgment by intruding upon the most intimate details of the marital relation with the full power of the criminal law." [131] It had determined that it could search houses for evidence of the use of contraceptives, seize contraceptives as evidence, and require married couples "to render account before a criminal tribunal of their uses" of the intimacy of their marriage.[132] In making this judgment it had exceeded the limits "to which a legislatively represented majority may conduct . . . experiments at the expense of [individual] dignity."[133] The anti-contraceptive legislation, as applied to married persons, had thus violated the Fourteenth Amendment's due-process clause.

Harlan's dissent in *Poe v. Ullman* was remarkable in its deviation from the passive model of judging that process liberalism required. It subjected a state statute to a more rigorous than normal scrutiny merely by asserting that the rights offended by the statute were "fundamental," and it based that fundamentality not on any explicit language in the Constitution, but on judicial glosses and analogies. It openly gave substantive content to the due-process clause, and created a new area of constitutional law by defining a right, privacy, that had not previously been given constitutional protection. It openly gave substantive content to the due process clause, and able under the statute, and built that distaste into its decision-making calculus. It was, in short, an activist, value-oriented, free-wheeling piece of judicial lawmaking, despite its articulated support for Frankfurter's belief that "the vague contours of the Due Process Clause do not leave judges at large [to] draw on our merely personal and private notions."[134]

Poe v. Ullman was perhaps the sharpest example of the different points of emphasis in Frankfurter and Harlan. On many other occasions their views converged to such an extent that only subtle differences could be perceived. *Baker v. Carr*, in this sense, was a case more representative of the work of the Warren Court in its first phase. Warren and Black jointly supported an expansive judicial reading of constitutional language with the aim of protecting the rights of a disadvantaged minority, whereas Frankfurter and Harlan resisted that reading and the theory of constitutional adjudication that had produced it. On examination, Frankfurter's and Harlan's perspectives in *Baker v. Carr* differed in degree, but were sufficiently similar to suggest that Harlan would perpetuate many Frankfurterian tenets of judicial performance after the latter's retirement (shortly after *Baker v. Carr* in 1962).

The familiar facts of *Baker v. Carr* need only brief exposition here. The 1950s witnessed patterns of population growth and diffusion that altered the shape and character of urban centers. Inner cities had become more ethnically and racially heterogeneous; discrete homogeneous suburbs had surrounded the inner city; the population of rural areas had declined. Those patterns often produced discernible differences in voting behavior between inner cities, suburbs, and rural areas. Existing state statutes creating voting districts on a geographical basis often did not reflect the new patterns, with the consequence that rural areas with a small population and urban or suburban areas with a huge population were treated as essentially equivalent for the purpose of electing state officials. The interaction of the existing statutes with the new demographic patterns resulted in a disproportionate increase in the political value of the votes of residents of rural districts, so that the consensus on an issue or candidate reached by a district in which 150 persons voted could offset that in which 100,000 voted. The problem was made acute by the divergence of rural and urban areas on major social issues—racial integration, the prevention of crime, tax support for welfare programs—whose ramifications were primarily felt in the cities. Rural districts in a state legislature could, through their disproportionate voting power, prevent state funds from being channeled into distinctly urban needs.

In response to this difficulty urban and suburban residents sought to challenge, as violations of the Equal Protection Clause, state statutes that apportioned voting on other than a population basis. They argued that their votes "counted less" than those of residents of rural districts, and that the equal-protection clause required that the two sets of votes "count" the same. One statute so challenged was that of Tennessee. This statute, enacted in 1901, had tied legislative representation to population patterns of that time, and since then the Tennessee legislature had undertaken no reapportionment of voting districts or seats in its general assembly. In *Baker v. Carr* the Court, in a 6–2 decision, held that allegedly underrepresented Tennessee voters had standing to challenge the statute and that their challenge presented a bona-fide constitutional claim that could be adjudicated in court.

Black and Warren both joined Justice Brennan's majority opinion in *Baker v. Carr*, but one may surmise that their perspectives on the case were not precisely the same. Black believed that the equal protection clause was an absolute bar to all state discriminatory classifications infringing Bill of Rights freedoms. But there was no mention in the Bill of Rights of a right to vote, let alone to have one's vote count equally with another's. Thus Black's support for Brennan's opinion, in terms of his own attitude toward constitutional adjudication, could be based only on an appeal to the actual design of the Constitution, which he may have read as assuming that voting rights were precious and inviolate. This was a more "liberal" reading of the constitutional text than Black had ever made. His vote in *Baker v. Carr* constituted his primary departure from literalism in constitutional adjudication; it came close to being an aberration.

Warren also came to the conclusion that equal voting representation was compelled by the Constitution. He believed, however, that the judiciary had a further obligation: to scrutinize the activities of other branches of government to insure that they were not perpetuating inequalities or injustices. In this sense he did not confine the sweep of the Court's jurisdiction to those areas explicitly covered by constitutional language. He did not see judicial activism solely as an obligation following upon a reading of the Constitution, but viewed it more positively, as an affirmative exercise in enlightened governing. In *Baker v. Carr* his position coalesced with that of Black, but the coalescence was exceptional, given the fact that a judge-made gloss on the constitutional text was required to reach the result. Normally Warren diverged from Black precisely at the point where fairness and justice could be promoted only by departures from the text. Hence Warren's position in *Baker v. Carr* was representative of his jurisprudence, and Black's was highly unrepresentative of his.

Frankfurter and Harlan were likewise paired but not indistinguishable. Frankfurter's dissent confined itself to reasons, jurisprudential and historical, why the Court should not decide the case. Harlan's separate dissent incorporated Frankfurter's views by reference but went on to find that the Tennessee statute did not violate the equal protection clause (since that clause did not impose "rigid equality" [135]) but merely prohibited state discriminatory classifications that could be shown to be arbitrary or capricious. The overlap between the two dissents was considerable. Both maintained that "continuing national respect for the Court's authority depends in large measure upon its wise exercise of self-restraint and discipline in constitutional adjudication"; [136] both spoke of the value of legislative experimentation on the part of the states in a federal republic; and both argued that the framers of the Fourteenth Amendment

had no intention "to fix immutably the means of selecting representatives for state governments." [137] Harlan, however, was prepared,
as he had been in *Poe*, to make a more explicit statement of the substantive values underlying his approach. In protesting the decision
in *Baker v. Carr*, he was doing more than decrying judicial involvement in traditionally legislative areas; he was identifying himself
with a tradition of American intellectual thought that juxtaposed
the ideal of equality against a discomfort with total commitment to
that ideal in practice.

Baker v. Carr was something of a milestone for the Warren
Court. Not only did it signify the Court's willingness to extend its
scrutiny of legislative activity to areas beyond that of race, thus
auguring a redefinition of the relations between legislatures, courts,
and the Constitution, it also marked the last term of service for
Frankfurter, whose retirement deprived the Court of a spokesman
for process liberalism in its most thoroughgoing form. Although the
Warren Court in its last seven years remained divided on the desirability of active judicial promotion of humanitarian causes, none of
its Justices envisaged so limited a role for the Court as had Frankfurter, none maintained a jurisprudential stance in which procedural technicalities played such a dominant part, and none defined
his position as a judge in so self-abnegated a fashion. Consequently,
few internal brakes existed for the Court's buoyant momentum in
behalf of the constitutional imperatives that it perceived.

The area in which the Warren Court in its second phase made its
deepest impact and engendered the most controversy was criminal
procedure. The crucial analytical step in its criminal procedure
reforms was the rejection by a majority of two Frankfurterian principles; first, that, because of the federal character of the American
republic, state law enforcement officials were not restricted in their
activities by the Bill of Rights in the same manner in which were
federal officials; second, that the due process clause of the Fourteenth Amendment protected against state infringement of "basic
values implicit in the concept of ordered liberty" [138]—nothing more
and nothing less. The rejection of these propositions marked a
triumph for Black, albeit not a complete one, since his counterprin-
ciple—that the due process clause incorporated against the states all
the specific protections of the Bill of Rights, and nothing more—
was never accepted by a Court majority. Instead the Court "selectively" [139] incorporated various Bill of Rights provisions against the

states. Those making the strongest impact on state administration of criminal practice were the search-and-seizure clause of the Fourth Amendment, the self-incrimination clause of the Fifth Amendment, and the Sixth Amendment's speedy trial, confrontation, and assistance of counsel clauses.

Although most of the Court's significant criminal procedure innovations took place after Frankfurter's retirement, one of its most far-reaching decisions, *Mapp v. Ohio*,[140] had been handed down during his tenure. *Mapp* squarely raised the issue of the applicability, against the states, of the Fourth Amendment's protection against unreasonable search and seizures. The Court held that all evidence obtained by searches in violation of the Fourth Amendment was inadmissible in a criminal trial in a state court. Warren was part of the majority; Black concurred, arguing that although the Fourth Amendment alone did not prevent the admission of such evidence, that the Fifth Amendment's self-incrimination clause and the Fourth Amendment's search-and-seizure clause, taken in tandem, did; Harlan and Frankfurter dissented, affirming the values of federalism and declaring their allegiance to the "ordered liberty" doctrine of the Fourteenth Amendment rather than to the incorporation theory.

Mapp was an important case in at least two respects: not only did it signify that a majority of the Court was prepared to accept incorporation in some form; it also threatened to upset existing systems of law enforcement in the states. Convictions of thousands of criminals incarcerated in state prisons had been secured through the use of evidence that *Mapp* now declared to have been illegally obtained and therefore inadmissible at trial. Even prisoners convicted before Mapp apparently had the right to challenge their convictions on habeas corpus, by reason of the then-existing principle that judge-made changes in constitutional law were presumed to have retroactive effect. The validity of this principle, which Traynor had identified as a manifestation of a jurisprudential climate in which law was "found" and changes in legal rules were seen as discoveries of the correct rule, had never been explicitly considered by the Court because it had never before had such concrete effects. Now its application threatened to empty the state prisons.

The criminal procedure reformers of the Warren Court were thus faced with a delicate trade-off. Retroactive application of new criminal procedure rules might seriously disrupt state administration of criminal justice and create a political nightmare for the Court. On the other hand, prospective application of new rules meant that some persons would receive their benefit and others not—merely by fortuities of timing. Prospective application required the judicial imposition of a cut-off date for each new rule's effect; as the Court's criminal procedure reforms continued apace, the selection of each date would mean the difference between continued incarceration and potential freedom for countless numbers of convicts. The choice of total retroactivity might identify the Court with a mass exodus from the prisons. The choice of prospectivity suggested the kind of apparently arbitrary classifications that the Court scrutinized in legislatures.

Linkletter v. Walker,[141] a 1965 decision, represented the Court's response to this dilemma. In that case a majority opted for prospective application of *Mapp,* meaning that while the petitioner in *Mapp* received the benefit of the new rule, the petitioner in *Linkletter,* whose conviction had become finalized before the date *Mapp* was handed down, did not. In choosing prospectivity the majority traded off the seemingly arbitrary exclusion of some prisoners from the benefits of its reforms against the power to continue making criminal procedure reforms. It made an implicit political judgment that disruption of state law enforcement systems would ultimately foreclose the Court from making future rulings restraining law enforcement practices. To prevent such a checkmate, the majority was prepared to limit the number of criminals who could challenge their convictions on the basis of a new rule.

Warren was part of the majority in *Linkletter* and one of the architects of the prospectivity doctrine.[142] In subsequent cases involving the retroactivity of new criminal procedure rules, the Court showed little coherence either on rationales for prospective application or on the appropriate cut-off dates.[143] Warren, however, never failed to vote for prospective application of a new rule when that option was seriously entertained, and he showed willingness to utilize any number of analytical techniques to support his position[144]—although his calculus was in fact more pragmatic than analytical, as he indicated in a 1969 opinion, *Jenkins v. Delaware.*[145] "Incongruities" resulting from the arbitrariness of the prospectivity doctrine, he maintained in *Jenkins,* "must be balanced against the impetus the technique provides for the implementation of long overdue reforms, which otherwise could not be practicably effected." [146]

The primary value furthered by decisions supporting prospective application was, for Warren, the retention of power in the Court to continue its reformist stance. Here Warren showed how closely judicial activism and the implementation of humanitarian goals were linked in his mind. The reforms were "long overdue"; they could be "practicably effected" if they did not disrupt the law enforcement process of the states; the judiciary was in a position not only to implement the reforms but to control their effect; hence, prospectivity went hand in hand with close scrutiny of state law enforcement procedures. Justice at large transcended justice for the individual litigant. The preservation of the judicial power to keep state officials from violating the Constitution surmounted the desires of individual criminals to secure their freedom.

Black's calculus in retroactivity cases was just the reverse of Warren's. He dissented in *Linkletter* and from all subsequent Warren Court decisions giving prospective application to criminal procedure rule changes. His reasons were the same in every instance: no justification existed for singling out one of many similarly situated litigants to receive the benefit of a new rule change. Justice to individual persons outweighed the potential for justice in the abstract. Here Black again revealed the purity and rigidity of his philosophy of constitutional interpretation. The "Bill of Rights safeguards," he said in *Linkletter*, "should be faithfully enforced by the courts without regard to a particular judge's judgment as to whether more people could be convicted by a refusal of courts to enforce the safeguards." [147] Black, in constitutional law cases, was concerned more with the preservation of his theory of adjudication than with the results it produced. An expansive reading of the mandates of the Bill of Rights excluded curtailment of their scope for reasons of convenience. But if the reading itself was wrong, as in a few search and seizure cases in which Black felt that a Court majority had read the Fourth Amendment too expansively, retroactive application was wrong as well. In those instances Black reiterated his *Linkletter* position but concurred in a prospectivist result. [148]

A final revealing sidelight of these cases was Harlan's emergence as an advocate of retroactive application. In *Linkletter* Harlan was a silent member of the prospectivist majority, and he continued to support prospective application for the next four terms.[149] But in *Desist v. United States*,[150] a 1969 decision, Harlan reversed his position and announced a complicated test that was designed to keep prospective application to a minimum. He had become offended, he stated in *Desist*, by the "incompatible rules and inconsistent principles"[151] engendered by prospectivist decisions and by the "pick-[ing] and choos[ing] from among similarly situated defendants"[152] that prospectivity required. He confessed that he had once welcomed prospectivity because he "thought it important to limit the impact"[153] of criminal procedure rule changes he opposed, but he could no longer "remain content with the [resulting] doctrinal confusion."[154] True to his word, Harlan opposed the next prospective application of a rule change, even though he found himself "in the uncomfortable position of having to dissent from a holding which actually serves to curtail the impact" of a decision with which he had never agreed.[155] From vastly different vantage points, he and Black had become a singular pair of allies.

Harlan's evolution from *Linkletter* to *Desist* suggests that he had self-limiting jurisprudential principles that were as strong as those of Frankfurter. Foremost among them, perhaps, was "principled adjudication," under which similarly situated litigants were to be given like treatment by a court unless principles of general applicability could be found for distinguishing between them. Harlan was prepared to subordinate his social instincts to these institutional constraints, but he found the necessity for this subordination less frequent than did Frankfurter. The retroactivity decisions showed, however, that his fidelity to what he called the "classical view of constitutional adjudication"[156] was not lip service. In this sense his approach was closer to Black's than it might have appeared, and seemingly incompatible with Warren's. The first two men built perceived constraints and obligations into their jurisprudence to a far greater extent than did the third.

As prospectivity was emerging to shield future reforms, the Court maintained its reform momentum in the criminal procedure area. Perhaps its high-water mark was *Miranda v. Arizona*,[157] in which the Fifth Amendment's privilege against self-incrimination was transposed into a set of precise guidelines for police conduct during the interrogation of suspects. In the 1960s the Court shifted its focus in coerced confession cases from the "voluntariness" requirement to the atmosphere surrounding the interrogation. The very presence of police officers in authoritarian roles, the Court reasoned, was an intimidating device that put suspects "in such an emotional state as to impair [their] capacity for rational judgment." [158] *Malloy v. Hogan*, [159] a 1964 decision, applied the Fifth Amendment's privilege against self-incrimination against the states. The Court in *Escobedo v. Illinois*, [160] decided a week later, held that a "protective device" was necessary to insure that persons being interrogated by the police would not be coerced into incriminating themselves. *Escobedo* focused on the presence of counsel for the suspect as the necessary device, and held that a request by a subject for the assistance of counsel could not be denied.

Miranda went well beyond that relatively narrow holding to build a set of judicially-created procedural safeguards into the interrogation process. Once a person was "taken into custody" or "otherwise deprived of his freedom" by the police and "subjected to questioning," [161] the police were required to warn him that he had the right to remain silent, that any statement he made could be used against him in a trial, that he had the right to the presence of an attorney, and that if he could not afford an attorney one would be appointed for him. Questioning could not begin until those warnings had been given and the suspect's rights "knowingly and intelligently" waived. The burden of proof was on the police to show that such a waiver had taken place; a waiver could be withdrawn at any time; once a waiver had been withdrawn, even through the implicit act of silence, the interrogation was required to cease. [162] The holding in *Miranda*, said Warren, author of the majority opinion, was "not an innovation in our jurisprudence," but merely, like *Escobedo*, "an application of basic rights that are enshrined in our Constitution." [163] The judiciary had an "obligation to apply these constitutional rights." [164] It was "in this spirit, consistent with our role as judges," [165] that *Miranda* was decided.

Of all Warren Court decisions, *Miranda* has been the most controversial in the short run. Not even the noncompliance or grudging compliance with *Brown* or with *Engel v. Vitale* [166] (the decision outlawing prayers in the public schools) rivaled the furor engendered by *Miranda*. Statistical studies attempted to demonstrate that the *Miranda* warnings were being ignored by the police or were having no real impact on the interrogation process. [167] Congress sought to legislate the warnings out of existence. [168] The Court's "coddling" of criminals became a major issue in the 1968 elections;

new appointees to the Court after Warren's retirement were selected in part on their commitment to law enforcement and their
hostility to "criminal forces." But the significance of the decision,
for present purposes, has little to do with the outcry it engendered
or the efficacy of its result. *Miranda's* importance here is as a means
of identifying the character of the Warren Court at large.

Miranda symbolized the interweaving of two jurisprudential
threads to produce a stance and tone that distinguished the Warren
Court from any of its twentieth-century predecessors. One thread
was the constitutional liberalism of Black, the other was the messianic paternalism of Warren. In *Miranda* these threads, which ran
in separate paths on many other occasions, united so completely
that Warren's language on the judiciary's obligation to apply basic
constitutional rights perfectly expressed Black's thoughts. For Black
there was no issue of judicial encroachment on the prerogatives of
law enforcement officials in *Miranda*. The privilege against self-
incrimination was written into the Constitution; it was to be given
an expansive reading; and that reading was obligatory for the judiciary. All *Miranda* did was to conform conduct to the mandates of
the Bill of Rights. The most important function of the Court was to
give the language of the Constitution meaning in the context of contemporary events, and that it did in *Miranda*. No question of "activism" was involved, for the Court was restrained by the literal
language of the Constitution as much as it was compelled to give
meaning to that language.

In the context of *Miranda*, Warren would not have disagreed with
any of these sentiments. His quarrels with Black were in those
areas in which expansive but literal interpretations of the Constitution unfairly failed to prohibit activity that Warren found offensive
to human rights. Warren's mission in *Miranda* and elsewhere was to
suppress behavior that he found obnoxious or repressive from his
perspective of deep commitment to the freedoms inherent in American citizenship. The Constitution was one source of Warren's perspective, but there were others: his instincts about what was fair
and just, his humanitarian premises, his outrage at brutal or im-
moral acts. In *Miranda* constitutional imperatives were a means of
curtailing conduct he found deplorable, but the starting place for
his thinking was the character of the conduct. Black's starting
place, on the other hand, was his philosophy of interpreting the
Constitution.

The harmony of Black and Warren in *Miranda* symbolized the jurisprudential paradigm of the Warren Court that has most often
served to identify the Court, albeit incompletely, in the minds of
observers. In summary form, the paradigm was as follows. The
Constitution was the supreme law of the land; its mandates displaced all competing laws, whether legislative, executive, administrative, or judicial. The judiciary, in the person of the Court, had
alone been given the responsibility of being the ultimate interpreter
of the Constitution. Its interpretative responsibilities amounted to
duties. It was bound by its interpretations of constitutional language, and a formula existed for the process of interpretation, essentially the same formula as that employed by Marshall. One
began with the literal words of the Constitution and gave those
words as expansive a reading as possible within their linguistic
ambit. In instances where the literal words would bear alternative
readings, one turned to the words of the Founding Fathers or those
of the framers of later amendments to find their meaning. This
formula gave changing content to citizens' rights without disturbing
their original meaning. It foreclosed the particular criticism that
judges were substituting their own preconceptions for those of the
framers by requiring them to work only within the original text and
supplementary historical sources. It avoided all discussions of the
reach of judicial power, the appropriate balance to be struck between competing values, and the proper substantive content of
vague clauses like equal protection or due process. The judiciary did only what the Constitution compelled it to do, but it was
faithful to that obligation in a very full sense. Its power was limited
only by the boundaries of the constitutional text, and although in
one sense only its members knew those boundaries, in another
sense they were in plain sight for everyone to see and understand.

This was the underlying stance of one pole of the Warren Court,
the justification for its substantive crusades and also its link to the
American tradition of an independent yet accountable judiciary.
But the mosaic of the Court did not consist of that view alone. Accompanying it was a counterview, advanced by Frankfurter and
refined by Harlan, that sought to expose two crucial difficulties
with the paradigm outlined above. The first difficulty, according to
Frankfurter, was that constitutional interpretation was never so
clear a process as the paradigm made it out to be. The literal words
of the Constitution did not explicitly anticipate coverage of evolving

areas in American life, and the process of inclusion or exclusion was a matter of judicial art. An expansive reading of constitutional language was not categorically mandated; at times a restrictive reading might be necessary. Hence the Court in its interpretation of the Constitution was making value choices after all. Whether contemporary acts were to receive constitutional protection was a matter, in ambiguous cases, of how much value contemporary American society placed on the protection of those acts. Since this value choice was necessary, what justified the antidemocratic, unrepresentative judicial branch of government from making it? Why should the Court not defer to the value choices of more popularly-oriented branches? From these rhetorical questions the canons of Process Jurisprudence were derived. Their purpose was to prevent value choices in constitutional adjudication from being made by the judiciary and to insure that the process of judicial balancing of competing values, where unavoidable, would be fully articulated.

Harlan, who had dissented in *Miranda* and from most of the Court's innovations in criminal procedure, focused on a second difficulty, one stemming from Frankfurter's insight that a restrictive reading of the constitutional text was as possible as an expansive one. Through a combination of historical scholarship and policy-oriented ruminations Harlan showed that courts and legislatures had chosen restrictive interpretations of constitutional clauses as often as expansive ones; that those restrictive interpretations embodied counteregalitarian and counterlibertarian values that were an equally important part of the future of American civilization; that those interpretations also affirmed other liberties, such as privacy, that competed on occasion with constitutional rights, such as freedom of speech; and that, in short, there was abundant evidence that the process of constitutional interpretation was not linear and uni-dimensional, with the Constitution itself even embracing contradictory principles such as "ordered liberty." Thus, alongside the pathbreaking jurisprudential stance of one element of the Warren Court emerged a sophisticated critique of that stance that ultimately reaffirmed the validity of an earlier twentieth-century approach to judging.

The Warren Court, viewed from this perspective, embodied the dominant features of the American judicial tradition. It offered, in separate parts, the eighteenth-century linguistics of Marshall and his bold, creative use of power; the subtle philosophical insights of

Holmes, along with his fatalistic acceptance of the dictates of legislative majorities; the humanitarian impulses of modern liberalism in heaping doses; the professionalist impulses of that same ideology at the crest of their academic influence; the constant clashes in American history between egalitarian ideals and elitist practices, with their resultant dilemmas for the elitist judiciary. Yet the Warren Court also added a dimension to American jurisprudence by producing and operationalizing a theory of substantive judging that stood in opposition to the dominant, passive model of the middle twentieth century.

The Burger Court is not within the scope of this study, and at any event it may be premature to attempt to characterize jurisprudential trends on that Court. But it is abundantly clear that substantive judging has, if anything, gained momentum since Warren's retirement.[169] Perhaps Process Jurisprudence, in its purest, Frankfurterian form, may no longer be in a position of prominence, on the Supreme Court or elsewhere. Perhaps, further, clashes between process and substantive liberalism have ceased to be a major theme of Supreme Court adjudication. The momentum of modern egalitarianism may have crested in the last phase of the Warren Court; the terms "liberalism" and "conservatism" may be in for yet another redefinition. Out of this possible flux may emerge a fourth twentieth-century jurisprudential perspective.

15

The Tradition and the Future: A Summary

A prime concern of this study has been to describe the elements of a tradition of appellate judging in America, and simultaneously to explore its meaning. One area of emphasis has been the special set of freedoms and limitations that have defined the office of judge since Marshall. Because appellate judging has often been defined by judges and commentators in terms of constraints, one may incline to underemphasize its freedoms, which are worthy of recapitulation. First among them is the power to declare, in a final sense, what "the law" is. American judges function as the primary interpreters of the meaning of the Constitution or a statute, until the sovereign people, through their legislative representatives, choose to change that meaning. That is no minor perquisite, constitutional amendments being rare and statutes invariably being open to further interpretation. It was not always identified with the judiciary in America; it is not thought to be fully possessed by judges in other common-law nations.[1] Judges in America can declare and thereby make law. If one takes seriously the notion of law as a set of guidelines for social conduct, American appellate judges have had abundant opportunities to establish those guidelines.

Federal appellate judges and many state appellate judges have also had the freedom of life tenure. That freedom has been minimized by the oracular theory of the nineteenth century and by twentieth-century theories of judicial self-restraint. It has meant, however, that one holding the office of judge is beholden to far fewer persons than are other occupants of comparably powerful offices. Nowhere, perhaps, but on the United States Supreme Court could governing officials as powerful, independent-minded, and outspoken as Harlan the Elder, Jackson, or McReynolds remain relatively insulated from direct political pressures. American appellate judges have been allowed to make decisions affecting fundamentally the lives of others with (in most cases) minimal fear of having those decisions rebound to their personal disadvantage. In America few offices with such power have had such relatively low personal visibility.

These freedoms in the judiciary, we have seen, have continually interacted with equally important constraints. One can recognize the inherently restrained nature of appellate adjudication in America simply by noting the incompatibility of a democratic theory of government and the office of the judiciary. If judges make decisions of such importance, if their decisions are exercises of power rather than of mechanical logic, and if so few checks exist on the character of their performance, how is their presence tolerated in a democracy? Numerous explanations have been offered over time in response to this query, among them responses that would invest the judiciary with a guardianship of antidemocratic and antiegalitarian prerogatives. But the response most regularly accepted has been one emphasizing the distinctive technical skills of judges. The judiciary is allegedly entrusted with power because its representatives alone understand the intricacies of the law and can make them intelligible to laymen.

The attractiveness of this explanation has been its confining effect. The power of judges pertains only to those matters peculiarly "legal," as distinguished from political. Outside their field of competence judges become mere citizens and thus as subject to the whims of public opinion as anyone else. Part of the burden of judicial opinion-writing, then, has been to show that a decision has not been grounded on other than "legal" considerations, and that within that ambit it analyzes legal issues in an intelligible fashion. The legitimacy of a judicial decision in America is somehow linked with the degree to which it meets this requirement.

Were the lines between the "legal" and "political" spheres hard and fast, the foregoing explanation might be more satisfactory. But the history of American government suggests that questions of law, especially constitutional law, have been so intermingled with questions of politics as to often be indistinguishable. In reality, judges are not asked to refrain from deciding political questions at all; rather they are asked to refrain from deciding political questions in too openly partisan a fashion. Judges cannot become so isolated from contemporary conditions that their views are obsolescent—as witness the Four Horsemen. On the other hand, they cannot reveal by their opinions too passionate a concern with partisan issues or too strong an interest in passing on orthodox political questions—as witness *Dred Scott*. Paradoxically, the effectiveness of an appellate judicial decision is related to its ability to transcend mere partisanship; and yet the more effective a decision, the wider its political impact.

But if the judiciary has functioned as a political force, its decisions have resisted characterization in conventional political terms. Throughout American history judging has taken place against a backdrop of changing ideological currents; yet those currents, insofar as they themselves are capable of characterization, have not often proved to be fruitful vehicles for analyzing the performance of individual justices. To call Marshall a "Federalist," Taney a "Jacksonian," Field a "conservative," or Holmes a "liberal" not only lends a false unity to the terms, it distorts the thrust of the individual contributions of those justices.

The view of appellate judging on which this book rests emphasizes, rather than political characterizations, differences between the judiciary and other governmental institutions in America. One way in which the judiciary differs from other branches is in the necessarily limited scope of the office of judge. Judges, we have seen, were originally pictured as being not only able to follow the dictates of "the law," but also as free to declare what those dictates were. And as the oracular theory of judging disintegrated with time, its conception of the judicial function as independent but constrained has remained. All the twentieth-century jurisprudential theories described in this study, including Realism, have assumed that judges make law, but have continued to associate judging with a perception of limitations on the lawmaking power of judges. Some limitations have been intellectual (an obligation to give adequate reasons for results), some institutional (an obligation to defer to the power of another branch of government), some political (a

need to avoid involvement in hotly partisan issues), some psychological (a need to recognize the role of individual bias in judicial
decision-making). Emphasis on one or another set of limitations had
varied with the theory of judging propounded. All the theories,
however, have implicitly given the appellate judiciary a limited
mandate to dispense justice as it sees fit.

"Activism" and passivity—or "self-restraint"—have been the
common terms employed in this century to describe judicial responses to the above mandate. But, as indicated throughout this
study, activism in the judiciary has not always been compatible
with liberalism, nor have passivity and conservatism always harmonized. Marshall took an expansive view of his powers, and used
them to further the interests of selected established propertyhol-
ders; Field in a later age acted in an analogous fashion. But Warren
adopted an equally expansive approach toward the pursuit of very
different substantive ends. His activism stimulated change and favored disadvantaged persons. Brandeis, Frankfurter, and Harlan II,
in varying degrees, were apostles of judicial self-restraint. It does
not capture the essence of any of those last three judges to designate them "liberals" or "conservatives" without further refinement
of terms. American appellate judges have had to ask themselves not
simply what social goals they believe in but also whether current
perceptions of the office of judge are compatible with a judicial
implementation of those goals. Because they have had to ask this
additional question, their decisions, in some instances, have constituted a deviation from or a subordination of their social views. Orthodox political characterizations do not ordinarily address this institutional dimension of appellate judging.

A second distinctive aspect of appellate judging has been the
presence of a professional constituency of courts that can be said to
differ, both in composition and in expectations, from the constituencies of other governmental branches. To recapitulate: in handing
down their opinions, appellate courts are communicating to at least
two differing sets of audiences—the public at large, whose lives
may be influenced in a general sense by the impact of their decisions, and a professional constituency, including the lower courts,
similarly situated potential litigants, and counsel for those litigants,
which is influenced by a decision in a much more specific sense. An
appellate opinion can be a clear signal to a select group of persons
that their conduct must be adjusted in accordance with the deci-

sion, or, alternatively, that it need not be so adjusted. It functions, at this level, to give specialized guidance to other courts and private persons on particular legal questions.

These two constituencies of a top-level appellate court need not always be on the same side of a conflict. Thus, in cases such as the *Gold Clause* cases of 1935, in which a decision is both a generalized response to a political controversy—the soundness of the existing monetary system—and a specialized directive to a defined class of persons—holders of United States bonds—innovation by a court may be politically satisfying in the general sense and yet highly disruptive of existing expectations in the class of persons it directly affects. From this perspective, judicial innovation often clashes with the values of certainty and predictability, and service to a professional constituency becomes a counterweight to change. If a judge believes that appellate courts have an obligation not to upset drastically the expectations of their professional public, he may decline to implement a change in the law, even though he might welcome it as a general political response. In that case his calculus again contains a dimension that standard political characterizations cannot easily portray.

Finally, the relation between ideas and judicial decisions is more complex than the conventional terms representing ideological postures would seem to suggest. The ideological terms used in this study—e.g., federalism, paternalism, liberalism, conservatism—have had different meanings at different times, and have been identified with judicial responses pointing in a variety of directions. Complexities arise partially from the ambivalent character of the terms themselves. Federalism may connote either strength in the national government or a balance of strength between that government and the states. Paternalism can embrace both active participation by the judiciary in behalf of disadvantaged persons or tolerance by judges of the social welfare schemes of legislatures. Liberalism contains within itself mutually contradictory impulses. Complexities arise also from the adversary nature of appellate decision-making, which emphasizes ambivalences and invites the use of a single rationale to justify opposite results. Terms such as federalism may become tools in the hands of lawyers and judges: they may be perceived as being capable of pointing in more than one direction, but employed without clarification of their ambiguities. All this makes the characterization of judges as representatives of varie-

ties of social thought a difficult and dangerous enterprise. The relation between ideological change and appellate adjudication is not a
linear one.

If one accepts the thesis that the American judicial tradition has
been composed of certain core elements, will those elements continue to remain relatively constant in the future? Some observations
are suggested by the experience of the past. Political controversies
have a way of infiltrating the courts, and no theory of judicial performance, however confining, can prevent the courts from eventually passing upon sufficiently serious and divisive issues, provided
that an adequate doctrinal framework exists for their consideration.
The delicate relation between the judiciary and politics seems destined to endure, and highly charged "political" issues such as the
constitutionality of "benign" racial quotas in public education will
continue to require resolution. Various "passive" devices exist to
enable the judiciary to postpone the time of decision, but not the
ultimate responsibility.[2] Many such issues will be divisive, as were
those in *Charles River Bridge, Brown* v. *Board of Education,* or *Griswold*
v. *Connecticut,* in representing clashes between cherished values
rather than between one desirable and one obnoxious set of attitudes. The Constitution, like other sources of law in America, em-
bodies contradictory principles. Free speech may clash with privacy, egalitarianism with racial justice, liberty with patriotism,
freedom to hold property with freedom to acquire it. Appellate
courts will have to make hard, temporary choices between those
values.

In the process of making such decisions the independence of the
judiciary will continue to manifest itself individually, unless the future of appellate judging in America differs markedly from the
past. Personal skills of persuasion and expression can affect the content of a decision and can give an opinion a more secure place in
history. The influence of a person in a leadership position at a given
time can make subtle alterations in the course of legal development,
as in the cases of Marshall and Warren. Appellate judicial decision-
making is small-group decision-making; the process makes heavy
use of the written opinions of individual judges in the past; judges
are insulated to an important extent from outside pressures, although never immune from them. In that context individual pres-
ences will continue to make themselves felt. The judges in this
study upon whom one might wish to confer the label of greatness

were more than simply suited to their times or to the dictates of their office. They gave a new dimension to judging in America, stretching its meaning a little to accommodate their own convictions.

Yet the intellectual options of individual judges will remain limited by time and place. Influence in an American appellate judge has not been solely a product of the force of personality; it has required a certain conformity to currently acceptable standards of institutional performance. Marshall could not have advanced the theory that judges openly "made" law and retained his intellectual respectability. Conversely, no justice on the Warren Court could have seriously maintained, with Kent, that the judiciary's primary function was that of a buffer against democratic excesses. The tolerated limits on judicial use of power have varied over time, but a rough conformity to the predominantly accepted limit has been essential. Although one may not be able to discern in advance the boundaries of respectability, they nonetheless exist.

Finally, a mode of minimally acceptable professional competence has followed the judiciary through time, despite changes in the styles and forms of opinions.[3] Oracular and mechanical jurisprudence have given way to various twentieth-century theories, but analytical soundness, intelligibility, and rationality have been continuously associated with competent judging. These minimum requirements have been transcended in the great appellate opinions of American history, opinions in which judging has resembled high art and statecraft; yet they have thus far not been abandoned. They will remain in the future unless the appellate judiciary adopts an approach in which institutional power utterly replaces rational analysis, the euphemism becomes the sole means of communication, and the tension between independence and accountability accordingly evaporates. At that point the American judicial tradition will have lost its meaning.

Appendix: Chronology of Judicial Service

John Marshall   1801–35

James Kent   1798–1823

Joseph Story   1811–45

Lemuel Shaw   1830–60

Roger Taney   1836–64

Samuel Miller   1862–90

Joseph Bradley   1870–92

Stephen Field   1857–63
                       (Supreme Court of California)
                       1863–97
                       (U.S. Supreme Court)

Thomas Cooley   1865–85

Charles Doe   1859–74, 1876–96

John Harlan I   1877–1911

Oliver Wendell Holmes   1882–1902
                               (Supreme Court of Massachusetts)
                               1902–32
                               (U.S. Supreme Court)

Louis Brandeis   1916–39

Willis Van Devanter   1903–10
                               (U.S. Court of Appeals for
                                  the Eighth Circuit)
                               1910–37
                               (U.S. Supreme Court)

George Sutherland   1922–38

Pierce Butler   1922–39

James McReynolds   1914–41

Charles Evans Hughes   1910–16
                               (Associate Justice, U.S.
                                  Supreme Court)
                               1930–41
                               (Chief Justice, U.S.
                                  Supreme Court)

Harlan Fiske Stone   1925–46

Robert Jackson   1941–54

Benjamin Cardozo   1914–32
                               (New York Court of Appeals)
                               1932–38
                               (U.S. Supreme Court)

Learned Hand	1909–23
	(U.S. District Court for the
	   Southern District of New York)
	1923–61
	(U.S. Court of Appeals for
	   the Second Circuit)

Jerome Frank	1941–57
Roger Traynor	1940–70
Felix Frankfurter	1939–62
Hugo Black	1937–71
Earl Warren	1953–69
John Harlan II	1954–55 (U.S. Court of Appeals for the Second Circuit) 1955–71 (U.S. Supreme Court)

Notes

1

1. See generally R. Ellis, *The Jeffersonian Crisis* 5–6 (1971). On Massachusetts, see Nelson, "The Legal Restraint of Power in Pre-Revolutionary America," 18 Am. J. Legal Hist. 1 (1974).

2. Nelson, *supra* n. 1 at 13–26. See generally W. Nelson, *Americanization of the Common Law* (1975).

3. See J. Goebel, 1 *History of the Supreme Court of the United States: Antecedents and Beginnings to 1801* 662–793 (1971); E. Corwin, *John Marshall and the Constitution* 15–24 (1919).

4. Corwin, *supra* n. 3 at 20–23.

5. The Judiciary Act of February, 1801 reduced the Court to five members. Thomas Jefferson, on assuming the Presidency in March of that year, resolved to repeal the Act, and succeeded in 1802. The new Act postponed the opening of the Supreme Court until February 1803 and increased the size of the Court to six.

6. 2 Dall. 419 (1793).

7. For the political overtones of judicial activity in this period, see R. Ellis, *supra* n. 1. See generally Wheeler, "Extrajudicial Activities of the Early Supreme Court," 1973 Sup. Ct. Rev. 123.

8. Quoted in Corwin, *supra* n. 3 at 23–24.

9. 1 Cranch 137 (1803).

10. 4 A. Beveridge, *The Life of John Marshall* 321 (4 vols., 1919). At one time in the writing of his biography, Beveridge was given to serious doubts about Marshall's character. His preliminary research into the Marshall family's purchase of portions of the Fairfax Estate in the Northern Neck region of Virginia, described below, suggested that Marshall may have had a conflict of interest in the cases of *Fairfax's Devisee v. Hunter's Lessee*, 7 Cranch 625 (1813) and *Martin v. Hunter's Lessee*, 1

Wheat. 317 (1816), which grew out of a controversy over the disposition of title to sections of that estate. At one time Beveridge wrote Edward Corwin that he suspected that Marshall had done "some crooked work" in connection with the cases. Beveridge to Corwin, March 12, 1919, quoted in J. Braeman, *Albert J. Beveridge* 264 (1971). Subsequent research revealed for Beveridge that Marshall had no financial interest in the sections of the estate whose ownership was under dispute. See Braeman at 264–65.

11. Quoted in Corwin, *supra* n.3 at 223.
12. William Wirt, in W. Wirt, *The Letters of the British Spy* 110 (1831).
13. 2 Beveridge, *supra* n.10 at 168.
14. Quoted in 3 J. Dillon, *John Marshall* 363 (1903).
15. 2 Beveridge, *supra* n.10 at 194, 177.
16. Wirt, *supra* n.12 at 112.
17. Charles Campbell, quoted in L. Baker, *John Marshall* 709 (1974).
18. F. Gilmer, *Sketches, Essays and Translations* 23 (1828); 3 F. La Rochefoucald-Liancourt, *Travels Through the United States of North America* 120 (4 vols., 1800).
19. Marshall notebook, Library of Congress.
20. 2 Beveridge, *supra* n.10 at 180.
21. Quoted in Corwin, *supra* n.3 at 116.
22. Wirt, *supra* n.12 at 113.
23. Rutherford B. Hayes reported hearing this anecdote from Story while a law student in one of Story's classes at Harvard. See C. Williams, 1 *Diary and Letters of Rutherford Birchard Hayes* 116 (5 vols., 1922).
24. La Rochefoucald-Liancourt, *supra* n.18 at 347.
25. See generally Corwin, *supra* n.3 at 198–99.
26. 2 C. Warren, *The Supreme Court in United States History* 273n (3 vols., 1922).
27. Federal Judicial Center, *Report of the Study Group on the Caseload of the Supreme Court* A7 (1972).
28. 3 Beveridge, *supra* n.10 at 239–41.
29. 3 Beveridge, *supra* n.10 at 226.
30. Id. at 227.
31. Two recent discussions of the ambivalent meaning of the term "sovereignty" in Revolutionary America are Kettner, "The Development of American Citizenship in the Revolutionary Era," 18 Am. J. Legal Hist. 208 (1974), and Reid, Book Review, N.Y.U. L. Rev. (1974).
32. See, e.g., *United States v. Wiltberger*, 5 Wheat. 76 (1820); *Meade v. Deputy Marshal*, 1 Brock. 324 (1815); *Fletcher v. Peck*, 6 Cranch 87 (1810).
33. See 2 J. Marshall, *The Life of George Washington* 447 (1803–5).
34. See, e.g., 2 Marshall, *supra* n. 33 at 68.
35. See generally R. Faulkner, *The Jurisprudence of John Marshall* 19ff. (1968).
36. See *Johnson and Graham's Lessee v. McIntosh*, 8 Wheat. 543, 591 (1823).
37. See generally 4 Beveridge, *supra* n.10 at 472–79; Faulkner, *supra* n.35 at 51.
38. *Fletcher v. Peck*, *supra* n.32 at 139.
39. 9 Wheat. 1 (1824).
40. 4 Wheat. 316 (1819).
41. 12 Wheat. 419 (1827).
42. *Gibbons v. Ogden*, *supra* n.39.
43. *Willson v. Black Bird Creek Marsh Co.*, 2 Pet. 245 (1829).
44. Initially by Chief Justice John Bannister Gibson of the Supreme Court of Pennsylvania in *Eaken v. Raub*, 12 Sergeant & Rawle 330, 347–48 (1825) (dissent).
45. See generally Goebel, *supra* n.3 at 338. It was not, however, a dominant one.

See Nelson, "Changing Conceptions of Judicial Review," 120 U. Pa. L. Rev.
1166, 1168 (1972).
46. See generally G. Wood, *The Creation of the American Republic* (1969).
47. 3 Beveridge, *supra* n.10 at 585; see generally C. Magrath, *Yazoo* (1966).
48. This tactic was also employed by Marshall in *Marbury v. Madison*, where he
used the occasion of confining the jurisdictional reach of the Court in a particular
instance to assert a far broader judicial power in the abstract.
49. 6 Cranch at 133–34.
50. Id. at 135.
51. Id. at 137.
52. Id. at 139.
53. Jefferson to William Johnson, June 12, 1823, quoted in Baker, *supra* n.17 at
413.
54. E.g., 4 Beveridge, *supra* n.10 at 290.
55. 4 Wheat. at 405–06.
56. Id. at 406–07.
57. Id. at 408.
58. Id. at 421.
59. Id. at 426.
60. Id. at 436.
61. Quoted in 1 Warren, *supra* n.26 at 517.
62. See generally G. Gunther, *John Marshall's Defense of McCulloch v. Maryland*
(1969).
63. See 2 Warren, *supra* n.26 at 72–80.
64. *Livingston v. Van Ingen,* 9 Johns. 507 (1812).
65. 9 Wheat. at 187–88.
66. Id. at 190–93.
67. Id. at 193–96.
68. Id. at 203–4, 205–6.
69. Id. at 221.
70. Id. at 272.
71. Quoted in 2 Warren, *supra* n.26 at 71–72.
72. Quoted in Corwin, *supra* n.3 at 124.

2

1. *Osborn v. Bank,* 9 Wheat. 738, 866 (1824).
2. J. Horton, *James Kent: A Study in Conservatism* 55 (1939).
3. Harrison Gray Otis to Robert Goodloe Harper, April 19, 1807, quoted in 1 S.
Morison, *Life and Letters of Harrison Gray Otis* 283 (2 vols., 1913).
4. Quoted in J. Loring, *The Hundred Boston Orators* 375–76 (1852).
5. See generally Horton, *supra* n.2 at 52–60.
6. James Kent to Moss Kent, Aug. 20, 1790, quoted in Horton, *supra* n.2 at 47.
7. See generally Horton, *supra* n.2 at 99–108.
8. See I. Browne, *Short Studies of Great Lawyers* 232 (1878).
9. See Roper, "Justice Smith Thompson: Politics and the New York Supreme
Court in the Early Nineteenth Century," 51 N.-Y. Hist. Soc. Q. 128 (1967).

10. See Cassoday, "James Kent and Joseph Story, 12 Yale L. J. 146, 152 (1903).
11. Quoted in 1 W. W. Story, *Life and Letters of Joseph Story* 333 (2 vols., 1851).
12. G. Dunne, *Justice Joseph Story* 20 (1970).
13. Quoted in Dunne, *supra* n.12 at 33.
14. Story to Harrison Gray Otis, Dec. 27, 1818, quoted in 1 Morison, *supra* n.3 at 122–23.
15. Story to Ezekiel Bacon, Aug. 3, 1828, quoted on 1 Story, *supra* n.11 at 538.
16. G. Dunne, *supra* n.12 at 328.
17. See *Ramsay v. Allegre*, 12 Wheat. 611, 626–38 (1827) (Johnson, J., concurring); G. Dunne, *supra* n.12 at 263–65.
18. G. Dunne, *supra* n.12 at 364–65.
19. Henry Wheaton to Eliza Lyman, May 14, 1837, quoted in E. Baker, *Henry Wheaton* 131 (1937).
20. Quoted in 1 Story, *supra* n.11 at 185.
21. See generally L. Levy, *The Law of the Commonwealth and Chief Justice Shaw* 10–20 (1957).
22. "Memorandum," Shaw Papers, Massachusetts Historical Society, quoted in Levy, *supra* n.21 at 20.
23. See Levy, *supra* n.21 at 16.
24. Quoted in Levy, *supra* n.21 at 23, 20.
25. See generally F. Chase, *Lemuel Shaw* 275–85 (1918).
26. Shaw to Lemuel Shaw, Jr., March 5, 1853, quoted in Levy, *supra* n.21 at 27.
27. Quoted in Chase, *supra* n.25 at 286; quoted in Levy, *supra* n.21 at 27.
28. Shaw, "A Sketch of the Life and Character of the Hon. Isaac Parker," 9 Pick. 577 (1830), quoted in Levy, *supra* n.21 at 24.
29. See generally Horwitz, "The Emergence of an Instrumental Conception of American Law, 1780–1820," in D. Fleming and B. Bailyn, *Law in American History* 287 (1971).
30. R. Pound, *The Formative Era of American Law* 8 (1938).
31. John Dudley, quoted in D. Boorstin, *The Americans: The Colonial Experience* 201 (1958).
32. Kent to Thomas Washington, Oct. 6, 1828, quoted in Horton, *supra* n.2 at 154.
33. Erastus Root in N. Carter and W. Stone, *Reports of the Proceedings and Debates of the Convention of 1821* 616 (1821).
34. *Packard v. Richardson*, 17 Mass. 121 (1821).
35. Quoted in Horton, *supra* n.2 at 211.
36. Dunne, *supra* n.12 at 199, 200.
37. See 1 Story, *supra* n.11 at 283.
38. See Dunne, *supra* n.12 at 169.
39. Story to Henry Wheaton, April 11, 1816, quoted in Dunne, *supra* n.12 at 149.
40. Wheaton to Story, April 19, 1816, quoted in Dunne, *supra* n.12 at 149–50.
41. Quoted in P. Miller, *The Life of the Mind in America* 225 (1966).
42. Quoted in Miller, id.
43. J. Kent, 4 *Commentaries* 20 (1832).
44. Id. at 19.
45. Kent, 2 *Commentaries* 319–28 (1832).
46. See generally Kent, 2 *Commentaries* 338ff (1832).
47. *Livingston v. Van Ingen*, 9 Johns. 507 (1812).
48. E.g., *Croton Turnpike Co. v. Ryder*, 1 Johns. Ch. 611 (1815).
49. See generally Kent, 3 *Commentaries* 459 (1832).
50. Kent in Carter and Stone, *supra* n.33 at 221.

51. Kent, "The Law of Corporations," 1 Law Reporter 57, 58 (1838).
52. Kent, 2 *Commentaries* 271 (1832).
53. See generally Kent, 2 *Commentaries* 272ff. (1832).
54. Quoted in H. S. Commager, "Joseph Story," in *Gaspar Bacon Lectures on the Constitution of the United States* 33, 57 (1953).
55. Quoted in id. at 58.
56. Quoted in Miller, *supra* n.41 at 226.
57. *Wilkinson v. Leland*, 2 Pet. 627, 657 (1829).
58. *Dartmouth College v. Woodward*, 4 Wheat. 518 (1819); *Green v. Biddle*, 8 Wheat. 1 (1823).
59. *Society for the Propagation of the Gospel v. Wheeler*, 22 Fed. Cas. 756 (1814).
60. *Terrett v. Taylor*, 9 Cranch 43 (1815).
61. See generally L. Friedman, *A History of American Law* 174–75 (1973).
62. See generally Scheiber, "The Road to *Munn*: Eminent Domain and the Concept of Public Purpose in the State Courts," in Fleming and Bailyn, *supra* n.29 at 329.
63. 4 Wheat. at 638–40 (1819).
64. See generally A. Beveridge, 4 *John Marshall* 276–81 (4 vols., 1919).
65. 4 Wheat. at 669–71, 708.
66. See J. Hurst, *Law and the Conditions of Freedom* 27, 66–70 (1964 ed.).
67. *Proprietors of the Charles River Bridge v. Proprietors of the Warren Bridge*, 11 Pet. 420 (1837).
68. Story to Mrs. Joseph Story, Feb. 14, 1837, quoted in 2 Story, *supra* n.11 at 268; Kent to Story, June 23, 1837, quoted in Horton, *supra* n.2 at 294.
69. 11 Pet. at 552.
70. *Hazen v. Essex Co.*, 12 Cush. 475, 477–78 (1853).
71. See Kent, 2 *Commentaries* 275 (1832).
72. 16 Pick. 512 (1835); 18 Pick. 472 (1836).
73. *Boston Water Power Co. v. Boston and Worcester R.R.*, 23 Pick. 360 (1839).
74. *Boston and Lowell Railroad v. Salem & Lowell Railroad*, 2 Gray 1 (1854).
75. Id. at 28.
76. *Inhabitants of Springfield v. Connecticut River R.R.*, 4 Cush. 63 (1849).
77. *Dodge v. County Commissioners of Essex*, 3 Metc. 380 (1841).
78. See, e.g., *Inhabitants of Worcester v. Western R.R.*, 4 Metc. 564 (1842); *Lexington & West Cambridge R.R. v. Fitchburg R.R.*, 14 Gray 266 (1859).
79. *Fisher v. McGirr*, 1 Gray 1 (1854); *Commonwealth v. Murphy*, 10 Gray 1 (1857); *Commonwealth v. Howe*, 13 Gray 26 (1859).
80. Shaw in *Commonwealth v. Alger*, 7 Cush. 53, 85 (1851).
81. Id. at 84–85.
82. *Davidson v. B & M·R.R.*, 3 Cush. 91 (1849).
83. *Wellington v. Petitioners*, 16 Pick. 87 (1834).
84. *Commonwealth v. Blackington*, 24 Pick. 352 (1837).
85. *Commonwealth v. Farmers and Mechanics Bank*, 21 Pick. 542 (1839).
86. *Commonwealth v. Alger*, *supra* n.80.
87. *Commonwealth v. Howe*, *supra* n.79.
88. *Norway Plains Co. v. Boston & Me. R.R.*, 1 Gray 263, 267 (1854).
89. Id.
90. See generally *Wellington v. Petitioners*, *supra* n.83.
91. *Commonwealth v. Proprietors of New Bedford Bridge*, 2 Gray 339 (1854); *Commonwealth v. Essex Co.*, 13 Gray 239 (1859); *Central Bridge Corp. v. Lowell*, 15 Gray 106 (1860).
92. *Commonwealth v. Proprietors of New Bedford Bridge*, *supra* n.91.

93. *Commonwealth v. Essex Co., supra* n.91; *Central Bridge Co. v. Lowell, supra* n.91.
94. See Miller, *supra* n.41, at 148–55.
95. Quoted in Levy, *supra* n. 21 at 335.

3

1. *Dred Scott v. Sandford,* 19 How. 393 (1857).
2. E.g., C. Swisher, *Roger B. Taney* 115 (1935); Harris, "Chief Justice Taney: Prophet of Reform and Reaction," 10 Vand. L. Rev. 227 (1957).
3. Quoted in D. Martin, *Trial of the Rev. Jacob Gruber* 43–44 (1819).
4. Swisher, *supra* n.2 at 94.
5. Quoted in id. at 154, 158.
6. John H. B. Latrobe, quoted in J. Semmes, *John H. B. Latrobe and His Times* 202 (1917).
7. Story to Charles Sumner, Jan. 25, 1837, quoted in 2 W. Story, *The Life and Letters of Joseph Story* 266 (1851).
8. Quoted in C. Fairman, *Mr. Justice Miller and the Supreme Court* 52 (1939).
9. See C. Swisher, *The Taney Period* 17 (1972).
10. *New York v. Miln,* 11 Pet. 102 (1837); *Briscoe v. Bank of the Commonwealth of Kentucky,* 11 Pet. 257 (1837).
11. *Proprietors of the Charles River Bridge v. Proprietors of the Warren Bridge,* 11 Pet. 420 (1837).
12. Taney to Andrew Jackson, Aug. 5, 1833 in 5 J. Bassett, *Correspondence of Andrew Jackson* 147 (7 vols., 1926–35).
13. *Dred Scott v. Sandford, supra* n.1.
14. See Swisher, *supra* n.2 at 571–72.
15. C. Warren, 2 *The Supreme Court in United States History* 250 (1922).
16. 11 Pet. at 547–48.
17. *Philadelphia, W & B R.R. v. Maryland,* 10 How. 376 (1850); *Ohio Life Ins. Co. v. Debolt,* 16 How. 416 (1854).
18. *West River Bridge Co. v. Dix,* 6 How. 507 (1848).
19. *Bronson v. Kinzie,* 1 How. 311 (1843).
20. *State Bank of Ohio v. Knoop,* 16 How. 369 (1854).
21. 9 Wheat. 1 (1824).
22. *Supra,* n.10.
23. 5 How. 504 (1847).
24. *The Passenger Cases,* 7 How. 283, 464 (1849) (dissent).
25. *Pennsylvania v. Wheeling and Belmont Bridge Co.,* 13 How. 518, 627 (1852) (dissent).
26. *Almy v. California,* 24 How. 169 (1861).
27. *Cook v. Moffat,* 5 How. 295 (1847).
28. *Prevost v. Greneaux,* 19 How. 1 (1857).
29. *Propeller Genesee Chief v. Fitzhugh,* 12 How. 443 (1852).
30. *Swift v. Tyson,* 16 Pet. 1 (1842).
31. *Louisville, C & C R.R. v. Letson,* 2 How. 497 (1844).
32. See *Ohio Life Ins. Co. v. Debolt, supra* n.17; *State Bank of Ohio v. Knoop, supra* n.20.

33. *Bank of Augusta v. Earle*, 13 Pet. 519 (1839).
34. *Bronson v. Kinzie, supra* n.19.
35. *Ohio Life Ins. Co. v. Debolt, supra* n.17 at 428.
36. *Ableman v. Booth*, 21 How. 506, 521 (1859).
37. Id.
38. *Luther v. Borden*, 7 How. 1 (1849).
39. *Kennett v. Chambers*, 14 How. 38 (1852).
40. *Rhode Island v. Massachusetts*, 12 Pet. 657, 752 (1838) (dissent).
41. *United States v. Ferreira*, 13 How. 40 (1852).
42. *Gordon v. United States*, 2 Wall. 561 (1864); Taney's opinion was reported in 117 U.S. 697 (1886).
43. 16 Pet. 1 (1842).
44. J. Wallace, *The Want of Uniformity in the Commercial Law between the Different States of Our Union* 27 (1851).
45. 15 Pet. 449 (1841).
46. 15 Pet. at 503ff. See generally 2 Warren, *supra* n.15 at 346.
47. 16 Pet. 539 (1842).
48. Andrew P. Butler of South Carolina, quoted in 2 Warren, *supra* n.15 at 497.
49. See 2 Warren, *supra* n.15 at 498.
50. 10 How. 82 (1850).
51. See generally 3 Warren, *supra* n.15 at 5–6.
52. 5 J. Richardson, *A Compilation of the Messages and Papers of the Presidents* 431 (20 vols., 1917).
53. 19 How. at 404–7.
54. See 3 Warren, *supra* n.15 at 25.
55. 19 How. at 446–50.
56. See citations in 3 Warren, *supra* n.15 at 28–31.
57. Id. at 30.
58. Id. at 29.
59. Id. at 32.
60. *New York Tribune*, March 17, 1857, quoted in id. at 41.
61. Timothy Farrar, "The Dred Scott Case," 85 North American Review (1857), quoted in id. at 38.
62. Taney to Franklin Pierce, Aug. 29, 1857, quoted in Swisher, *supra* n.1 at 518–19.
63. See generally Swisher, *supra* n.1 at 571–72.

4

1. See generally Nelson, "The Impact of the Antislavery Movement Upon Styles of Judicial Reasoning in Nineteenth Century America," 87 Harv. L. Rev. 513 (1974); A. Paul, *Conservative Crisis and the Rule of Law* (1960); P. Buck, *The Road to Reunion* (1947); E. Kirkland, *Dream and Thought in the Business Community* (1956).
2. Compare E. McKitrick, *Andrew Johnson and Reconstruction* (1960), with W. Brock, *An American Crisis* (1963), and H. Hyman, *A More Perfect Union* (1973).
3. See P. Temin, *The Jacksonian Economy* (1969); Nelson, *supra* n.1 at 519.
4. See generally J. Higham, *Strangers in the Land* (1955); R. Wiebe, *The Search for Order* (1967).

5. For a contrary view with regard to Chief Justice Morrison Waite, see C. Magrath, *Morrison R. Waite* (1963).

6. Charles Evans Hughes characterized the Court in the late nineteenth century as "brutal . . . in its personal relations," stating that he had "heard that [the Justices] actually shook fists at one another." Hughes to Felix Frankfurter, in Diary, April 25, 1947, Frankfurter Papers, Library of Congress.

7. Quoted in C. Fairman, *Mr. Justice Miller and the Supreme Court* 53 (1939).

8. Gray to Samuel Williston, related in id. at 320.

9. Miller to William P. Ballinger, Oct. 15, 1876, quoted in id. at 251–52.

10. Quoted in id. at 409.

11. "C.H.," New York *Sun*, Sept. 26, 1892, quoted in id. at 417.

12. Id. at 427.

13. Miller to Ballinger, Dec. 31, 1869, quoted in id. at 344.

14. Miller to Ballinger, March 21, 1874, quoted in id. at 348.

15. Miller to Ballinger, Oct. 28, 1877, quoted in id. at 366.

16. Miller to Ballinger, Jan. 18, 1874, quoted in id. at 265.

17. Quoted in id. at 391.

18. Quoted in id. at 279.

19. Miller to Ballinger, Dec. 5, 1875, quoted in id. at 373–74.

20. Remark attributed to Miller by Charles Fairman in conversation with Felix Frankfurter. Diary, April 25, 1947, Frankfurter Papers, *supra* n.6.

21. *Gelpcke v. Dubuque*, 1 Wall. 175, 214 (1864).

22. Quoted in Fairman, *supra* n.2 at 67.

23. Compare *Slaughter House Cases*, 16 Wall. 36 (1873) with Miller's dialogue with counsel in *San Mateo Co. v. Southern Pacific R.R.*, quoted in *Oral Argument on Behalf of Defendant by S. W. Sanderson* 24–25 (1883).

24. E.g., *Civil Rights Cases*, 109 U.S. 3 (1883).

25. Miller, "The Conflict in this Country between Socialism and Organized Society," quoted in C. Gregory, *Samuel Freeman Miller* 143ff. (1907).

26. Quoted in Fairman, "Mr. Justice Bradley," in A. Dunham and P. Kurland, *Mr. Justice* 65, 69 (1964).

27. Id. at 68.

28 Cortland Parker, quoted in id. at 68.

29. See Fairman, *supra* n.7 at 362.

30. See Bradley, *Miscellaneous Writings of the Late Hon. Joseph P. Bradley* (1902).

31. Quoted in Friedman, "Joseph P. Bradley," in 2 L. Friedman and F. Israel, *The Justices of the United States Supreme Court 1789–1969* 1181, 1199 (4 vols., 1969).

32. Bradley to Caroline Bradley, June 4, 1871, quoted in Fairman, *supra* n.26 at 81.

33. John Spalding Flannery, quoted in id.

34. Quoted in 2 Friedman, *supra* n.31 at 1183.

35. See id. at 1199.

36. *Hepburn v. Griswold*, 8 Wall. 603 (1870).

37. *Legal Tender Cases*, 12 Wall. 457 (1871).

38. Miller to Ballinger, April 21, 1870, quoted in Fairman, *supra* n.7 at 170.

39. See Fairman, "Mr. Justice Bradley's Appointment to the Supreme Court and the Legal Tender Cases," 54 Harv. L. Rev. 977, 1128 (1941).

40. See 2 Friedman, *supra* n.31 at 1192.

41. Id.

42. Quoted in id. at 1193.

43. Id.

44. Ballinger to Miller, quoted in Fairman, *supra* n.26 at 80.

45. W. Turner, *Documents in Relation to the Charges Preferred by Stephen J. Field and Others* 17–18 (1853).
46. Quoted in C. Swisher, *Stephen J. Field* 343 (1930).
47. See id. at 359.
48. *In re* Neagle, 135 U.S. 1 (1890).
49. Stephen A. White to James McCreery, quoted in Swisher, *supra* n.46 at 356.
50. Quoted in id. at 343.
51. Graham, "Justice Field and the Fourteenth Amendment," 52 Yale L. J. 851, 857ff (1943).
52. Field to Matthew P. Ready, May 17, 1886, quoted in Graham, *supra* n.58 at 857n.
53. E.g., T. Cooley, *A Treatise on the Constitutional Limitations* (1868); J. Pomeroy, *Constitutional Law* (1868).
54. *Hepburn v. Griswold, supra* n.36.
55. 12 Wall. at 560ff.
56. 12 Wall. at 661ff.
57. *Trebilcock v. Wilson*, 12 Wall. 687 (1872).
58. *Dooley v. Smith*, 13 Wall. 604 (1872); *The Vaughan and Telegraph*, 14 Wall. 258 (1872); *Railroad Co. v. Johnson*, 15 Wall. 195 (1873); *Juilliard v. Greenman*, 110 U.S. 421 (1884).
59. 110 U.S. at 470.
60. *Washington University v. Rouse*, 8 Wall. 439, 443 (1869).
61. Some instances were *Stone v. Washington*, 94 U.S. 181 (1877) and *Ruggles v. Illinois*, 108 U.S. 526 (1883).
62. 12 How. 299 (1851).
63. *The Clinton Bridge*, Fed. Case No. 2900 (1867).
64. *The Clinton Bridge*, 10 Wall. 454 (1870).
65. *Pound v. Turck*, 95 U.S. 459 (1878).
66. *Munn v. Illinois*, 94 U.S. 113 (1877).
67. *Wabash v. Illinois*, 118 U.S. 557 (1886).
68. *State Tax on Railway Gross Receipts*, 15 Wall. 284, 299 (1873).
69. *Woodruff v. Parham*, 8 Wall. 123 (1869).
70. *Cook v. Pennsylvania*, 97 U.S. 566 (1878).
71. See Fairman, "The So-Called Granger Cases, Lord Hale, and Justice Bradley," 5 Stan. L. Rev. 587 (1953).
72. 134 U.S. 418, 461 (1890).
73. *Brown v. Houston*, 114 U.S. 622 (1885).
74. *Coe v. Errol*, 116 U.S. 517 (1886).
75. *Pullman's Palace Car Co. v. Pennsylvania*, 141 U.S. 18, 29 (1891) (dissent).
76. *Walling v. Michigan*, 116 U.S. 446 (1886).
77. *Robbins v. Shelby County Taxing District*, 120 U.S. 489 (1887).
78. *Philadelphia & Southern Steamship Co. v. Pennsylvania*, 122 U.S. 326 (1887); *Maine v. Grand Trunk Railway*, 142 U.S. 217, 230 (1891) (dissent).
79. *California v. Central Pacific Railroad Co.*, 127 U.S. 1 (1888).
80. *Transportation Co. v. Parkersburg*, 107 U.S. 691 (1883).
81. *State Tax on Railway Gross Receipts, supra* n.68 (dissent); *Gloucester Ferry Co. v. Pennsylvania*, 114 U.S. 196 (1885); *Philadelphia and Southern Steamship Co. v. Pennsylvania, supra* n.78; *Pullman's Palace Car Co. v. Pennsylvania, supra* n.75.
82. *The Delaware Railroad Tax*, 18 Wall. 206 (1874); *Railroad Co. v. Maryland*, 21 Wall. 456 (1875); *Maine v. Grand Trunk Railway, supra* n.78.
83. *Georgia Railroad & Banking Co. v. Smith*, 128 U.S. 174 (1888).
84. *Stone v. Wisconsin*, 94 U.S. 181, 183 (1877) (dissent).

85. *Stone v. Farmers' Loan & Trust Co.*, 116 U.S. 307 (1886).
86. Id. at 331.
87. On the "original meaning" of the Reconstruction Amendments, compare Fairman, "Does the Fourteenth Amendment Incorporate the Bill of Rights? The Original Understanding," 2 Stan. L. Rev. 5 (1950), with Bickel, "The Original Understanding and the Segregation Decision," 69 Harv. L. Rev. (1955), and Kinoy, "The Constitutional Right of Negro Freedom," 21 Rutgers L. Rev. 387 (1967).
88. *Slaughter House Cases*, 1 Woods 21, 28–29 (1870).
89. Id. at 29, 31.
90. *Slaughter House Cases*, 16 Wall. 36, 81 (1873).
91. Cf. *Crandall v. Nevada*, 6 Wall. 35 (1867).
92. 16 Wall. at 82.
93. 16 Wall. at 111ff.
94. 16 Wall. at 83ff.
95. 18 Wall. 129 (1874).
96. 94 U.S. at 152.
97. 99 U.S. 700 (1879).
98. *Georgia Railroad & Banking Co. v. Smith, supra* n.83.
99. See, e.g., *Ex parte* Newman, 9 Cal. 502 (1858); *People v. Burr*, 13 Cal. 343 (1859); *McCauley v. Brooks*, 16 Cal. 11, 56 (1860); *Ex parte* Andrews, 18 Cal. 678 (1861).
100. *In re* Ah Fong, 1 Fed. Cas. 213 (1874); *Ho Ah Kow v. Nunan*, 12 Fed. Cas. 252 (1879); *In re* Quong Woo, 13 F. 229 (1882).
101. *Livestock Dealers & Butchers Ann. v. Crescent City Livestock Landing & Slaughter House Co.*, 4 Fed. Cas. 891 (1870).
102. *Chicago-Alton R.R. v. People*, 67 Ill. 11 (1873) (Lawrence, C. J.).
103. *Continental Insurance Co. v. New Orleans*, 13 Fed. Cas. 67 (1870).
104. 13 F. 145; 13 F. 722, 744 (1882).
105. See Graham, "The 'Conspiracy Theory' of the Fourteenth Amendment," 47 Yale L. J. 371 (1938), 48 Yale L. J. 171 (1938).
106. *Santa Clara v. Southern Pacific R.R.*, 118 U.S. 394 (1886).
107. E.g., *Ex parte* Virginia, 100 U.S. 339 (1879).
108. *United States v. Reese*, 92 U.S. 214 (1876); *United States v. Cruikshank*, 92 U.S. 542 (1876).
109. E.g., *United States v. Cruikshank*, 25 Fed. Cas. 707 (1874).
110. 109 U.S. 3 (1883).
111. *Ex parte* Siebold, 100 U.S. 371 (1880).
112. *Virginia v. Rives*, 100 U.S. 313 (1880).
113. 168 U.S. 717 (1897).

5

1. See Jones, "Thomas M. Cooley and the Michigan Supreme Court: 1865–1885," 10 Am. J. Legal Hist. 97 (1966).
2. See Horwitz, "The Emergence of an Instrumental Conception of American Law," in D. Fleming and B. Bailyn, eds., *Law in American History* 287 (1971); Nelson, "The Impact of the Antislavery Movement Upon Styles of Judicial Reasoning

in Nineteenth Century America," 87 Harv. L. Rev. 513 (1974); White, "From Sociological Jurisprudence to Realism," 58 Va. L. Rev. 999 (1972).

3. See generally E. Kirkland, *Business in the Gilded Age* (1952); R. Wiebe, *The Search for Order* (1967).

4. H. Hutchins, "Thomas McIntyre Cooley," in 7 W. Lewis, *Great American Lawyers* 440 (8 vols., 1909).

5. Hutchins in Lewis, *supra* n.4 at 444.

6. Id. at 455.

7. Vander Velde, "Thomas McIntyre Cooley," in E. Babst and L. Vander Velde, *Michigan and the Cleveland Era* 92 (1948).

8. See Cooley, "The Next Half-Century," *Michigan Expositor*, April 8, 1851.

9. B. Twiss, *Lawyers and the Constitution* 18 (1942). See also M. Bernstein, *Regulating Business by Independent Commission* (1955). My discussion of Cooley complements interpretations advanced in Jones, "Thomas M. Cooley and 'Laissez-Faire' Constitutionalism: A Reconsideration," 53 J. Am. Hist. 751 (1967), and Paludan, "Law and the Failure of Reconstruction: The Case of Thomas Cooley," 33 J. Hist. Ideas 597 (1972).

10. Two recent overviews of the Jacksonians are E. Pessen, *Jacksonian America* (1969), and F. Gattel, *Essays on Jacksonian America* (1970).

11. T. Cooley, *A Treatise on Constitutional Limitations* 355 (1868).

12. 20 Mich. 452 (1870).

13. See generally C. Goodrich, *Government Promotion of American Canals and Railroads 1800–1890* (1960).

14. Cooley, *supra* n.11 at 488ff.

15. *People v. Salem*, *supra* n.12 at 487.

16. See, e.g., *East Saginaw Manufacturing Co. v. City of East Saginaw*, 19 Mich. 259 (1869).

17. *Gale v. Kalamazoo*, 23 Mich. 344 (1871).

18. *Flint & Fentonville Plank Road Co. v. Woodhull*, 25 Mich. 99 (1872).

19. *Sutherland v. Governor*, 29 Mich. 320 (1874).

20. *Benjamin v. Manistee River Improvement Co.*, 42 Mich. 628 (1880).

21. *State of Michigan v. Iron Cliffs Co.*, 54 Mich. 350, 361 (1884).

22. Compare *Constitutional Limitations* 356 (1868):

> When the government . . . interferes with the title to one's property . . . and its action is called in question as not in accordance with the law of the land, we are to test its validity by those principles of civil liberty and constitutional protection which have become established in our system of laws, and not generally by rules that pertain to forms of procedure merely.

with *Weimer v. Bunbury*, 30 Mich. 201, 214 (1874):

> Administrative process of the customary sort is as much due process of law as judicial process. . . . To [hold otherwise] would be to give the judiciary a supremacy in the state and seriously to impair and impede the efficiency of executive action.

23. See Cooley, "Limits to State Control of Private Business," 1 Princeton Review 233 (1878).

24. See remarks of Charles A. Kent, quoted in 7 Lewis, *supra* n.4 at 483.

25. Judge John Dudley, quoted in D. Boorstin, *The Americans: The Colonial Experience* 201 (1958).

26. Doe to Wigmore, July 9, 1889 quoted in J. Reid, *Chief Justice* 176 (1967).

27. See generally Reid, *supra* n.26 at 82–84.

28. *Lisbon v. Lyman*, 49 N.H. 553, 602 (1870).
29. *Stebbins v. Lancashire Ins. Co.*, 59 N.H. 143 (1879).
30. *Lisbon v. Lyman*, *supra* n.28.
31. *Haverhill Iron Works v. Hale*, 64 N.H. 426 (1887).
32. *Darling v. Westmoreland*, 52 N.H. 401 (1872).
33. *State v. Pike*, 49 N.H. 399, 427 (1870) (dissent).
34. *Brown v. Collins*, 53 N.H. 442 (1873).
35. *Brown v. Bartlett*, 58 N.H. 511 (1879).
36. *Edgerly v. Barker*, 66 N.H. 434 (1891).
37. *Wooster v. Plymouth*, 62 N.H. 193 (1882).
38. *Opinion of the Justices*, 66 N.H. 629 (1891).
39. *Orr v. Quimby*, 54 N.H. 590, 640 (1874) (dissent).
40. *State v. U.S. & Canada Express Co.*, 60 N.H. 219, 246 (1880) (concurrence).
41. *Boston, Concord & Montreal Railroad v. State*, 60 N.H. 87 (1880).
42. Doe to John M. Shirley, undated, quoted in Reid, *supra* n.26 at 250.
43. *Dow v. Northern R.R.* 67 N.H. 1 (1886).
44. Doe to Shirley, quoted in Reid, *supra* n.26 at 263.

6

1. In *Adamson v. California*, 332 U.S. 46, 62 (1947).
2. Watt and Orlikoff, "The Coming Vindication of Mr. Justice Harlan," 44 Ill. L. Rev. 13 (1949).
3. *New York Times*, May 23, 1954, §4, p. 10E, cols. 1, 2.
4. See A. Dunham and P. Kurland, *Mr. Justice* (1964).
5. See Blaustein and Mersky, "Rating Supreme Court Justices," 58 A.B.A.J. 1183 (1972).
6. That characterization of Harlan has been attributed to Justice David P. Brewer. See, e.g., Waite, "How 'Eccentric' Was Mr. Justice Harlan?" 37 Minn. L. Rev. 173, 181 (1953).
7. 16 Wall. 36 (1873).
8. 94 U.S. 113 (1877).
9. 109 U.S. 3 (1883).
10. 118 U.S. 557 (1886).
11. Harlan, "Address," 134 U.S. 751, 755 (1890).
12. For newspaper accounts of these speeches, see Hartz, "John M. Harlan in Kentucky," 14 Filson Club Hist. Q. 17 (1940). Harlan's reference to the Reconstruction Amendments is quoted at 31.
13. Quoted in id. at 34.
14. Quoted in id. at 39.
15. Harlan, "The Know-Nothing Organization," reprinted in 46 Ky. L. J. 321, 332 (1958).
16. Malvina Shanklin Harlan, "Some Memories of a Long Life," reprinted in id. at 329.
17. Quoted in Westin, "John Marshall Harlan and the Constitutional Rights of Negroes," 66 Yale L. J. 637, 639n (1957).
18. Quoted in Hartz, *supra* n.3 at 34.
19. See, e.g., Civil Rights Cases, *supra* n.9 at 33–59.

20. See *Clyatt v. United States*, 197 U.S. 207, 222 (1905) (dissent). A possible exception is *Cumming v. Board of Education*, 175 U.S. 528 (1899), where Harlan, for the majority, sustained a Georgia state court's finding that Richmond County's failure to maintain a high school for blacks did not violate the equal protection clause of the Fourteenth Amendment. *Cumming* needs to be read in its context. The black petitioners asked for an injunction closing the white high school in Richmond County; the Georgia court found only that injunctive relief was improper because the County Board of Education, in temporarily closing the black high school "for economic reasons," had not abused its discretion. Id. at 545. The precise question before the Supreme Court was whether the state court's action constituted "a clear and unmistakable disregard" of Fourteenth Amendment rights. Harlan held only that the state court's action did not, on its face, violate the Amendment. He expressly left open the question whether sanction of an affirmative refusal by the Richmond County Board to establish and maintain a black high school would violate the Fourteenth Amendment. *Cumming*, of course, appeared three years after *Plessy v. Ferguson*, in which "separate but equal" facilities were held to satisfy the equal protection clause. See discussion *infra*, text accompanying notes 88–92.

21. E.g., *United States v. Clark*, 96 U.S. 37, 44, 47 (1877) (dissent); *Standard Oil Co. v. U.S.*, 221 U.S. 1, 82 (1911) (dissent).

22. *Smyth v. Ames*, 169 U.S. 466, 527–28 (1898).

23. E.g., *Geer v. Connecticut*, 161 U.S. 519, 542 (1896) (dissent).

24. E.g., *Adair v. U.S.*, 208 U.S. 161 (1908).

25. *Atkin v. Kansas*, 191 U.S. 207, 223 (1903).

26. *Adair v. U.S.*, *supra* n.24 at 180.

27. Quoted in Abraham, "John Marshall Harlan," 41 Va. L. Rev. 871, 876 (1955).

28. White, "Proceedings on the Death of Mr. Justice Harlan," 222 U.S. xxvii (1912).

29. See *New York Sun*, May 21, 1895, p. 1, col. 7; *New York Tribune* May 21, 1895, p. 1, col. 5.

30. See Farrelly, "Harlan's Dissent in the *Pollock* Case," 24 S. Cal. L. Rev. 174, 179 (1951).

31. *Supra* n.21.

32. *U.S. v. American Tobacco Co.*, 221 U.S. 106 (1911).

33. *Northern Securities Co. v. U.S.*, 193 U.S. 197 (1904).

34. *Supra* n.21 at 104–5.

35. White, *supra* n.28 at xxvi.

36. A. Kelly and W. Harbison, *The American Constitution* 585 (1963).

37. G. Myers, *History of the Supreme Court* 678n (1912).

38. Westin in Dunham & Kurland, *supra* n.4 at 118, attributing characterization to "most commentators."

39. Westin, *supra* n.17 at 697.

40. M. Porter, "John Marshall Harlan and the Laissez-Faire Court," 1 (doctoral dissertation, University of Chicago, 1971).

41. Harlan to Augustus Willson, June 1, 1895, quoted in Westin, *supra* n.4 at 121.

42. Cf. R. Bremner, *From the Depths* (1956).

43. E.g., *Taylor v. Ypsilanti*, 105 U.S. 60 (1882); *Thompson v. Perrine*, 106 U.S. 589 (1883); *Brenham v. German-American Bank*, 144 U.S. 173, 189 (1892) (dissent).

44. E.g., *Stone v. Farmers' Loan & Trust Co.*, 116 U.S. 307, 337 (1886) (dissent).

45. *Plaquemines Tropical Fruit Co. v. Henderson*, 170 U.S. 511 (1898).

46 *Macon v. Atlantic Coast Line*, 215 U.S. 501, (511) (1910) (dissent); *Tennessee v. Union Planters' Bank*, 152 U.S. 454, 464 (1894) (dissent).

47. *Smyth v. Ames, supra* n.22.

48. E.g., *Hooper v. California,* 155 U.S. 648, 659 (1895) (dissent).

49. *County of Tipton v. Locomotive Works,* 103 U.S. 523 (1880); *Concord v. Robinson,* 121 U.S. 165 (1886).

50. *Mugler v. Kansas,* 123 U.S. 623 (1887); *Powell v. Pennsylvania,* 127 U.S. 678 (1888).

51. *Hennington v. Georgia,* 163 U.S. 299 (1896); *Lake Shore & Michigan South Ry. v. Ohio,* 173 U.S. 285 (1899); *Northern Pacific v. Dustin,* 142 U.S. 492, 509 (1892) (dissent).

52. *Adair v. U.S., supra* n.24.

53. *Lochner v. New York,* 198 U.S. 45, 65 (1905) (dissent); *Atkin v. Kansas, supra* n.25.

54. *Standard Oil Co. v. U.S., supra* n.21 at 83.

55. *Texas & Pacific Ry. Co. v. ICC,* 162 U.S. 197, 239 (1896) (dissent); *ICC v. Alabama Midland Ry. Co.,* 168 U.S. 144, 176 (1897) (dissent); *Harriman v. ICC,* 211 U.S. 407, 423 (1908) (dissent).

56. *Standard Oil Co. v. U.S., supra* n.21 at 82 (dissent).

57. *U.S. v. E. C. Knight Co.,* 156 U.S. 1, 18 (1895).

58. *Pollock v. Farmers' Loan & Trust Co.,* 157 U.S. 429, 652 (1895) (dissent).

59. Harlan to Augustus Willson, June 1, 1895, quoted in Westin, *supra* n.4 at 121.

60. Harlan to Willson, Dec. 1, 1905, quoted in id. at 120.

61. *International Postal Supply Co. v. Bruce,* 194 U.S. 601, 606 (1904) (dissent).

62. *Adair v. U.S., supra* n.24.

63. *Lochner v. New York, supra* n.53.

64. See cases cited at n.43 *supra.*

65. E.g., *Galveston, Harrisburg & San Antonio Ry. Co. v. Texas* (Texas Gross Receipts Tax Case), 210 U.S. 217, 228 (1908) (dissent).

66. Cf. O. W. Holmes, "The Path of the Law," in *Collected Legal Papers* 184 (1920).

67. *Supra* n.9 at 53.

68. E.g., *Murray v. Louisiana,* 163 U.S. 101 (1896); *Thomas v. Texas,* 212 U.S. 278 (1909).

69. *Strauder v. West Virginia,* 100 U.S. 303 (1880).

70. *Virginia v. Rives,* 100 U.S. 313 (1880).

71. *Ex parte* Virginia, 100 U.S. 339 (1880).

72. *Neal v. Delaware,* 103 U.S. 370 (1881). See also *Cumming v. Board of Education, supra* n.20.

73. *Bush v. Kentucky,* 107 U.S. 110 (1883); *Williams v. Mississippi,* 170 U.S. 213 (1898).

74. *Carter v. Texas,* 177 U.S. 442 (1900); *Rogers v. Alabama,* 192 U.S. 226 (1904).

75. *Smith v. Mississippi,* 162 U.S. 592 (1896); *Brownfield v. South Carolina,* 189 U.S. 426 (1903); *Thomas v. Texas, supra* n.68.

76. *In re* Wood, 140 U.S. 278 (1891); *Gibson v. Mississippi,* 162 U.S. 565 (1896).

77. 110 U.S. 651 (1884).

78. 190 U.S. 127 (1903).

79. 189 U.S. 475 (1903).

80. Id. at 493, 503–4.

81. *Clyatt v. U.S., supra* n.20 (dissent).

82. *Hodges v. U.S.,* 203 U.S. 1, 20 (1906) (dissent).

83. *Bailey v. Alabama,* 211 U.S. 452, 455 (1908) (dissent).

84. *Robertson v. Baldwin,* 165 U.S. 275, 288 (1897) (dissent).

85. Id. at 301. Italics in original.

86. *Bailey v. Alabama*, 219 U.S. 219 (1911).
87. *Supra* n.9 at 47.
88. 133 U.S. 587 (1890).
89. *Hall v. DeCuir*, 95 U.S. 485 (1878).
90. *Supra* n.88 at 594–95.
91. 163 U.S. 537 (1896).
92. Id. at 560 (dissent).
93. See Westin, *supra* n.17 at 702.
94. Id. at 704–5.
95. *Elk v. Wilkins*, 112 U.S. 94, 110 (1884) (dissent).
96. *Baldwin v. Franks*, 120 U.S. 678, 694 (1887) (dissent).
97. *O'Neil v. Vermont*, 144 U.S. 323, 366, 370 (1892) (dissent).
98. *Hurtado v. California*, 110 U.S. 516, 538 (1884) (dissent); *Baldwin v. Kansas*, 129 U.S. 52, 57 (1889) (dissent); *O'Neil v. Vermont*, supra n.97; *Boln v. Nebraska*, 176 U.S. 83 (1900); *Maxwell v. Dow*, 176 U.S. 581, 605 (1900) (dissent); *Twining v. New Jersey*, 211 U.S. 78, 114 (1908) (dissent).
99. Brewer, "The Movement of Coercion," 1893 address before the New York State Bar Association, quoted in R. Gabriel, *The Course of American Democratic Thought* 233 (1940).

7

1. Cf. C. Hughes, *The Supreme Court of the United States* 50 (1928). Hughes listed *Pollack v. Farmers Loan & Trust Co.*, invalidating the income tax, as a third such "wound." Id. at 53.
2. For an elaboration of this observation, see White, Book Review, 59 Va. L. Rev. 1130 (1973).

8

1. See generally L. Hartz, *The Liberal Tradition in America* (1955).
2. The discussion to follow draws on insights in H. May, *The End of American Innocence* (1959); R. Wiebe, *The Search for Order* (1967), and P. Conkin, *The New Deal* (1967).
3. E.g., H. Laski, *Authority in the Modern State* (1919).
4. No effort is made here to deny the possibility of a divergence between the publicly expressed and the privately held views of supporters of either populism or progressivism. Both movements attracted persons from a variety of social and economic backgrounds, and various theories have been advanced as to their collective motivations for reform. Compare J. Chamberlain, *Farewell to Reform* (1932), with R. Hofstadter, *The Age of Reform* (1955), and G. Kolko, *The Triumph of Conservatism* (1963). In contrast to that of the New Dealers, the rhetoric of populists and progressives appears laden with moral appeals and visions of an idyllic society. For an expression of the contrasting tone taken by liberals, see T. Arnold, *The Symbols of*

Government (1935). These different angles of vision may have reflected fundamentally different social perspectives. See H. Graham, *Encore for Reform: The Old Progressives and the New Deal* (1967).

5. For the late-nineteenth-century version of this view, see J. Sproat, *The Best Men* (1971). See generally White, "The Social Values of the Progressives: Some New Perspectives," 70 South Atlantic Quarterly 62 (1971).

6. See, e.g., Pound, "Mechanical Jurisprudence," 8 Colum. L. Rev. 605 (1908); Dodd, "Social Legislation and the Courts," 28 Pol. Sci. Q. 1 (1913).

7. Examples of the two schools in the period discussed are Pound, "The Theory of Judicial Decision," 36 Harv. L. Rev. 641, 802, 940 (1923); Oliphant, "A Return to Stare Decisis," 14 A.B.A.J. 71, 159 (1928). See generally White, "From Sociological Jurisprudence to Realism," 58 Va. L. Rev. 999 (1972).

8. E.g., R. Jackson, *The Struggle for Judicial Supremacy* 312 (1941): "Holmes and Brandeis have not only furnished the highest expression but they have been the very source and the intellectual leaders of recent liberalism in the United States."

9. See White, "The Rise and Fall of Justice Holmes," 39 U. Chi. L. Rev. 51, 56 (1971).

10. O. W. Holmes, Sr., 3 *The Complete Writings of Oliver Wendell Holmes* 59, 142 (13 vols., 1900).

11. William James, Oct. 2, 1869, quoted in R. Perry, 1 *The Thought and Character of William James* 307 (2 vols., 1935).

12. Holmes to Felix Frankfurter, June 26, 1928, in Holmes Collection, Harvard Law School.

13. Holmes, "Notes on Albert Dürer," 7 *Harvard Magazine* 41, 43–44 (October 1860).

14. Holmes, "The Path of the Law" (1896), reprinted in *Collected Legal Papers* 167, 172 (1920).

15. Holmes, "Law in Science and Science in Law" (1899), reprinted in id. at 210, 242.

16. See discussion of free-speech cases *infra*.

17. *Buck v. Bell*, 274 U.S. 200 (1927).

18. *Patsone v. Pennsylvania*, 232 U.S. 138 (1914).

19. Holmes to Harold Laski, in M. Howe, ed., 1 *Holmes-Laski Letters* 217 (2 vols., 1953).

20. Holmes, "Law in Science and Science in Law," *supra* n.15 at 239.

21. Id.

22. See Holmes to Harold Laski, January 13, 1923, in 1 Howe, ed., *supra* n.19, at 473–74.

23. Holmes to Sir Frederick Pollock, in M. Howe, ed., 2 *Holmes-Pollock Letters* 22 (2 vols., 1961).

24. Holmes to Pollock, in 1 Howe, ed., *supra* n.23 at 163.

25. Quoted in H. Pringle, 2 *The Life and Times of William Howard Taft* 969 (2 vols., 1939).

26. Charles G. Ross, *St. Louis Post-Dispatch*, quoted in I. Dillard, ed., *Mr. Justice Brandeis, Great American* 14 (1941).

27. Brandeis to Otto Wehle, March 12, 1876, in *Public Papers of Louis D. Brandeis*, U. Louisville Law School.

28. A. Mason, *Brandeis: A Free Man's Life* 42 (1946).

29. See id. at 103.

30. Brandeis to Charles Nagel, July 12, 1879, in *Public Papers*, *supra* n.27.

31. Brandeis to Amy Brandeis Wehle, Jan. 2, 1881, in id.

32. Brandeis to Alice Goldmark, quoted in Mason, *supra* n.28 at 75.

33. Testimony before the Committee of the Board of Aldermen in the Case and Management of Public Institutions, 3 *Report* 3631–32 (1874).
34. L. Brandeis, *Business—A Profession* 321 (1914).
35. See generally A. Link, *Wilson: The New Freedom* (1956).
36. Brandeis, "A Call to the Educated Jew," 1 *Menorah Journal* 15 (1915).
37. Brandeis to Alfred Brandeis, June 18, 1907 in *Public Papers, supra* n.27.
38. Brandeis, *Business—A Profession, supra* n.32, at liv-lvi.
39. Brandeis, "The Living Law," 10 Ill. L. Rev. 461, 465 (1916).
40. 244 U.S. 590 (1917).
41. Id. at 597, 600 (dissent).
42. Holmes wrote Laski that on one occasion he had told Brandeis that the latter was "letting partisanship disturb his judicial attitude." 1 M. Howe, ed., *supra* n.19 at 128.
43. *Duplex Co. v. Deering*, 254 U.S. 443, 479, 488 (1921) (dissent).
44. E.g., *In re* Jacobs, 98 N.Y. 98 (1885); *Millett v. People*, 117 Ill. 294 (1886); *Godcharles v. Wigeman*, 113 Pa. 431 (1886).
45. *Powell v. Pennsylvania*, 127 U.S. 678, 687 (1888) (Field, J., dissenting); *Hooper v. California*, 155 U.S. 648, 659 (1895) (Harlan, Brewer, Jackson, JJ., dissenting); *Frisbie v. United States*, 157 U.S. 160 (1895); *Allgeyer v. Louisiana*, 165 U.S. 578 (1897); *Holden v. Hardy*, 169 U.S. 366 (1898).
46. E.g., *Lochner v. New York*, 198 U.S. 45 (1905); *Adair v. United States*, 208 U.S. 161 (1968); *Adkins v. Children's Hospital*, 261 U.S. 525 (1923).
47. Theodore Roosevelt, *Autobiography* (1919), reprinted as *The Autobiography of Theodore Roosevelt* 334 (1958).
48. Pound, "Liberty of Contract," 18 Yale L. J. 454, 462 (1909).
49. Id. at 464.
50. 187 U.S. 606 (1903).
51. Id. at 608–9.
52. Holmes to Laski, in 1 Howe, ed., *supra* n.19 at 51.
53. Id. at 42.
54. Holmes, *Collected Legal Papers, supra* n.14 at 306.
55. *Lochner v. New York, supra* n.46 at 75 (dissent).
56. *Adair v. United States, supra* n.46 at 191 (dissent).
57. Holmes to Laski, in 1 Howe, ed., *supra* n.19 at 21.
58. 236 U.S. 1 (1915).
59. Id. at 26, 27 (dissent).
60. *Adams v. Tanner, supra* n.40.
61. *Truax v. Corrigan*, 257 U.S. 312, 354 (1922) (dissent).
62. *Burns Baking Co. v. Bryan*, 264 U.S. 504, 517 (1924) (dissent).
63. Brandeis, "The Anti-Bar Law," address before the Joint Committee on Liquor Law of the Massachusetts Legislature, Feb. 27, 1891, in *Public Papers, supra* n.27.
64. *Hamilton v. Kentucky Distilleries Co.*, 251 U.S. 146 (1919).
65. *Jacob Ruppert v. Caffey*, 251 U.S. 264 (1920).
66. *United States v. One Ford Coupe*, 272 U.S. 321 (1926).
67. *Lambert v. Yellowley*, 272 U.S. 581 (1926).
68. Holmes to Laski, in 1 Howe, ed., *supra* n.19 at 8.
69. *Abrams v. United States*, 250 U.S. 616, 630 (1919) (dissent).
70. Id.
71. 205 U.S. 454 (1907).
72. 236 U.S. 273 (1915).
73. 249 U.S. 47 (1919).
74. Id. at 52.

75. *Abrams v. U.S.*, *supra* n.69 at 624 (dissent).
76. 251 U.S. 466 (1920).
77. Id. at 482 (dissent).
78. Id. at 482–83.
79. 252 U.S. 239, 253 (1920) (dissent).
80. 254 U.S. 325 (1920).
81. Quoted in Z. Chafee, *Free Speech in the United States* 290 (1941).
82. 268 U.S. 652 (1925).
83. Id. at 673 (dissent).
84. 274 U.S. 357 (1927).
85. Id. at 372, 379 (concurrence).
86. 283 U.S. 697 (1931).
87. Id. at 708.
88. 282 U.S. 251 (1931).
89. *Thomas v. Collins*, 323 U.S. 516 (1945).
90. See generally R. Cushman, "Clear and Present Danger in Free Speech Cases," in M. Konvitz and A. Murphy, *Essays in Political Theory* 311 (1948).
91. J. Frank, *Law and the Modern Mind* 253 (1930).
92. See generally Rogat, "Mr. Justice Holmes: A Dissenting Opinion," 15 Stan. L. Rev. 3, 254 (1963).
93. E.g., Mason, *supra* n.28 at 567: Brandeis's "stand in [cases involving] 'moral' issues" was "strangely out of key with his customary liberalism."

9

1. See generally R. Murray, *The Harding Era* (1969).
2. Blaustein and Mersky, "Rating Supreme Court Justices," 58 A.B.A.J. 1183, 1186 (1972).
3. No claim is made here that a single individual, even a President, can determine the nomination of a Supreme Court Justice. The process of securing a nomination to the Court is a complex one involving the interactions of numerous individual people, not to mention outside events.
4. William Howard Taft to Horace D. Taft, Oct. 6, 1921, William Howard Taft Papers, Library of Congress.
5. Taft to Helen Taft Manning, id., June 11, 1923.
6. Mason, "William Howard Taft," in 3 L. Friedman and F. Israel, *The Justices of the Supreme Court* 2103, 2113 (4 vols. 1969).
7. Id. at 2114. The case was *Sonneborn Bros. v. Cureton*, 262 U.S. 506 (1923).
8. Taft to Helen Taft Manning, *supra* n.5.
9. Taft to Horace D. Taft, June 7, 1921, *supra* n.4.
10. Taft to Helen Taft Manning, *supra* n.5.
11. W. Taft, *The Anti-Trust Act and the Supreme Court* 33 (1914).
12. Taft to Horace D. Taft, Sept. 13, 1922, Taft Papers.
13. Taft to Walter H. Sanborn, Dec. 15, 1910, Taft Papers.
14. See generally Bickel, "Mr. Taft Rehabilitates the Court," 79 Yale L. J. 1, 25–45 (1969).
15. Id. at 36.
16. Taft to Sanborn, *supra* n.13.

17. See Taft, "The Right of Private Property," 3 Mich, Law Journal 215 (1894).
18. See generally L. Gould, *Wyoming: A Political History, 1868–1896* (1968).
19. *United States v. Northern Securities Co.*, 120 F.721 (C.C.D. Minn. 1903); *United States v. Standard Oil Co.*, 173 F.177 (C.C.E.D. Mo. 1909).
20. *United States v. Union Pacific R.R.*, 188 F.102 (C.C.D. Utah 1911).
21. *National Photograph Co. v. Schegel*, 128 F. 733 (8th Cir. 1904).
22. *Dr. Miles Medical Co. v. Park & Sons Co.*, 220 U.S. 373 (1911).
23. E.g., *Chicago & N.W. Ry. v. Andrews*, 130 F.65 (8th Cir. 1904); *St. Louis & S.F.R.R. v. Dewees*, 153 F.56 (8th Cir. 1907); *Great Northern Ry. v. Hooker*, 170 F.154 (8th Cir. 1909).
24. *Chicago, M. & St. P. Ry. v. Voelker*, 129 F.522; (8th Cir. 1904); *Great Northern Ry. v. United States*, 155 F.945 (8th Cir. 1907); *Union Stockyards Co. v. United States*, 169 F.404 (1909).
25. See Philadelphia North American, Dec. 14, 1910; Saturday Evening Post, March 18, 1911, quoted in Bickel, *supra* n.14 at 43–44.
26. Taft to Warren G. Harding, Dec. 4, 1922, Taft Papers.
27. Sutherland, "The Law and the People," Sen. Doc. No. 328, 63d Cong., 2d Sess. 3 (1913).
28. Id. at 3–5.
29. See generally J. Paschal, *Mr. Justice Sutherland* 3–36 (1951).
30. Id. at 111.
31. Taft to George Sutherland, July 2, 1921, Taft Papers.
32. John Clarke to Taft, Sept. 12, 1922, Taft Papers.
33. D. Danelski, *A Supreme Court Justice Is Appointed* 67 (1964).
34. New York World, Nov. 25, 1922, quoted in id. at 90.
35. See id. at 18–19.
36. Id. at 13.
37. Taft to Pierce Butler, Oct. 25, 1922, Taft Papers.
38. See S. Early, "James Clark McReynolds and the Judicial Process" 43–45 (doctoral dissertation, University of Virginia, 1954).
39. Taft to Helen Taft Manning, *supra* n.5.
40. Id.
41. The comments are from, respectively, D. Pearson and R. Allen, *The Nine Old Men* 222 (1936); H. Robinson, *Fantastic Interim* 257 (1943); 13 Fortune 85 (May, 1936); Time, Dec. 4, 1939, at 14.
42. McReynolds, extemporaneous dissent in *Norman v. Baltimore & Ohio R.R.*, 294 U.S. 240, 361 (1935), reprinted in *Wall Street Journal*, Feb. 23, 1935.
43. *Home Bldg. & Loan Assn. v. Blaisdell*, 290 U.S. 398 (1934); *Nebbia v. New York*, 291 U.S. 502 (1934).
44. 291 U.S. 502, 556 (1934).
45. Taft to Horace Taft, June 8, 1928, Taft Papers.
46. *Panama Refining Co. v. Ryan*, 293 U.S. 388 (1935).
47. *Norman v. Baltimore & Ohio R.R.*, *supra* n.42; *Nortz v. United States*, 294 U.S. 317 (1935); *Perry v. United States*, 294 U.S. 330 (1935).
48. Extemporaneous dissent in *Norman v. Baltimore & Ohio R.R. supra* n.42.
49. J. McReynolds to R. P. McReynolds, Feb. 23, 1935, McReynolds Papers, Alderman Library, University of Virginia.
50. Id.
51. *Schechter Corp. v. United States*, 295 U.S. 495 (1935); *Humphrey's Executor v. United States*, 295 U.S. 602 (1935); *Jones v. Securities Commission*, 298 U.S. 1 (1936).
52. *Retirement Board v. Alton R. Co.*, 295 U.S. 330 (1935).
53. *United States v. Butler*, 297 U.S. 1 (1936).

54. *Carter v. Carter Coal Co.*, 298 U.S. 238 (1936).
55. *Ashton v. Cameron County Dist.*, 298 U.S. 513 (1936).
56. *Morehead v. New York ex rel. Tipaldo*, 298 U.S. 587 (1936).
57. *Associated Industries v. Dept. of Labor*, 229 U.S. 515 (1936).
58. F. Rodell, *Nine Men* 221 (1955).
59. Id. at 249.
60. *West Coast Hotel Co. v. Parrish*, 300 U.S. 379, 390 (1937).
61. 261 U.S. 525 (1923).
62. *Labor Board v. Jones & Laughlin*, 301 U.S. 1 (1937).
63. *Associated Press v. Labor Board*, 301 U.S. 103 (1937).
64. *Senn v. Tile Layers Union*, 301 U.S. 468 (1937).
65. *Carmichael v. Southern Coal Co.*, 301 U.S. 495 (1937).
66. *Steward Machine Co. v. Davis*, 301 U.S. 548 (1937).
67. *Mulford v. Smith*, 307 U.S. 38 (1939).
68. *United States v. Bekins*, 304 U.S. 27 (1938).
69. *Electric Bond Co., v. Comm'n*, 303 U.S. 419 (1938); *Tennessee Electric Power Co. v. Tennessee Valley Authority*, 306 U.S. 118 (1939).
70. *United States v. Morgan*, 307 U.S. 183 (1939).
71. *United States v. Caroline Products Co.*, 304 U.S. 144 (1938).
72. Cushman, "Constitutional Law in 1938–1939," 34 Am. Pol. Sci. Rev. 249 (1940).
73. Sutherland was ranked a "near great" justice in the 1972 survey cited in Blaustein and Mersky, *supra* n.1 at 1185.
74. *United States v. Butler*, *supra* n.53 at 62.
75. See White, "The Evolution of Reasoned Elaboration," 59 Va. L. Rev. 279, 281–82 (1973).

10

1. See, e.g., G. Gunther, ed., *John Marshall's Defense of McCulloch v. Maryland* (1969).
2. Oliver Wendell Holmes to Sir Frederick Pollock, Sept. 24, 1910, in 1 *Holmes-Pollock Letters* 170 (M. Howe ed., 1961).
3. 18 Stat. 470.
4. F. Frankfurter and J. Landis, *The Business of the Supreme Court* 60 (1928).
5. Act of April 9, 1866, 14 Stat. 27; Act of April 20, 1871, 17 Stat. 13.
6. Act of Feb. 18, 1861, 12 Stat. 130.
7. Act of Feb. 25, 1889, 25 Stat. 693.
8. Act of Feb. 5, 1867, 14 Stat. 385; Act of March 3, 1885, 23 Stat. 437.
9. Act of June 1, 1872, 17 Stat. 196.
10. 26 Stat. 826.
11. Act of Feb. 13, 1925, 43 Stat. 936.
12. C. Hughes, *The Autobiographical Notes of Charles Evans Hughes* 164–65 (D. Danelski and J. Tulchin, eds., 1973). See generally H. Hart and H. Wechsler, *The Federal Courts and the Federal System*, 36–41 (2d ed., 1973).
13. Quoted in Putnam, "Recollections of Chief Justice Fuller," 22 Green Bag 526, 529 (1910).

14. Hughes to Merlo J. Pusey, May 15, 1946, quoted in 1 M. Pusey, *Charles Evans Hughes* 283 (1951).

15. Hughes, *supra* n.12 at 164.

16. See generally Dunham, "Mr. Chief Justice Stone," in A. Dunham and P. Kurland, eds., *Mr. Justice* (1964).

17. *Girouard v. United States*, 328 U.S. 61 (1946). The earlier case which the *Girouard* majority disapproved was *United States v. Macintosh*, 283 U.S. 605 (1931).

18. Mary Connelly Hughes to Charles Evans Hughes, quoted in 1 Pusey, *supra* n.14 at 39.

19. McElwain, "The Business of the Supreme Court as Conducted by Chief Justice Hughes," 63 Harv. L. Rev. 5, 6 (1949).

20. Id. at 9.

21. Id.

22. See generally S. Haber, *Efficiency and Uplift* (1964).

23. Chafee, "Charles Evans Hughes," 93 Proceedings of the American Philosophical Society 267, 279 (1949); Danelski and Tulchin in Hughes, *supra* n.12 at xv.

24. Quoted in 1 Pusey, *supra* n.14 at 377.

25. Quoted in B. Glad, *Charles Evans Hughes and the Illusions of Innocence* 121 (1966).

26. F. Frankfurter, in *Of Laws and Men* 147 (P. Elman, ed., 1956).

27. C. Hyde, "Charles Evans Hughes," in 10 S. Bemis, ed., *The American Secretaries of State and Their Diplomacy* 327–28 (1929).

28. Holmes to Pollock, June 12, 1916, in 1 *Holmes-Pollock Letters*, *supra* n.2 at 237.

29. *Proceedings of the Bar and Officers of the Supreme Court of the United States in Memory of Charles Evans Hughes* 127 (1950).

30. Frankfurter, *supra* n.26 at 147–48.

31. E.g., Hughes to Antoinette Carter Hughes, Aug. 8, 1894, Papers of Charles Evans Hughes, Library of Congress.

32. Quoted in Glad, *supra* n. 25 at 109.

33. Hughes, 9 *Proceedings of American Law Institute* 44, 49 (1931).

34. C. Hughes, *Addresses 1906–1916* 247 (1916).

35. In this vein Paul Freund's "unperceptive" and "unfriendly" critic who said that Hughes "possessed one of the finest minds of the eighteenth century" was perhaps not so blind, if unsympathetic. See Freund, "Mr. Justice Brandeis," in A. Dunham and P. Kurland, *supra* n.16 at 177.

36. *Minnesota v. Blasius*, 290 U.S. 1 (1933).

37. *Minnesota Rate Cases*, 230 U.S. 352 (1913); *Houston & Texas Ry. v. United States* (Shreveport Case), 234 U.S. 342 (1914).

38. *Schechter Corp. v. United States*, 295 U.S. 495 (1935).

39. *Crowell v. Benson*, 285 U.S. 22 (1931).

40. *St. Joseph Stock Yards Co. v. U.S.*, 298 U.S. 38 (1936).

41. *Bailey v. Alabama*, 219 U.S. 219 (1911); *Norris v. Alabama*, 294 U.S. 587 (1935); *United States v. Macintosh*, *supra* n.17.

42. *Stromberg v. California*, 283 U.S. 359 (1931); *Near v. Minnesota*, 283 U.S. 697 (1931).

43. *Minersville School District v. Gobitis*, 310 U.S. 586 (1940); *Cox v. New Hampshire*, 312 U.S. 569 (1941).

44. *St. Joseph Stock Yards Co. v. U.S.*, *supra* n.40.

45. Hughes, Address to the Federal Judges of the Fourth Circuit at Asheville, N.C. (1932), quoted in 2 Pusey, *supra* n.14 at 693.

46. Id. quoted in 2 Pusey, *supra* n.14 at 691.

47. Stone, "The Tenement House Decision," quoted in A. Mason, *Harlan Fiske Stone* 117 (1956).

48. Hand to Harlan Fiske Stone, May 29, 1930, Stone Papers, Library of Congress.

49. *Norman v. Baltimore & O. R. Co.*, 294 U.S. 240 (1935); *Nortz v. United States*, 294 U.S. 317 (1935); *Perry v. United States*, 294 U.S. 330 (1935).

50. *Retirement Board v. Alton R. Co.*, 295 U.S. 330 (1935).

51. D. Danelski, *A Supreme Court Justice Is Appointed* 185 (1964).

52. E.g., Charles Collier on a portion of Roberts's opinion in *United States v. Butler:* "a genuine logical disaster." Collier, "Judicial Bootstraps and the General Welfare Clause," 4 Geo. Wash. L. Rev. 211, 227 (1936).

53. *Labor Board v. Jones & Laughlin*, 301 U.S. 1 (1936); *Labor Board v. Clothing Co.*, 301 U.S. 58 (1936); *Associated Press v. Labor Board*, 301 U.S. 103 (1936).

54. *Senn v. Tile Layers Union*, 301 U.S. 468 (1937).

55. *Carmichael v. Southern Coal Co.*, 301 U.S. 495 (1937).

56. *Steward Machine Co. v. Davis*, 301 U.S. 548 (1937).

57. *Mulford v. Smith*, 307 U.S. 38 (1938).

58. *United States v. Bekins*, 304 U.S. 27 (1938).

59. *Ashton v. Cameron County Dist.*, 298 U.S. 513 (1936).

60. *Alabama Power Co. v. Ickes*, 302 U.S. 464 (1938); *Tennessee Electric Power Co. v. Tennessee Valley Authority*, 306 U.S. 118 (1939).

61. *Mahnich v. Southern Steamship Co.*, 321 U.S. 96, 105, 112 (1944) (dissent).

62. *Smith v. Allwright*, 321 U.S. 649, 666, 669 (1944) (dissent).

63. *Mahnich v. Southern Steamship Co.*, supra n.61 at 113.

64. Freund, Book Review, 65 Harv. L. Rev. 370 (1951).

65. Quoted in Mason, *supra* n.47 at 789.

66. Stone to John Bassett Moore, May 17, 1932, Papers of Harlan Fiske Stone, Library of Congress.

67. See 2 H. Ickes, *The Secret Diary of Harold L. Ickes* 552 (1953).

68. C. Hughes, *The Supreme Court of the United States* 67 (1928).

69. 287 U.S. 45 (1932).

70. Attributed to Stone by Mason, *supra* n.47 at 488.

71. Unidentified Justice to Stone, quoted in id. at 794.

72. Hughes told Merlo Pusey that he felt that "every Justice should have a chance to demonstrate through the writeup of opinions the wide range of his reasoning powers and not be kept before the public as an extremist or specialist working in one particular groove." Hughes to Pusey, May 28, 1947, quoted in Pusey, "Charles Evans Hughes" in Dunham and Kurland, *supra* n.16 at 161.

73. Quoted in E. Gerhart, *America's Advocate* 165 (1958).

74. See, e.g., *United States v. Morgan*, 307 U.S. 183 (1939).

75. E.g., *South Carolina Highway Department v. Barnwell Bros.*, 303 U.S. 177 (1938); *United States v. Carolene Products Co.*, 304 U.S. 144 (1938); *Minersville School District v. Gobitis*, 310 U.S. 586 (1940).

76. See, e.g., *Bailey v. Alabama*, supra n.41; *Frank v. Mangrum*, 237 U.S. 309, 345 (1915) (dissent); *Stromberg v. California*, supra. n.42; *United States v. Macintosh*, supra n.42; *Near v. Minnesota*, supra n.42; *Brown v. Mississippi*, 297 U.S. 278 (1936); *Lomax v. Texas*, 313 U.S. 544 (1941).

77. Cf. Stone, "The Common Law in the United States," 50 Harv. L. Rev. 4, 25 (1936).

78. [N. Butler], *Annual Report of the President of Columbia University* 27–28 (1922).

79. Stone to John Bassett Moore, April 24, 1923, Stone Papers.

80. 201 N.Y. 271 (1911).

81. H. Stone, *Law and Its Administration* 152 (1915).
82. Quoted in Mason, *supra* n.47 at 116.
83. Stone, "Introduction," in T. Beale, ed., *Man versus the State* (1916), quoted in Mason, *supra* n.66 at 119.
84. Stone, *supra* n.81 at 43–44.
85. [Morris Cohen], Book Review, 11 New Republic 227 (1917).
86. Stone, "Some Aspects of the Problem of Law Simplification," 23 Colum. L. Rev. 319, 334 (1923).
87. Id. at 328.
88. Stone to Beryl H. Levy, Oct. 1, 1938, Stone Papers.
89. Stone, *supra* n.77 at 23.
90. E.g., *United States v. Classic*, 313 U.S. 299 (1941).
91. Cf. Dunham in A. Dunham and P. Kurland, *supra* n.16 at 242.
92. *South Carolina Highway Department v. Barnwell Bros.*, *supra* n.75.
93. Stone, Address to Twelfth Annual Judicial Conference of the Fourth Circuit, June 19, 1942, quoted in Mason, *supra* n.47 at 591.
94. *Supra*, n.90.
95. 295 U.S. 45 (1935).
96. *Supra*, n.62.
97. See Mason, *supra* n.47 at 615–16.
98. *Supra* n.62 at 670 (dissent).
99. Stone to Hugo L. Black, Jan. 17, 1946, Stone Papers.
100. 327 U.S. 1 (1945).
101. 320 U.S. 81 (1943).
102. Id. at 100.
103. 323 U.S. 214 (1944).
104. 327 U.S. 304 (1946).
105. 323 U.S. 214, 242 (dissent).
106. Id. at 233 (dissent).
107. 327 U.S. 304, 322.
108. Stone to Black, Stone Papers, *supra* n.99.
109. *Viereck v. United States*, 318 U.S. 236 (1943); *Schneiderman v. United States*, 320 U.S. 118 (1943); *Baumgartner v. United States*, 322 U.S. 655 (1944); *Hartzel v. United States*, 322 U.S. 680 (1944); *Cramer v. United States*, 325 U.S. 1 (1945); *Keegan v. United States*, 325 U.S. 478 (1945).
110. Quoted in A. Mason, *supra* n.47 at 684.
111. *N.L.R.B. v. Fainblatt*, 306 U.S. 601 (1939); *N.L.R.B. v. Fansteel Metallurgical Co.*, 306 U.S. 240, 263 (1939) (partial concurrence).
112. 49 Stat. 449.
113. *Apex Hosiery Co. v. Leader*, 310 U.S. 469 (1940).
114. *Allen Bradley Co. v. Brotherhood of Electrical Workers*, 325 U.S. 797 (1945).
115. See generally Mason, *supra* n.47 at 131–38.
116. Quoted in id. at 401.
117. Stone to D. Lawrence Groner, Aug. 17, 1941, quoted in P. Fish, *The Politics of Federal Judicial Administration* 259 (1973).
118. Mason, *supra* n.47 at 791. Frankfurter privately referred to "the habit of Stone . . . of carrying on a running debate with any Justice who expresses views different from his," which Frankfurter felt produced "an inevitable dragging out of the discussion." Diary, Jan. 9, 1943, Frankfurter Papers, Library of Congress.
119. Quoted in Mason, *supra* n.47 at 792.
120. Stone to Joseph Strauss, May 5, 1937, Stone Papers.
121. Stone, "The Chief Justice," 27 A.B.A.J. 407, 408 (1941).

122. Quoted in Mason, *supra* n.47, at 591.

123. Quoted in id. at 769.

124. Quoted in id. at 627.

125. See, e.g., id. at 616.

126. *Mercoid Corp. v. Mid-Continent Investment Co.*, 320 U.S. 661, 672 (1944). By 1943 Frankfurter was referring to "the earlier days here when Black talked more freely to me." He complained to Jackson that "every time we have that which should be merely an intellectual difference [it] gets into a championship by Black of justice and right and decency and everything and those who take the other view are impliedly always made out to be the oppressors of the people and the supporters of some exploiting interest." Diary, January 30, 1943, *supra* n.118.

127. *Jewell Ridge Coal Corp. v. United Mine Workers of America*, 325 U.S. 161 (1945).

128. The details of the Roberts letter incident are described in chap. 11.

129. *Houston Post*, quoted in Mason, *supra* n.47 at 624.

130. Sears, "The Supreme Court and the New Deal—An Answer to Texas," 12 U. Chi. L. Rev. 140, 176 (1945).

131. Stone, *supra* n.121 at 408.

11

1. See generally W. Twining, *Karl Llewellyn and the Realist Movement* (1973); E. Purcell, *The Crisis of Democratic Theory* (1973).

2. The relation of Process Jurisprudence to Realism is discussed in Ackerman, Book Review, 103 Daedalus 119 (1974), and White, "The Evolution of Reasoned Elaboration," 59 Va. L. Rev. 279 (1973). In the latter article I used the term "reasoned elaboration" primarily to denote an aspect of the general perspective I am now characterizing as Process Jurisprudence. "Reasoned elaboration" most accurately refers to an approach to the writing of judicial opinions; it is a particular canon of a larger "process" theory. But portions of my article suggested also that "reasoned elaboration" could be used to designate a school of jurisprudence. I now withdraw that suggestion.

3. The phrase was coined by Karl Llewellyn in "A Realistic Jurisprudence—The Next Step," 30 Colum. L. Rev. 431 (1930). For a fuller discussion of Realism see chap. 13.

4. Purcell, "American Jurisprudence Between the Wars," 75 Am. Hist. Rev. 424 (1969); White, *supra* n.2.

5. For examples see L. Fuller, *The Law in Quest of Itself* (1940); Fuller, "Reason and Fiat in Case Law," 59 Harv. L. Rev. 376 (1943); H. Hart and A. Sacks, *The Legal Process* (tent. ed., 1958).

6. Frankfurter, "Mr. Justice Jackson," 68 Harv. L. Rev. 937, 938 (1954).

7. *United States v. Women's Sportswear Mfg. Assn.*, 336 U.S. 460, 464 (1949).

8. A collection is found in E. Gerhart, *Lawyer's Judge* 121–38 (1961).

9. Jackson to Eugene C. Gerhart, Oct. 8, 1948, quoted in E. Gerhart, *America's Advocate* 36 (1958).

10. Quoted in id. at 62.

11. R. Jackson, "Reminiscences," Columbia University Oral History Project, quoted in Kurland, "Robert H. Jackson," 4 L. Friedman and F. Israel, *The Justices of the United States Supreme Court* 2543 (4 vols., 1969).

12. Quoted in Gerhart, *supra* n.9 at 63.

13. Quoted in Kurland, *supra* n.11 at₂.
14. Quoted in Gerhart, *supra* n.9 at 63.
15. Quoted in Gerhart, *supra* n.9 at 63.
16. Quoted in Kurland, *supra* n.11 at 2563.
17. Quoted in ibid.
18. H. Ickes, 3 *The Secret Diary of Harold L. Ickes* 267 (3 vols., 1954).
19. See generally Gerhart, *supra* n.9 at 229–31.
20. See Kurland, *supra* n.11 at 2547–48.
21. Quoted in Gerhart, *supra* n.9 at 41.
22. Gerhart, *supra* n.11 at 241.
23. Arthur Krock to Eugene Gerhart, May 7, 1949, quoted in Gerhart, *supra* n.11 at 242.
24. 315 U.S. 289 (1942).
25. *Tennessee Coal, Iron & R.R. Co. v. Muscoda Local 123*, 321 U.S. 590 (1944); *Jewell Ridge Coal Corp. v. United Mine Workers of America*, 325 U.S. 161 (1945).
26. The full text of the letter is quoted in A. Mason, *Harlan Fiske Stone* 765–66 (1956).
27. Hugo Black to Stanley Reed, Aug. 20, 1945, quoted in id. at 766.
28. Jackson to Stone, Sept. 8, 1945, Stone Papers, Library of Congress.
29. See A. Mason, *Harlan Fiske Stone* 768 (1956).
30. Id. at 769.
31. Stone to Jackson, March 1, 1946, Stone Papers.
32. Gerhart, *supra* n.9 at 280.
33. Jackson to Eugene C. Gerhart, Oct. 8, 1948, quoted in Gerhart, *supra* n.9 at 278.
34. Rodell, "Supreme Court Postcript," 10 Progressive 5 (May, 1946).
35. Jackson to Eugene C. Gerhart, Oct. 25, 1949, cited in Gerhart, *supra* n.9 at 493n–94n.
36. Gerhart, *supra* n.9 at 494n.
37. *Washington Evening Star*, May 16, 1946, p. 15.
38. *New York Times*, June 11, 1946, p. 2.
39. Id.
40. *Jordan v. DeGeorge* 341 U.S. 223, 241 (1951).
41. *Massachusetts v. United States*, 333 U.S. 611, 635, 639–40 (1948) (dissent).
42. 317 U.S. 111 (1942).
43. *Duckworth v. Arkansas*, 314 U.S. 390, 397, 400 (1941) (concurrence).
44. Id. at 401.
45. Id.
46. *McCarroll v. Dixie Greyhound Lines, Inc.*, 309 U.S. 176, 183, 188–89 (1940) (dissent).
47. Id., at 189.
48. *H. P. Hood & Sons, Inc. v. DuMond*, 336 U.S. 525, 545, 554 (1949) (dissent).
49. R. Jackson, *The Supreme Court in the American System of Government* 66–67 (1955).
50. Id. at 67.
51. Id.
52. *Duckworth v. Arkansas, supra* n.43.
53. *H. P. Hood & Sons, Inc. v. Dumond, supra* n.48.
54. *Independent Warehouses Inc. v. Scheele*, 331 U.S. 70 (1947).
55. *Miller Bros. Co. v. Maryland*, 347 U.S. 340 (1954).
56. *General Trading Co. v. State Tax Comm'n*, 322 U.S. 335 (1944).
57. *State Tax Comm'n v. Aldrich*, 316 U.S. 174, 185 (1942) (dissent).
58. *H. P. Hood & Sons, Inc. v. DuMond, supra* n.48 at 533–34.

59. Jackson, *supra* n.49 at 67.

60. *West Virginia State Bd. of Educ. v. Barnette*, 319 U.S. 624, 638 (1943).

61. Id. at 640.

62. *Brinegar v. United States*, 338 U.S. 160, 180 (1949) (dissent).

63. *Harris v. United States*, 331 U.S. 145, 195 (1947) (dissent); *McDonald v. United States*, 335 U.S. 451, 457 (1948) (concurrence). But see *On Lee v. United States*, 343 U.S. 747 (1952).

64. *Saia v. New York*, 334 U.S. 558, 566 (1948) (dissent).

65. *Terminello v. Chicago*, 337 U.S. 1, 13 (1949) (dissent).

66. *Beauharnais v. Illinois*, 343 U.S. 250, 287 (1952) (dissent). Jackson's dissent in the case, in which an Illinois statute providing criminal penalties for slanderous remarks based on race was sustained as applied against a white resident of Chicago who had distributed racist leaflets, did not quarrel with the majority's holding that such forms of speech could be adjudged criminal offenses.

67. *Dennis v. United States*, 341 U.S. 494, 561 (1951) (concurrence).

68. *Watts v. Indiana*, 338 U.S. 49, 58 (1949) (concurrence).

69. *Brinegar v. United States*, *supra* n.62 at 183.

70. *Price v. Johnston*, 334 U.S. 266, 295, 301 (1948) (dissent).

71. *United States ex rel. Knauff v. Shaughnessy*, 338 U.S. 537, 550, 551 (1950) (dissent).

72. *Watts v. Indiana*, *supra* n.68 at 61–62.

73. See generally C. Pritchett, *Civil Liberties and the Vinson Court* (1954).

74. Jackson to Eugene C. Gerhart, Oct. 8, 1948, quoted in Gerhart, *supra* n.8 at 304.

75. Jackson, *supra* n.49 at 79.

76. Id. at 57–58.

77. *Jewell Ridge Coal Corp. v. United Mine Workers*, *supra* n.25 at 170 (dissent); *Wallace Corp. v. NLRB*, 323 U.S. 248, 257 (1944) (dissent); *Farmers Reservoir & Irrigation Co. v. McComb*, 337 U.S. 755, 770 (1949) (dissent).

78. With the exception of certain wartime cases involving persons of Japanese or German ancestry. See discussion above, chap. 10.

79. *Terminello v. Chicago*, *supra* n.65 at 37.

80. *State Tax Comm'n v. Aldrich*, *supra* n.57 at 185.

81. Stone to Sterling Carr, Dec. 4, 1945, Stone Papers.

82. See Gerhart, *supra* n.9 at 256–57.

83. Jackson, "The Rule of Law among Nations," 39 Am. Soc'y Int'l L. Proc. 10, 15–16 (1945).

84. 19 International Military Tribunal, *Trial of the Major War Criminals* 400, 415–17 (42 vols., 1947).

85. 2 id. at 155, 99.

86. 2 id. at 101, 155.

87. Jackson, Introduction, in W. Harris, *Tyranny on Trial* xxvii (1954).

88. 2 International Military Tribunal, *Trial of the Major War Criminals* 101.

89. E.g., Hart and Sacks, *supra* n.5.

12

1. See generally E. Purcell, *The Crisis of Democratic Theory* (1973).

2. W. Twining, *Karl Llewellyn and the Realist Movement* 10–55 (1973); Purcell, *supra* n.1 at 3–11.

3. Examples are Pound, "The Scope and Purpose of Sociological Jurisprudence," 24 Harv. L. Rev. 591 (1911), and Pound, "The Theory of Judicial Decision," 36 Harv. L. Rev. 641, 802, 940 (1923).

4. A "representative" example of the multifaceted theory of judging articulated by Realists is more difficult to set forth. Articles illustrating various aspects of the theory are Moore, "Rational Basis of Legal Institutions," 23 Colum. L. Rev. 609 (1923); Cook, "Scientific Method and the Law," 13 A.B.A.J. 303 (1927); Llewellyn, "Realistic Jurisprudence—The Next Step," 30 Colum. L. Rev. 431 (1930); and Frank, "Realism in Jurisprudence," 7 Am. L. School Rev. 1063 (1934).

5. E.g., Bickel and Wellington, "Legislative Purpose and the Judicial Process: The *Lincoln Mills* Case," 71 Harv. L. Rev. 1 (1957); H. Hart and A. Sacks, *The Legal Process* (tent. ed., 1958); Wechsler, "Toward Neutral Principles of Constitutional Law," 73 Harv. L. Rev. 1 (1959).

6. Hutcheson, "The Judgment Intuitive: The Function of the 'Hunch' in Judicial Decision," 14 Corn. L. Q. 274 (1929).

7. Hart and Sacks, *supra* n.5 at 161ff; see above, chap. 11, n.2.

8. Hand's address was delivered on May 14, 1933. It has been reprinted in I. Dilliard, ed. *The Spirit of Liberty: Papers and Addresses of Learned Hand* 103 (1952). Hereafter cited as Hand, *Spirit of Liberty*.

9. Hand, *Spirit of Liberty*, *supra* n.8 at 178.

10. Among members of Cardozo's family was the author of the words on the base of the Statue of Liberty. See generally Kaufman, "Benjamin Nathan Cardozo," in A. Dunham and P. Kurland, eds., *Mr. Justice* 251 (1964).

11. G. Hellman, *Benjamin N. Cardozo* 10–11, 23 (1940); Kaufman, *supra* n.10 at 252.

12. Cardozo to Aline Goldstone, quoted in Hellman, *supra* n.11 at 49.

13. See Columbia College Yearbook, Cardozo Papers, Rare Book and Manuscript Library, Columbia University. Hereafter cited as Cardozo Papers.

14. Rabbi Stephen S. Wise, a close friend of Cardozo for many years, referred a year after Cardozo's death to "very, very intimate and personal letters exchanged between Cardozo and Ellen. Wise was uncertain whether the letters ought to be published. They are not included in the Cardozo Papers. Wise to George S. Hellman, Jan. 16, 1939, Cardozo Papers, id.

15. Lloyd Stryker, Wall Street Journal, July 12, 1938, Cardozo Papers.

16. Hand orally to Hellman, Nov. 15, 1938. A memorandum of the conversation is in the Cardozo Papers.

17. The comments, in order, are from Wise, New York Times, May 23, 1930; William Lyon Phelps to Hellman, Dec. 14, 1938, Cardozo Papers; Stryker, *supra* n.15; and Judge Ferdinand Pecora, Wall Street Journal, July 12, 1938, Cardozo Papers.

18. Hand to Hellman, *supra* n.16.

19. Kaufman, *supra* n.10, at 254.

20. Corbin, "The Judicial Process Revisited: Introduction," 71 Yale L. J. 195, 197 (1961).

21. See Cardozo, "The Altruist in Politics" (1889) and "Communism" (1889), Cardozo Papers.

22. Butler to Hellman, quoted in Hellman, *supra* n.11 at 21.

23. Hand to Hellman, *supra* n.16.

24. Memorandum, Cardozo Papers.

25. B. Cardozo, *The Nature of the Judicial Process* 28 (1921).

26. Id. at 35–36.

27. Cardozo borrowed this quote from Holmes's "Path of the Law." See id. at 54–55.

28. Id. at 96, 98.

29. Id. at 67.

30. See description in Corbin, *supra* n.20 at 197–98.

31. Kaufman, *supra* n.10 at 260.

32. Cardozo, *supra* n.25 at 105; B. Cardozo, *The Growth of the Law* 56 (1924).

33. B. Cardozo, *The Paradoxes of Legal Science* 135 (1928).

34. Id. at 59.

35. Cardozo, "Law and Literature," 52 Harv. L. Rev. 471, 477 (1939).

36. Cardozo, *supra* n.33 at 57.

37. Hand, "Mr. Justice Cardozo," in Hand, *supra* n.8 at 129, 131.

38. Hand, *supra* n.8 at 122.

39. Hand to Clark, Feb. 23, 1950, quoted in M. Schick, *Learned Hand's Court* 304 (1970).

40. Charles C. Burlingham, "Judge Learned Hand," 60 Harv. L. Rev. 330, 331 (1947).

41. Quoted in H. Shanks, ed., *The Art and Craft of Judging* 6 (1968).

42. Shanks, id. at 7–8.

43. Quoted in id. at 9.

44. Taft to Harding, Dec. 4, 1922, William Howard Taft Papers, Library of Congress.

45. See M. Freedman, *Roosevelt and Frankfurter* 671–76 (1967).

46. Quoted in Shanks, *supra* n.41 at 13.

47. The letter was reprinted in the *New York Times*, June 18, 1961.

48. See Chief Judge J. Edward Lumbard's remarks in 33 N.Y.S. B. J. 410 (1961).

49. Holmes to Frederick Pollock in 2 M. Howe, ed. *Holmes-Pollock Letters* 114 (1961).

50. Cardozo to Peter B. Olney, Feb. 7, 1925, reprinted in Learned Hand Centennial Exhibit, Harvard Law School, Sept. 5–Nov. 5, 1972, p. 7.

51. See A. Mason, *Harlan Fiske Stone* 335 (1956).

52. Hamburger, "The Great Judge," 21 Life 116 (Nov. 4, 1946).

53. Burlingham, "Judge Learned Hand," *supra* n.40 at 332.

54. "Proceedings in Commemoration of Fifty Years of Federal Judicial Service," 264 F. 2d 6, 20 (1959).

55. M. Schick, *supra* n.39 at 155.

56. Id. at 12n, 156.

57. See generally White, "The Rise and Fall of Justice Holmes," 39 U. Chi. L. Rev. 51 (1971).

58. Hand to Stone, February 6, 1934, quoted in Mason, *supra* n.51 at 384.

59. Quoted in Shanks, *supra* n.41 at 14.

60. Hand, *supra* n.8 at 101.

61. Id.

62. Id.

63. Id. at 181.

64. Id. at 109.

65. Id.

66. Id. at 174.

67. L. Hand, *The Bill of Rights* 26 (1958).

68. Hand, "A Plea for the Open Mind and Free Discussion," in I. Dilliard, *The Spirit of Liberty* 274 (1960 ed.).

69. Hand, *supra* n.8 at 180.

70. Hand, *supra* n.67, at 34.

71. Hand *supra* n.8, at 178.

72. Hand, "Proceedings," *supra* n.54, at 28.
73. Hand, *supra* n.68, at 278.
74. Hand, *supra* n.8, at 107.
75. Wyzanski, "Judge Learned Hand's Contributions to Public Law," 60 Harv. L. Rev. 348, 349 (1947).
76. Wyzanski, "Introduction," in L. Hand, *The Bill of Rights* viii (1964 ed.).
77. Hand, "Presentation to the Harvard Law School of a Portrait of Mr. Justice Holmes," quoted in Pepper, "The Literary Style of Learned Hand," 60 Harv. L. Rev. 333 (1947).
78. Hand, *supra* n.8 at 107.
79. Id. at 108.
80. Frank, "Some Reflections on Learned Hand," 24 U. Chi. L. Rev. 666, 668 (1957).
81. *United States v. Rubenstein,* 151 F.2d 915, 919, 920 (2d. Cir., 1945) (dissent).
82. Hand to Mrs. Jerome N. Frank, Jan. 20, 1957, quoted in Schick, *supra* n.39 at 245.
83. See comments by Rebecca West and others, quoted in id. at 34.
84. Clark, "Jerome N. Frank," 66 Yale L. J. 817, 818 (1957).
85. Frank, *supra* n.80 at 666.
86. Pound apparently first used the term in "The Need of a Sociological Jurisprudence," 19 Green Bag 607 (1907).
87. See, e.g., Hand, "The Speech of Justice," 29 Harv. L. Rev. 617 (1916); Pound, "The Theory of Judicial Decision," 36 Harv. L. Rev. 641, 802, 940 (1923).
88. *Supra* n.33 at 60.
89. Hutcheson, *supra* n.6.
90. J. Frank, *Law and the Modern Mind* 239 (1930).
91. See Llewellyn, "Some Realism about Realism," 44 Harv. L. Rev. 1222 (1931), an article identifying and describing leading Realists. Frank had contributed heavily to the article.
92. Cardozo, untitled address, 55 Report of the New York State Bar Association 263, 290 (1932).
93. Id. at 272.
94. Id. at 288–90.
95. Frank, "Cardozo and the Upper Court Myth," 13 Law & Contemp. Prob. 369, 384 (1948).
96. [Frank], "The Speech of Judges: A Dissenting Opinion," 29 Va. L. Rev. 625, 620–32 (1943).
97. Hand to Andrew Kaufman, quoted in Kaufman, *supra* n.10 at 253.
98. *Supra* n.96 at 634.
99. Id. at 636.
100. Id. at 634.
101. Id. at 637.
102. Professor Philip Kurland, who clerked for Frank during the 1944 term, has said in conversation that Frank subsequently regretted the anonymity of the essay. Walton Hamilton, in a eulogy of Frank in 1957, maintained that Frank had nonetheless told him that he "had a hell of a good time" writing the essay. See Hamilton, "The Great Tradition—Jerome Frank," 66 Yale L. J. 821, 822 (1957).
103. See Frank, *supra* n.80 at 672–74.
104. Professor Kurland has maintained that Frank "found it next to impossible to dislike anyone whom he got to know at all well." Kurland, "Jerome N. Frank: Some Reflections and Recollections of a Law Clerk," 24 U. Chi. L. Rev. 661, 663 (1957).

105. See generally Schick, *supra* n.39 at 219–23, and correspondence there cited.
106. Frank to Clark, June 1, 1950, quoted in id. at 219.
107. See, e.g., Yntema, "The Hornbook Method and the Conflict of Laws," 37 Yale L. J. 468 (1928); Moore and Hope, "An Institutional Approach to the Law of Commercial Banking," 38 Yale L. J. 703 (1929).
108. Llewellyn, *supra* n.4 at 444.
109. Frank, *supra* n.90 at 130.
110. Id. at 154.
111. Id. at 147.
112. Id. at 147n.
113. See Frank, "Realism in Jurisprudence," *supra* n.4.
114. See the debate between Hand and Frank in *Repouille v. United States*, 165 F.2d 152 (2d Cir., 1947), where an alien who had administered euthanasia to his monstrously deformed son was denied citizenship on the ground of his "moral character."
115. Frank, "Realism in Jurisprudence," *supra* n.4.
116. Seagle, Book Review, 29 Va. L. Rev. 664 (1943).
117. Lehman, "Judge Cardozo in the Court of Appeals," 52 Harv. L. Rev. 364, 371 (1939); Hand, "Mr. Justice Cardozo," 52 Harv. R. Rev. 361, 362 (1939).
118. *MacPherson v. Buick Motor Co.*, 217 N.Y. 382 (1916).
119. *Palsgraf v. Long Island R.R.*, 248 N.Y. 339 (1928).
120. See generally G. Calabresi, *The Cost of Accidents* (1970).
121. *Sundstrum v. State of New York*, 213 N.Y. 68 (1914); *Wood v. Lucy, Lady Duff-Gordon*, 222 N.Y. 88 (1917).
122. *DeCicco v. Schweizer*, 221 N.Y. 431 (1917); *Allegheny College v. National Chataugua County Bank*, 246 N.Y. 369 (1927).
123. *Helgar Corp. v. Warner's Features*, 222 N.Y. 449 (1918); *Holden v. Efficient Craftsman Corp.*, 234 N.Y. 437 (1923).
124. *Marks v. Cowden*, 226 N.Y. 138, 144 (1919): see *Imperator Realty Co. v. Tull*, 228 N.Y. 447, 453 (1920) (concurrence); *Saltzman v. Barson*, 239 N.Y. 332 (1925).
125. E.g., *DeCicco v. Schweizer*, *supra* n.122, where he enforced an informal promise without any consideration. This decision was reflected in the first edition of the Restatement of Contracts, § 90 (1932).
126. *Wood v. Lucy, Lady Duff-Gordon*, *supra* n.121 at 91.
127. *Winterbottom v. Wright*, 10 M. & W. 109 (1842).
128. 6 N.Y. 397 (1852).
129. *MacPherson v. Buick Motor Co.*, *supra* n.118 at 385.
130. Id. at 386.
131. Id.
132. Id. at 387.
133. Id. at 385.
134. Id. at 387.
135. Brett, J. (Lord Esher) in *Heaven v. Pender*, 11 Q.B.D. 503, 510 (1883).
136. *MacPherson v. Buick Motor Co.*, *supra* n.118 at 389–90.
137. Id. at 389.
138. Id. at 391.
139. Id. at 391.
140. *Torgeson v. Schultz*, 192 N.Y. 156 (1908).
141. Cardozo, *supra* n.25 at 165.
142. Hand, "The Speech of Justice," *supra* n.87.
143. Hand, *supra* n.8 at 109.
144. *Lehigh Valley Coal Co., v. Yensavage*, 218 F.547 (E.D. N.Y., 1914).

145. Hand, *supra* n.8 at 108: see *Borella v. Borden Co.*, 145 F.2d 63 (2d. Cir., 1944).
146. Hand, *supra* n.8 at 181.
147. E.g., *Massachusetts Fire & Marine Ins. Co. v. Commissioner*, 42 F.2d 189 (2d. Cir., 1930); *Niagara Falls Power Co. v. FPC*, 137 F.2d 787 (2d Cir., 1943).
148. Hand, *supra* n.8 at 109.
149. *Fleming v. Arsenal Building Corporation*, 125 F.2d 278 (2d. Cir., 1933); Borella v. Borden Co., *supra* n.142.
150. *Helvering v. Gregory*, 69 F.2d 809 (2d Cir., 1934).
151. *Cabell v. Markham*, 148 F.2d 737 (2d Cir., 1945).
152. *Peter Pan Fabrics, Inc. v. Martin Weiner Corp.*, 274 F.2d 487 (2d Cir., 1960).
153. E.g., *Yale Electric Corporation v. Robertson*, 26 F.2d 972 (2d Cir., 1928); *American Chicle Co. v. Topps Chewing Gum, Inc.* 208 F.2d 560 (2d Cir., 1953).
154. E.g., *Masses Publishing Co. v. Patten*, 244 F.535 (S.D. N.Y., 1917); *United States v. Dennis*, 183 F.2d 201 (2d Cir., 1950).
155. Friendly, "Learned Hand: An Expression From the Second Circuit," 29 Brooklyn L. Rev. 6, 12 (1962).
156. Frank, "On Holding Abe Lincoln's Hat," in B. Kristein, ed., *A Man's Reach* 3, 7 (1965).
157. Frank, "Red, White and Blue Herring," 214 Saturday Evening Post 9 (Dec. 6, 1941); J. Frank, *If Men Were Angels* (1942).
158. E.g., "Cardozo and the Upper Court Myth," *supra* n.95; Frank, " 'Short of Sickness and Death': A Study of Moral Responsibility in Legal Criticism," 26 N.Y.U. L. Rev. 545 (1951).
159. See discussion in J. Frank, *Courts on Trial* 266–80 (1950).
160. For some Warren Court decisions illustrating this view, see *Mapp v. Ohio*, 367 U.S. 643 (1961); *Gideon v. Wainwright*, 372 U.S. 335 (1963); *Miranda v. Arizona*, 384 U.S. 436 (1966).
161. The first expansive reading of the guaranties of the Bill of Rights after World War II came in Justice Black's dissent in *Adamson v. California*, 332 U.S. 46, 68 (1947). No majority of the Warren Court ever adopted Justice Black's position that all of the Bill of Rights was incorporated into the due process clause of the Fourteenth Amendment. But Black's dissent set the stage for the "selective" incorporation of portions of the First, Fourth, Fifth, and Sixth Amendments in the 1950s and 1960s. The subject is considered in more detail in chap. 14.
162. E.g., *United States v. Ebeling*, 146 F.2d 254, 257, 258 (2d Cir., 1944) (dissent).
163. Id. at 258.
164. *United States v. St. Pierre*, 132 F.2d 837, 840 (2d. Cir., 1942) (dissent).
165. *United States v. Mitchell*, 137 F.2d 1006, 1011 (2d Cir., 1943) (dissent).
166. *United States v. Ausmeier*, 152 F.2d 349, 356 (2d Cir., 1945).
167. *United States v. Liss*, 137 F.2d 995, 1001 (2d Cir., 1943) (dissent).
168. *United States v. Rubenstein*, 151 F.2d 915, 919, 924 (2d Cir., 1945) (dissent).
169. *United States v. Antonelli Fireworks Co., Inc.*, 155 F.2d 631, 642 (1946) (dissent).
170. *United States v. Leviton*, 193 F.2d 848, 857 (1951) (dissent.)
171. *In re Fried*, 161 F.2d 453, 457, 458–59 (2d Cir., 1947).
172. *United States v. Leviton*, *supra* n.170; *United States ex rel. Caminito v. Murphy*, 222 F.2d 698 (1955).
173. *United States v. Masciale*, 236 F.2d 601, 604 (2d Cir., 1956) (dissent).
174. *United States v. Scully*, 225 F.2d 113, 116 (2d Cir., 1955) (concurrence).
175. *United States v. Gordon*, 236 F.2d 916 (2d Cir., 1956).
176. *United States v. On Lee*, 193 F.2d 306, 311 (2d Cir., 1951) (dissent).
177. *United States ex rel. Caminito v. Murphy*, *supra* n.172 at 706.

178. E.g., Harris, "Idealism Emergent in Jurisprudence," 10 Tul. L. Rev. 169 (1936); Mechem, "The Jurisprudence of Despair," 21 Iowa L. Rev. 669 (1936). These sentiments were expressed also in two books published in 1940: E. Bodenheimer, *Jurisprudence*, and L. Fuller, *The Law in Quest of Itself.*
179. E.g., *United States v. Ullmann*, 221 F.2d 760 (2d Cir., 1955).
180. 195 F.2d 583 (2d Cir., 1952).
181. Id. at 595–96.
182. J. Frank and B. Frank, *Not Guilty* (1957).
183. H. Hart and A. Sacks, *supra* n.5 at iii.

13

1. For examples, see H. Hart and A. Sacks, *The Legal Process* (tent. ed., 1958); Wechsler, "Toward Neutral Principles of Constitutional Law," 73 Harv. L. Rev. 1 (1959).
2. See Miller & Howell, "The Myth of Neutrality in Constitutional Adjudication," 27 U. Chi. L. Rev. 661 (1960); Clark, "A Plea for the Unprincipled Opinion," 49 Va. L. Rev. 660 (1963). A fuller discussion of the controversy appears in White, "The Evolution of Reasoned Elaboration," 59 Va. L. Rev. 279 (1973).
3. L. Hand, *The Bill of Rights* (1958). Hand's views on constitutional interpretation were more restrictive than those of leading adherents of the process theory. See Wechsler's comments on *The Bill of Rights* in Wechsler, *supra* n. at 2–13.
4. Traynor, "Law and Social Change in a Democratic Society," 1956 U. Ill. L. F. 230, 231.
5. Id. at 232.
6. Traynor, "Badlands in an Appellate Judge's Realm of Reason," 7 Utah L. Rev. 157, 167, 168 (1960).
7. Traynor, "La Rude Vita, La Dolce Giustizia; Or Hard Cases Can Make Good Law," 29 U. Chi. L. Rev. 223, 234 (1962).
8. E.g., Arnold, "Professor Hart's Theology," 73 Harv. L. Rev. 1298 (1960).
9. 24 Cal. 2d 453 (1944).
10. *Goetten v. Owl Drug Co.*, 6 Cal. 2d 683 (1936); *Ward v. Great Atlantic & Pacific Tea Co.*, 231 Mass. 90 (1918), cited in *Escola v. Coca Cola Bottling Co.*, *supra* n.8 at 464.
11. 24 Cal. 2d at 463. Res ipsa loquitur (literally, "the thing speaks for itself") is a doctrine that shifts the burden of proof to tort defendants having sole control over relevant evidence.
12. Id. at 464.
13. Id. at 465.
14. Id. at 466.
15. Id. at 462.
16. *Greenman v. Yuba Power Products, Inc.*, 59 Cal. 2d 57 (1963).
17. 24 Cal. 2d at 467.
18. Traynor, *supra* n.7 at 234.
19. Id. at 235.
20. Id. at 234.
21. Traynor, *supra* n.6 at 163.

22. Id. at 170, 157.
23. Traynor, *supra* n.4 at 236.
24. Traynor, "Statutes Revolving in Common-Law Orbits," 17 Cath. U. L. Rev. 401, 402 (1968).
25. Id. at 402.
26. Traynor, "Reasoning in a Circle of Law," 56 Va. L. Rev. 739, 742 (1970).
27. Id. at 751.
28. Traynor, *supra* n.25 at 402.
29. Id. at 403.
30. Traynor, *supra* n.6 at 164.
31. Id.
32. Traynor, *supra* n.26 at 743.
33. Traynor, *supra* n.23 at 403.
34. Id. at 405.
35. Traynor, *supra* n.6 at 165.
36. Traynor, *supra* n. 25 at 406.
37. Traynor, "Fact Skepticism and the Judicial Process," 106 U. Pa. L. Rev. 635, 638 (1958).
38. Id.
39. Id. at 638, 639.
40. Traynor, "No Magic Words Could Do It Justice," 49 Calif. L. Rev. 615, 622 (1961).
41. Traynor, "Better Days in Court for a New Day's Problems," 17 Vand. L. Rev. 109 (1963).
42. Id.
43. Comment, "Real Property: Landlord and Tenant: The Rule in Dumpor's Case," 14 Calif. L. Rev. 328, 333 (1926).
44. Traynor, *supra* n.40 at 622.
45. Traynor, *supra* n.26 at 753.
46. Traynor, *supra* n.40 at 627.
47. Id. at 627, 628, 629.
48. Traynor, *supra* n.4 at 233.
49. *Freedman v. The Rector*, 37 Cal. 2d 16, 21 (1951); *Barkis v. Scott*, 34 Cal. 2d 116, 122 (1949).
50. *Escola v. Coca Cola Bottling Co.*, *supra* n. 9 at 466.
51. *Seely v. White Motor Co.*, 63 Cal. 2d 9, 15 (1965).
52. *Bernkrant v. Fowler*, 55 Cal. 2d 588, 595, 596 (1961).
53. Traynor, *supra* n.41 at 115n.
54. Traynor, *supra* n.25 at 425.
55. *In re* Estate of Mason, 62 Cal. 2d 213 (1965).
56. Traynor, *supra* n.23 at 419.
57. Traynor, *supra* n.26 at 747–48.
58. Id. at 747.
59. Id. at 748.
60. Id. at 749.
61. Id.
62. Id. at 749, 750, 751.
63. Traynor, *supra* n.37 at 636.
64. Traynor, *supra* n.40 at 628.
65. Id. at 621, 623.
66. Wechsler, *supra* n.1 at 19.
67. Traynor, *supra* n.40 at 624, 625.

68. Id. at 624.
69. Traynor, *supra* n.41 at 121–22.
70. Id. at 124.
71. Traynor, *supra* n.6 at 169. See *Startup v. Pacific Elec. Ry. Co.*, 29 Cal. 2d 866, 872 (1947).
72. Traynor, *supra* n.40 at 616.
73. Traynor, *supra* n.41 at 115.
74. Id. at 112.
75. Id. at 119–21.
76. See generally Traynor, "*Mapp v. Ohio* at Large in the Fifty States," 1962 Duke L. J. 319.
77. *Escola v. Coca Cola Bottling Co.*, *supra* n.9; *Greenman v. Yuba Power Products Co.*, *supra* n.16; *Vandermark v. Ford Motor Co.*, 61 Cal. 2d 256 (1964); *Elmore v. American Motors Corp.*, 70 Cal. 2d 578 (1969).
78. *Malloy v. Fong*, 37 Cal. 2d 356 (1951).
79. *Muskopf v. Corning Hospital Dist.*, 55 Cal. 2d 211 (1961).
80. *Emery v. Emery*, 45 Cal. 2d 421 (1955).
81. *Knight v. Kaiser Co.*, 48 Cal. 2d 778 (1957) (dissent).
82. *State Rubbish, Etc. Ass'n v. Siliznoff*, 38 Cal. 2d 330 (1952).
83. *Laux v. Freed*, 53 Cal. 2d 512, 525 (1960) (concurrence); Estate of Rule, 25 Cal. 2d 1, 17 (1944) (dissent).
84. *Union Oil Co. v. Union Sugar Co.*, 31 Cal. 2d 300 (1948).
85. *Gelhaus v. Nevada Irr. Dist.*, 43 Cal. 2d 779 (1955); *Quader-Kino A. G. v. Nebenzal*, 35 Cal. 2d 287, 297 (1950) (dissent).
86. *Monarco v. Lo Greco*, 35 Cal. 2d 621 (1950).
87. *Drennan v. Star Paving Co.*, 51 Cal. 2d 409 (1958).
88. *Lewis & Queen v. N. M. Ball & Sons*, 48 Cal. 2d 141 (1957); *Fewel & Dawes, Inc. v. Pratt*, 17 Cal. 2d 85 (1941).
89. *Osborn v. Osborn*, 42 Cal. 2d 358 (1954).
90. *Sorenson v. Costa*, 32 Cal. 2d 453 (1948).
91. *Coast Bank v. Minderhout*, 61 Cal. 2d 311 (1964).
92. *Jordan v. Talbort*, 55 Cal. 2d 597 (1961).
93. *Barkis v. Scott*, *supra* n.49.
94. *Bernhard v. Bank of America*, 19 Cal. 2d 807 (1942).
95. Id. at 813. Abandonment of mutuality was not original with Traynor. See *Coca Cola Co. v. Pepsi Cola Co.*, 36 Del. 124 (1934). Traynor's innovation was to foreswear deciding *Bernhard* through use of a widely recognized exception to mutuality in cases involving derivative liability and to face the mutuality doctrine head-on.
96. *Perez v. Sharp*, 32 Cal. 2d 711 (1948).
97. *McLaughlin v. Florida*, 379 U.S. 184 (1964).
98. *Danskin v. San Diego Unified School District*, 28 Cal. 2d 536 (1946).
99. *Speiser v. Randall*, 48 Cal. 2d 903, 904 (1957) (dissent).
100. *Black v. Cutter Laboratories*, 43 Cal. 2d 788, 809 (1955) (dissent).
101. *People v. Gonzales*, 20 Cal. 2d 165 (1942).
102. *People v. Cahan*, 44 Cal. 2d 434 (1955).
103. *Castenda v. Superior Court*, 59 Cal. 2d 439 (1963); *People v. Gorg*, 45 Cal. 2d 776 (1955).
104. *People v. Brown*, 45 Cal. 2d 640 (1955).
105. *Willson v. Superior Court*, 46 Cal. 2d 291 (1956).
106. *People v. Simon*, 45 Cal. 2d 645 (1955).
107. *Jones v. Superior Court*, 58 Cal. 2d 56 (1962).

108. See generally *Pennoyer v. Neff*, 95 U.S. 714 (1878); *Restatement of Conflict of Laws* (1934).

109. *Grant v. McAuliffe*, 41 Cal. 2d 859 (1953); *Emery v. Emery*, 45 Cal. 2d 421 (1955).

110. *Bernkrant v. Fowler, supra* n.52.

111. *Reich v. Purcell*, 67 Cal. 2d 551 (1967).

112. *Bernkrant v. Fowler, supra* n.52.

113. Traynor and Surrey, "New Roads Toward the Settlement of Federal Income, Estate and Gift Tax Controversies," 7 Law & Contemp. Prob. 336 (1940).

114. Traynor, "National Bank Taxation in California," 17 Calif. L. Rev. 83, 232, 456 (1929).

115. See Traynor and Keesling, "Recent Changes in the Bank and Corporation Franchise Tax Act," 21 Calif. L. Rev. 543 (1933), 22 Calif. L. Rev. 499 (1934), 23 Calif. L. Rev. 51 (1934).

116. Ratner, "Reflections of a Traynor Law Clerk," 44 S. Cal. L. Rev. 876A (1971).

117. *West Publishing Co. v. McColgan*, 27 Cal. 2d 705 (1946).

118. *Forster Shipbuilding Co. v. County of Los Angeles*, 54 Cal. 2d 450 (1960).

119. *De Luz Homes, Inc. v. County of San Diego*, 45 Cal. 2d 546 (1955).

120. *Roehm v. County of Orange*, 32 Cal. 2d 280 (1948).

121. *Von Hamm-Young Co. v. San Francisco*, 29 Cal. 2d 798 (1947).

122. Traynor, quoting Justice Charles D. Breitel in Traynor, *supra* n.23 at 402n.

123. See, e.g., Fuller, "Reason and Fiat in Case Law," 59 Harv. L. Rev. 376, 393–94 (1946); R. Dahl, *Who Governs?* (1961); H. Hart and A. Sacks, *The Legal Process, supra* n.1.

14

1. See, e.g., Meyer v. Nebraska, 262 U.S. 390 (1923); Gitlow v. New York, 268 U.S. 652 (1925); Whitney v. California, 274 U.S. 357 (1927).

2. See above, chap. 8.

3. *Minersville School District v. Gobitis*, 310 U.S. 586 (1940); *West Virginia Board of Education v. Barnette*, 319 U.S. 624 (1943).

4. In Justice Frankfurter's Diary for March 12, 1943, the following alleged colloquy between Frankfurter and Justice Douglas is recorded: "Douglas said, 'Hugo [Black] would now not go with you in the Flag Salute Case.' I said, 'Why, has he reread the Constitution during the summer?' Douglas replied, 'No, but he has read the papers.' " Felix Frankfurter Papers, Library of Congress.

5. *Sweatt v. Painter*, 339 U.S. 629 (1950); *McLaurin v. Oklahoma State Regents*, 339 U.S. 637 (1950).

6. *Smith v. Allwright*, 321 U.S. 649 (1944); *Terry v. Adams*, 345 U.S. 461 (1953).

7. *Shelly v. Kraemer*, 334 U.S. 1 (1948); *Hurd v. Hodge*, 334 U.S. 24 (1948).

8. E.g., *Dennis v. United States*, 341 U.S. 494 (1951).

9. 319 U.S. at 643.

10. 371 U.S. x (1962).

11. See, e.g., "Why I Shall Vote For La Follette—VI," 40 New Republic 199 (1924).

12. See generally R. Wiebe, *The Search for Order* (1967); White, "The Social Values of the Progressives," 70 South Atlantic Quarterly 62 (1971).

13. Frankfurter, "The Manager, the Workman, and the Social Scientist," 3 Bull. Taylor Soc'y 8 (1917).

14. Frankfurter, "Law and Order," 9 Yale Rev. 225 (1920).

15. See Levinson, "The Democratic Faith of Felix Frankfurter," 25 Stan. L. Rev. 430, 433 (1973).

16. Frankfurter, *supra* n.11.

17. Frankfurter to Learned Hand, April 6, 1921, quoted in Levinson, *supra* n.15 at 439.

18. Frankfurter to Learned Hand, June 5, 1923, quoted in id. at 440.

19. [Frankfurter], "The Supreme Court as Legislator," 46 New Republic 158 (1926).

20. Frankfurter, "Can the Supreme Court Guarantee Toleration," 43 New Republic 85 (1925).

21. Frankfurter to Charles P. Howland, June 10, 1932, Frankfurter Papers, Library of Congress.

22. F. Frankfurter, *The Public and Its Government* 159 (1964 ed.).

23. V. Hamilton, *Hugo Black: The Alabama Years* 46 (1972).

24. Durr, "Hugo L. Black: A Personal Appraisal," 6 Ga. L. Rev. 1, 6 (1971).

25. J. Frank, *Mr. Justice Black* 46 (1949).

26. D. Meador, *Mr. Justice Black and His Books* 2 (1974).

27. Id. at 9–11.

28. Id. at 13–29.

29. Id. at 14.

30. Id. at 13–29.

31. Frankfurter, "The Red Terror of Judicial Reform," 40 *New Republic* 110, 113 (1924).

32. Frank, "Hugo L. Black," in 3 L. Friedman & F. Israel, *The Justices of the United States Supreme Court* 2321, 2330 (1969).

33. Sacks, "Felix Frankfurter," in 3 id. at 2401, 2403.

34. Frankfurter's Diary, in the Frankfurter Papers in the Library of Congress, is filled with characterizations of his fellow justices that could not have been calculated to win their admiration.

35. A notable exception was Black's nation-wide radio address in 1939 admitting but downplaying his membership in the Ku Klux Klan. That information had become public knowledge during the confirmation proceedings pursuant to his nomination to the Court. See generally J. Frank, *supra* n.25.

36. E.g., *Rochin v. California*, 342 U.S. 165 (1952).

37. *McCart v. Indianapolis Water Co.*, 302 U.S. 419, 423 (1938) (dissent).

38. *Indiana ex rel. Anderson v. Brand*, 303 U.S. 95, 109 (1938) (dissent) (academic tenure holders); *Wood v. Lovett*, 313 U.S. 362, 372 (1941) (dissent) (purchasers of homes).

39. *SEC v. Chenery Corp.*, 318 U.S. 80, 95 (1943) (dissent).

40. *NLRB v. Columbian Enameling & Stamping Co.*, 306 U.S. 292, 301 (1939) (dissent).

41. *Hirabayshi v. United States*, 320 U.S. 81 (1943); *Korematsu v. United States*, 323 U.S. 214 (1944), discussed above, chap. 10.

42. *Bridges v. California*, 314 U.S. 252 (1941).

43. *Milk Wagon Drivers Union v. Meadormoor Dairies*, 312 U.S. 287, 299 (1941) (dissent); *Cox v. New Hampshire*, 312 U.S. 569 (1941).

44. *Palko v. Connecticut*, 302 U.S. 319 (1937).

45. *Giboney v. Empire Storage & Ice Co.*, 336 U.S. 490 (1949).

46. *Kovacs v. Cooper*, 336 U.S. 77, 98 (1949) (dissent).

47. E.g., *Schulz v. Pennsylvania R.R.*, 350 U.S. 523 (1956); *Allen Bradley v. Local No. 3*, 325 U.S. 797 (1945).

48. Cf. Cahn, "Justice Black and First Amendment 'Absolutes,' " 37 N.Y.U.L. Rev. 549 (1962).

49. 332 U.S. 46, 68 (1947) (dissent).

50. Black's interpretation of history was challenged in Fairman, "Does the Fourteenth Amendment Incorporate the Bill of Rights?" 2 Stan. L. Rev. 5 (1949).

51. *Kovacs v. Cooper, supra* n.46.

52. *New York Times Co. v. Sullivan*, 376 U.S. 254, 293 (1964) (concurrence).

53. *Ginzburg v. United States*, 383 U.S. 463, 476 (1966) (dissent).

54. *Cox v. Louisiana*, 379 U.S. 536, 575 (1965) (partial dissent).

55. *Brown v. Louisiana*, 383 U.S. 131, 151 (1966) (dissent).

56. *Berger v. New York*, 388 U.S. 41, 70 (1967) (dissent).

57. *Schmerber v. California*, 384 U.S. 757, 773 (1966) (dissent).

58. *Griswold v. Connecticut*, 381 U.S. 479, 507 (1965) (dissent).

59. *Harper v. Virginia Board of Elections*, 383 U.S. 663, 670 (1966) (dissent).

60. *Connecticut Gen. Life Ins. Co. v. Johnson*, 303 U.S. 77, 83 (1938) (dissent).

61. E.g., in *Adamson v. California, supra* n.49.

62. See Reich, "Mr. Justice Black and the Living Constitution," 76 Harv. L. Rev. 673, 694–700 (1963).

63. See generally Symposium, 58 Calif. L. Rev. 1 (1970).

64. *Adamson v. California, supra* n. 49.

65. *Foster v. Illinois*, 332 U.S. 134 (1947) (assistance of counsel in state proceedings).

66. *Dennis v. United States*, 341 U.S. 494 (1951).

67. *Foster v. Illinois, supra* n.65 at 140.

68. *Adamson v. California, supra* n. 49 at 67.

69. See A. Mason, *Harlan Fiske Stone* 469 (1956).

70. Justice Douglas said that Black was "an ardent proselytizer of his constitutional views, seeking to convert any 'wayward' Brother on the Court." W. Douglas, *Go East, Young Man* 452 (1974).

71. 163 U.S. 537 (1896).

72. Douglas, *supra* n.70 at 451; R. Kluger, *Simple Justice* 586–616 (1976).

73. As exemplified in *Missouri ex rel. Gaines v. Canada*, 305 U.S. 337 (1938); *Sipuel v. Board of Regents*, 332 U.S. 631 (1948); *Sweat v. Painter, supra* n.5; *McLaurin v. Oklahoma State Regents, supra* n.5.

74. Lewis, "Earl Warren," in 4 L. Friedman and F. Israel, *supra* n.32 at 2721, 2728–29.

75. *Irvine v. California*, 347 U.S. 128 (1954); *Barsky v. Board of Regents*, 347 U.S. 442 (1954).

76. *Watkins v. United States*, 354 U.S. 178 (1957); *Sweezy v. New Hampshire*, 354 U.S. 234 (1957).

77. *Greene v. McElroy*, 360 U.S. 474 (1959).

78. *Miranda v. Arizona*, 384 U.S. 436 (1966), discussed below.

79. *Ginzburg v. United States, supra* n.53.

80. *Marchetti v. United States*, 390 U.S. 39, 77 (1968) (dissent).

81. E.g., *Harper v. Virginia Board of Electors, supra* n. 59, outlawing poll tax requirement for voting in the face of a pending constitutional amendment; *Jones v.*

Alfred H. Mayer Co., 392 U.S. 409 (1968), reviving an 1866 Civil Rights Act prohibiting racial discrimination in the sale of housing in the context of a proposed Congressional open-housing statute.

82. Harlan, "The Frankfurter Imprint as Seen by a Colleague," 76 Harv. L. Rev. 1, 2 (1963).

83. See D. Shapiro, *The Evolution of a Judicial Philosophy* xvii (1969).

84. *Harper v. Virginia Board of Elections, supra* n.59 at 686 (dissent).

85. 356 U.S. 86 (1958).

86. 367 U.S. 497 (1961).

87. 369 U.S. 186 (1962).

88. *Barsky v. Board of Regents, supra* n. 75.

89. See *Watkins v. United States* and *Sweezy v. New Hampshire, supra* n.76.

90. 356 U.S. 44 (1958).

91. 356 U.S. at 64–65.

92. Id. at 76.

93. Id at 78.

94. Id. at 92.

95. Id. at 93.

96. Id.

97. Id. at 110.

98. Id. at 107.

99. Id. at 94.

100. Id. at 98.

101. Id. at 97.

102. Id.

103. Id. at 101.

104. Id.

105. Id. at 119–20.

106. Id. at 121–22.

107. Id. at 124.

108. Id. at 125.

109. Id. at 126.

110. Id. at 128.

111. *State v. Nelson*, 126 Conn. 412 (1940).

112. Cf. Bickel, "The Passive Virtues," 75 Harv. L. Rev. 40 (1961).

113. *Griswold v. Connecticut, supra* n.58.

114. 367 U.S. at 503.

115. Id.

116. Id. at 508.

117. Id.

118. Id. at 532.

119. Id. at 534.

120. Id. at 537.

121. Id. at 538–39.

122. Id. at 508 (Frankfurter's phrase).

123. Id. at 538.

124. Id. at 536.

125. Id. at 540.

126. Id. at 542.

127. Id.

128. Id. at 543.
129. Id. at 548.
130. Id. at 550.
131. Id. at 548.
132. Id. at 553.
133. Id. at 555.
134. Id. at 544.
135. 369 U.S. at 334.
136. Id. at 340.
137. Id. at 333–34.
138. Harlan in *Griswold v. Connecticut, supra* n.58, quoting Cardozo for the Court in *Palko v. Connecticut,* 302 U.S. 319, 325 (1937).
139. "Selective incorporation," as a doctrine, has not been expressly accepted by a majority of the Court, although it has been practiced. See D. Shapiro, *supra* n.83 at 26n.
140. 367 U.S. 643 (1961).
141. 381 U.S. 618 (1965).
142. E.g., *Johnson v. New Jersey,* 384 U.S. 719 (1966); *Jenkins v. Delaware,* 395 U.S. 213 (1969).
143. Compare *Linkletter v. Walker, supra* n.141, with *Johnson v. New Jersey, supra* n.142, and *Desist v. United States,* 394 U.S. 244 (1969).
144. Compare *Johnson v. New Jersey, supra* n.142 with *Jenkins v. Delaware, supra* n.142.
145. *Supra* n.142.
146. *Supra* n.142 at 218.
147. 381 U.S. at 640, 650 (dissent).
148. See *Desist v. United States, supra* n.143 at 254; *United States v. White,* 401 U.S. 745, 754 (1971).
149. E.g., *Tehan v. Shott,* 382 U.S. 406 (1966); *Stovall v. Denno,* 388 U.S. 293 (1967); *De Stefano v. Woods,* 392 U.S. 631 (1968).
150. *Supra* n.143.
151. 394 U.S. at 258.
152. Id. at 259.
153. Id. at 258.
154. Id.
155. *Jenkins v. Delaware, supra* n.142 at 222.
156. 394 U.S. at 258.
157. 384 U.S. 436 (1966).
158. Id. at 465 (Warren, C. J.).
159. 378 U.S. 1 (1964).
160. 378 U.S. 478 (1964).
161. 384 U.S. at 478.
162. Id. at 444, 467–79.
163. Id. at 442.
164. Id. at 443.
165. Id. at 444.
166. 370 U.S. 421 (1962).
167. E.g., Note, "Interrogations in New Haven: The Impact of *Miranda,*" 76 Yale L. J. 1519 (1967); Seeburger and Wettick, *"Miranda* in Pittsburgh—A Statistical Study," 29 U. Pitt. L. Rev. 1 (1967); Medalie, Zeitz and Alexander, "Custodial

Police Interrogation in our Nation's Capitol," 66 Mich. L. Rev. 1347 (1968).
168. Omnibus Crime Control and Safe Streets Act, 82 Stat. 197(1968).
169. For only some examples, see *Weber v. Aetna Casualty & Surety Co.*, 406 U.S. 164 (1972); *Roe v. Wade*, 410 U.S. 113 (1973); *Cleveland Board of Education v. La-Fleur*, 414 U.S. 632 (1974); *Memorial Hospital v. Maricopa County*, 415 U.S. 250 (1974).

15

1. See L. Jaffe, *English and American Judges as Lawmakers* (1969).
2. In *DeFunis v. Odegaard*, 416 U.S. 312 (1974), the Court postponed decision on the constitutionality of minority admissions programs in state law schools by invoking the requirement that a controversy not be moot by the time it reaches the Court. Four dissenters said that the *DeFunis* issues "must inevitably return . . . to this Court." Id. at 350.
3. K. Llewellyn, *The Common Law Tradition* (1960), and J. Welter, *The Styles of Appellate Judicial Opinions* (1960), discuss changing modes of opinion-writing over time. Llewellyn's "grand" and "formal" styles are as much prescriptive as descriptive: see W. Twining, *Karl Llewellyn and the Realist Movement* 203–69 (1973).

Bibliographical Note

A variety of primary and secondary source materials forms the basis for my assessment of the judges portrayed in this study. A fuller listing of sources appears in the notes. This essay comments briefly on some of the principal sources.

Marshall's *Autobiographical Sketch* (John S. Adams, ed., 1937) is a detailed account of his early years. His *The Life of George Washington* (1805–7) contains numerous comments on the political and jurisprudential climate in which the Constitution was framed. Leonard Baker has a recent biography, *John Marshall: A Life in Law* (1974). Albert Beveridge's four-volume *Life of John Marshall* (1919) remains the liveliest account of Marshall's career; both Edward Corwin's *John Marshall and the Constitution* (1919) and Robert Faulkner's *The Jurisprudence of John Marshall* (1968) are more revealing of Marshall's thought and his approach to judging. Frances Mason's *My Dearest Polly* (1961), a collection of letters from Marshall to his wife, also provides a social history of Richmond at the time of Marshall and some anecdotes about the Marshall family. Melville Jones has edited a valuable collection of essays on various aspects of Marshall's thought, *Chief Justice John Marshall, A Reappraisal* (1956). William Winslow Crosskey has provocative comments on Marshall in his *Politics and the Constitution in the History of the United States* (1953) and in "Mr. Chief Justice Marshall," in Allison Dunham and Philip

Kurland, eds., *Mr. Justice* (1964). Gerald Gunther has discovered and published Marshall's extrajudicial *Defense of McCulloch v. Maryland* (1969). Charles Warren's *The Supreme Court in United States History* (3 vols., 1922) is a good source for public reaction to Marshall's decisions. A collection of Marshall papers is housed in the Institute of Early American History and Culture at the College of William and Mary, and another is in the Library of Congress.

James Kent's papers and journals are in the Library of Congress. His son William Kent edited the *Memoirs and Letters of James Kent* (1898). Holmes's edition of Kent's *Commentaries on American Law* was published in four volumes in 1873. The fullest treatment of Kent's life remains John Horton's *James Kent: A Study in Conservatism* (1939). Joseph Dorfman has related Kent's decisions and writing to the economic context of his time in "Chancellor Kent and the Developing American Economy," 61 Colum. L. Rev. 1290 (1961). Lawrence Friedman has some perceptive comments on Kent in his *A History of American Law* 290–92 (1973).

Story's continuous concern with putting his views on paper has resulted in several primary source collections, including a set of papers in the Massachusetts Historical Society, one in the Clements Library at the University of Michigan, one in the Library of Congress, one in the University of Texas Library, and one in the Essex Institute in Salem, Massachusetts. Story also published a collection entitled *The Miscellaneous Writings of Joseph Story* (1852), which contains an "Autobiography." His son William Story produced a *Life and Letters* of his father (1851) that is a source of correspondence, as is Charles Warren's *The Story-Marshall Correspondence* (1942). Two biographies have recently appeared, Gerald Dunne's *Justice Joseph Story and the Rise of the Supreme Court* (1970) and James McClellan's *Joseph Story and the American Constitution* (1971). Three other sources give significant insights into Story: Henry Steele Commager's "Joseph Story" in the *Gaspar Bacon Lectures on the Constitution of the United States* (1953); Perry Miller's *The Life of the Mind in America* (1965); and Morton Horwitz's "The Conservative Tradition in the Writing of American Legal History," 17 Am. J. Legal Hist. 275 (1973).

The Shaw Papers are in the Massachusetts Historical Society and Boston Social Law Library. Two interesting contemporary accounts of Shaw's life are found in volumes of the Massachusetts Reports, 15 Gray 599 (1860) and 16 Gray 598 (1861). In Frederic Chase's biography entitled *Lemuel Shaw* (1918), the last chapter has some observations on Shaw's character and personality. Leonard Levy's *The Law of the Commonwealth and Chief Justice Shaw* (1957) is a thorough account of the corpus of Shaw's decisions. Robert M. Cover's *Justice Accused* (1975) treats Shaw's slavery opinions with imagination and insight. A revealing source of Shaw's thought before his appointment to the Massachusetts Supreme Court is an address he delivered to the Suffolk Bar in 1827, reprinted as "Profession of the Law in the United States," 7 *American Jurist and Law Magazine* 56 (1832).

Taney's own account of his youth, entitled "Early Life and Education," appeared in Samuel Tyler's *Memoir of Roger Brooke Taney* (1872). There is a collection of Taney papers in the Maryland Historical Society. Taney's account of his role as Secretary of the Treasury during the Jackson Administration's attack on the National Bank of the United States is in a collection of his papers in the Library of Congress. Letters from Taney to Jackson are found in John S. Bassett, ed., *Correspondence of Andrew Jackson* (6 vols., 1926–34). The best biography is Carl B. Swisher's *Roger B. Taney* (1935); the best short account of his career, Robert J. Harris's "Chief Justice Taney: Prophet of Reform and Reaction," 10 Vand. L. Rev. 227 (1957); and the best history of the Taney Court, Swisher's monumental *The Taney Period*, vol. 5 of the Holmes Devise *History of the Supreme Court of the United States* (1974). "The Unjust Judge: A Memorial of Roger Brooke Taney" (Anonymous, 1865) gives a sample of the "villain" literature on Taney after *Dred Scott*.

The literature on Miller is dominated by Charles Fairman's *Mr. Justice Miller and the Supreme Court* (1939), which relied heavily on a series of letters between Miller and his brother-in-law, William Pitt Ballinger, on deposit at the University of Texas Library. Fairman published two shorter accounts: "Justice Samuel Miller: A Study of a Judicial Statesman," 50 Pol. Sci. Q. 15 (1935), and "Samuel F. Miller, Justice of the Supreme Court," 10 Vand. L. Rev. 193 (1957). Charles N. Gregory's *Samuel Freeman Miller*, a sketchy biography, appeared in 1907. A contemporary characterization may be found in *Proceedings of the Bench and Bar of the Supreme Court of the United States, in Memoriam Samuel F. Miller* (1891).

To date there has been no biography of Bradley, whose papers are in the New Jersey Historical Society. Bradley's *Family Notes Respecting the Bradley Family of Fairfield*, a source of information on his youth, appeared in 1894. Charles Fairman's articles are the best treatment of his career: "The Education of a Justice," 1 Stan. L. Rev. 217 (1949); "What Makes a Great Justice?," 30 B. U. L. Rev. 49 (1950); "The So-called Granger Cases, Lord Hale, and Justice Bradley," 5 Stan. L. Rev. 587 (1953); and "Mr. Justice Bradley" in Allison Dunham and Philip Kurland, eds., *Mr. Justice* (1964). Another more recent contribution is John A. Scott, "Justice Bradley's Evolving Concept of the Fourteenth Amendment From the Slaughterhouse Cases to the Civil Rights Cases," 25 Rut. L. Rev. 552 (1971).

Collections of Field's papers are housed in the library of the University of California at Berkeley and at the Oregon Historical Society in Portland. Field has an account of his California years in *Personal Reminiscences of Early Days in California* (1893). William Turner's side of his controversies with Field may be found in W. Turner, *Documents in Relation to the Charges Preferred by Stephen J. Field* (1853). Contemporary views on Field's personal influence in the Supreme Court are included in Charles Fairman, *Mr. Justice Miller and the Supreme Court* (1939), and Alan Westin, "Stephen Field and the Headnote to *O'Neill v. Vermont*," 67 Yale L. J. 363 (1958). Carl B. Swisher's *Stephen J. Field* (1930) is an excellent biography. Three important shorter studies are Howard J. Graham, "Justice Field and the Fourteenth Amendment" 52 Yale L. J. 851 (1943); Robert G. McCloskey, "Stephen J. Field," in 2 Leon Friedman and Fred Israel, eds., *The Justices of the United States Supreme Court* 1069 (4 vols., 1969); and Charles W. McCurdy, "Justice Field and the Jurisprudence of Government Business Relations," 61 J. Am. Hist. 970 (1975).

No biography of Cooley exists; his papers are in the University of Michigan Historical Collections. Cooley has been treated in four specialized studies: Philip S. Paludan, *A Covenant with Death* (1975); Sidney Fine, *Laissez-Faire and the General Welfare State* (1956); Clyde E. Jacobs, *Law Writers and the Courts* (1954); and Benjamin Twiss, *Lawyers and the Constitution* (1942). Among the articles on Cooley as a commentator and·a judge the most revealing are Alan Jones, "Thomas M. Cooley and the Michigan Supreme Court: 1865–1885," 10 Am. J. Legal Hist. 97 (1966); Jones, "Thomas M. Cooley and 'Lassez Faire Constitutionalism': A Reconsideration," 53 J. Am. Hist. 759 (1967); and Paludan, "Law and the Failure of

Reconstruction: The Case of Thomas Cooley," 33 J. Hist. Ideas 597 (1972).

Piecing together information from the Doe Collection in the New Hampshire Historical Society, the Doe Papers at the Supreme Court of New Hampshire, and various other contemporaneous documents, John Reid produced a biography of Doe, *Chief Justice* (1967), which is a classic of its kind. Among the sources Reid relied on were Elmer Doe, *The Descendants of Nicholas Doe* (1917); Jeremiah Smith, *Memoir of Hon. Charles Doe* (1897); Joshua Hall, "Memoir of Hon. Charles Doe," 2 Proc. So. N.H. Bar Ass'n 84 (1896); Crawford D. Hening, "Charles Doe," in 8 W. D. Lewis, ed., *Great American Lawyers* 241 (1909); and Note, "Doe of New Hampshire: Reflections on a Nineteenth Century Judge," 63 Harv. L. Rev. 513 (1950). For a collection of observations by contemporaries, see 2 Proc. So. N.H. Bar Ass'n 84 (1896).

There is no full-length scholarly biography of Harlan, some of whose papers are deposited at the Library of Congress and at the University of Louisville Law School. A study of Harlan's decisions, Floyd B. Clark's *The Constitutional Doctrines of Justice Harlan*, appeared in 1915. The best source on his early years is Louis Hartz, "John M. Harlan in Kentucky, 1855–1877," 14 Filson Club Historical Quarterly 17 (1940). Some Harlan speeches and personal anecdotes are reprinted in 46 Ky. L. J. 321ff (1958). Important articles are Loren Beth, "Justice Harlan and the Uses of Dissent," 49 Am. Pol. Sci. Rev. 1085 (1955); Alan Westin, "John Marshall Harlan and the Constitutional Rights of Negroes," 66 Yale L. J. 637 (1957); and Westin, "Mr. Justice Harlan," in Allison Dunham and Philip Kurland, eds., *Mr. Justice* (1964).

Holmes has been written on extensively, and there are two excellent biographies with different perspectives, Catherine Drinker Bowen's, *Yankee from Olympus* (1943), which emphasizes his family background, and Mark De Wolfe Howe's *Justice Oliver Wendell Holmes: The Shaping Years* (1957) and *Justice Oliver Wendell Holmes: The Proving Years* (1963), which stress the development of his ideas. Grant Gilmore is currently completing the Howe biography. Among the best articles are Walton Hamilton, "On Dating Justice Holmes," 9 U. Chi. L. Rev. 1 (1941); Daniel Boorstin, "The Elusiveness of Mr. Justice Holmes," 14 New England Q. 478 (1941); Yosal Rogat, "The Judge as Spectator," 31 U. Chi. L. Rev. 213

(1964); and Robert Faulkner's appendix comparing Holmes with Marshall in his *The Jurisprudence of John Marshall* (1968). For a compilation and evaluation of the literature, see G. Edward White, "The Rise and Fall of Justice Holmes," 39 U. Chi. L. Rev. 51 (1971). The Harvard Law School and the Library of Congress have collections of the Holmes papers.

Alpheus Mason has an extensive biography of Brandeis, *Brandeis: A Free Man's Life* (1946), and two earlier analytical studies of Brandeis's ideas, *Lawyer and Judge in the Modern State* (1933); and *The Brandeis Way* (1938). Mason's best work on Brandeis is found in his essay "Louis D. Brandeis," in 4 Leon Friedman and Fred Israel, eds., *The Justices of the United States Supreme Court* 2043 (1969). A collection of articles is edited by Felix Frankfurter, *Mr. Justice Brandeis* (1932). Alexander Bickel's *The Unpublished Opinions of Mr. Justice Brandeis* (1957) contains some valuable insights. Louis Jaffe's "Was Brandeis An Activist?: The Search for Intermediate Premises," 80 Harv. L. Rev. 986 (1966), undertakes to evaluate Brandeis's contributions in the light of more recent jurisprudential controversies. Melvin Urofsky's *A Mind of One Piece: Brandeis and American Reform* (1971) is a more recent discussion of Brandeis's ideas. Two studies assessing Brandeis's distinctive legacy to administrative law are Jaffe, "The Contributions of Mr. Justice Brandeis to Administrative Law," 18 Iowa L. Rev. 213 (1933), and G. Edward White, "Allocating Power between Agencies and Courts: The Legacy of Justice Brandeis," 1974 Duke L. J. 195 (1974). Collections of Brandeis papers are held at the law schools of the University of Louisville and Harvard University.

The Cardozo papers, deposited in the Columbia University Library, were severely edited at one time by friends of Cardozo, and are in consequence not particularly revealing. George Hellman, a family friend, published an undocumented biography, *Benjamin N. Cardozo*, in 1940. Hellman's notes are in the Columbia University collection. Remarkably little has been written on Cardozo as a judge or a person. The best work includes a collection of essays in 52 Harv. L. Rev. 261ff (1939)—especially those by Irving Lehman, Arthur Corbin, and Warren Seavey; and Andrew L. Kaufman's two essays, "Mr. Justice Cardozo," in Dunham and Kurland, *supra*, and "Benjamin Cardozo," in Friedman and Israel, *supra*. Kaufman has a biography in progress.

The Learned Hand papers are in the possession of Gerald

Gunther, who is preparing a biography. A student of Gunther's, Michael A. Kahn, has recently used the papers in a note entitled "The Politics of the Appointment Process: An Analysis of Why Learned Hand Was Never Appointed to the Supreme Court," 25 Stan. L. Rev. 251 (1973). Two full-length studies have appeared: Marvin Schick, *Learned Hand's Court* (1970), an account of the inner workings of the Court of Appeals for the Second Circuit while Hand was its Chief Justice, and Kathryn Griffith, *Judge Learned Hand and the Role of the Federal Judiciary* (1973), an analysis of his jurisprudence. The two best treatments of Hand to have appeared are Philip Hamburger's "The Great Judge," 21 Life 116 (1946), and Hershel Shanks's introduction to *The Art and Craft of Judging: The Decisions of Judge Learned Hand* (1968). Some articles of interest are collected in 60 Harv. L. Rev. 325ff (1947). Hand's *Spirit of Liberty* (1953) is a revealing collection of essays. His *The Bill of Rights* (1958) contains his advocacy of a limited judicial review of constitutional cases.

Three book-length works have appeared on Frank: Julius Paul, *The Legal Realism of Jerome N. Frank* (1959), J. Mitchell Rosenberg, *Jerome Frank: Jurist and Philosopher* (1970), and Walter E. Volkomer, *The Passionate Liberal: The Political and Legal Ideas of Jerome Frank* (1970). Several perceptive articles appeared in 1957, the year of his death, among them Thurman Arnold, "Judge Jerome Frank," 24 U. Chi. L. Rev. 633 (1957); Charles E. Clark, "Jerome N. Frank," 66 Yale L. J. 817 (1957); Sidney M. Davis, "Jerome Frank—Portrait of a Personality," 24 U. Chi. L. Rev. 627 (1957); and Philip B. Kurland, "Jerome N. Frank: Some Reflections and Recollections of a Law Clerk," 24 U. Chi. L. Rev. 661 (1957). Wilfred E. Rumble has a skillful discussion of Frank's ideas in "Jerome Frank and His Critics: Certainty and Fantasy in the Judicial Process," 10 J. Pub. Law 125 (1961). Frank's own essay, "Some Reflections on Judge Learned Hand," 24 U. Chi. L. Rev. 66 (1957), is a better source for Frank's ideas than for Hand's. William Twining has some interesting comments on Frank in *Karl Llewellyn and the Realist Movement* (1973). The Oral History Project at Columbia University contains a memoir by Frank.

The Van Devanter Papers are in the Library of Congress. Very little has been written on Van Devanter, and the best source of background information is Lewis L. Gould, *Wyoming: A Political History* (1968). Alexander Bickel's "Mr. Taft Rehabilitates the

Court," 79 Yale L. J. 1 (1969), has a full account of Van Devanter's appointment. "Proceedings in Memory of Mr. Justice Van Devanter," 316 U.S. (1941), contains commentaries on Van Devanter by his colleagues. David Burner's "Willis Van Devanter," in Friedman and Israel, *supra*, is a narrative account.

Of all the Four Horsemen, Sutherland has been subjected to the most critical analysis—a fact that may have contributed to his higher reputation. Joel F. Paschal's *Mr. Justice Sutherland* (1951) is a worthwhile treatment of Sutherland's ideas and decisions. In a briefer essay, "Mr. Justice Sutherland," in Dunham and Kurland, *supra*, Paschal asserts that Sutherland "towers over Van Devanter, McReynolds, and Butler, with whom he was so often associated." (217). John P. Frank, in a book review, 61 Yale L. J. 598 (1952), focuses on the outmoded status of Sutherland's ideas at the time he was on the Court. Sutherland's early career is discussed more fully by Paschal in "The Education of a Justice," 1 J. Legal Ed. 333 (1949). Revealing addresses by Sutherland are "Private Rights and Government Control," 42 A.B.A. Rep. 197 (1917), and "Principle or Expedient," 44 N.Y. State Bar Ass'n Rep. 263 (1921).

The Butler Papers are at the Minnesota Historical Society. Short of a biography, the fullest sketch of Butler's personality and career is David J. Danelski, *A Supreme Court Justice Is Appointed* (1964), a study of his nomination and confirmation to the Court. Frances J. Brown's *The Social and Economic Philosophy of Pierce Butler* (1945) treats Butler's ideas. Contemporary estimates may be found in *Proceedings of the Bar and Officers of the Supreme Court in Memory of Pierce Butler* (1940), and *In Memoriam, Hon. Pierce Butler, Proceedings Before the United States Court of Appeals for the Eighth Circuit* (1941). Two shorter pieces are Richard J. Purcell, "Mr. Justice Pierce Butler," 42 Catholic Educational Review 193 (1944), and David Burner, "Pierce Butler," in Friedman and Israel, *supra*.

The McReynolds Papers, in the Alderman Library at the University of Virginia, are unrevealing. The best account of McReynolds's career and attitudes is Stephen T. Early, "James Clark McReynolds and the Judicial Process," Ph.D. dissertation, University of Virginia, 1952. S. Price Gilbert's *James Clark McReynolds* (1946), a testimonial published on the occasion of his death, contains some interesting anecdotes. David Burner's "James C. McReynolds," in Friedman and Israel, *supra*, is a helpful synthesis.

The Hughes Papers, in the Library of Congress, should be supplemented by the David Danelski and Joseph Tulchin edition of *The Autobiographical Notes of Charles Evans Hughes* (1973). Hughes's notes are deliberately official and ponderous but revealing nonetheless. The introduction by Danelski and Tulchin is the finest single piece on Hughes. Merlo Pusey's two-volume biography, *Charles Evans Hughes* (1951), is thorough but the fact that it is authorized makes it somewhat less than detached. Edwin McElwain, "The Business of the Supreme Court as Conducted by Chief Justice Hughes," 63 Harv. L. Rev. 5 (1949), is an excellent source of information on Hughes as an administrator. Hughes's *The Supreme Court of the United States* (1928), in which he set forth theories on the proper function of the Court, should be compared with his practices as Chief Justice. Other helpful studies of Hughes are Samuel Hendel, *Charles Evans Hughes and the Supreme Court* (1951), and "The 'Liberalism' of Chief Justice Hughes," 10 Vand. L. Rev. 259 (1959); F. D. G. Ribble, "The Constitutional Doctrines of Chief Justice Hughes," 41 Colum. L. Rev. 1190 (1941); and Paul Freund, "Charles Evans Hughes: Chief Justice," 81 Harv. L. Rev. 4 (1967).

Alpheus Mason's *Harlan Fiske Stone* (1956) surpasses his biography of Brandeis and is one of the fine judicial biographies. Mason had access to Stone's personal correspondence during his incumbency on the Court, and the yield was a wealth of normally unrevealed information. The best brief essay on Stone is Allison Dunham's "Mr. Justice Stone," in Dunham and Kurland, *supra*. Other helpful works are Noel T. Dowling's "Mr. Justice Stone and the Constitution," 36 Colum. L. Rev. 351 (1936); Dowling's "The Methods of Mr. Justice Stone in Constitutional Cases," 41 Colum. L. Rev. 1160 (1941); John P. Frank, "Harlan Fiske Stone: An Estimate," 9 Stan. L. Rev. 621 (1957); Herbert Wechsler, "Stone and the Constitution," 46 Colum. L. Rev. 793 (1946); and Learned Hand, "Chief Justice Stone's Conception of the Judicial Function," 46 Colum. L. Rev. 696 (1946), the last as much for what it says about the author as for the subject. Stone's classic essay, "The Common Law in the United States," appeared in 50 Harv. L. Rev. 4 (1936).

The Oral History Project at Columbia University has an extensive collection of interviews with Jackson, and on this material Philip Kurland based an interesting sketch, "Robert H. Jackson," in Friedman and Israel, *supra*. Eugene Gerhart's authorized biography of Jackson, *America's Advocate,* appeared in 1958; Gerhart's brief analysis of his decisions, *Lawyer's Judge,* in 1961. The best analysis presently available is Louis Jaffe's "Mr. Justice Jackson," 68 Harv. L. Rev. 940 (1955). Other important articles are Paul Freund, "Individual and Commonwealth in the Thought of Mr. Justice Jackson," 8 Stan. L. Rev. 9 (1955); Charles Fairman, "Robert H. Jackson," 55 Colum. L. Rev. 445 (1955); Felix Frankfurter, "Mr. Justice Jackson," 68 Harv. L. Rev. 937 (1955); Warner Gardner, "Robert H. Jackson, 1892–1954—Government Attorney," 55 Colum. L. Rev. 438 (1955); and Telford Taylor, "The Nuremberg Trials," 55 Colum. L. Rev. 488 (1955). Jackson contributed three works of his own: *The Struggle for Judicial Supremacy* (1941), *Full Faith and Credit: The Lawyer's Clause of the Constitution* (1946), and *The Supreme Court in the American System of Government* (1955).

The most revealing writing on Traynor is his own, in the numerous law-review articles cited in the notes for Chapter 13. Three symposia contain most of the significant scholarly analyses of Traynor: 13 Stan. L. Rev. 717 (1961), 53 Calif. L. Rev. 5 (1965), and 44 So. Calif. L. Rev. 876 (1971). See especially Walter V. Schaefer, "Justice Roger J. Traynor," 13 Stan. L. Rev. 717; Brainerd Currie, "Justice Traynor and the Conflict of Laws," 13 Stan. L. Rev. 719; Wex S. Malone, "Contrasting Images of Torts—The Judicial Personality of Justice Traynor," 13 Stan. L. Rev. 779; Stewart Macaulay, "Justice Traynor and the Law of Contracts," 13 Stan. L. Rev. 812; Robert B. McKay, "Constitutional Law: Ideas in the Public Forum," 53 Calif. L. Rev. 67; Barbara N. Armstrong, "Family Law: Order Out of Chaos," 53 Calif. L. Rev. 121; James E. Sabine, "Taxation: A Delicately Planned Arrangement of Cargo," 53 Calif. L. Rev. 173; Harry Kalven, "Torts: The Quest for Appropriate Standards," 53 Calif. L. Rev. 189; Leonard G. Ratner, "Reflections of a Traynor Law Clerk," 44 So. Calif. L. Rev. 876A; Geoffrey C. Hazard, Jr., "Res Nova in Res Judicata," 44 So. Calif. L. Rev. 1036; and Page Keeton, "Roger Traynor and the Law of Torts," 44 So. Calif. L. Rev. 1045.

With Frankfurter, as with Story but with few other Justices in this study, a problem of selectivity arises. In addition to the Frankfurter Papers at the Library of Congress, there is an edition of Frankfurter's correspondence with Franklin Roosevelt (Max Freedman, ed., *Roosevelt and Frankfurter, Their Correspondence 1928–1945* (1967); three volumes of essays and reminiscences, *Of Law and Men*

(Philip Elman, ed., 1956), *Felix Frankfurter Reminisces* (Harlan Phillips, ed., 1962), and *Of Law and Life and Other Things That Matter* (Philip Kurland, ed., 1965); several books, among them *The Public and Its Government* (1930), *The Commerce Clause under Marshall, Taney, and Waite* (1937), *Mr. Justice Holmes and the Supreme Court* (1938), and *The Case of Sacco and Vanzetti* (1962 ed.); and numerous articles and essays, both scholarly and otherwise. Two biographies have appeared: Helen Thomas, *Scholar on the Bench* (1960), and Liva Baker, *Felix Frankfurter* (1969). Wallace Mendelson's *Justices Black and Frankfurter: Conflict on the Court* (1961) discusses the charged relations between the two Justices. Mendelson's edited volume, *Felix Frankfurter, A Tribute* (1964), contains an important essay by Alexander Bickel: "Applied Politics and the Science of Law: Writings of the Harvard Period." Albert Sacks's "Felix Frankfurter" in Friedman and Israel, *supra*, is a perceptive overview. The best source of Frankfurter's early years is Sanford V. Levinson's note, "The Democratic Faith of Felix Frankfurter," 25 Stan. L. Rev. 430 (1973). Louis Jaffe's "The Judicial Universe of Mr. Justice Frankfurter," 62 Harv. L. Rev. 357 (1949), remains the best single analysis of Frankfurter's thought, even though it was written in the middle of Frankfurter's judicial career.

The Hugo Black papers have now been made available in the Library of Congress, but do not appear to be complete. John P. Frank's early biography, *Mr. Justice Black: The Man and His Opinions* (1949), is informative and lively. Virginia V. Hamilton, *Hugo Black: The Alabama Years* (1972), is an account of his background; another revealing source is Clifford Durr, "Hugo Black, Southerner," 10 Am. U. L. Rev. 27 (1961). Charles Reich's "Mr. Justice Black and the Living Constitution," 76 Harv. L. Rev. 673 (1963), is an imaginative attempt to describe the development of Black's philosophy of constitutional adjudication. Edmund Cahn, "Justice Black and First Amendment 'Absolutes,' " 37 N.Y.U. L. Rev. 549 (1962), constitutes an interview with Black and Cahn's comments, which are of interest. Sylvia Snowiss," The Legacy of Justice Black," 1973 Sup. Ct. Rev. 187, is a perceptive overview of Black's thought. Daniel P. Meador's *Justice Black and His Books* (1974) lists the sources of Black's reading, along with an illuminating introduction. Two rewarding contributions by Black himself are "Reminiscences," 18 Ala. L. Rev. 3 (1965), and *A Constitutional Faith* (1968).

The literature on Warren is very scanty. Warren's papers have been deposited, with restrictions, in the Earl Warren Oral History Center at the University of California at Berkeley. *The Public Papers of Chief Justice Earl Warren* (1959), are largely unrevealing. John D. Weaver and Louis Katcher completed biographies of Warren in 1967, which both emphasize his political career. (Weaver, *Warren: The Man, the Court, the Era*; Katcher, *Earl Warren—A Political Biography*). Two symposia contain pieces on Warren. The first is in 67 Mich. L. Rev. 219 (1968), especially A. Kenneth Pye, "The Warren Court and Criminal Procedure," at 249; Harry Kalven, "A Note on Free Speech and the Warren Court," at 289; John P. MacKenzie, "The Warren Court and the Press," at 303; Thomas E. Kauper, "The 'Warren Court' and the Antitrust Laws," at 325; and Philip B. Kurland, "Earl Warren, The 'Warren Court', and the Warren Myths," at 353. The second is 58 Calif. L. Rev. 1ff (1970), which contains a series of reminiscences on Warren by persons associated with him during his career. Two additional helpful articles are Archibald Cox's brief treatment, "Chief Justice Earl Warren," 83 Harv. L. Rev. 1 (1969), and especially Anthony Lewis, "Earl Warren," in Friedman and Israel, supra. Cox's *The Warren Court* (1968) is a fine account of the philosophical direction of the Court under Warren.

David Shapiro's *The Evolution of A Judicial Philosophy: Selected Opinions and Papers of Justice John M. Harlan* (1969) is the best single source on Harlan yet available. It contains a brief biographical essay as well as selections from Harlan's opinions and extrajudicial writings. Among the writings those of greatest interest are "The Frankfurter Imprint as Seen by a Colleague," 76 Harv. L. Rev. 1 (1963); "Thoughts at a Dedication: Keeping the Judicial Function in Balance," 49 A.B.A.J. 943 (1963); "The Bill of Rights and the Constitution," 50 A.B.A.J. 918 (1964); and "Introduction" to Justice Potter Stewart's "Robert H. Jackson's Influence on Federal-State Relationships," 23 Rec. Ass'n of the Bar of the City of New York 7 (1968). In addition to Shapiro's introduction, the following selections shed light on Harlan as a person or a judge: Whitney North Seymour, "John Marshall Harlan," 1 N.Y. Law Forum 1 (1955); Norman Dorsen, "The Second Mr. Justice Harlan: A Constitutional Conservative," 44 N.Y.U. L. Rev. 249 (1969); J. Harvie Wilkinson, "Justice John M. Harlan and the Values of Federalism," 57 Va. L. Rev. 1185 (1971); Gerald Gunther's remarks on Harlan in his "In Search of Judicial Quality on a Changing Court: The

Case of Justice Powell," 24 Stan. L. Rev. 1001, 1004–14 (1972); Nathan Lewin, "Justice Harlan: The Full Measure of the Man," 58 A.B.A.J. 579 (1972); and Henry Friendly, "Mr. Justice Harlan As Seen by a Friend and Judge of an Inferior Court," 85 Harv. L. Rev. 382 (1971).

Index